THE GREAT WAR
in
HOLLYWOOD
MEMORY
1918–1939

THE SUNY SERIES

HORIZONS OF CINEMA

MURRAY POMERANCE | EDITOR

THE GREAT WAR in HOLLYWOOD MEMORY 1918–1939

MICHAEL HAMMOND

Cover: Poster art for *Wings* (1927), directed by William A. Wellman. Paramount Pictures/Photofest © Paramount Pictures.

Published by State University of New York Press, Albany

© 2019 State University of New York Press

All rights reserved

No part of this book may be used or reproduced in any manner whatsoever without written permission. No part of this book may be stored in a retrieval system or transmitted in any form or by any means including electronic, electrostatic, magnetic tape, mechanical, photocopying, recording, or otherwise without the prior permission in writing of the publisher.
For information, contact State University of New York Press, Albany, NY
www.sunypress.edu

Library of Congress Cataloging-in-Publication Data
Names: Hammond, Michael, 1954– author.
Title: The Great War in Hollywood memory, 1918–1939 / Michael Hammond.
Description: Albany, NY : State University of New York Press, [2019] | Series: SUNY series, horizons of cinema | Includes bibliographical references, filmographies and index.
Identifiers: LCCN 2018059959 | ISBN 9781438476971 (hardcover : alk. paper) | ISBN 9781438476988 (e-book) | ISBN 9781438476964 (paperback : alk. paper)
Subjects: LCSH: World War, 1914–1918—Motion pictures and the war. | Motion pictures—United States—History—20th century. | War films—United States—History—20th century. | Historical films—United States—History—20th century. | Collective memory and motion pictures.
Classification: LCC D522.23 .H46 2019 | DDC 791.43/658—dc23
LC record available at https://lccn.loc.gov/2018059959

10 9 8 7 6 5 4 3 2 1

*For Betty Lou
and
Kelly Hammond*

CONTENTS

List of Illustrations	ix
Acknowledgments	xi
Introduction: Dr. Otternschlag Goes to Hollywood	xv

PART I KLEOS: GLORY

1	The War on the Ground: From Edenic to Blasted	3
2	The War in the Ground: "I am the grass, let me work"	23
3	The War in the Air	65
4	Forbidden Zones: Women, Vernacular, and "War as it really is"	99

PART II NOSTOS: HOME

5	Veterans: "Sweet jangled bells, out of tune"	127
6	War Relic and Forgotten Man: Richard Barthelmess as Celluloid Veteran	175
7	The After-Images	193

Notes	239
Bibliography	257
Filmography	271
Index	275

ILLUSTRATIONS

I.1. "Every object around him was a sham." Ferdinand Gottschalk as Piminov, John Barrymore as the Baron, and Lewis Stone as Dr. Otternschlag in *Grand Hotel*. xvi
1.1. Charlie in the trenches reading another soldier's letter from home in *Shoulder Arms*. 7
1.2. *The Lost Battalion* featured footage of Lt. Col. Whittlesey (who had been promoted from major) as well as other surviving members of the 77th Battalion. 11
1.3. Filling the frame with cross-covered hills at the end of *The Four Horsemen of the Apocalypse*. 20
2.1. C.R.W. Nevinson's *Road from Arras to Bapaume* (1917). 29
2.2. Vidor's version of moving up to the front in *The Big Parade*. 30
2.3. Reneé Adorée in *The Big Parade*. 30
2.4. *The Veteran in a New Field*, by Winslow Homer. 56
2.5. Ford's visual quote of Homer's *Veteran in a New Field* in *Pilgrimage*. 57
2.6. A Gold Star mother seeking redemption. Henrietta Crosman as Hannah Jessop in *Pilgrimage*. 59
3.1. "Looking up": Charles Rogers as Jack Powell in *Wings*. 71
3.2. Behind-the-pilot shot from *Hell's Angels*. 79
3.3. "I'm going to stop the whole rotten mess." Frederic March and Cary Grant in *The Eagle and the Hawk*. 93
4.1. Mary (Clara Bow) rescues Jack (Charles Rogers) at the end of the Folies Bergère scene in *Wings*. 107
4.2. Cushie (Zasu Pitts), Rosalie (Marie Provost), Joy (Anita Page), Helen (Martha Sleeper), and Babs (June Walker) wisecracking in *War Nurse*. 112
4.3. Monica (Evelyn Brent) dies in No Man's Land in *The Mad Parade*. 120
5.1. Frederic March as Kenneth and Norma Shearer as Kathleen in *Smilin' Through*. 137
5.2. Katherine Hepburn and John Barrymore in *A Bill of Divorcement*. 145

5.3. David Manners (Shep), Helen Chandler (Nikki), Richard
Barthelmess (Cary), John Mack Brown (Bill), and Elliot
Nugent (Francis) in *The Last Flight*. 160
5.4. Lewis Stone (Doctor Otternschlag), Lionel Barrymore
(Kringelein), and John Barrymore (Baron Geigern)
in *Grand Hotel*. 168
5.5. Circular motif in Cedric Gibbons's set for the lobby of
Grand Hotel underpins the downward spiral of the various
characters' stories. 170
6.1. Richard Barthelmess in *Heroes for Sale*. 178
6.2. Richard Barthelmess and May McAvoy in *The Enchanted Cottage*. 185
7.1. Lon Chaney as Blizzard in *The Penalty*. 200
7.2. "Penderel didn't seem to have escaped the war yet." Melvyn
Douglas as Roger Penderel and Brember Wills as Saul Femm
in *The Old Dark House*. 215
7.3. Caught in the mud at the site of the battle of Marmaros:
"The greatest graveyard in the world." David Manners,
Jacqueline Wells, and Bela Lugosi in *The Black Cat*. 224

ACKNOWLEDGMENTS

With a project of this size there are inevitably many people to whom I am deeply grateful for assistance along the way. First and foremost I would like to thank my editor Murray Pomerance. His enthusiasm for the project was essential in ensuring the book's completion. I would also like to thank Rafael Chaiken, Jenn Bennett and James Peltz at SUNY Press for making this book happen on a practical level, and James Harbeck for his detailed and thoughtful copyediting. I am also grateful to the readers of this manuscript who offered such positive comments and recommendations. The Southampton University Film and English Departments have provided solid support in granting me periods of sabbatical leave in which to research and write. I want to thank Shelley Cobb, Linda Ruth Williams, Lucy Mazdon, Michael Williams, Tim Bergfelder, Kevin Donnelly, Malcolm Cook, and Beth Carroll for reading and discussing various aspects of this work. I also want to thank my colleagues in the English Department, where I worked for over a decade. Clare Hanson, Stephen Bygrave, Steve Bending, John McGavin, Stephen Morton, Peter Middleton, Bella Millett, David Glover, and Cora Kaplan all gave me helpful advice and encouragement. Colleagues from the History Department were very helpful in encouraging my interdisciplinary approach to this book: Eve Colpus, Kendrick Oliver, Mark Cornwall, and Joan Tumblety were always supportive in reading and discussing the work.

I would like to thank my colleagues and friends in the Film Studies world: Christine Gledhill, Roberta Pearson, Yvonne Tasker, David Mayer, Helen Day Mayer, Rebecca Harrison, Nick Hiley, Lee Grieveson, Tom Gunning, Charles Maland, Lawrence Napper, Helen Hanson, Thomas Slater, Richard Maltby, Peter Krämer, Ian Christie, and Bryony Dixon, all of whom at one stage or another either read or discussed the project with me and offered valuable perspectives. I am grateful to Kevin Brownlow for his generosity with his own personal archive and his depth of knowledge, which were indispensible. Thanks also to Kate MacLoughlin, who introduced me to the War and Representation Network, which has in turn kept me in touch with scholars whose interest in the cultural memories of the Great War were of great value in shaping my own understanding of cinema's role. Alice Kelly, Emma Hanna, Mark Connelly, Dominiek Dendooven, and David Lubin have all been helpful in discussing sections of this book. I would like to especially thank Mara Keire for her generosity and enthusiasm in sharing her invaluable perspectives on the impact of the war on American culture. Martin Hurcombe and the anonymous readers at *Journal of War and Culture Studies* offered valuable early advice on a version of chapter 6 that appeared in volume 6, issue 4, 2013.

My research was initiated by a grant from the British Academy and I am grateful for that support which enabled me to visit archives across the United States. Ned Comstock at Special Collections at the Cinematic Arts Library at the University of Southern California gets a special mention for his ability to anticipate and recommend material such as script files, recorded script meetings with Irving Thalberg at MGM and many other primary sources that help to make up much of the book's evidence base. Jonathan Auxier at the Warner's Archive at USC provided much needed guidance through the script files and notes held there. I would also like to thank Barbara Hall and the staff at the Margaret Herrick Library for their guidance to production materials and rare archived films, and for their interest in this project. The staff at the Billy Rose Collection at the New York Public Library were very helpful in guiding me through the clippings files and set photographs there. Daniel Watts at the L. Tom Perry Special Collections in the Harold B. Lee Library at Brigham Young University pointed me to essential script materials from their King Vidor collection. Researcher Richard Fraser found material for me held at the UCLA Film and Television Archive; he had a keen idea of what was valuable to the project. I also want to thank the staff at the UCLA Cinema and Television Library who kept me busy watching films during a hot summer in Westwood.

When working in archives in varied places it helps to have friendly faces to go to and relax with. I want to thank my very good friends Pat Kirkham and the late and much missed Andy Hoogenboom for their generosity and hospitality in New York City; David and Kim Danielsen, who truly gave me a home away from home while I worked at the Los Angeles archives; and Katie Moy and Bob Brimson, whose refuge in London was essential.

On a more personal level, I want to thank Adrian Smith, Neil Ewen, Mark Kermode, and Aly Hirji for their expertise, friendship, and encouragement. I also want to thank Neil Brand for his support for my work on the Great War throughout my career. To Lloyd Trimble and Jay Watson, both veterans, I owe any perspective I have on the experiences of conflict and of coming home from it. Lloyd once told me that the problem he had with war films was that the soldiers "were always walking too close together" . . . an important perspective when thinking about realism and the combat genre.

It will not go unnoticed that the title *The Great War in Hollywood Memory* is in part a reference to Paul Fussell's classic study *The Great War and Modern Memory*. The differences in method and approach between this book and that one are evident, but the idea that cinema had similarly contributed to the cultural memory of the war first occurred to me as a postgraduate at the University of East Anglia. I was encouraged to pursue this by Charles Barr and I would like to especially thank him for his intellectual generosity and his long-standing support for the idea.

I am grateful to my grown-up children, Alex and Sarah Hammond, for getting on with their careers, listening patiently about films they had never seen, commenting wisely on those they had, and looking on with affection, and some amusement, over the years I was researching and writing. I have dedicated this book to Betty Lou and Kelly Hammond, who did not live to see it come into print but never had any doubt that it would. Finally, I want to thank my partner, Mary Hammond, who read and commented on the chapters at every stage. Her enthusiasm and willingness to discuss the ideas in here, regardless of setting or time of day, was, and remains, humbling.

Introduction

DR. OTTERNSCHLAG GOES TO HOLLYWOOD

Vicki Baum introduces the anomic Doctor Otternschlag in the first few pages of her 1929 novel *Menschen im Hotel* as if she is describing the automaton movements of a ghost. "A tall gentleman in the Lounge got up stiffly out of an easy chair and came with bent head towards the porter's desk. He loitered for a bit round the Lounge before approaching the entrance hall. The impression he made was emphatically one of listlessness and boredom." He is not a ghost; the Doctor is a wounded veteran of the Great War. Baum casually ties his behavior to his physical appearance and, in an economy of understatement, provides a characterization of the Doctor as the human debris of the trenches.

> His face, it must be said, consisted of one-half only, in which the sharp and ascetic profile of a Jesuit was completed by an unusually well shaped ear beneath the sparse grey hair on his temples. The other half of his face was not there. In place of it was a confused medley of seams and scars, crossing and overlapping, and among them was set a glass eye. 'A Souvenir from Flanders' Doctor Otternschlag was accustomed to call it when talking to himself.[1]

Her description provides the novel with a pervasive sense of post-traumatic ennui, a matter-of-fact-ness that loads the phrase "nothing ever happens" that he repeats throughout the novel with a symptom, a trace of an unimaginable past. The "Jesuit" half of his face provides evidence of a past devotion to duty that the scarred and misshapen other half abnegates. He is removed by his experiences to a condition beyond carelessness and cynicism—he is described as "cut-off from life." As *genius loci* of the novel he acts as the still axis around which the stories and the characters in the Hotel revolve. He watches them commenting "It's a ghastly business . . .

This is no life. No life at all. But where is there any life? Nothing happens. Nothing goes on. Boring. Old. Dead. Ghastly. Every object around him was a sham."[2] Each of the characters' motivations and actions are depicted and understood through his attitude, his *Weltanschauung*, as if seen through the dead lens of his glass eye. Paradoxically, it is his static torpor that animates the novel.

Such an attitude seems antithetical to the kind of positivist, energetic "Americanism" of the Hollywood studio cinema of the post-war period. Yet in early 1930 Irving Thalberg and MGM bought the rights to the novel, retitled *Grand Hotel* in the English translation, and co-produced the Broadway play. He then enlisted Baum's services in the adaptation of the film and made the innovative decision to make it a multi-star production casting MGM's biggest stars—Greta Garbo, Wallace Beery, John Barrymore, Joan Crawford, and Lionel Barrymore—in the major roles, with the venerable Lewis Stone as the Doctor. What in this novel, apart from the pre-marketing assurance of having been a success, attracted Thalberg? What

FIGURE I.1. "Every object around him was a sham." From left to right: Ferdinand Gottschalk as Piminov, John Barrymore as The Baron, and Lewis Stone as Dr. Otternschlag in *Grand Hotel* (Edmund Goulding, 1932). Digital frame enlargement.

did he see in this that suggested enough potential to justify a major production investment of capital and star power? Most certainly it was the rhythm of the hum and bustle of the hotel lobby, the jazz playing in the tea room, the potential for rapid cutting between storylines, and the modern décor of the Grand Hotel itself that drove the novel and the play. These elements could be taken to spectacular extremes cinematically through camera movement and editing and the new and by now fully integrated technology of sound. The art deco–inspired sets of Cedric Gibbons and the costumes by Adrian would provide an elegant and sumptuous mise-en-scène. Against this background each star could be shown to their advantage in keeping with the studio's strategy of star development. These were all compelling reasons to take the project to production, and indeed Thalberg and director Edmund Goulding's final film version did exploit all of the technical and creative possibilities of the studio system. Yet from the first scene of the film Dr. Otternschlag remains the hollow center of the piece. The publicity, reviews, and fan magazine stories highlighted the romance of Garbo as the aging and disillusioned ballet dancer Grusinskaya and John Barrymore's broke Baron-turned-jewel-thief. But still the characters circle around the mysterious and profoundly disfigured Doctor.

Through Doctor Otternschlag the Great War lingers over *Grand Hotel* as a presence, an embodied memory of the cultural impact of the first catastrophic global war of the twentieth century. Neither highlighted by the MGM production nor removed as a distasteful reminder to an entertainment-minded public, the Doctor represents the subject of this book, the representation of the Great War in the Hollywood cinema between the wars and its contribution to American cultural memory as it ebbed and flowed across the 1920s and '30s. I will argue that the memory of the war, like the Doctor, permeates the post-war Hollywood system as a mnemonic, an aid to processing the traumas not only of the war itself but of the broader shifts in cultural and social practices wrought by consumer capitalism and modernity. *Grand Hotel* is often cited as a salient example of the incorporation of modernism and its association with "luxury, glamour and affluence" and "the perfect visual style to complement Thalberg's urban strategy of producing pictures based on contemporary sources and themes."[3] It is also an example of the excessive or surplus meanings, references, and cultural currents that run alongside the cooptation of modernism as spectacle and backdrop for romance. The denizens of Baum's world are part of the traumatized population of Weimar Germany. Thalberg's film relies on that as a means of providing a setting for the European glamor and gloom of Greta Garbo, the old-world nobility of

John Barrymore's Baron Geigern, Wallace Beery's bourgeois brute General Direktor Preysing, and Lionel Barrymore's pitiable and terminally ill clerk Kringelein. Along with Doctor Otternschlag these characters, their pasts, and their motivations demonstrate the war's latent presence in the film's visual style.

Thalberg and his team's revisioning of Baum's novel and play acted to suppress the post-war malaise and ennui through spectacular sets, camera work, and high-profile stars to enhance the romantic tragedies of the characters' lives. The war's impact on them is muted in favor of spectacle, motivations, and character traits that serve and enhance the personas of each star. Greta Garbo's identifying line from the film, "I want to be alone," remained with her for her entire career. The economic imperatives of the Hollywood studios were paramount in such adaptations and in this way, different from official forms of memorializing the war such as monuments and public holidays, Hollywood's contribution to the memory of the Great War is largely the product of the distortions and selectivity created by the various commercial and regulatory restraints under which the industry operated during the interwar period. Consequently, Hollywood's contribution to the broader public memory of the war in America is reactive, or responsive within those boundaries.

The specific nature of the memory of the war in Hollywood films can be understood through how it differs from another approach to film and the Great War. Anton Kaes's study of Weimar cinema incorporates the phrase "the lingering effects of the war" to refer to what he calls "shell shock cinema." In Kaes's incisive analysis he sees the war's "tragic aftermath" refracted through the films' visual motifs and narrative structures. In *The Cabinet of Dr. Caligari* (Robert Weine, 1920), *Nosferatu* (F. W. Murnau, 1922), and *Metropolis* (Fritz Lang, 1927) lies "the shock of the war" expressed in fantastic scenarios as a means of uttering Germany's national experience of the trauma of war and defeat.[4] Through mechanisms of displacement and latency that mimic Freudian psychic responses to trauma, Kaes argues that these films "document distressed communities in a state of shock."[5] The key word for my purpose here is his use of the term "aftermath," which connotes the consequences of catastrophe. Kaes's concern is not only with the films' evocation of the real consequences of the war but also with how they connected with the widespread grief and loss that pervaded German everyday life in the 1920s. The trauma of loss and the sheer numbers of dead and wounded suffered by Germany meant that the war was an inescapable but also unspeakable experience. His contribution to the enduring question of what role cinema played in articulating this and in the descent into fascism that came later is to focus on the Weimar culture's trauma and the way in which specific films "allude to, displace, and relive the experience of war and defeat."[6]

The term *aftermath* is as appropriate for Kaes's study of a nation traumatized by loss and defeat in the Great War as it is inappropriate for a study of that war's impact on Hollywood. The United States' experience of the Great War in terms of the length of time involved and the cost in dead and wounded does not match that of Germany or the Allied countries of France and Great Britain. Although considerable in terms of losses and returning wounded—approximately 117,000 dead and 205,000 wounded—it amounts to 0.13% of the population, compared to almost 4% of that of Germany, 2% for Britain, and over 4% for France. In the years that followed the war its effects in Europe were publicly visible in the prevalence of wounded veterans and the public ceremonies of remembrance and privately in the grief and suffering of veterans and the bereaved families of those lost. Kaes notes the significance of the "twelve million soldiers [who] came back physically disabled, and untold numbers [who] endured long term psychological damage."[7] The Weimar years were marked by the cultural humiliation of defeat, and the films that Kaes focuses on differed from the main body of films the German industry produced. Kaes's subjects of analysis, the expressionist cinema, were artistic endeavors that recast that sense of "doom and despair." His study reads these films for cultural forces that were suppressed and never explicitly articulated publicly. In that sense he is dealing with an artistic movement that is responding to the effects of defeat and cultural trauma, the *aftermath* of the war.

The United States' experience was fundamentally different. While the war effort and return of veterans had a high profile in terms of media visibility, the effect was in many ways the converse of that of Germany. Rather than being defeated, the country emerged from the war an enormous economic powerhouse. Wages rose steadily from 1917 and continued throughout the 1920s until the crash of 1929. The social impact of new technologies such as the telephone and the automobile added to a sense of the increasing rhythm of modernization. Cinema culture through the films, the fan magazines, the press, and the social space of the cinema theatres developed alongside these phenomena and became a primary, and very public, visual manifestation of modernity. From 1900 and throughout the war years the American film industry had developed along the lines of the rest of the nation's industrial transformation by incorporating Taylorist "scientific management" techniques and a variation of Fordist principles of serial manufacturing, which standardized production practices but still allowed a flexibility among craftsmen and creatives.[8] As with other forms of American industry, these practices, along with protectionist policies toward imports and extensive distribution networks worldwide, resulted in the dominance of the domestic market, which in turn aided the predominance of Hollywood product internationally.[9] Outside of the boundaries of the United States this phenomenon offered a different version of modernity than that of post-war Europe. In Europe this American modernity of mass production and consumption offered a competitive contrast to European versions and had the effect of superseding "the dichotomously understood assault on traditional culture" of modernity with a discourse of "Americanization."[10] But within the boundaries of the United States the dichotomy persisted. With the rise of the studio system the basis of most Hollywood narratives lay in a response to the challenges of modernization for traditional social mores. Throughout the narratives of the films, the stories in the magazines, and the "real life" stories of the stars, the primary conflict remained to an extent the traditional versus the modern, whether it lay in sensational melodramas set in urban environments, in the encroaching of civilization (modernity) on the wilderness in Westerns, or in the prevalence of dramas concerned with the behavior of the "new woman." The war in Hollywood cinema was incorporated into these broader concerns as a setting as in war films or as a motivation for character behavior and conflict in films featuring veterans and relationships affected by the war. Rather than the war's cultural impact and trauma being expressed through strategies of displacement that articulated its *aftermath*, its consequences, or indeed a national unconscious, the memory of the Great War in Hollywood cinema culture acted as a storehouse of motifs and tropes able to be drawn on in the service of an industry actively seeking to produce clearly told, entertaining stories to paying audiences.

In considering how cultural memory persists and changes across public spaces, Joan Ramón Resina has used the term *after-image* in his work on urban environments and architecture to refer to "a visual sensation that lingers after the stimulus that provoked it has disappeared."[11] Resina invokes after-image to refer to a way of conceiving the ongoing development of urban spaces by underscoring their fluidity across historical and social frameworks. Incorporating "image" in a wider semantic sense, he expands the "image" metaphor beyond the optical to a "general sense of 'visuality,' which includes tropes, mental arrangements of spatial information and the effects of perceptual organization."[12] He sees image-like structures that emerge at points in the urbanizing process as "precipitates from social and historical solutions" and as solid manifestations or imprints of their historical and social moment. Moreover, these precipitates influence and affect those that follow and perpetuate, shape, and distort the original stimulus. Architecture shares with cinema the goal of organizing space and creating narratives with preferred meanings, and this nuanced concept of after-image allows a means of understanding how a historical event, like the Great War, is co-opted by and incorporated into the processes of cinema culture. After-image conceived in this wider way affords a means for accounting for the processes and phenomenon associated with the Hollywood industry, where repetition of successes prompts production cycles and where receptions help to shape and distort the original event and its consequences, giving rise to further, reshaped versions. Films, then, are not only texts but part of events in the same way as those "solid" architectural objects that arise as moments from the flow of their social and historical processes. In this way it is possible to account for the shifts, refractions, distortions, and concealments that shape the memory of the war in specific films, their stars, the advertising and framing stories that surround them, and the critical responses to them.

Seeing films as not only texts but "events" helps to extend the available evidence for their contribution to public memory of the war beyond the text. Demonstrating how specific films, their advertising campaigns, and instances of critical and popular reception mobilize broader discursive trends has provided a rich field for investigation, if not a complete account of a national memory. This is critical for understanding the way films are situated within their historical moment and offers a means of diachronic comparison with other films within previous and subsequent time periods. It is also effective in allowing for a productive selection of texts. The Great War is referred to in numerous ways throughout many films in the interwar period. There is an abundance of choice of texts in this period, and each would provide an important nuance, however slight, to the broader trends and trajectories of how the memory of the Great War developed in Hollywood productions across the two decades. However, in order to trace the often contradictory currents of the cultural memory of the war in the United States in depth I have had to make specific choices. The controlling criteria here for selection operate slightly differently with each chapter. For part I, "Kleos: Glory," the choice of war films selected was guided by their presentation as memorials to those who experienced the war. From *The Lost Battalion* (1919) to *The Fighting 69th* (1940), the films I have chosen to focus on in one way or another offer themselves up as a cinematic memorial to the war. Not all of these are specific to the American experience; critically, two films that profoundly affected the way Hollywood remembered the Great War, *All Quiet on the Western Front* (1930) and *Journey's End* (1930), are not about the American experience. But they were central to the articulation of pacifism and anti-war sentiment that was pervasive in the later part of the 1920s and into the mid-'30s. In many ways these films were able to present a harder-hitting treatise against war precisely because they were not centered on the American Expeditionary Force's experience. Similarly, the choice of war-in-the-air films was driven by their presentation as memorials, such as *Wings* (1927), and similar to *All Quiet* and *Journey's End* were often set with not the American Expeditionary Force but the Royal Flying Corps. *Hell's Angels* (1930), *The Dawn Patrol* (1930), and *The Eagle and the Hawk* (1933) are all examples of using the British flying experience. These films differ from the war-on-the-ground films in that they hold within them the contradictory appeal of the pity of war and war as laboratory for technological progress and the source of cinematic thrills. My choice of the war-nurse cycle was driven not by a criterion of popularity, as these films in this short-lived cycle were modest successes at best, but by an attempt to demonstrate how the studios were "trying out" scenarios that would appeal to wider audiences, in this case women. Here a close look at the production history—for example the various script versions of *War Nurse* (1930) annotated by Becky Gardiner, or the reception of *The Mad Parade* (1931)—reveals, through the changes imposed on Gardiner and the resistant critical responses to wisecracking women, the important contribution women script writers had been making throughout the 1920s and '30s in demonstrating, however coded, gender power imbalances not only in the military but in American society more generally.

Veterans as characters make up part II, "Nostos: Home." I found the more films I considered, the more I found traces of veterans. The basis of the second part of this book is that the veteran as a character was, and remains, a malleable figure in a narrative system built on requirements of plausible actions with identifiable motivations. The Hollywood narrative system developed through the need to tell stories clearly and efficiently to paying audiences. The veteran is a particularly useful type for this system in that veterans are unpredictable and the very fact that they have been in war makes them so. The way that veterans are written into films and how they are responded to by other characters indicates the shifting currents of the memory of the war. Veterans are in fact the embodied memory of the war and its impact and consequences, either mental or physical. The Greek term *xenos*, which refers to stranger but also to guest-friend, applies here not simply because it outlines the veteran as stranger in his own land but because they are familiar, uncanny. The veteran comes home changed, the same but different. Kate McLoughlin points to the veteran as serving as "a gauge for a community's attitudes towards those who are different, those who are vulnerable, those who are threatening and even those who pose problems because they exceed normal standards of fortitude, strength and bravery."[13] McLoughlin's attribution of those traits lines up with the way veterans function in the Hollywood system. They illuminate the nature of the other characters around them. Their unpredictable behavior, whether threatening or not, provides narrative information and character development across a range of films. The veteran's ability to prompt attitudes in other characters provides a guide to how the memory of the war functions within the Hollywood system. The three chapters in part II are concerned with veteran characters as they functioned in the Hollywood system in three ways. The first is as central characters: Leon Kantor in Frank Borzage's *Humoresque* (1920), Kenneth Wayne in two versions of Jane Cowl and Jane Murfin's *Smilin' Through* (1922 and 1932), Hilary Fairfield in George Cukor's *A Bill of Divorcement* (1932), and Dr. Otternschlag in *Grand Hotel*. Each of these films was chosen because the veteran characters in their different manifestations display the evolving memory of the war, illustrating the conflict between traditional and modern ways of living, one of the main preoccupations of the Hollywood narrative system in this period. The second chapter demonstrates the way the veteran character was incorporated by the studio star system and shaped the star persona of Richard Barthelmess, which in turn illustrates the changing and contradictory nature of the memory of the war in American culture. Finally, the veteran was the main criterion for choosing the films in the last chapter, on production cycles. Gangster films and social-problem films often incorporated veteran characters; less common were veterans in horror films. However, there is considerable scholarly writing about the way that horror films feature a return of repressed war trauma via the disfigured features of monsters. While I take that scholarship into account I limit my discussion of horror films to two that feature veterans: *The Black Cat* (Edgar Ulmer, 1934) and *The Old Dark House* (James Whale, 1932).

Because this study is limited to Hollywood production, the representation of race—particularly that of African Americans—is present by its absence. The representation of ethnicity was central to the development of the war film, but precisely in its exclusion of the African American experience. Instead the "melting pot" myth that is apparent in *The Big Parade*

(1925), *The Lost Battalion* (1919), *What Price Glory?* (1926), and *The Fighting 69th* (1940) focused on those of white European origins and mapped across specific immigrant populations in the urban areas of Chicago and New York. African American representation was limited to the portrayal of servants or minstrel figures like the character of Molasses played by Ray Turner in *The Patent Leather Kid* (1927). African American filmmakers did, however, take the Great War and its impact on the African American community as topics in films such as *The Flying Ace* (1926), written, directed and produced by Richard E. Norman for Norman films, and *Absent* (1928), a story of a returning shell-shocked veteran who is helped on the road of recovery by a woman and the American Legion. This was produced and directed by Harry A. Gant for Rosebud Film Corporation.

METHOD

My method incorporates the production histories, the critical receptions, the advertising campaigns, and the film texts as a means of tracing the process of change in the Hollywood studios' interpretation and contribution to the American memory of the Great War. This entails connecting specific films, the "solid objects" of cinema culture, and their industry and reception histories with the broader cultural history of the memorialization of the war in the 1920s and '30s. Throughout this period, the war was a consistent theme and setting for many Hollywood productions as the industry anticipated and responded to audience demand. From big-budget epics such as *The Four Horsemen of the Apocalypse* (1921) and *Wings* (1927) through the Warner Brothers' social-problem production cycle of the early '30s, this "dialogue" between producers and audiences was influenced by the broader cultural changes in the American public's attitudes about the war. Through specific examples, the book traces the industry's perception of those attitudes and charts the decisions that shaped the types of stories chosen for production, the choice and creation of specific stars, and the ways in which new demands both gave rise to new production cycles and also adapted pre-existing ones.

This book explores three interconnected and overlapping areas: story selection and script development, production design, and the generation and reception of production cycles. It places these within the context of wider cultural and historical trends and events. For example, the representations of returning veterans alter considerably between the early to mid-1920s and the early 1930s. In films from the '20s, injury and mental illness often appear as afflictions that are dealt with in the private realm. In *The Enchanted Cottage* (John S. Robertson, 1924), for example, the wounded veteran Oliver Bashforth finds resolution in a fantasy world and the love of the "plain" woman he meets in his country retreat. But a mere decade later the veteran of the social-problem and crime film emerges as the "forgotten man" and is seen as a potential threat to social order. This shift from personal conflict to social problem is evident in the motivations that the classical style attributes to veterans, who often operate as a "shorthand" for narrative clarity. When a veteran commits a crime, for example, as in *I Am a Fugitive from a Chain Gang* (Mervyn LeRoy, 1932), the motivation is unspoken and recognized as driven by an inability to return unaffected to civilian life. Often, too, as in William Dieterle's *The Last Flight* (1931), these characters exhibit symptoms that reflect the current medical debates concerning "shell shock." In this way the character motivations attributed to veterans relate directly to broader social issues and discourses around mental illness, social dis/functionality, and political division.

In selecting stories, the main studios each had slightly different approaches as they constructed their annual production schedules, but these were broadly similar. For example, they all acquired pre-marketed material in the form of stories from popular magazines, from literature, and from successful theatre productions, thus tying their particular responses to the war to a range of pre-circulated narratives. Here I look in detail at key examples of such adaptations, including plays such as Arthur Wing Pinero's *The Enchanted Cottage* (1922) and Clemence Dane's *A Bill of Divorcement* (1920) and novels such as Vicki Baum's *Grand Hotel* and John Monk Saunders's 1929 stories for *Liberty* magazine, "Nikki and Her Warbirds," which were adapted for Warner Brothers as *The Last Flight* in 1931.

Script selection was also developed in house, where studios generated their own material, creating stories of wartime romances and adventures out of previously unpublished scripts. For example, John Monk Saunders sold his story *Wings*, from which the highly successful 1927 production was adapted, directly to Paramount. This influential film initiated the popular aviation production cycle, which included Saunders's work *The Eagle and the Hawk* (1933) and *The Dawn Patrol* (1930). Studios who lost out in in acquiring successful novels and plays generated original stories that were clear derivations. The war is a central setting for some high-profile examples. Laurence Stallings was brought in by Thalberg to write an original story and script for *The Big Parade* (1925), following on the heels of his success with the play *What Price Glory* on Broadway in 1924, for which he subsequently co-wrote the film version for Fox (1926). Darryl Zanuck, well known for his predilection for hard-boiled stories drawn from newspapers, exploited the plight of veterans and events such as the Bonus March and Roosevelt's "Forgotten Man" speech in his commissioning of the original screenplay for *Heroes for Sale* (1933).

One of the key areas of focus here is the role that women scriptwriters played in constructing the cinematic memory of the Great War in this period, during which the studios' conversion to sound meant a new attention to scripts and new opportunities for writers. Almost half of all of the films with a war setting or theme made between 1919 and 1939 were scripted or coscripted by women. Part of the work of this book is in addressing the impact the coming of sound had on the development of an American female vernacular language in cinema through the work of Anita Loos, Hope Loring, and Becky Gardiner, all professionally successful and highly influential during the move from intertitles to soundtrack. I maintain that this vernacular also offered a means by which the social, sexual, and physical conflicts and disruptions brought about by the Great War as experienced by women could be expressed within the developing aesthetic parameters of the war-film production cycle, and that this was often achieved through the efforts of women scriptwriters. Little previous scholarly work has been done on these women's contribution to a nascent cinematic language, and none at all on the fact that among their most common subjects was the effect of war and its returning veterans on civilian life.

The war's impact on production design lay both in the aesthetic changes and strategies adopted by production teams and in the input of particular personnel, many of whom were European émigrés who had experienced the war first-hand. For example, the production team for F.W. Murnau of Karl Rosher, Edgar Ulmer, and Rochus Gliese had a considerable influence on other directors and their production teams at Fox, such as that of Frank Borzage. The example of some of these Weimar émigrés who brought a "trauma aesthetics" to Hollywood demonstrates that the aftermath of the war in Germany triggered in their work in Hollywood a memory of the war, refracted through the studio system for audiences and an American cinema culture with different expectations and experiences. The expressive set designs and intricate camerawork for Borzage's films with war themes such as *7th Heaven* (1927), *Lucky Star* (1929), and *A Farewell to Arms* (1932) exhibit these influences in terms of cinematography and mise-en-scène, particularly in the visual rendering of the characters' interior states. For example, Jean Negulesco, himself a veteran, created a modernist montage of the retreat from Caporetto in *A Farewell to Arms*. This incorporation of visual techniques associated with modernism and expressionism as a means of cinematically rendering Hemingway's celebrated prose offers a clear example of the interconnection between film aesthetics and the wider palette of cultural forms that were influenced by the war or were products of it.

PRODUCTION CYCLES

The war film is only the most obvious example of a type of film that used the war as a centerpiece, however, and this book considers the production and reception of other production cycles that incorporated the war and its social impact into their narratives in less overt ways. I offer detailed examinations of the crime and social-problem film, the aviation or "flying film" cycle from 1927 to '36, and the horror/thriller cycle from 1930 to '34. The war-film cycle covers the entire interwar period and will chart the shift in emphasis from adventure films through the anti-war or pro-pacifist films led by films such as *Journey's End* (1931) and *All Quiet on the Western Front* (1932) to films that reinvigorate the cycle in the late 1930s such as William Keighly's *Fighting 69th*, filmed in 1939 and released in January 1940. The crime and social-problem cycle also extends across this period. The focus here will be on the subject of characterization and the depiction of the returning veteran character. The emphasis of the study of these films is on script development and the use of the veteran and the war itself as plausible motivating characteristics. I will explore the persistence of this character as a marker of the intersection of medical and public discourse concerning the issues of shell shock and mental illness more broadly.

The chapter for the aviation cycle roughly follows the career of novelist and playwright John Monk Saunders, who wrote *Wings*, is credited with *The Dawn Patrol* (1930), and wrote eight other aviation films with the Great War as their setting. The exploration will not be solely confined to Saunders's work, but his career from *Wings* up to the remake of *The Dawn Patrol* in 1938 offers a central guide to the development of the cycle as well as to the film industry's relationship to publishing and theatre trends.

THE STRUCTURE

The book is divided into two parts, "Kleos: Glory" and "Nostos: Home." These are Greek terms used to describe the themes of "glory" in the *Iliad* and of "homecoming" in the *Odyssey*. Part I, "Kleos: Glory," is concerned with films that are set at the front, while part II, "Nostos: Home," considers those films concerned with the aftermath of the war on those who returned and on the families and communities they returned to. Chapter 1, "The War on the Ground," introduces Charles Chaplin's *Shoulder Arms* (1918), a remarkable film that through comedy presciently depicts the sense of futility that becomes more fully realized in the later films of the period. The chapter then focuses on the war-on-the-ground production cycle that immediately followed the war with *The Lost Battalion* (Burton King, 1919), D.W. Griffith's *The Girl Who Stayed at Home* (1919), and *The Four Horsemen of the Apocalypse* (Rex Ingram, 1921), early attempts at ennobling the memory for the war through more traditional tropes of glory and sacrifice. Chapter 2, "The War in the Ground," represented by *What Price Glory* (1926), *The Big Parade* (1925), and *The Unknown Soldier* (1926), offers a set of competing versions of the war's memory in the interwar period as romantic sacrifice and/or grim reality. I incorporate Jay Winter's concept of a "geometry of memory" as a means of charting the way these films move from casting the war as a heroic and glorious enterprise to one of futility and melancholy:

> At any single site, remembrance of war can move in many directions, but its center of gravity, its core, is grief mourning and bereavement, described as such in so much of Western art through an emphasis on the horizontal axis. The vertical is the language of hope, the horizontal the language of loss.[14]

Throughout the '20s there is a discernible shift toward putting the blame for the war onto militarism itself. This move, developed through *What Price Glory* and *The Big Parade,* reached an apotheosis with *Journey's End* (James Whale, 1930) and *All Quiet on the Western Front* (Lewis Milestone, 1930). The chapter examines this shift as it manifested itself through the studios' story selection and choices of source material, particularly the relationship between concurrent examples in literature and theatre. This continues with the sound films of the early 1930s, and specifically *Journey's End* (1930) and *All Quiet on the Western Front* (1930). The shift toward the anti-war sentiment highlights the relationship between the Hollywood industry and literary modernism.

Chapter 3, "The War in the Air," considers the aviation cycle beginning with *Wings* up to the mid-1930s. It focuses primarily on the work of John Monk Saunders and on Howard Hughes's *Hell's Angels* (1930). This enduring cycle offered the combination of aerial spectacle and the underlying melancholy of the war films on the ground. *Wings* and *Hell's Angels* provided the template for depicting aerial combat, but the cycle was most fully developed in the work of Saunders. His stories for films such as *The Legion of the Condemned* (1929), *The Dawn Patrol* (both versions, 1930 and 1938), *The Eagle and the Hawk* (1933), and *Ace of Aces* (1933) explored the relationship between war and trauma in ways that resolved the commercial imperative for thrills with a corresponding reverence for sacrifice.

Chapter 4, "Forbidden Zones," concludes the "Kleos: Glory" section with an examination of the role of women scriptwriters in developing both this cultural memory and an influential American vernacular. It focuses primarily on the roles of Hope Loring in writing *Wings* (1927) and of Becky Gardiner in writing the sound film *War Nurse* (1930). The use of vernacular to render realism in the male adventure war films provides a turning point not only in the development of an anti-sentimental American voice but also in the modern American woman's voice.

The next three chapters make up part II, "Nostos: Home," focusing on the returning veteran. Chapter 5, "Veterans," considers the veteran as a motif in social dramas such as *Grand Hotel* (1932), *A Bill of Divorcement* (1932), and *The Last Flight* (1931). It examines Hollywood's relationship with adaptations from the stage, including their production and reception. Picking up on the insights from *Journey's End* and *All Quiet On the Western Front*, it examines the transnational nature of the representation of the war in these anti-war plays. The returning veteran is considered through the fantasy scenarios of *The Enchanted Cottage* and *Smilin' Through* (1932), which feature the traumas of the war played out in a bucolic England and negotiated through spiritualist fantasy.

Chapter 6, "War Relic and Forgotten Man," offers a star study of Richard Barthelmess. Across the interwar period the Hollywood industry's attempts to imagine the World War I veteran's experience on screen were characterized by tensions between traditional and modern versions. Throughout much of the 1920s the veteran was a "relic" of the past to be honored and feted. But during periods of social unrest and particularly the financial crises of the 1930s, the veteran became an unwelcome reminder of the war's cost and a threat to the social order, a "forgotten man." Richard Barthelmess was a star whose career traversed this period and this representational trajectory. His roles as a wounded flyer in *The Enchanted Cottage* (1924) and as a reformed addict in *Heroes for Sale* (1933) offer an example of the relationship between the construction and commemoration of the World War I veteran in American culture and Hollywood industry practice. By highlighting Barthelmess, the chapter explores the policy of Daryl Zanuck at Warner Brothers in developing a realist, "hard-boiled" aesthetic and the role played in this by returning veterans and the deeper issues of war trauma in the 1930s. Such production decisions were directly linked to the wider debates that surrounded Great War veterans exemplified by events such as the Bonus March on Washington in 1932.

The final chapter is inspired by a 1927 novel by J.B. Priestley, entitled *Benighted*, which describes the unreliable and unpredictable behavior of the veteran characters that stand out as generic tropes in the gangster and the horror cycles that incorporated the war. The chapter, "The After-Images," considers the war as a motivating force in the crime and social-problem films such as *The Public Enemy* (William A. Wellman, 1931), *Scarface* (Howard Hawks, 1931), *I Am a Fugitive from a Chain Gang* (1932), and *Heroes for Sale* (1933). It focuses on setting and performance in the thriller/horror cycle from Lon Chaney through to the horror cycles of the early 1930s, considering whether the relationship between the development of the thriller in the '20s (and then the horror cycle in the '30s) and the impact of the Great War is as direct as some historians suggest. The chapter seeks to show the social function of the thriller production cycle as having an oblique connection to the war. While in the United States there was certainly a general social anxiety around the results of mechanized warfare on the human body, these films also need to be seen in the context of the variety of issues, public discourses, debates, and traditions of performance that, while related to the war, have a much longer and often neglected history. I will further suggest that the almost direct relationship between the war and the more highbrow film culture through expressionism, dada, and the European avant-garde—represented in part by the European émigré directors and personnel such as Paul Leni, F.W. Murnau, and Karl Freund and actors such as Emil Jannings and Conrad Veidt—is much less clear with Hollywood's more lowbrow fare. This is the case with many of Chaney's films, but particularly with the Browning-Chaney collaborations.

Throughout this period the war's impact on the bodies of veterans accelerated shifts in public perceptions of disability and mental illness through concerns for veterans' rehabilitation. Categories of "lunatic" and "cripple" were already in the process of being redefined through public debate and legislation as well as in the cultural forms of literature, theatre, and eventually cinema. It is important to recognize the influence of and dialogue with European and British medical communities on both physical and mental disability. Some of these nomenclatures and medical taxonomies entered popular discourse, often in distorted and incomplete ways. *The Enchanted Cottage* dealt with the return of a shattered flyer in a fantasy scenario. Pinero's play was designed to draw attention to the plight of those returning British soldiers and to offer an accessible account of their mental torment. J.B. Priestley's *Benighted* is the story of three people caught in a violent storm who seek shelter in an old manor house occupied by strange eccentrics. The trio is a couple and a single man. The two men are veterans, and the single man is "benighted" by his experiences in the war. The novel was retitled for the US market as *The Old Dark House* (1928). The title was an attempt by the US publishers to fit the novel as a smart satire of the "haunted house genre" of popular fiction and theatre of the '20s. It was then adapted in 1932 by Universal as a follow-up to *Frankenstein*, directed by British war veteran James Whale. The film was faithful to the novel and succeeds for the most part in imparting a sense of dread and, like Dr. Otternschlag in *Grand Hotel*, is imbued with a touch of the traumatic past. The plot's conflict in the novel and film is between the disenchanted trio, who act as representatives of the forces of modernity and the ancient and decaying aristocracy of the occupants of the house. For the film the replacement of the original downbeat ending was the only real change and this was made following test screenings to audiences. The placement of both novel and film within a larger production cycle and the decision to use it as a follow-up to Whale's *Frankenstein* demonstrates how marketing and aesthetic choices twist, reshape, and refract the image of the war and its effects. While Hollywood exploited European and British novels and plays dealing with the aftermath of the war, the industry's marketing and the films' receptions also contributed to wider cultural discourses concerning disability and mental illness. In this way, for the American market, these films construct and offer "solid" examples of the after-image of the Great War.

The chapter concludes with a focus on the legacy of the war as embedded memory to look forward to the returning soldier of World War II and the lessons learned from history. From there it points to the persistent after-image of the war in Hollywood up to the present day: from Kubrick's *Paths of Glory* (1957) through the cycle of Vietnam films in the 1980s, where the inheritance of the Great War lies as an underlying obbligato of melancholy, futility, and irony. The returning veteran films of the post–World War II period also owe a debt to the almost-forgotten returning-veteran films of the 1920s and '30s. *The Men* (Fred Zinnemann, 1950), *Captain Newman M.D.* (David Miller, 1963), *Coming Home* (Hal Ashby, 1978), *Born on the Fourth of July* (Oliver Stone, 1989), *Dead Presidents* (Hughes Brothers, 1995), and *In the Valley of Elah* (Paul Haggis, 2007) all offer examples of scriptwriting and characterizations that draw on the precedent of incorporating contemporary and popularized trauma discourse as a means of attributing causal motivations to veteran characters. The Great War's legacy lies not only in the generic traditions of the war film, the aviation film, and the crime film established in the interwar period but also in its role as a counterweight to prevailing discourses about the war's purpose. The Great War's after-image hovers over the post–World War II returning veteran film in the internal conflict the veteran characters confront. In some cases these characters are almost unchanged from some of the earliest examples, such as Oliver Bashforth in *The Enchanted Cottage*, which was remade by RKO with director John Cromwell in 1945. The later version updates the setting, but the anger and bitterness of the veteran remains curable only through his newfound vision of beauty in his "plain" wife and in himself. While his symptoms are recognizable as shell shock, his "cure" is in the whimsical magic of the cottage. It is not until the Hollywood Vietnam War film cycle that the explicit trauma discourse becomes evident as a recognizable character motivation.

At the end of *Grand Hotel* Dr. Otternschlag stands by the revolving door of the hotel, all the guests having left, the "Jesuit" side of his face to camera. He states the film's epitaph: "Grand Hotel. Always the same. People come, people go. Nothing ever happens." The camera pulls back and we see him through the glass of the revolving panels as he disappears into the hotel, an apparition destined to remain confined in the eternal ennui of the endless flow of the hotel's paying customers, a revenant of the Great War uttering blank judgments on their anomic existence. It is a surprising contrast to the celebration of the modern extravagance of the films' glittering set and yet it is an apt metaphor for the celluloid memory of the Great War. The Doctor could just as well be pronouncing on the parade of films, scripts, publicity campaigns, and reviews that make up Hollywood cinema culture. However, each film, like each hotel guest, holds its own difference, its own iteration of the interplay between fiction, history, and memory. It is the interaction between the memory of the war the Doctor represents and the diversity of Hollywood film productions and their receptions that is the subject of this book.

PART I

Kleos: Glory

Chapter 1

THE WAR ON THE GROUND
From Edenic to Blasted

D.W. Griffith's oft-quoted declaration that the Western Front as a drama was "disappointing" underscores the problems that faced Hollywood filmmakers during and immediately after the war. There were no glorious charges on horseback, and while there were battles with charges they were sporadic in a war of attrition. Soldiers spent their time in the trenches, surrounded by sandbags and earth, or even underground. Any attachment to war and romance ran counter to a commitment to authenticity. The promise of cinema as recorder of truth was rendered ineffective by the logistics of modern trench warfare, where being seen meant being killed. The tension between the romance of war as a setting for adventure stories and the realities of the Western Front, a moonscape framed by barbed wire, set the terms of the aesthetic development of the Hollywood war film in the 1920s. Similar tensions between the traditional and the modern typified debates about the way the war should be remembered, the way soldiers should be memorialized, and whether the war had been a worthwhile endeavor or an exercise in futility. Hollywood as an entertainment industry tended to react to broader cultural responses to the question of remembering and memorializing the war. The debates concerning the heroics on the battlefield, the repatriation of the dead, the ceremonial Unknown Soldier, the plight of veterans, or the Gold Star Mothers' pilgrimages were represented in various ways by the industry. In that sense Hollywood's contribution to the developing American memory of the Great War was contradictory. Its currents often ran in opposite directions; some films focused on action and adventure and glorified the endeavor, while others were more contemplative and humanized the terror and anguish of war. These currents ebbed and flowed with the broader public discourses that informed the memory of the war throughout the '20s and '30s.

As the decade progressed, Hollywood war films' relationship with landscape altered. At times they contrasted the pastoral land or western vistas of the New World with the blasted and decadent landscapes of the Western Front; at others, the bustle and speed of the American city and its own decadence were countered by the serene pastoral of the rural land in Europe or the contemplative spaces of military cemeteries. Along with these themes came specific aesthetic practices in depicting the front. There was a discernible trajectory across the decade from a romantic panorama—with sweeping armies rendered through high-angle epic shots and a focus on the characters caught up in a universe where ultimately innocence and justice prevail—to frames filled with dirt, dying soldiers, and explosions, with editing practices that work to decenter the audience and to render war as chaos, physically, morally, and ethically. This trajectory is literal as the camera, and later also the microphone, moves to smaller and lower spaces in the landscape. Jay Winter's focus on the spatial logic of memorials is pertinent here for two reasons. The first is that war films are in themselves memorials, albeit commercial in intent. For reasons of profit, but also uplift and respectability, Hollywood films about the war often advertised and presented themselves as memorials. Secondly, the broader shift in representing warscapes cinematically from epic to prosaic, from high-angle to low-angle, from clearly constructed space to chaos, aligns well with the term "geometry of remembrance" that Winter applies to war memorials. Hollywood films, like memorials, construct a spatial logic, and similarly, across the interwar years, those films possess within them a tension between a vertical heroic axis and a horizontal contemplative axis. In Winter's terms for some artists and architects of memorials, following the "mass violence and mass death" of the Great War "There is both a logic and force of gravity in the preference for the horizontal."[1] This chapter will focus on a similar trajectory that ran through films that depicted, or had as their setting, the war on the ground and the experience of the infantry, a force that moved toward the indexical and metaphorical properties of landscape, earth, and dirt, and a tendency to descend to the troglodyte worlds of the mise-en-scène of *The Big Parade*, *Journey's End*, or *All Quiet on the Western Front*.

Charles Chaplin offered an uncannily prescient example of this descent into the earth a month before the armistice with his comedy *Shoulder Arms* (1918). Trading his crumpled derby and moth-eaten coat for a helmet and doughboy's uniform, Chaplin's character wreaks havoc in the barracks and in the trenches, then disguises himself as a tree, rescues a French peasant woman from the clutches of comically terrible "Huns" and, disguised as a chauffeur, drives the Kaiser back across enemy lines. Then he wakes up back in the training camp: it has all been a dream. While a summary of the narrative implies a superficiality in the treatment of the trench experience, the film in its subject matter, its mis-en-scène, the comic business around soldiers' discomfort, danger, and fear, and the fantasy of heroics hinted at the darkly pathetic picture of the front presented by later war films such as *All Quiet on the Western Front* and *Journey's End*.

The intended structure of Chaplin's film was to begin with his familiar tramp figure Charlie joining the army. The father of three children tormented by a comic virago wife, he receives a letter outlining the adventures and romance of life in Uncle Sam's army. It is written in the vertical language of wartime propaganda. "Have you ever thought what a romantic life a soldier in the army of Uncle Sam leads?" The letter promises all of the attributes that he lacks, his "expenses paid, even his clothes furnished . . . a few hours a day at work that is more like play" and promising "You can be a big handsome man too." Chaplin's comedy, and his unprecedented popularity, had been built on the tramp figure who moved from film to film, from chaos to chaos, always the outsider. He described the character he had invented to Mack Sennett as "many-sided, a tramp, a gentleman, a poet, a dreamer, a lonely fellow, always hopeful of romance and adventure. He would have you believe he is a scientist, a musician, a duke, a polo player. However he is not above picking up cigarette butts or robbing a baby of its candy."[2] Charlie's character in uniform was another example of the tramp as imposter that appealed to soldiers who saw themselves as more than a "Government Issue" cog in the military machine.

At the same time, his military masquerade, the unstable and innervated tramp in uniform, subtly pointed to the con that was the myth of war as a transformative experience. However, Chaplin must have recognized that his character conveyed these qualities as soon as he donned the uniform, and in the final film he dispensed with this beginning and plunged Charlie straight into boot camp. By 1918 Chaplin was recognizable through his trademark mustache, oversized shoes, and erratic walk. The doughboy uniform on Charlie was the visual counter to its intended function of erasing individuality. Charlie in boot camp responds to the regimen in the same way he did in his "work" films, disrupting the order and rationale of the training process. As he marches, the drill sergeant shouts at him about his turned-out feet. He turns them in and marches straight until the sergeant turns away and then the feet go out again, only to come back when the sergeant looks at him. This visual gag is repeated along with the rhythm of the marching soldiers' feet but in effect disrupting it.

Treating the military experience in this way connected with soldiers, for whom the anomic existence of the front was a constant.

The comic possibilities of Charlie in uniform appealed to Chaplin enough for him to risk satirizing the war, the devastating effects of which were certainly evident by 1918. The effort was made more perilous because Chaplin had been singled out by the British press two years earlier for enjoying the riches of Hollywood rather than fighting for his country.[3] Much of this critique had subsided by 1918 due to a concerted effort by Chaplin and Essanay, particularly their London publicist Langford Reed. In his 1916 book *The Chronicles of Charlie Chaplin* Reed quoted British soldiers' comments endorsing his effect on their morale. He quoted W. Murphy, a major in the Royal Army Service Corps, who wrote of Chaplin's films, "It is impossible to make you realize how they were appreciated, and I truly wish you could have heard the cheer that went up when Charlie appeared on the screen."[4] Chaplin's financial contributions to the war effort and his appearances, along with Mary Pickford and Douglas Fairbanks, on a countrywide War Bond junket in 1918 helped to assuage any further accusations of slackerism. More forcefully, a consensus seemed to have been reached that his positive impact on troop morale was his most valued contribution. Nevertheless, those close to him had expressed their concern that a comedy about the catastrophic war could backfire.[5]

The full effect of Chaplin's war comedy lay in its prescient treatment of the trench experience. Able to lampoon the vertical language of heroism, Chaplin takes Charlie straight from the training ground to the trench. Here the frame is filled with sandbags and dirt, death and injury whirls above the parapet, and bombs explode nearby, giving clear cause for his otherwise unmotivated erratic and jerky movements. Below him in the dugout, a set not dissimilar to those in *Journey's End* and *All Quiet on the Western Front*, water runs in and fills it so that Charlie and his comrades and their belongings float on the rising water. Chaplin's trench set invokes the soldiers' troglodyte world and inverts its miseries. These trench scenes bring Chaplin's ability for what Noël Carroll has called "mime metaphor" together with the state of his body as a permeable barrier to outside stimulus. Carroll notes that Chaplin's primary comic quality was as a mime and that he transformed objects into other things.[6] In the dugout he uses a cheese grater as a back scratcher. While hunkered down in the trench as the bullets and shrapnel fly overhead, he holds up a match and uses the flying metal to light it for his cigarette, then he holds up a beer bottle and the bullets act as a bottle opener. His body becomes extrinsically connected to the concussion of explosions, jerking as each one hits closer to him as he stands in the trench. He combines these qualities in the mail-call scene where, failing to get any mail himself, he reads a letter over the shoulder of a fellow soldier. The soldier's emotions, as he reads the letter, seem to transfer to Charlie, who mimics his responses so that they move and emote together in tandem until the soldier looks up at him angrily and Charlie leaves him to his privacy. Moments later Charlie gets a package, significantly addressed to no one, that contains a Limburger cheese. Upon opening it he quickly dons his gas mask and weaponizes it by hurling it into the German trench like a hand grenade. It hits the martinet German officer in the face.

Chaplin's war in the ground goes a step farther than embedding the comedy beneath the earth. He "volunteers" to occupy an observation post and dons the disguise of a tree. He literally becomes a part of the landscape. The scene opens up with an apparent shot of the battlefront with a dead blasted tree in the foreground. Only when Charlie moves is his camouflage, as that tree, obvious. The sight gag offers a play on the very

FIGURE 1.1. Charlie in the trenches reading another soldier's letter from home in *Shoulder Arms* (1918). Chaplin's focus on the troglodyte world of the trenches anticipates that of later war films such as *Journey's End* (James Whale, 1930) and *All Quiet on the Western Front* (Lewis Milestone, 1930). Digital frame enlargement.

real danger of being seen above ground at the front. It also uses the consistent trope of Charlie's extrinsic nature, of taking on the energies and appearance of his surroundings. In this case the masquerade is as nature, the impact of which is only fully felt when a German soldier, looking for firewood, approaches Charlie's "tree" with an ax. That disguise turns to visual trickery in the following scenes, where Henry Bergman as the portly German soldier chases the tree into a forest. *Film Daily* saw this scene as a highlight of the film, "an awful lot of fun" where "Charlie was chased by a fat German soldier through a wood where he would occasionally hide while the German stabbed the various trees trying to find him . . . [and it] . . . was great stuff because the audience had an awful time with each new flash (shot) trying to locate the comedian."[7] The visual conceit, in keeping with Chaplin's approach to this war comedy, leverages his persona as "always hopeful of romance and adventure" to blur the distinctions between persons and the environment and sheds some light on the devastation and futility of the war to nature and humanity.

The reviews for the film were uniformly positive. Showcased prior to the armistice, however, it did prompt some reviewers to note the somber subject matter. Sime Silverman of *Variety* wrote that "the laughs were many" but that it might have been even more successful had Chaplin waited till the war was over. But Silverman's review seems to indicate a deeper resonance for the film across the coming decade. "One must still laugh heartily notwithstanding what the subject matter forces into memory."[8] The drift downward toward a horizontal futility is predicated in the toppling of the vertical heroics of Charlie's dream. Charlie's antics present the nightmare of war in a humorous frame but he awakens to an altogether more somber reality. Louis Delluc, writing in 1921, noticed the proximity of Chaplin's humor to the tragedy of the war. He saw the film as "An hour of laughter if you like—but say, rather, an hour of lashes, one after the other. . . . When dogs are wretched they bay at the moon. That war film of Chaplin bays most terribly at the moon."[9] *Shoulder Arms* in this regard offers a first glimpse into the trajectory of Hollywood's memory of the war through the 1920s.

DOWN TO EARTH

One of the earliest memorial films was Edward McManus Productions' *The Lost Battalion*, released on the September 8, 1919, two months before the first anniversary of the armistice. The film was a reenactment of the story of the 77th "New York's Own" Division. Made up of men from a cross-section of ethnic and class backgrounds, the division took part in the Allied advance in the Argonne Forest in October 1918. They advanced far into the German lines, where they were surrounded and then heroically held out against repeated German attacks until rescued. Widely reported in the press at the time, the event had come to represent the courage and bravery of the US forces on the Western Front by the end of the war. The film was heralded by the *Moving Picture Age* as a "most valuable historical document" due to its "fidelity to detail."[10] The intent of McManus and director Burton King was to combine the sensation of realism with the reverence of a memorial. Much of the purported realism was provided through the inclusion of surviving members of the 77th alongside actors in a fiction concocted by scriptwriter Charles A. Logue. Logue had written three war-themed films the previous year: *The Service Star, My Four Years in Germany*, and *Too Fat to Fight. My Four Years in Germany* was based on James W. Gerard's account of his time as US Ambassador to Germany and combined newsreel footage with melodramatically staged scenes to catalog the atrocities of the Kaiser and his troops. Logue's approach to the scenario of *The Lost Battalion* was similar in that it combined US Signal Corps footage, reenacted scenes, and fictional vignettes into a story that centered on the melting pot theme that had become central to the popular myth of the Lost Battalion. Included in the cross-class range of characters were a middle-class clerk, a son of a wealthy industrialist who tries to pull strings with the army, and a ne'er-do-well burglar. In addition Logue added comic scenes of army camp life while incorporating pathos through depicting the relationships between the soldiers and their loved ones at home. The early scenes are taken up with depicting the leveling and regenerative effects of the military experience. The wealthy son is relegated to KP duty. The clerk, who was ineffectual in his job in civilian life, learns the value of work. When the police arrive to arrest the burglar, the camp commander sends them away, a gesture of solidarity.

The film highlighted all of the elements of the story that had been circulating in the press since the news of the Lost Battalion first broke on October 3, 1918. The press at the time had been running updates until the Battalion was rescued five days later.[11] The film highlighted main elements that had been central to the press reports, its "last stand" status, the heroics of commander Major Charles Whittlesey, and the diverse ethnicity of the 77th, who were mainly from the streets of New York City. Logue built the story around the event by weaving together vignettes of actual and fictional characters. His story embellished these elements through romanticized scenarios that emphasized the men's comradeship and the trials of those waiting at home, but throughout touched on the well-known aspects of the story. The division had advanced farther and achieved their objectives only to be cut off; the heroics of Private Abraham Krotoshinsky, who escaped and made contact with rescuing forces, and the story of the carrier pigeon Cher Ami, which delivered the message that halted US shells landing on their own men, were all high-profile episodes in the press reports at the time. The best known of these stories was Whittlesey's response "Go to hell" to a German request to surrender. The film's memorializing form is evident in its emphasis on these vignettes rather than in the kind of character development that was central to the dominant Hollywood form by that time or to the way that D.W. Griffith's films such as *Birth of a Nation* and *Hearts of the World* built pathos into their battle sequences.

McManus's strategy for marketing the film adhered to the same theme of authenticity by inviting the comments and endorsements of well-known and respected public figures. In June 1919 *Moving Picture World* noted that "While most of the film industry is busy combating oppressive censorship, the McManus corporation comes out this week with the announcement that it has invited . . . [a] powerful group of censors to pass judgment on its feature 'The Lost Battalion.'"[12] It was indeed an impressive group that included future president Calvin Coolidge; Theodore Roosevelt; Maud Ballington Booth, prominent leader of the Salvation Army and founder of the charity Volunteers of America; and Alfred E. Smith, Governor of New York. McManus promised to print their comments "good, bad or indifferent." McManus built on this kind of publicity to capitalize on the high public awareness of the subject matter before interest waned.

The transparent attempt to exploit one of the most publicized episodes of the American involvement in the war was encouraged in *Moving Picture World* (*MPW*). Highlighting cinema's ability to preserve the heroic deeds on celluloid, exhibitors were told to "Sell History": "The battle of Bunker Hill would be good today. So would Sheridan's ride. So would any chapter of American military history re-enacted by the men who came out of the battle alive." *MPW* highlighted Calvin Coolidge's telegram to McManus praising the "celluloid film" as permanent record and "proof to the rising generations that Americans are ready to die for their country."[13] The reverent tone of memorial rang through the article while the romance of the fictitious characters added a "universal touch." Multiple angles on exploitation, from the humor of camp life to the excitement of battle

FIGURE 1.2. *The Lost Battalion* featured footage of Lt. Col. Whittlesey (right; promoted from Major after the events of the movie) as well as other surviving members of the 77th Battalion. Digital frame enlargement.

scenes, belied concern among the producers that the film might appeal only to the Manhattan area from where most of the 77th were originally drawn. The advice was to stress that many of the replacements for the division were from all areas of the nation and the appeal would stretch beyond Manhattan to the rest of the country. The main worry, however, was that the war, by the summer of 1919, was old news. *Wid's Daily*, in its column on advice to exhibitors, labeled the film "history" and recommended exploiting the film accordingly. "It is a conceded fact now that Peace is at hand people's minds have turned to other things than war."[14] Describing the film as a "visualized news story," *Wid's* review criticized the inclusion of "home scenes, before and after" and complained that the film was too long.

Whether McManus, Logue, or King included the home scenes as a means of addressing the problem of war-weariness is unclear. *Wid's Daily*'s critique was borne out in the relatively unfulfilled expectations of the film at the box office. It ran for two weeks at the George M. Cohan theatre in Manhattan, respectable but not exceptional. Yet *Wid's* critique also offers an insight into the film's place in the evolving cinematic memory and memorialization of the war. While it dismisses the photography as "nothing special," it describes the battle scenes as having been guided by "someone who knew something of military affairs." Although described as "conventionally done," close-ups dominate in the depiction of the "fighting, starving and thirsty men."[15] The close camera work has the effect of bringing out the physical and mental ordeal of the men holding out in the wooded area. Significantly for what was to become a visual theme in depictions of the front throughout the 1920s, the close-ups had the effect of filling the frame with the foliage and dirt of the ground the soldiers occupy.

The conventions of filming battle scenes had been set by Griffith's *The Birth of a Nation* in 1915 with sweeping panoramas and the movement of armies in long shot combined with the close-ups of the struggles of the Little Colonel and hand-to-hand fighting. *The Lost Battalion*'s promotion stressed its relationship with Griffith's film by commissioning a score from *The Birth of a Nation*'s composer, Joseph Carl Breil, while the reviews they chose to feature in the advertisements for the film connected the use of actual survivors with Griffith's cinematic artistry.[16] In keeping with the link with history, the film was "like viewing 'The Birth of a Nation' with the original cast of its Civil War heroes."[17] However, in *The Lost Battalion*, the emphasis is on close-ups; there are few panoramic shots of the battlefield and those that are there are not from elevated platforms or high-angle camera placement. Rather, the camerawork is exclusively at ground level. The first battlefield shot introduces General Alexander inspecting the troops with the camera in the trench and the horizon high in the frame. The progression of the battle as the 77th move from the trench through the woods of the Argonne Forest overtaking the German trenches and finally ending up surrounded in "the Pocket" is also a progression of enveloping the soldiers in the landscape, pictorially engulfing them in the ground. Budget restrictions, intentionally or not, enabled an aesthetic reordering of the depiction of the Great War into one of claustrophobia and suffocation by the scarred and shattered battlefield itself. The shots of the men in their funk holes feature no sky at all. To underscore the immersion of bodies into the earth, at one point a soldier is shot dead trying to get water from a filthy pond; he falls, his head immersed in the water, his body framed by the woods and the ground. The dominance of close-ups and tight framing in the battle sequences was in fact the consequence of budgetary and time restraints on a production meant to capitalize on a well-known story while it was still fresh in the public mind, but regardless of the cause, *The Lost Battalion* provides an early version of the move away from the epic sweep of battle scenes toward the troglodyte experience of soldiers in the Great War.

The influence of Griffith was still apparent in the editing between the fighting and those waiting at home. Contemporary criticisms of the scenes from home as "extraneous matter"[18] underscored the flaws of trying to link the two spaces. The intercutting from home to front here was intended as a *memoria* designed to highlight the sacrifices made at the front and at home. It is significant that the soldiers whose deaths were depicted were played by actors with fictional names, which rendered explicit the action and suffering that is entombed in memorials, referred to but never expressed. The scene of the soldier who is killed beside the pond, immersed in water, carries with it the implication of baptism and absolution. As the battle rages the soldier identified as "the burglar" leaves his funk hole to rescue a wounded comrade. He is shot, and then a cut-in frames him in iris as he lies dying, followed by a cut to his mother reading the Bible with the girl next door. As the girl looks down the mother closes the Bible, establishing the spiritual link between mother and son, acknowledging his death (and regeneration) and her sacrifice.

The film's network structure binding the personal stories of the soldiers depended on public understanding of the actual personalities involved. Major Whittlesey's response "Go to hell" to the German demand for surrender and Private Krotoshinsky's break-through of German lines to bring the rescuing forces were widely known by the time of the film's release. The fictional vignettes were also emblematic of the wider experience of both Western Front and home front. The burglar's story was one of regeneration through death and sacrifice; the "hyphenates," i.e., the Chinese American, German American, and Jewish American, reenacted earning the right of citizenship, while the middle-class romances negotiated the impact of the war on gender relationships, albeit as a means of recuperating them. The burglar's mother acts as the representative of the sacrifice and this is carried through in the function of the service flag with the blue star that the girl next door holds, which becomes the gold star held by his mother at the end of the film.[19]

In keeping with the film's symbolic system of the authentic through "relics," the actual survivors' reenactment, the film ends in the Argonne Forest with a long shot of the fresh graves of the dead of the 77th. Preceding the final funerary image are actual scenes of the parade held on May 6,

1919, in New York of the 77th intercut with the fictitious women characters watching the proceedings. The film continues the Western Front/home front binary between the women and the soldiers on parade in this way and sets up the final shot of the graves. The wooden crosses on the graves in France are surrounded by the foliage and earth of the land, with just a hint of sky in the top left corner of the frame. The cross-cutting of the film between home and front culminates here in an unintended provocation. By the summer of 1919 the question of identifying the dead, or preserving their remains and bringing them home, had become a matter of debate within the federal government. The film seems to tacitly support the creation of memorials in France, but the debate about the return of the bodies was far from settled at this time and in fact played out over the next five years.[20] Ending with soldiers literally buried in the ground offers a final set of objects in the film's symbolic system as reliquary. They are the culmination of the image–objectification dynamic in the reenactment by the survivors, the fetishization represented by the artifacts in the film of the written German surrender demand, or the depiction of Cher Ami, the carrier pigeon. Yet in terms of the impact of the war on American cinematic style and the representation of battle on the ground, *The Lost Battalion* points to an inexorable move toward engulfing the frame with dirt, foliage, and blasted landscape.

LANDSCAPES: EDENIC AND BLASTED

Two months before McManus had submitted *The Lost Battalion* to his esteemed panel for approval, D.W. Griffith had already incorporated reference to the Lost Battalion in *The Girl Who Stayed at Home*. In that film Ralph Gray, the upstanding older brother played by Richard Barthelmess, leads his company, joined by his younger brother, the ne'er-do-well "Oily Jim" (Robert Harron), in the advance. The titles indicate they become "lost beyond their objective" and then "surrounded, the little company refuse to surrender." The scene is set for Oily Jim to escape to get help, effectively reenacting Private Krotoshinsky's role in the real action. Griffith builds into this section other aspects of the popular narrative of the Lost Battalion: the desperate hunger and thirst of Barthelmess's company and the airdrop of supplies (although in this case they actually reach them, whereas in reality the drops fell into German hands). Audiences were meant to recognize these elements as standing in for the whole of the experience of the American troops in the war.

The two films also share a visual inscription of the nature of the Western Front. McManus and King necessarily incorporated alternating low-angle and high-angle compositional frames using primarily close-ups and midshots. The effect fills the frames with dugouts and the churned earth of No Man's Land. Griffith, who had a more expanded budget, was a first-hand witness of trench warfare and purposefully incorporated the same kind of compositional system. Once the American troops are in "the trenches" the frames are filled with sandbags and blasted shell holes while night-time sequences erase or obliterate the open sky altogether.

Griffith's film employs the contrast of traditional and modern as a running motif throughout the film. The brothers Ralph and Jim, and their romantic partners Atoline and Cutie Beautiful respectively, embody those polarities. Griffith extends this in his use of landscape. Atoline's father, "Mr. France" (Adolph Lestina), the ex-Confederate soldier, presides over his rural estate in France. The opening title sets out the pastoral scene: "On a June day gold with spring and blossoms in an old chateau in the pleasant Valley of the Marne Monsieur France sits dreaming." The portending tragedy is inscribed on the ill-fated Marne Valley. Reinforcing this emphasis on the pastoral landscape is the depiction of the old man's memory of the visual setting at the end of the Civil War, the moment when he refused to surrender to the Yankees and escaped to France. It is a tableau of reunification and reconciliation. Propped against a split-rail fence benevolently aiding a wounded Union soldier in the foreground, the young Confederate is embedded in idealized wilderness woodland with a creek passing through the middle of the frame. Smoke from an explosion in the background appears but does not disrupt the bucolic setting as the late afternoon sun is reflected in the creek backlighting the two soldiers, giving them a halo effect.

The scene serves to establish a metaphorical landscape that will contrast with the blasted fields of No Man's Land. It foreshadows the coming destruction in France while presenting a New World landscape barely touched by war. At the same time the narrative problem of solving the old man's bitterness in his self-imposed exile is introduced. Thus Griffith weaves a memory of a reunifying nation after the Civil War into the memory of the US involvement in the Great War. The promise of reconciliation is built into the scene at the levels of setting, lighting, and character motivation. The setting recalls the antebellum painters of the Hudson River School in their idealization of landscape. Familiar to Griffith and his cameraman Billy Bitzer, these paintings had been reprinted throughout the mid-nineteenth century and hung in middle-class homes throughout the country. Specifically resonant is Asher Brown Durand's 1849 painting *Kindred Spirits*, depicting Thomas Cole, the founder of the Hudson River School, and his friend the poet William Cullen Bryant standing on a rock promontory overlooking a valley in the Catskill Mountains. The parallel of Griffith's two soldiers with *Kindred Spirits* is combined with another tendency in the Hudson River painters that is illustrated in Durand's 1853 painting *Progress (The Advance of Civilization)*. Angela Miller notes a narrative structure of "progress" and "nation building" in this painting that is reflected in the foreground, middle ground, and distance. The reality of settlement of the North American wilderness was the destruction of natural formations and ecosystems that in *Progress* is depicted as reconciled. The wilderness in the foreground gives way to a cultivated field, then a settlement, and further on smoke-billowing factories, but beyond is a setting sun over the large lake that casts a unifying glow over the whole. Miller notes, "The painting celebrates the triumph over nature while recalling a time of child-like submersion in the natural world, a phase of Wordsworthian wonder and magical awareness that preceded the movement into adulthood, and the great upheaval of nation-building."[21] Similarly, Griffith's setting sublimates the shell explosion into an idealized landscape, the wafting vapors of factories replaced by the smoke of war, and a setting sun that acts as a metaphor for both the nostalgic end of the Antebellum South and the post-war progress of the nation.

In the old man's memory his younger self faces east, away from the landscape, while telling the wounded Yankee "I shall never surrender! I shall go to a foreign land." A cut-in to the two soldiers reveals their faces to convey their emotions. Young Mr. France's motivation, set out in this memory, equates his character with the past and precipitates one of the film's narrative projects, which is to modernize and repatriate him under the Stars and Stripes. He looks toward Europe, an older (white) order, to escape from the modernizing force of the newly recombined America. This part of the narrative is directly derived and follows on from the Reconstruction chapter in *The Birth of a Nation*. The unfinished strand of that conflict butts up against the new European war, which itself serves as a force for unifying ethnic differences as it does in *The Lost Battalion*. Significantly, both films, in making these links, are explicit in their erasure of African Americans, rather than explicitly violent in their inclusion as Griffith is in *The Birth of a Nation*.[22] Griffith here uses the Great War to reinforce the reunification of white America.

The theme of reunification at the center of the Reconstruction structure of the Civil War play with all its ideological distortions was a formative influence on Griffith. David Mayer points to the shift away from partisan depictions of victory over a vanquished enemy in the earliest post–Civil War amateur melodramas to a more inclusive reunification message in the professional productions. This was achieved through acknowledging the grief and tragedies both sides had suffered at the war's end. "Differences acknowledged and set aside, the characters achieved mutual and personal closure. . . . Such a realignment of concern usually obliged a final act set in the war's aftermath."[23] It was a reunification at the expense of denying African Americans equal rights and ushering in the Jim Crow era in the South. Through the Mr. France character, Griffith and screenwriter Stanner E.V. Taylor open the film as a continuation of the Reconstruction, thereby articulating the Great War memory as a product of the conflict of the past and the future of the nation, the modern and the traditional, and the continuum of trauma and recovery that persists from one generation to the next.

The Lost Battalion and the Mr. France story in *The Girl Who Stayed at Home* are narratives of "recovery." In the case of *The Lost Battalion* the story is literally one of a recovery of a "lost" group of soldiers, but also of a "lost" sense of unity, an Anglo-white entitlement threatened by hyphenates and by immigration, then reordered to accommodate the new Americans who had earned their citizenship by fighting, suffering, and dying. Mr. France thinks he is recovering his antebellum Eden in France but the forces of the modern world are bearing down on him and he finally accepts an altered but tolerable, still white, world. Environmental historian Carolyn Merchant notes that a "recovery narrative" is fundamental to Western culture, where the idea of an Eden corrupted by various forms of Original Sin is a constant. This pertains to the reordering of the New World throughout the last three centuries in the service of agriculture, industrial capitalism, consumer culture, and patriarchy.[24] In the context of the emerging American nation as a global power in the post-war 1920s such a recovery narrative seems central to both of these films, and the landscapes, be they pastoral or blasted, act as vehicles for the cinematic memory of the Great War.

As a recovery narrative the Griffith film introduces a somewhat complex metaphorical relationship between that of America and of Europe. Mr. France's original antebellum Southern "Eden" has been corrupted, he has been cast out, while at the same time he refuses to recognize the reunited American nation. His solution is to return to the pastoral world of the French countryside where his family originated. This move is transitory; his land in France becomes devastated beyond that depicted in his departure scene on American land with the Union soldier at the beginning of the film. Griffith's intention in showing the destruction of the French ancestral home is clearly to make an equivalence with the destruction of the South, but the film does not fully resolve Mr. France's dilemma. He simply salutes the American flag while holding onto the folded Confederate flag. No more resolved with the new order, Atoline's and Ralph's relationship idealizes an eternal traditional past, their last scene spent in a well-tended garden standing at a "an old shrine sacred in their memories." It is only the modern couple, Cutie and Oily Jim, shown on his return to a modern America—an urban setting of apartments, phonographs, nightclubs, factories, and newspapers—who seem fully comfortable in the new reordered nation.

The Girl Who Stayed at Home introduces a parallel between the wide horizons of the Edenic west and the charred and scarred landscape of the front in Europe that approaches something of a topos, a common rhetorical strategy, in subsequent war pictures. We see a similar dichotomy set up in in the titles that open *The Four Horsemen of the Apocalypse*, released two years later in 1921. The opening title declares Europe "a world old in hatred and bloodshed, where nation is crowded against nation and creed against creed" as a dark contrast to the New World where, in the following title, "boundless space offers a haven to the alien, and ancient hatreds are forgotten." The opening shot of the landscape of Argentina reinforces the contrast. In long shot, Don Madariaga, the landowner, known as the Centaur, sits astride a horse in the foreground, his land spreading out into the horizon behind him. In this way producer and screen writer June Mathis's script places the recovery narrative inherent in the contrast between the New World and the Old at the center of the film. Her adaptation of Vicente Blasco Ibáñez's novel reorganizes the structure to emphasize the dark/light disparity. The novel begins in the days before the war in Paris and then flashes back to the idyllic ranch setting in Argentina. Mathis replaces this with a chronological structure in telling the story of an Argentine dynastic family split by loyalties, German and French, in the Great War. The film focuses on Don Madariaga's grandson, Julio Desnoyers, played by Rudolph Valentino. Julio begins his life as the favored grandson. Don Madariaga dotes on him and initiates Julio into the pleasures and excesses of nightlife in the La Boca district of Buenos Aires. When Don Madariaga dies, Julio's father, Marcel Desnoyers, moves his family back to Paris, while his uncle, the militaristic Karl Von

Hartrott, takes *his* family back to Germany. Julio, an aspiring artist, leads a life of Bohemian dissipation while his father, who refuses to support him, spends the family fortune on a country chateau and on antiques with which to fill it. During his time as an artist Julio befriends Tchernoff, a Russian mystic and sage who foretells the coming of the Great War via the biblical Four Horsemen of the Apocalypse. Julio begins an affair with Marguerite Laurier, wife of family friend Etienne Laurier. When war does break out Etienne joins up and is blinded in battle. Rather than carry on the affair, Marguerite becomes a nurse at Lourdes. When Julio sees her attending the blind Etienne he joins up and for the four years of the war fights heroically. In the last days before the Armistice he meets his last remaining German cousin in No Man's Land, where they are both blown apart by a shell. Marguerite, about to leave Etienne, is visited by the ghost of Julio, who gestures to her to stay with her husband. The film ends with the elder Marcel and his wife searching the graves of the dead. When they find Julio's marker the mystic Tchernoff joins them. When asked by Marcel if he knew his son, Tchernoff gestures to the massive gravesite, followed by the title "I knew them all." The film ends with Tchernoff foretelling that while the Four Horsemen have now left they will always return, "until hatred is dead and only love reigns in the heart of mankind."

Mathis's changes that bookend the film emphasize the regeneration through sacrifice of Julio and Marguerite. She accomplishes this through a transition of landscape, from the Edenic fields of Argentina, the New World, to the cross-laden cemeteries of Europe's blasted battlefields. The wide horizons and endless sky of Madariaga's ranch are replaced with the high dark hills of the buried dead, thousands of crosses dotting the landscape with only a chevron of sky pointing down the middle of the frame. The visual strategy of the scene is literally a revelation: first the hills appear in silhouette with their crosses visibly prominent on the horizon, and then the foreground is flooded with light to reveal a crowded necropolis, with Julio's mother and father, his sister and her wounded husband standing in the middle. Both novel and film bring the narrative to a close by piling it with references to the earth. Ibáñez describes Marcel Desnoyers's thoughts as he stands at Julio's grave:

> "He imagined him sleeping unshrouded below, in direct contact with the earth. . . . The bereaved father wished to transfer his son . . . he would erect for him a mausoleum fit for a king. . . . And what good would that do? He would merely be changing the location of a mass

of bones, but his body—all that had contributed to the charm of his personality would be mixed with the earth . . . [and] become an inseparable part of a poor field in Champagne."[25]

Mathis renders these thoughts visible through the dominance of earth and the crosses of remembrance; Julio is one of many who are "inseparable" from the dirt of the field.

For this last scene in the film Mathis appears to have used as reference material photographs and newsreel footage of the battlefield cemeteries in France. She noted in an early version of the script that she needed to see the "graveyard scenes" from the *News Weekly* before she could write the scene accurately.[26] This is not surprising given the context of national debate about the repatriation of American dead from France that had been prominent in the press during the early months of 1920.[27] In January the War Department had offered to return the dead to their families should they request it. This prompted a public debate that was joined by the newly formed American Legion veterans group and

FIGURE 1.3. Filling the frame with cross-covered hills at the end of *The Four Horsemen of the Apocalypse* (Rex Ingram, 1921). Metro Pictures Corporation. Digital frame enlargement.

the American Field of Honor Association. These organizations were in favor of leaving the dead in France and they employed rhetoric marked by a discourse of "sacred soil." American Expeditionary Force chaplain Bishop Charles H. Brent referred to "that sacred dust which, though mingled with the soil of France, is forever American."[28] Lisa Budreau argues that the terms of these debates played out against a background of reunification and renewal and the "myth of the melting pot" and at times served to highlight the participation of immigrant and African American soldiers, if ultimately it merely worked to suppress those histories. Mathis's choice of filling the frame with the cross-covered hills echoed the repatriation debate but along with it came the uncomfortable realities repatriation raised. Accounts in the public press of families seeking to bring their loved ones home reported on the difficulties of finding the bodies and, when found, transporting them. Reports of malfeasance by morticians further highlighted the often-gruesome nature of the effort.[29]

The Four Horsemen of the Apocalypse was released at the height of the debate in February 1921. Its initial review in *Film Daily* directly referenced it as a potential problem. First in its category of "Character of Story" it warned, "Good enough for any house, but question whether any of your people want war stuff." Pointing to specifics, the reviewer declared, "why there should be acres of graves for the final shot is difficult to conceive. It is so unnecessarily gruesome." Beneath the review the column dedicated to suggestions for marketing and publicity thought the film had appeared three years too late, and would have done better business in 1918. "The question is whether or not it is too late, will your people want to see it?" As it transpired, the film was a clear success, broke box office records, and if anything the memorial tone of the ending was in tune with the time.

Mathis, like Griffith and McManus in their earlier films, developed themes of national reunification and recovery by invoking sacred soil and land. In the novel Marcel is left bereft by his son's death and resigned to his own: "The world was going to its ruin. . . . He was going to his rest." Written in 1916, Ibáñez's novel ends in the second year of the war. Mathis brings the ending up to the armistice, which enables her to return to the Old World/New World dichotomy: "The nations of the Old World were torn asunder and lay bleeding, crying out to a just God to release them from the forces of evil." The solution comes from the New World bringing "men to cheer and help their brothers." Mathis's adaptation brings an emphasis on the choice of ending on a larger theme of sacrifice than

Ibáñez's novel. By contrast, the dark Old World operates to heighten the luminous and heroic New World, and this plays out with specific reference to distinctly American sources. When Tcharnoff spreads his arms and gestures toward the whole of the vast field of wooden crosses his words "I knew them all" reprise Walt Whitman's refrain for the Civil War dead: "the dead, the dead, the dead, *our* dead—or North or South—ours all (all, finally dear to me)"[30] with its insistent theme of reconciliation, reunification, recovery. Hence it redirects the story to one of American sacrifice.

Chapter 2

THE WAR IN THE GROUND

"I am the grass, let me work"

The contrast between the peaceful, verdant land of rural France and the blasted landscapes of No Man's Land continued a trope evident in the Great War poetry published by 1925. Carl Sandburg employed it in 1918: "And pile them high at Ypres and Verdun . . . I am the grass, let me work."[1] So too did English poet Wilfred Owen in his poem of the same year "Spring Offensive." Owen's soldiers walked toward the battle line while brambles "clung to them like sorrowing hands," and then as they raced toward the German lines "instantly the sky burned."[2] By 1925 the art that had emerged from the war offered a number of examples of such irony in their use of landscape. The once-pastoral-now-blasted landscapes of English war artists Paul Nash and C.R.W. Nevinson were echoed by those of American artists such as Charles Burchfield and Claggett Wilson, or implied in works such as Georgia O'Keeffe's 1915 *No. 9 Special*.[3] Nash's 1918 *We are Making a New World* employs in abstract the bitter contrast of a sunrise revealing a shattered and pockmarked landscape with broken leafless trees standing and leaning like tombstones, their upward reach stunted and futile. C.R.W. Nevinson's *The Road from Arras to Bapaume* (1917) employs the tradition of English landscape painting in its rolling contours of the road as it vanishes in the horizon, high in the frame, its strength derived from the viewer's position of relative safety on a road to oblivion. David Lubin has noted that American artist Claggett Wilson's watercolor *First Attack on the Bois de Belleau*, painted in 1919, though published in 1928, three years after the release of *The Big Parade* (1925), uncannily depicts the advance in the wood of that film with the line of doughboys, some in the process of falling to gunfire, all being swallowed up by the golden grass they traverse.[4] The use of the nature/war counterpoint became a guiding thematic principle for MGM director King Vidor's approach to filming *The Big Parade* in developing the Edenic-to-blasted trope set out in literary and war art examples of the immediate post-war period and pushing it toward a more critical assessment of the American experience in the war than had *Four Horsemen* and *The Lost Battalion*.

The Big Parade seems to have arisen out of the convergence of Irving Thalberg's idea of producing a road-show spectacle for the newly formed MGM studios, Vidor's expressed wish to make an epic that lasted beyond the usual week or two of a standard feature run, and the fact that MGM had bought the rights to Laurence Stallings's 1924 novel *Plumes*. Added to this was the success of Stallings's and Maxwell Anderson's play *What Price Glory?* of the same year. In addition, the appearance in September of 1924 of two other plays with a Great War theme on Broadway, *Havoc* written by Harry Wall and *Nerves* written by John Farar and Stephen Vincent Benét, served to indicate a resurging interest in war subjects, albeit those concerned with its consequences. Thalberg sought to exploit the advantage of the relationship with Stallings by owning the rights to *Plumes*. However, as the novel was mainly an account of the reintegration of a wounded veteran into post-war life, he realized it lacked the epic proportions he had in mind. He landed instead on the idea of using the title of a short story that Stallings had published the same year in the *New Republic* magazine entitled *The Big Parade* as the basis for a film.[5] Stallings wrote a treatment for the film that bears little resemblance to the short story and instead includes a romantic relationship between Jim Apperson, his main character, and Melisande, a woman from the French village where most of the story takes place.

In his 1953 autobiography Vidor remembered that Thalberg had asked him what kind of subject he thought would make a road-show epic. He replied that he was not sure but that it would be either "steel, wheat or war."[6] While Thalberg settled on the war theme by making Jim a wealthy city dweller rather than the Southern gentleman of Stallings's original and by incorporating an ironic use of blasted farmland, Vidor managed to weave the other two themes into the film. Both resonated with previous war films' use of the melting-pot myth, as Jim is joined by Slim, a welder, and Bull, a bartender, and with the Edenic-to-blasted landscape trajectory.[7] The twist was to make these distinct through the ironic bitterness of Stallings's influence, i.e., the concentration on the war's aftereffects on the mind and body of the participants.

The narrative of *The Big Parade* is well known and usually cited as formative in the development of the Hollywood war-film genre; nevertheless, a summary is useful here to demonstrate how significant landscape was to the developing cinematic memory of the Great War. The film takes the similar geographic trajectory to *The Four Horsemen of the Apocalypse* and *The Lost Battalion*, between a New World Eden and the blasted Old World, albeit with a finale that reverses it. The story is based around the war experiences of Jim Apperson, a playboy turned doughboy, reiterating the boy-into-man theme of Julio in *The Four Horsemen of The Apocalypse* and Oily Jim in *The Girl Who Stayed at Home*. In *The Big Parade* Jim Apperson (played by John Gilbert) is the ne'er-do-well second son of industrialist Mr. Apperson (Hobart Bosworth) but is persuaded to join the army by his girlfriend, Justyn Reed (Claire Adams). He meets two working-class comrades in arms, Slim, a riveter (Karl Dane), and Bull (Tom O'Brien), a bartender, and they become friends. In France their company billets in the village of Champillons and after a few comic episodes he meets Melisande (Renée Adorée). They strike up a romance, even though he is engaged to Justyn back home. His regiment is called up to the line and their combat trials begin with a slow walk through a wood in the face of gunfire; then, as they get to the blasted landscape of the front, the three friends are together in a shell hole just yards from the German lines. Ordered to take a machine gun nest, they have a spitting contest to decide who will go out. Slim, who is the spitting champion of the regiment, wins and goes out only to be wounded. His cries for help drive Jim over the edge and he goes out to help Slim as Bull follows him. They find him and he dies in Jim's arms; Jim goes forward and Bull is shot. Jim, by now wounded in the leg, shoots an advancing young German soldier, and they both crawl into the same shell hole. He goes to kill the youth with his bayonet but realizes he is already dying and instead gives him a cigarette. Before he can light it the German soldier dies. The big push is sounded and as he lies in the foxhole his regiment advances over him. Taken to a field hospital in a church, he hears that the Champillons has been at the apex of the fighting and Melisande's farmhouse has changed hands four times. He escapes from the hospital to go back there to see the farmhouse in ruins; he collapses and is picked up by medics.

On his return home his father drives him to their front door. Before they get there his mother notices Justyn, his fiancée, kissing his brother, Harry (Robert Ober). As Jim stands in the doorway she sees he has lost his leg and as she embraces him a montage of memories of him as a baby, walking, running, and playing baseball flash on the screen. It is her memory. Behind her his brother says he looks great, and Jim flashes back, "Don't try to kid me! I know what I look like!" He tells his mother there is a girl in France and she says he must go to her. In the final scene of the film Melisande and her mother are plowing a field. As they are working to remake the soil that has been blasted by the war Melisande notices a movement on the hill above them. It is Jim, on crutches, he waves, and she runs to meet him. The film ends with them in each other's arms.

In his 1973 book on filmmaking, King Vidor stresses the importance of visual awareness in a filmmaker. He gives the example of taking a car journey:

> Every tree, every field, every barn, every house come under my graphic scrutiny. I am a Camera There are so many tell-tale landmarks on each route I take that I seldom need directions if I have to repeat the drive. In fact there can be so many points of visual identification in a route I have never travelled before that I very often arrive at a predetermined destination without having received specific directions.[8]

Having apprenticed in the emerging classical Hollywood narrative style, Vidor had a sensitivity to such visual forms of information that held to the maxim of reinforcing and repeating narrative information across the available planes of signifiers, the mise-en-scène, editing, shot size, etc. When we compare the final film with Stallings's twelve-page treatment of *The Big Parade*, Vidor's application of this visual technique is clearly evident. Stallings's treatment gives story and character information but very little visual detail. His outline of Jim's farewell to Melisande as they mobilize for the front, a scene that in the reviews of the finished picture was singled out as the most memorable, is a simple short paragraph:

> The big moment comes. The platoon is down at the bridge being loaded in camions for the test of fire that is to come. It is a fine picture and it has never been photographed. There are women of the town, of all ages, who are down to kiss goodbye to the men who have been living in their homes, speaking a different tongue but practicing the kindness that needs no language. The French women understand, where the Americans have no conception of it. It is a sentimental, humorous, tender, scene with Doughboys tearing off extra equipment and giving it to the women who have been kind to them.[9]

Vidor took Stallings's suggestion about throwing the extra equipment but refocused it to highlight the relationship between Jim and Melisande. He had Jim throw her his dog tags and then a spare boot. His dog tags are an obvious reference that he is leaving a token of his identity with her, emphasizing the anonymous obliteration that awaits, a visual rendering of Stallings's phrase, "The French women understand." The spare boot, however, continues a foreshadowing technique absent from Stallings's treatment that Vidor installed at the very beginning of the film. In an early scene Jim is seen tapping his foot to the music of the marching band as the new recruits parade by in his hometown. The motif continues when he first meets Melisande. He has put a barrel over his head in order to take it to his pals so they can fashion a makeshift shower from it. She, and the audience, sees only his legs, on one an unraveling mud-soaked puttee, as they go through their pantomime of courtship. Later when he gets a letter from Justyn he is lying down in a hay wagon and Melisande pulls at his leg to get his attention. Finally, just before Jim throws her his boot she hangs on to his leg as the camion he is riding on pulls away, then hangs onto a chain dangling from the back of the truck and finally, standing in the middle of the road, she clasps the boot and drops to her knees. In the original road-show film this sequence was the climax of the first section of the film, followed by an intermission. The role of the first section was to develop audience empathy for the characters by mixing romance with the comic elements of the training camp and the antics of Jim, Bull, and Slim in their encounter with the villagers in Champillons. Its function was also to set up the romance between Melisande and Jim. All of this worked to intensify the violence and turmoil of the second section.

The first section of the film, in its setup for the second, also echoes the Edenic-to-blasted landscape trajectory of previous films. While the city plays an important role in setting up Jim's backstory, the relationships central to his adventure are all developed within a setting of the rural countryside. Vidor's visual references surround Jim's pals as well as the lovers with the natural surroundings of rural France. Their training camp experience is brief, consisting of a shot of the new recruits in a field still in civilian clothes, indicating the various "types" that make up the melting pot. They are next seen marching through French countryside to Champillons with single shots of each "type" reinforcing their diversity. Once in Champillons the emphasis on the rural, while comic in intent, offers the first encounter with dirt as Bull, their corporal, orders them to shovel manure. Throughout the time in Champillons the three comrades, Jim, Bull, and Slim, are seen sleeping on straw, bathing in the lake, or digging manure piles. The romance between Jim and Melisande is at times framed by a set of two trees with a river running beside them. Standing between them in one scene, he steals a kiss, and she knocks him down. The scene is in long shot with the sun shining through the trees and the river flowing lazily in the background. The trees become their trysting place with two love scenes, one in the day and one at night with the moon shining through the two trees, both emblematic of their blossoming relationship, one that is genuine, if not chaste.

The last shot of the first section is a medium long shot of Melisande on her knees in the middle of the now-quiet road with rows of leaf-laden trees in the background. The lack of movement in the shot contrasts with the previous chaotic and passionate scene where Jim and Melisande, searching for each other as the troops run to embark for the front, finally embrace with the frantic movement of camions and marching troops in the background and foreground. Vidor called this his "music of silence" and wondered if it might be "action transformed into a kind of musical counterpoint."[10] He uses the visual planes in the frame in a kind of polyphonic and polyrhythmic movement and here it is a counterpoint of the couple touching each other tenderly as the military parade frantically moves around them. He used similar setups in his next film, *The Crowd* (1928), and effectively in the final scene in *Stella Dallas* (1937), a close-up of Stella (Barbara Stanwyck) looking through the iron bars toward the window at her daughter's wedding, while behind her on the street people move, indifferent to her tragic state. While in those two films the backgrounds serve to isolate the protagonists thematically in *The Big Parade*, the characters' isolation is played out against an inexorable movement in one direction with a purpose, toward the front.

The scene ends on alternating shots of Melisande in the middle of the road and the parade of troops. The alternation sets out a viewing position that will characterize the battle sequences that make up the second part of the film and reinforces the trajectory from Edenic to blasted landscape. The medium long shot of Melisande now alone in the road clutching Jim's shoe is from the side; she looks from screen left off to screen right. Then there is a cut to a long shot of the trucks moving along a straight road into the horizon. The camera's position, unmistakably paralleling Nevinson's painting *The Road from Arras to Bapaume*, initiates the second-section viewing position, one that looks on from behind the front. To reinforce this shift the camera casts a glance back to Melisande, this time in long shot facing the camera, now on her knees in the middle of the road. It seems as if it is Jim, and the viewer, taking one last look at her. The style brings the viewer closer into the action but maintains the distance of an outside observer. This serves the Edenic-to-blasted trajectory and enacts to move

FIGURE 2.1. C.R.W. Nevinson's *Road from Arras to Bapaume* (1917). Imperial War Museum, London.

FIGURE 2.2. Vidor's version of moving up to the front in *The Big Parade* (1925). Digital frame enlargement.

FIGURE 2.3. Reneé Adorée in *The Big Parade* (King Vidor, 1925). Digital frame enlargement.

the viewer through it just behind Jim and his comrades and establish a nexus of camera placement and editing that will characterize the battle scenes in part two.

Nevinson's painting is not referenced by Vidor but it enacts the framing of the battle sequence that Vidor employed where the trucks are seen going toward the front with tops down, the troops visible. In Nevinson's painting the traffic on the road is two-way. Vidor used two shots of the road so that later in the film, following the battle sequences, the same camera setup shows the camions returning now covered to hide the wounded. The returning ambulance shot has been masked so that the surrounding ground is now a warscape, the shrubs and trees of the first shot gone with only shattered stumps and shellholes remaining, similar to those in Nevinson's painting. Vidor's vision for this framing device was explicit and in his autobiography he recounts having sent a crew to Fort Sam Houston in San Antonio, Texas, to get that shot. When the film came back the crew had been persuaded by the military advisers there that "there were no long straight roads in France."[11] Instead they had shot footage of the trucks traveling in a series of cutbacks that traversed the screen. The script records bear this out. The first attempt by the crew took place on the 25th of June, 1925. One month later Vidor returned and the straight road sequence was shot on a section of the Blanco road. Vidor's directions were precise:

Scene Going up to the Front
1. Everything passing on camera's left preferably disappearing into the distance.
2. Speed about 20 miles an hour (18–25) *Hurry tempo is important* (handwritten).
3. No covers over body of trucks.
7. First try the shot from the slight elevation as we have always planned, then if it is possible try one from some other level, for example from the flat as they did in Covered Wagon.
8. Don't have any objects on the sides from the one effect we are striving for. If necessary gauze down the sides.
9. Don't have the long line concealed
14. Prefer equipment to be more or less clean.

On the return shot of the ambulances, which he labels Scene B, Vidor asks for the same setup and again emphases the tempo, directing them to be slower, at fifteen miles per hour, giving the "impression of a funeral."

He handwrites "Sad tempo." His emphasis on tempo and on composition of the landscape could hardly be more specific and matches precisely Nevinson's. The slight elevation, the gauzing down of the sides, the long unbroken line are employed to emphasize the direction away from the viewer and to create an ominous combination of a hurrying tempo and the vanishing point on the horizon. It also provides an open landscape as the point from which the descent into the desolate warscape that fills the frame with earth begins.[12]

In one section of his twelve-page treatment referring to the antics in the village before they move to the front, Stallings wrote to Thalberg, "In continuity, I can provide a million humorous details on this life."[13] Vidor's account supports this, stating that Stallings's stories made up much of the conversation he and his co-writer, Harry Behn, had on their train ride to New York. Following that trip, Vidor recounts that he and Behn then wrote the script on the return journey.[14] However, the visual rendering of the battle sequences is not apparent in the Stallings treatment and Vidor gives no real credit to Stallings for these. Vidor himself, though he had gone to a military school as a boy, had never experienced combat. There is another, less well known albeit documented, literary source for Vidor's visualization of the front. In a letter to Maxwell Perkins in 1933 F. Scott Fitzgerald wrote, "King Vidor told me that Stallings in despair of showing Vidor what the war was about gave him a copy of (Thomas Alexander Boyd's 1923 novel) *Through the Wheat*. And that's how Vidor, so he told me, made the big scenes of the *Big Parade*."[15] Fitzgerald had a stake in Boyd's career, as he had been instrumental in bringing *Through the Wheat* to the attention of Maxwell Perkins at Scribners' Sons.[16] Moreover, Boyd was a veteran of the war and his novel is a stark and unstinting account of Marine Corps Private William Hicks and his experiences in battles at Belleau Wood, Soissons, and Blanc Mont. Boyd tracks Hicks's increasing psychological undoing through these harrowing trials, and as he prepares for the last assault he begins to admit out loud that he is "all in." Boyd ends the novel with his protagonist shell-shocked, his soul "numbed," and feeling that "no longer did anything matter." Boyd's prose style, unlike Stallings's in his treatment, is primarily and brutally visual. His rendering of battle sequences is immersive and visceral in describing the sight, feel, and smell of battle. Late in the novel he renders the marines' advance toward the German wire by bringing all senses together:

> The ground, with the deep green of long, untrampled grass, was springy under the feet of men. Their mouths tasted as if they had

eaten mud. Breathless, the blunt air lay against them. From the somber purple trees on the hill, the unnatural stillness of the village, there was a portent of evil.[17]

Or:

Silently they deployed, mud caked ghosts, dragging wearily and uncertainly out in a long line that offered its front to the challenging boom of the enemy's long-range guns.[18]

Boyd buries his soldiers in the landscape, often contrasting the fear of the soldiers with the indifference of the once-pastoral fields and vistas: "Dazzling sunlight beat upon the full-topped yellow heads of wheat that weighted down the cool green stalks; on the flat absurdly shaped helmets of the soldiers." Then, as shells begin to rain down on them, "The platoon lay down in the wheat, trying to shield their bodies from the sight of the enemy."[19]

While Fitzgerald's claim may be hearsay and there is no account from Vidor that Boyd's novel was a source, the battle sequences in *The Big Parade* bear a remarkable resemblance to those in *Through the Wheat*. Driven by the same Edenic-to-blasted landscape trajectory, Vidor seems to have gained a visual palette, partly from Boyd's work, just as Stallings had intended by recommending he read it, and partly from the war art that he no doubt encountered in his research. The visual rendering of the wheat field as yellow and "dazzled by sunlight" hews close to Claggett Wilson's watercolor of 1919, *First Attack on the Bois de Belleau*. Wilson, like Boyd, served at Belleau Wood.

Vidor built the move toward the blasted landscape rhythmically and deliberately, from the initial enthusiasm in the rush to the front to the exhausted Jim lying in the shell hole with the dead German soldier, surrounded by earth and mud, watching the next wave of doughboys advance on the German lines, shell bursts illuminating them in the darkness. His well-known account of using a bass drummer playing a slow rhythm for the soldiers as they moved through the woods toward the Germans initiated the tempo of what would ultimately accelerate into the frenzy of the bombardment and attack. To prepare for the film Vidor had watched hundreds of feet of Army Signal Corps film made during the war. "One day in viewing a section of film I was struck by the fact that a company of men were passing the camera at a cadence decidedly different from the usual ones. It was a rhythm of suspended animation and their movement suggested an ominous event." It was a funeral cortege and he realized that using that he could employ that rhythm in his film in order to "illustrate the proximity of death."[20] Boyd's account of the advances has a similar tempo: "The sergeant in charge of the first wave set the pace, which was frightfully slow. . . . 'Yes' thought Kahl, 'it's amusing when we are right out in plain sight.'" Boyd describes their destination in terms that mirror Vidor's "ominous event": "Beyond lay mystery and a gargantuan demon who, taking whatever shape he chose, might descend with a huge funneled bag from which he might extract any number of fascinatingly varied deaths."[21]

Boyd's prose is often cinematic and he constructs the viewing position that anticipates Vidor's: the scenes are close but looked on from apart rather than solely from Hicks or Jim's point of view. Following the Belleau Wood sequence, Jim, Bull, and Slim behold a scene of No Man's Land framed by the woods as if a curtain has been drawn back to revealed blasted tree stumps and blasted earth. The camera is behind them. Boyd sets out a similar view taken from that of the batteries on a "swell in the earth. . . . Its face was pockmarked and scabbed with tin cans, helmets, pieces of equipment. Bones grayed in the sun. . . . Past the woods the barren earth continues, rising and disappearing at a distance."[22]

He also developed the relationship of Slim and Bull along the lines of Hicks's other comrades, King Cole and Jack Pugh. John Dos Passos's *Three Soldiers* is often cited as the influence for Vidor's three comrades, yet it seems that the link with Boyd is more tenable. A direct quote from the novel appears as a title in the film. When Hicks asks Pugh for a cigarette, his response is almost the same as Bull's to Slim's same request: "Ah doan mind givin' you cigarettes Hicksy, but I hate like hell to carry 'em around for you." Hicks witnesses the death of his friends in battle in his descent into traumatized numbness, as does Jim. The death of his friend Pugh describes exactly the way Vidor depicts Slim's death in the film: "Pugh was lying in a spot thoroughly without shelter. Around him the bullets spat viciously, covering him with fine dirt." Pugh is hit struggling to reach a mound of dirt that would protect him. "His head flattened against the earth, his body relaxing. From the left side of his head blood dripped, forming a little pool that was quickly absorbed by the dirt."[23] Boyd's vision is overtly cinematic and matches Vidor's attentiveness to visual storytelling; the main theme is the consumption of the bodies of the soldiers, living and dead, by the earth: "On the drab earth, beaten lifeless by carnage and corruption, drab bodies lay, oozing thin streams of pink blood." Vidor takes the viewer into this world, completely surrounded by dirt and overwhelmed by the fire of mechanized warfare, and presents Jim as a spectator as much as a participant. Daylight only reappears in the form of a spinning tire that is revealed to be that of a field ambulance, ironically stuck and spinning in the mud.[24]

The final scene completes and gives the nature/war trope its fullest expression. In his handwritten notes for the scene Vidor wrote at the top of the page "A beautiful field—pastoral."[25] His notes are worth recounting here:

> Two women and a crude plow—open.
> Follow shot—Melisande and her mother.
> c.u. Melisande chewing gum, she has learned to "work it—pull it out"—The thought of Jim cuts into her—she cries—she has thought of Jim too often—she gives up—she cries.
> "Come on" urges her mother—she bravely trudges on—she sees something away off—what looks familiar—
> Her mother—"What is the trouble"—"Nothing, lets plow on."
> But it is familiar, "Look mother"
> Mother: "I can't see anything"
> "But look" The figure comes over the hill.

The scene as it appears in the film echoes and answers motifs set up throughout the film. Infused with picturesque framings of the landscape, most of it is shot in a soft iris. The opening long shot of the field with the distant trees reaching into the horizon is interrupted by the two women plowing across from left to right, a reverse of the movement of the troops throughout the film in an approximation of the movement of the Allies from west to east. The hill on the horizon as Melisande looks up refers back to the engulfing earth that served as Jim's baptism. The small figure of Jim is an apparition, at first barely recognizable moving across the top of the hill. The hill fills up the frame so that the small figure is highlighted in silhouette in the top fifth of the frame, strikingly similar to the final cemetery scene in *The Four Horsemen of the Apocalypse*. The composition and shot size reinforce his emergence, his resurrection, as a revenant of the war and their love, recognizable by the combination of two motifs that Vidor has placed in the film; the first is the loss of his leg, a factor that determines the second, the rhythm of his gait. The final use of rhythm and pace demonstrate the permanent impact of the rhythms of modern warfare, and modernity on the body and the soul.

"WE ARE ALL DIRT."—CAPTAIN FLAGG

The move from pastoral to blasted in *The Big Parade* marked a shift from the sacred soil myth of *The Lost Battalion* and *The Four Horsemen of the Apocalypse*. The shift is not unequivocal and both *The Big Parade* and the film of *What Price Glory* (Raoul Walsh, 1926) demonstrate the studios' negotiation with the competing discourses that characterize the developing memory of the war in the 1920s. In *The Big Parade* the blasted, violated soil was no longer sacred but remained dirt mixed with the blasted bodies of soldiers, albeit with the hope of restoration through love. Similarly, where the title of the play *What Price Glory?* had a question mark that ameliorated the apparent sense of the war's futility, the film, *What Price Glory*, dropped it, making it more declarative. Walsh's film functions within the same realm of profane earth as the play but offers a more circumscribed version of the vernacular language that was the hallmark of the play and the subject of its controversy. The film retained the comic relief through the rivalries of Captain Flagg and Sergeant Quirt, first for the affections of Charmaine but ultimately for each other and the Marine Corps.

Lea Jacobs has recently shown how the Maxwell Anderson/Laurence Stalling play *What Price Glory?* of the 1924–25 season directly influenced the development of sentiment in the male adventure story and marked a change in the aesthetics of realism for studio pictures. Noting its basis in theatre production, Jacobs cites drama critic Kenneth MacGowan's point that realist drama in American theatre was initiated by *What Price Glory?* alongside O'Neill's *Anna Christie* and Sidney Howard's *They Knew What They Wanted*.[26] The two qualities the Anderson/Stallings play possessed were an unsentimental representation of war "as it really is" and the use of vernacular speech. Both of these presented problems for the film industry and, apart from the fact that Fox owned the rights to the play, were also a primary consideration for Thalberg when developing *The Big Parade*. In fact, beyond the title, the Stallings short story "The Big Parade" bears no resemblance either to Stallings's treatment or to the finished film. Stallings's short story, while less dependent on the vernacular language, is similar to the play *What Price Glory?* in that the story of a lieutenant's musings as he travels with the eight surviving members of his original company from the front line to parade in Paris mingles the memory of dirt and horror of the front, its "smell of roots and blood, of canned salmon and phosgene," with a carnal desire for the "fragrance of scented women" he marches past.[27]

Stallings's depiction of "war as it really is" entailed not only the physical and psychological impact of modern weaponry but also the moral compromises and transgressions that accompanied the all-male environment of the army and their behavior with women both at the front and left at home. In the play *What Price Glory?* the two main characters, Sergeant Quirt and Captain Flagg, compete for the affectionate attentions of Charmaine, the daughter of Pete de la Cognac, the village café bar owner. Much of the dialogue was in the male vernacular of the army, with double entendres and pidgin French. The realism of the depiction of war resided in the tough language used to describe the war experience. In the second act the wounded are being brought underground to a church cellar and the dialogue among the soldiers is stark. The stage directions for noises off in the promptbook from the New York production required explosions to come every 45 seconds to accompany and punctuate the speeches by various soldiers, culminating in the agonized soliloquy by Lt. Moore's with his exclamation of "What price glory now!" The following comes from a secondary character Mate on the existence of the soul:

> Mate: On the level, now. You know your souls go somewhere. You've seen too many men die. A fellow is walking alone, blood in his face and breath in his lungs and whizzzuuuu boommmmmm. . . . He's down on the ground and somethin's gone, something's gone, I tell you. What? Who Knows? But something. Something that was in the bird a minute before has left, and all you've got left is a pack of bloody rags and a lot of dirt. Well, for the want of a better name, you call that something—a soul. . . . And you can't kid me. . . . The soul's gone somewhere.[28]

The conjunction of vernacular ("something was in the bird") and the description of the grisly details of war ("bloody rags and a lot of dirt") was accompanied throughout the play by saucy sexual references among the soldiers' dialogue and in the love triangle between Flagg, Charmaine, and Quirt. Jacobs points out that the play made no effort to moralize Charmaine's promiscuity and that the romance plot remained suspended. Since "the men are likely to die anyway . . . the sexual dynamic of the play . . . dovetails with its pessimistic representation of the war."[29] Such unstinting reference to death and dying as well as sex caused problems for scriptwriters writing under the restrictions of Hollywood dictates.[30] The incorporation of vernacular language and gesture allowed the film versions of *What Price Glory* and Vidor's *The Big Parade* a kind of masculine sentimentality. John Gilbert and Renée Adorée's chewing gum scene is just such a scene, as is the comic banter between Flagg and Quirt in the film version of *What Price Glory*. At the end of the play, and the film, after having fought over Charmaine, Flagg is called back to lead his men to the front. Quirt, who has "won" Charmaine, leaves her and runs after Flagg shouting, "Wait for baby!"

Beyond the play and the Hollywood versions, visual sources for this type of masculine sentimentality are evident in the artwork of the period, particularly in that of Harvey Dunn. Dunn emerged as one of the key illustrators of war scenes in the interwar period. His work in this regard began when he was appointed one of eight civilian illustrators with the American Expeditionary Force (AEF).[31] Attached to the 167th infantry regiment, part of the 42nd Rainbow Division, he produced work during the war that underwent a transformation as he witnessed first-hand battles at Chateau Thierry in the summer of 1918 and then the Meuse-Argonne offensive that lasted from the September 26, 1918, to the armistice on November 11. Initially presenting figures of masculine assertiveness such as *The Machine Gunner* (1918), his work became more introspective as the effects of what he witnessed bore down on him.[32] A few months later his work demonstrates a clear introspection and sense of the precarious environment of the front lines. *The Sentry (Front Line in the Morning)*, Steven Trout observes, "depicts an American sentry, noticeably thin and narrow shouldered (as most men in the AEF actually were), peering into no-man's-land with eyes that simultaneously convey watchfulness and sleep deprivation." The haunted look of the figure in this painting contrasts sharply with *The Machine Gunner*'s assured gaze off to the right, by implication east toward the front. Both of these figure types are apparent in the film *What Price Glory*. The casting of Victor McLaglen as Captain Flagg, with his strong bearing and rugged features, owes something to Dunn's *Machine Gunner*, which had been widely circulated in the early post-war years. In the original Broadway play Louis Wollheim, a similarly rugged type, played the role of Flagg. The contrast between Dunn's *Machine Gunner* and *The Sentry* has a parallel in the film's fey rendering of the character Private Kenneth Lewisohn (Barry Norton), referred to as Mother's Boy. Lewisohn is an artist who writes long letters to his mother and is homesick. Lewisohn personifies the new poorly trained draftees who are sent to Flagg, which prompts his response in the title: "There's something rotten about a world that's got to be wet down every thirty years with the blood of boys like these." In the dressing-station scene following the battle, Lewisohn dies in Flagg's arms, asking him to "Stop the blood." McLaglen, in a performance of nuance and subtlety, relays sensitivity towards the boy that lends complexity to his character. Dunn's war sketches while with the AEF in

1918 gave way a decade later to more masculinized depictions in the illustrations for the covers of *The American Legion Monthly* magazines. These "exude masculine toughness" and are a "far cry" from his earlier war subjects.[33] Yet the inclusion of an empathetic but wholly masculine figure such as McLaglen's Flagg in the 1926 film resonates with the shifting discourses associated with the memory of the war in much the same way as Dunn's *Machine Gunner*. Flagg's strength and resolve are tempered by his clear-eyed understanding of the senseless and arbitrary nature of war. He is under no illusions about "saving the world for democracy"; his banter with Quirt and the battles over Charmaine operate as much as a coping mechanism in an environment where death, impersonal and capricious, looms just overhead. These characters and their relationships accommodate a more contested and nuanced account of the war as futile while at the same time offering an idealization of the male body through Flagg.

Directed by Raoul Walsh, who had been an assistant of D.W. Griffith on *Birth of a Nation*, *What Price Glory* offers a less immersive depiction of battle than Vidor's but, like *The Big Parade*, works to drive the characters into and under the ground. The ground into which they go is here a landscape that rationalizes their vernacular gestures as Quirt and Flagg perform war as their job, their purpose. Unlike Jim Apperton, they show resolve, suppressing fear with vulgar humor. The approach Walsh takes to the battle scenes certainly renders a genuine shock through its powerful depictions of explosions. There are times when the entire screen is filled with them. But Walsh's battle depictions also owe something to his experience with Griffith through the alternation of the high-angle "god's eye view" shots of the whole battlefield with close-ups of Flagg and Quirt leading their men out of the trenches. Griffith's older style of reenactment is on display here too as Walsh depicts one of the better-known stories of the war known as the Tranchée des Baïonettes, or the Trench of Bayonets, that supposedly happened to the 137th regiment of the French army in June of 1916. As the soldiers were preparing to go over the top to attack, artillery explosions were so extensive that they were buried in the trench with only the points of their bayonets sticking out of the earth. Walsh places this scene close to the climax of the explosions and depicts it with a special effect that is the reverse of Cecil B. DeMilles's parting of the Red Sea scene in the 1923 *Ten Commandments*. Throughout the battle scene Walsh uses the blasted landscape in this way as a force that threatens the soldiers. Not only is there a Belleau Wood scene like Vidor's in *The Big Parade* but the trees themselves begin to crash down, engulfing the soldiers as they walk rhythmically through the woods toward the enemy lines.

Rather than enacting the battle, the play depicted its consequences underground in the second act with the dead and dying being brought into a wine cellar set up as a dressing station. The film inserted the battle scenes between the first and second acts and introduced the dressing-station scene with a title that continues the into-the-ground trope: "Through the Scarlet Night—a dressing station beneath the earth—that earth to which so many will return before the mocking guns of glory cease." While this florid prose does contrast with the vernacular language and gesture of the first act, it chimes precisely with a particular discourse concerning the memory of the war that was closely associated with a broader sense that while the American entry into the war had not "made the world safe for democracy," the sacrifice of those who fought and died should be remembered. For example, the sanctified soldier, who performed his duty regardless of the failures of the politicians, was embodied by the American Legion. The conservative Legion was the dominant veterans' group that throughout the 1920s and '30s lobbied for better treatment of veterans, albeit at the same time segregating African American veterans. It took a main role in activities of public remembrance such as Armistice Day, Memorial Day, and the dedication of memorials at the national and local level. Moreover, the Legion had particularly close relationships with the central Hollywood establishment as well as owning and operating cinemas and participating in publicity stunts for war-related films.[34] Those links give an insight into the social function that the Hollywood industry attempted to perform via the guise of entertainment. The contentious complexion of war remembrance throughout the 1920s and '30s was palpable. For example, on the issue of disarmament the position of the Legion was military preparedness, a counter to national pacifist movements insistent on disarmament. Lisa Budreau has noted that in the late 1920s "This lack of consensus revealed the ambivalence still prevalent regarding America's intervention in the war, with political polarities playing out most vividly in commemorative ceremonies."[35] Films in the entertainment space of the matinee or the feature on a program of comedies, newsreels, and short subjects were not so obviously politically charged. A title such as "the earth to which so many will return before the mocking guns of glory cease" can be read with less gravitas and more latitude than if had they been inscribed on a memorial or read out in a commemoration speech.

The existence of varied positions implicit in war-related films at this time demonstrates that the privileging of the authenticity of Vidor and Walsh's films also obscured or reworked their pacifist undertones.

The *American Legion Weekly* praised *The Big Parade* for its realism—"The most authentic picturization of America's part in the World War yet produced"—and noted that a number of veterans had been used in the filming.[36] Even the original theatrical production of *What Price Glory?* was defended from the criticism and threatened censorship by Navy authorities as "great stuff" by veterans. Alfred Harding reported in the November 28, 1924, edition of *American Legion Weekly* that he had seen the show with Sgt. John Joseph Cole, who had been Stallings's orderly at Belleau Wood. Cole confirmed the authenticity of Charmaine le Cognac and her father "down to the make-up." Harding's most forceful endorsement was to recount Stallings's own war record.[37]

It is telling that *The Big Parade* and *What Price Glory*, both film and play, prompted controversy through their use of profane language and frank sexual relationships rather than through raising questions of memory and commemoration. By contrast, those films' spectacular depiction of the experience of war as violent and literally dirty worked in tandem with the Legion's intent to keep the veterans' experience at the forefront of the public imagination. The experience rendered in this way drove home the sacrifice made by the veterans—those who came home as well as those who did not. The sense that by the mid-1920s a shift had occurred in the receptiveness to such cinematic realism was expressed by Robert E. Sherwood. Writing about the spate of war films coming out of Hollywood for the *American Legion Monthly*, he observed,

> It is a strange unaccountable development, this sudden revival of interest in the war. All sorts of theories have been offered by way of explanation, but the real reason will probably be found in that honored adage, 'the truth will out.' . . . In 1917 and 1918 everyone was supposed (in patriotism's name) to look toward the trenches with rose-colored spectacles. It was treasonous to intimate that our boys in France were anything short of snow white crusaders. . . . If "What Price Glory?" had been offered for production in 1918, its authors would have been reported to the National Security League and both of them would have been in Leavenworth to this day. The scene in "The Big Parade" wherein the doughboy hero gives his last cigarette to a dying Heinie would have been hooted off the screen as a deplorable instance of "fraternizing with the enemy."[38]

While Sherwood, and by association the American Legion, saw the realism of *The Big Parade* and *What Price Glory* as part of a broader change in the cultural memorialization of the war, others read into that realism, if not pacificism, a marker of the passing of war as romantic and glorified.

Sacrifice and the consequences of the war were also the subject of *The Unknown Soldier* (1926). In his review, Mordaunt Hall of the *New York Times* compared it less favorably with *The Big Parade*. The film, a product of the short-lived Producers Distributing Corporation, was directed by Renaud Hoffman and scripted by E. Richard Shayer and James Tynan, from a story suggested by Dorothy Farnum. The story is a cross-class romance between a ballet dancer, Mary (Marguerite De La Motte), and a soldier, Fred (Charles Emmett Mack), who are from the same town. Coincidentally, they meet at the front during a show for the troops (although he had idolized her from afar back home, as she was the daughter of the owner of the factory where he worked). They get married, not knowing that the man who marries them is a fake. Fred then goes to the front line. He learns in a letter from Mary that the marriage is not legitimate and that she is pregnant. He volunteers for a suicidal mission that will get him closer to Mary, who has gone to Lourdes (for absolution), and he is apparently killed by an explosion. Returning home with her baby, she is shunned by her father (played by Henry B. Walthall). The pastor in her church takes pity on her and to make her child legitimate agrees to hold a posthumous marriage ceremony. The film had two endings, both taking place on Armistice Day. The first had Mary standing at the altar with Fred's helmet and then Fred appearing in the church as an apparition, in the manner of Valentino's Julio in *The Four Horsemen*, which serves to heal the rift between father and daughter. The alternative was a more upbeat version where Fred actually returns, having suffered amnesia.

The film was released on May 30, 1926 (Memorial Day), with the upbeat ending, and received poor notices. In his column "The Screen" in the *New York Times* Mordaunt Hall titled his review "A Lost Chance":

> The stirring title "The Unknown Soldier" ought in itself to have been an inspiration to any producer to make a really forceful photoplay. Unfortunately The Rivoli presentation of this title is so saturated with maudlin sentiment and silly comedy that the three words seem to be too sacred to be attached to any such chronicle. The climax of the film comes as a shock to anyone who might reasonably anticipate a sincere, earnest and courageous attempt at a story worthy of the theme.[39]

The palpable distaste for the sentiment that Hall displays draws its intensity from the fact that *The Big Parade* had been released the previous November: "Although they can hardly be mentioned in the same breath, there are in this current subject a few glimpses that are mindful of 'The Big Parade'. But the filming of these episodes, after comparison with King Vidor's picture, seems to have been beyond the ken of those responsible for this present pictorial feature."[40] Hall spoke in step with other critics of the film who also derided it for its sentimentality. *Film Daily* ran quotes from the major newspapers in New York, which reflect an ambivalence toward the film in varying degrees. The critic for the *New York Telegram* found its predictability made for a "slack and lackluster affair . . . it shuffles along uncertainly, pushing the audience a couple of leaps ahead," while *The World* noted that "common decency prevents anyone referring to a cinema based upon so sacred a subject in anything but the most generous, respectful tone. . . . Prod. Dist. Corp. Simply didn't know how to do it."[41] The ending, which Hall called a "shock" and *The Post* labeled "unconvincing," with its unlikely return of the amnesiac Fred, made the film seem passé.

The rejection of the sentiment in this film also indicates to some extent a sense that the "sacred" was either unconvincing or, as *The World* implied, out of place in the entertainment space of the cinema. This would have seemed even more the case by the time of the release of *What Price Glory* the following November. *The Unknown Soldier* as a title had a resonance that called up the deeper contradictions that had surrounded the adoption of the Unknown Soldier as a memorial to the war dead. The memorializing process in the US had been accompanied by what Steven Trout has called "a sense of liminality," where the question of how best to render the war and its impact through art and visual culture generally had been a question of whether to employ traditional methods and forms or modern ones. Hollywood film was no exception, and in some cases it fluctuated more given the uncertainty with which the industry viewed its market. But that liminal character of tradition versus the modern also attenuated deeper questions about America's past, in terms of race as well as the sectionalism that had resulted in the Civil War and continued through Reconstruction, the Jim Crow era, and the race riots of the early 1920s. Infamously, Hollywood's role in the construction of a dominant white supremacist historical narrative is represented most significantly in Griffith's *The Birth of a Nation* in 1915, a film that ushered in "tradition"—i.e., racist sensibilities—through a combination of melodramaturgy and modernist techniques of montage.

The ceremonial burial of the Unknown Soldier that took place in 1921 in Arlington Cemetery initiated instances of resistance to its intended meaning of a unifying sentiment. As Steven Trout has written, "What began as a top-down effort to impose a lasting interpretation of the First World War became a spectacle of contested meaning driven from the bottom up."[42] That unifying effort came with all of the dominant ideological assumptions of the period, that the body buried there was white and male, probably Protestant, and had fully embraced his sacrifice as having meaning. Throughout the 1920s and '30s as the meaning of the war continued to be contested, the Unknown Soldier was co-opted as a voice from the grave to speak from dissident positions.[43] The PDC's intent to capitalize on what they assumed to be a consensus of the sacred nature of the concept missed the mark. Released in May 1926, *The Unknown Soldier* was eclipsed first in its comparison to *The Big Parade* and then more completely by the release of *What Price Glory* the following November. Opting for the older, melodramatic tradition of plot coincidence, the trope of amnesia and the sacred nature of the fallen soldier in effect dated it when compared to the realism of the other two films. As we will see later in the production history of *The Enchanted Cottage* (John S. Robertson) in 1924, the Tomb of the Unknown Soldier was removed as the setting to the opening of the film in the early drafts of the shooting script. While this may have been due to the efficacies of pace and narrative focus, taking it out also removed the potentially contentious residue of the memorial.

The realistic portrayals of the war desacralized the blasted landscapes and dirt. As Flagg states in the play, "We are all dirt": the correlation between the soldier and the earth was both actual and metaphorical. Flagg's full statement comes in Act 2 after he has been given orders by newly arrived, inexperienced officers: "We are all dirt and we propose to die in order that corps headquarters may be decorated." The dirt here is metaphorical but profane; they are trod upon by foolish superiors. In Mate's words the dirt is also indistinguishable from their bodies if not their souls, "a pack of bloody rags and a lot of dirt," and in both cases it is their ultimate destination. His insistence on the separation of the soul from the earth belies a fear that they are not separate. Flagg's cynicism keeps the questioning of why, and Mate's search for a soul as reassurance, at arm's length. The difference with *The Unknown Soldier* is that the film's dependence on the title to make its narrative reverent ultimately exposed it as an exploitation of the Unknown Soldier memorial and concept. By confronting the viewers with vulgar humor and a "dirty," realistic narrative and spectacle of war, *The Big Parade* and *What Price Glory* marked out the space of the cinema and its social function as a site conducive to a vernacular memory rather than a sacred memorial. Moreover, by covering Flagg, Quirt, Jim, and the doughboys with dirt, they broke with the earlier trope of using the European battlegrounds to make shiny the promising horizons of the New World. Unlike the Unknown Soldier memorials in Paris and London, the Tomb of the Unknown Soldier at the sculpted landscape of Arlington cemetery is not buried but lifted above the ground and lies under the stars, exalted in a stone sarcophagus. In Paris and London the Unknown Soldier's burial sites lie in the heart of the capital cities, under the Arc de Triomphe and in Westminster Abbey respectively. At Arlington the landscape of the cemetery evokes the Arcadian tradition of Durand and the Hudson River painters. It is this apparent meaning that Julio in *Four Horsemen* and Ralph and Jim in *The Girl Who Stayed At Home* point to: sacrifice and an idealized west. The Tomb of the Unknown Soldier's dominant interpretation was similar. In what George L. Mosse has characterized as the "Cult of the Fallen," he notes, "The death of soldiers in combat, much romanticized, was a prelude to their resurrection."[44] The tomb's high position above ground in the pastoral setting of Arlington makes the link between that sacrifice and a rejuvenating, ever-expanding America. Ralph and Jim come home to the dynamo of modern America, while Julio's spirit, ennobled by his sacrifice for the Old World and resurrected as a ghost, lingers long enough to atone for his affair with Marguerite.

Yet Arlington itself was a contested site, sculpted out of land that belonged to Mary Anna Randolph Custis, great granddaughter of Martha Washington and wife of Confederate General Robert E. Lee. Set aside for the burial of Union dead toward the end of the Civil War, Arlington over time represented both sides and included the segregated graves of African American Union soldiers as well as Confederate soldiers. The site, Arcadian in its original intent, represents the reshaping of that tradition toward a more abstract representation of sacrifice and of national reunion. Naming the film *The Unknown Soldier* drew an equivalence with the concept of the memorial and in the process overlooked the competing discourses that the monument suppressed.

By contrast, Quirt and Flag continue their advance and, while dirty and chaotic, this war is their job and they do it as they will do it in the next one. They will never "go home." Jim Apperson abandons America altogether. Stallings was unequivocal, a bitterness that was in the earliest treatment. In his version of the final scene he describes Jim's life in France with Melisande: "There, with his wounded leg upon a chair, in a French farmer's smock and cap, sits Jim, long pipe in mouth." His brother, Conrad, visiting with his wife, sees Jim this way, living the rural life. They are both "horrified" and declare "Poor Jim!" Jim watches them as they walk by the canal: "From the tail of his eye he can see the Renault, the Chauffeur, the baggage, all the impediments of a Babbitt civilization. 'Poor Conrad' he says.—END—"[45] The contrast here with Vidor's emphasis on pastoral/blasted indicates the kind of cynical view of American life that Stallings had. There is no idealized American pastoral for Jim; it lies instead in tilling the very soil that had been desecrated by the war. The reference to Sinclair Lewis's *Babbitt*, the self-interested white-collar small-town capitalist, is evidence of a deeper undercurrent of resistance to the by then less dominant discourse of the war as noble sacrifice and resurrection, one that the critics of *The Unknown Soldier* such as Mordaunt Hall were alive to.

"SOMETHING ELECTRIC FROM THE GROUND"

About halfway through *All Quiet on the Western Front* (Lewis Milestone, 1930) the main character, Paul Bäumer, leaves the front-line hospital where his school friend Franz Kammerich has just died. He stands outside on the steps of the church used as a dressing station. The shot begins on Paul's boots, then the camera pans up slowly to reveal Franz's boots in his hands, then it tracks back to reveal Paul's erect body and keeps him centered in the frame as he begins to move. He starts to run but then the camera stops tracking and pans with him as he disappears along the road back to the front, running into and against groups of soldiers moving back toward the church. There is then a fade to black that suggests both a temporal ellipsis and a shutting down of the senses, a numbing. Next the camera opens its eyes to reveal Paul's comrades in a shelled-out house. Kat is lying in a canopy bed on screen right while Mueller, who wants Franz's boots, does math problems at the table screen left. In the back and dead center in the frame is a gaping hole in the wall, an echo of the archways and doors and windows that have been consistent frames within frames throughout the film. Paul enters through the doorway to the left of the blasted cavity and sits down next to Mueller:

> I saw him die. I didn't know what it was like to die before. I came outside . . . it felt so good to be alive. And I started then to walk fast and began to think of the strangest things, like being out in the fields, things like that, you know, girls and it felt there was

something electric from the ground up through me and I started and I began to run hard, past soldiers and I heard voices calling and I ran, I ran and I felt as if I couldn't breathe enough air into me. And now I'm hungry.

The ground here is neither sacred nor profane, it is innervating, a life-giving force that pays no attention to myth and behaves unpredictably. Throughout the film the earth fills up the frame and surrounds the characters as alternately both protection and threat. In the early scenes at training camp the ground is punishment; the recruits fall into the mud at the command of Himmelstoss, the local postman-turned-martinet. In later scenes they are driven to madness as they endure bombardments in their dugouts below the trenches and dirt trickles through the support boards above them. The safety the earth offers to the soldiers simultaneously threatens to bury them alive. During an advance Paul finds shelter in a shell hole in the middle of a cemetery only to find himself framed by the "viewing window" of a coffin that the earth has coughed up. He is appalled and scrambles out of the safety of the shell hole into the danger of the explosions and bullets on the surface and on to another shell hole, where he takes shelter as the French counterattack comes. The crater turns from shelter to threat when a French soldier seeking the same refuge jumps in. Paul stabs him and then watches him die, echoing Jim's episode with the dying German soldier in *The Big Parade*. This sublime quality of the dirt, the unbearable tension between life and death, is the vehicle for Paul's and his comrades' psychological disintegration.

Milestone's film offers an early example of a sound war film. In the considerable writing about *All Quiet* the use of sound is seen as both directorial innovation and a broader watershed in the realist aesthetic that accompanies all war films. Anton Kaes notes that the "voice humanizes" the characters and "creates melodramatic empathy."[46] In *War Beyond Words* Jay Winter sees the divide between silent and sound film one of abstraction and indirection over spectacle and metonym. He offers some important exceptions where sound does not direct the emotions of the viewer but notes by contrast that silent cinema offered a much greater range for interpretations.[47] Other critics have seen the film's use of sound as a means of using the cacophony of modern warfare to combine Hollywood's emphasis on spectacle with a need to demonstrate war's horror—if only as a means of capitalizing on the zeitgeist of the American public's disillusion by the late 1920s.[48] Critics at the time and since have noted that the anti-war message of the film was made more palatable for an American audience by the fact that it was not concerned with the plight of doughboys.[49] And yet as Paul, Lew Ayre gives his account of Franz's death to Mueller in a clear Midwestern accent. To the ears of American audiences it was the sound of innocence astonished at its loss. He shapes the words "I saw him die" with a kind of dark wonder, while his face contorts into a lascivious grimace over the word "girls." The electricity from the ground comes to him as a kind of guilty release from the misconceptions of youth and directly toward a recognition that he, and all of them, already belong to the earth.

Accompanying his use of sounds and silences, Milestone and cinematographer Arthur Edeson built into the film's visual track an immersive technique that combined tracking forward with a panoramic track from side to side. They introduce the combination in the opening shot of the film. A middle-aged man in front of two closed doors polishes the handles, while a woman is scrubbing the floor in the foreground. He opens the double doors as if opening a theatrical curtain and the camera moves forward through it out into the street. After a cut this motif is repeated again from inside the butcher's shop with the butcher standing in the doorway with his back to the camera. A third cut opens with a backward move from the schoolroom window; the camera tracks sideways, placing Professor Kantorek (Arnold Lucy) in center frame at his desk, then pulls back and up to reveal the whole of the schoolroom. As Kantorek makes his Dulce et Decorum Est speech, Edeson's camera tracks along the heads of the schoolboys sitting one after another at their desks. The motif is repeated later in the first battle scene, where the camera tracks along the same faces waiting in the trench looking out over No Man's Land for the French attack. This rhetorical strategy expressed in the camera tracking mobilizes the immersive early cinema tradition of the phantom ride, where the camera was mounted on the front of a train. Pointing out its difference from the rail traveler's view from a carriage window, Tom Gunning suggests the phantom ride, as it moves the spectator through space, worked to "substitute sensation for contemplation, overcoming effects of distance in a rush of visual motion."[50] Milestone and Edeson, as well as editor Edgar Adams, alternate the phantom ride tracking into the frame with the side-to-side tracking behind the machine gunners in the trench in a movement more in keeping with the view of the railway passenger. By combining these two contradictory types of perceptual regimes, one *into* the space in front of the trench to capture their faces, the other passing *across* the screen and looking out into No Man's Land, the film places the viewer directly in the line of fire, achieving a tense immersive effect that is only broken by alternations with high-angle bird's-eye views as the French attack takes place. Gunning sees contradictions in the two modes of representing landscape, the phantom ride and the railway passenger. There is "an anxiety about the nature of direct experience in the modern era, a desire for modes of representation intended to produce not simply a landscape, but the full sensual experience of being there, often employing sensual supplements."[51] Milestone et al. attenuate such an anxiety in the alternation of immersing and distancing the viewer. By 1930 the idea of the war being a true accounting and consequence of the modern age had gained traction and filmic warscapes such as Milestone's had become both a symptom of the war's consequences and the carrier of its deadly message via sensation.

The tension between immersion and distancing evident in the filmic techniques of *All Quiet* had its echo in the reception discourses as the memory of the war changed. In the US *All Quiet* was almost universally seen as an anti-war film. The novel presaged such a status and was endorsed by John Black in *The American Legion Monthly*.[52] It was a "scalding indictment" and the character Paul Bäumer's "process of disillusionment bitter." Yet for Black the American reader will be struck by the "almost utter lack of humor," which he put down to Germany's four hard years of war, but also to German militarism, and war as "more of a habit than an adventure." Invoking E.M. Viquesney's statue *Spirit of the American Doughboy*, Black wrote that the Americans "despised war" but "fought valiantly, audaciously and with a smile," while the German attitude to war was a "routine proposition." Such a qualified separation of the anti-war sentiment from the American experience echoed Milestone's *All Quiet* in the tendency to construct the American position as one of a spectator of a European debacle. Louella Parsons demonstrated a similar thinly veiled nationalism in her review of the film. It showed "no favoritism toward Germany" while at the same time "The blame for the slaughter of innocent boys is laid at the door of all those who were responsible for the war."[53] Yet the dichotomy between participant and onlooker, or in Gunning's terms phantom ride and railway passenger, was manifest in Llewellyn Miller's review for the Los Angeles *Record*:

> Though it sounds rather deadly as a recommendation for a show, All Quiet on the Western Front deserves the support of schools and churches. I can think of no more profitable way for a class of Modern History to spend two hours. And I can think of no more harrowing a way to for sensation seekers to spend an evening.[54]

The Record articulates here an educational discourse that was usually reserved for actuality footage during the war. Hence the "deadly" recommendation was referring to box office; exhibitors were reluctant to book "educational" films on the whole. The compensation lay in its appeal to sensation seekers. Sime Silverman's *Variety* review gave depth to how this combination of education and sensation worked. "A harrowing gruesome, morbid tale of war, so compelling in its realism, bigness and repulsiveness that Universal's 'Western Front' becomes at once a money picture." Silverman found in the film an anti-war message that would appeal through the kind of distancing effect that *The Record* had noticed. The realism of the film was so effective in Carl Laemmle's intent to "present a picture of Germans in war. . . . Universal has turned out a stern object lesson against war."[55] The interpretation of it as an anti-war film conjoined with a distancing that was more in keeping with the American onlooker onto Europe's disaster.

Both in the construction of the film and in its reception *All Quiet* reordered the metaphorical function of earth to one that was secular and fatalistic. *Variety* linked the two: "And when the German boy . . . a hardened war veteran . . . said to those young boys raring to go where he had been 'War is dirty. It is death . . .' the audience could not help but endorse that sentiment for those before the screen had endured with the German soldiers all of their horrors, frights, privations, amputations and death."[56] Put another way, the American positivism evident in the positions of the reviewers from *Variety* to *The American Legion Monthly*, however different in nuance, ran up against a warscape, on both image and sound tracks, constructed to alternate between participant and observer. From the sanctified soil of *The Lost Battalion* and *The Four Horsemen* through the vulgarized dirt of *What Price Glory* and *The Big Parade*, the Western landscape imagination remained invested with myth. *All Quiet*, with its immersive perceptual regime, takes it a step further and blasts the myth out of it altogether, with the caveat that the dirt remains foreign.

As noted earlier, each scene transition in *All Quiet* separated by fades to black effects the kind of disjointed arrangement of traumatic memory.[57] Each darkness enacts a kind of death and each scene a reanimation. Milestone's technique was an adaptation of the episodic nature of Remarque's novel and seems to be the cinematic expression of Paul's song of the earth:

"Oh earth thou grantest us the great resisting surge of new won life. Our being lost utterly carried away by the fury of the storm, streams back through our hands from thee, and we, thy redeemed ones, bury ourselves in thee, and through the long minutes in a mute agony of hope bite into thee with our lips!"

James Whale's film *Journey's End* (1930), another hymn to burial, takes place almost entirely in the dugout, a troglodyte chamber piece where Remarque's mute agonies play themselves out in the accents and manners of the British class system. Released a few weeks prior to *All Quiet*, and to less fanfare, Whale's adaptation of R.C. Sherriff's stage play gives some evidence to the tendency of American reviewers to praise the pathos while at the same time note the national differences. The film production differed from the play slightly by the inclusion of some external shots of No Man's Land. Although these are not full-fledged battle sequences, they are shot primarily at ground level or below; the earth, protector and threat, dominates the mise-en-scène. The film ends with the collapse of the dugout and flickering out of the candle, engulfed in earth.

The perceptual strategy of *Journey's End* sits in contrast to the push/pull, immersion/distancing of *All Quiet*. The economical use of analytical editing of the space of the dugout echoed the successful theatrical production Whale had directed in New York. Rather than place the viewer in the line of fire, *Journey's End* places the front just beyond the characters and the audience—a conscious choice by Whale, who apparently held off British producer George Pearson's insistence the film employ more editing and be more cinematic.[58] Whale, who had just come from working as dialogue director for Howard Hughes's *Hell's Angels*, understood that dialogue directed or informed editing in the new sound era. Whale had insisted on hiring the writer from *Hell's Angels*, Joseph Moncure March. March's careful editing produced a script that closely followed the play.[59]

The reviews for the film held this quality out as its primary virtue. Pare Lorentz, writing in *Judge*, noted that the drama "had reached the movies unblemished,"[60] a note that was in step with other reviewers' concerns that Hollywood would be incapable of doing justice to the play. Harry Evans of *Life* magazine wrote, "Frankly, this reviewer expected that some stupid motion picture official would step in and insist that the war angle of the story be given the attention that could not be afforded on the stage." Evans praised the film as "meticulously faithful."[61] Such comments on the cinematic rendering of the front offer a clue into how far the sacred soil myth had receded by the end of the decade. The critic for *The New Yorker* found the sparse use of cinematic technique highly justified by the scope of the movies as a special medium, and justified too by their own intrinsic success. These are scenes of the trenches outside the dugout, interpolated views of the front, of lines of sandbags and hideous mud-drenched passages as effective and realistic as any shown anywhere on the screen.[62]

Time magazine blasted the remaining myth out of the dirt: "These soldiers are heroic but with a kind of heroism never before depicted on the screen—a makeshift heroism, concocted in despair as the best way to behave in circumstances which are absurd, insane, horrible." *All Quiet*'s and *Journey's End*'s mythless, fatalistic warscapes are an X-ray of the sublime western landscapes of the Hudson River School and moreover of the landscapes of epic westerns of the 1920s. Alongside *The Big Parade* and *What Price Glory* they form a foundation, a tectonic plate for cinematic representations of the Western Front through the 1930s.

"SOIL ENNOBLED BY THE BLOOD OF YOUR SONS"

Although the "sacred soil" of the early 1920s films appeared to have given way to fatalism, the cross-currents of discourses on the memory of the American involvement in the Great War continued to run into the 1930s. Throughout the 1920s the right-leaning American Legion had been arguing for "preparedness" even as a wave of international cooperation had become evident with the signing of the Kellogg-Briand Pact in 1928, which promoted peaceful settlement among nations and was endorsed by the US Congress. However, the sense of optimism toward international peace contrasted with suspicion in conservative quarters of anti-war plays such as *Journey's End* as being pacifist and hence communist. Such attitudes bring the positive receptions of *All Quiet* and *Journey's End* into perspective.[63] The initial accolades in the urban press for both films demonstrate sympathy with their anti-war message both in the receding animosity toward Germany for *All Quiet* and in the admiration for the British display of emotion and compassion. However, this did not necessarily mean that films and plays with the US military experience at the center were considered irrelevant or of any less quality. In November 1929 theatre critic Richard Watts wrote a thought piece for the *Herald Tribune* entitled "Our Ways, Their Ways and a Play: Inevitable Comparisons of What Price Glory to Journey's End." "One could hardly deny that Journey's End was the more heartbreaking of the two," Watts wrote. He then turned his attention to the concept of national character to praise both plays:

> It is rather interesting to note how in their best war play, the Americans, the most frankly sentimental of peoples, conceal their tears behind a show of roistering, while the usually reticent English are far more frank in the appeal to pathos. It is I suppose only natural that the finest drama of the sentimentalists is the one where a mask of rowdiness is placed over their national vice, and the war masterpiece of the usually colder British is not afraid to cast aside for the moment the extremity of reticence that may easily become as great an artistic sin as romantic tearfulness."[64]

The film versions of each draw out more clearly Watts's distinctions. Lea Jacobs has demonstrated how Walsh's *What Price Glory* had diverged from the play by enhancing the character of Charmaine and toning down its vulgar vernacular language, hence resolving the problems the play posed for studio concerns about censorship and, as importantly, its appeal to women audiences. These script resolutions exerted considerable influence on subsequent Hollywood genres from the war and gangster films to comedies and westerns. Paradoxically, these films recast sentiment as "anti-sentiment" through their limited reworking of the romance plot (compared to the play) in favor of a male pair whose rivalries are expressed through "vernacular language and gesture."[65] Watts's prescient outline of just such a strategy in the play *What Price Glory?* claims it as a uniquely American voice, one that dons its sentiment in a "mask of rowdiness."

Similarly, the sacred soil sentiment of the early '20s war films gave way as much to such "anti-sentiment" as it did to the fatalism of *All Quiet* and *Journey's End*. This is not to say that other Hollywood films of the 1930s eschewed fatalism altogether. Films such as *All Quiet*'s sequel, *The Road Back* (James Whale, 1937), and *The Road to Glory* (Howard Hawks, 1936), a loose remake of the French anti-war film *Wooden Crosses* (*Les croix de bois*, Raymond Bernard, 1932), all set in Europe, had messages of despair and futility similar to *All Quiet* and *Journey's End*. Films centering on the American military experience at the front as futile were fewer. *Beyond Victory* (1931) was a story of four soldiers remembering the reasons they enlisted as they hold off the enemy from an isolated position at the front. In the end only two survive. Another was *Private Jones* (1933), a low-budget Universal picture about a reluctant draftee. Neither of these was well received critically. *Film Daily* found *Beyond Victory* a "fairly good war drama," emphasizing Marion Shilling, "the heart interest," as the main selling point.[66] *Variety* thought it lacked "screen entertainment" but should "fit in pacifistic spots."[67] *Private Jones* was dismissed by *Variety* as "lightweight" and considering the "mixed American reaction to anything German creates an uncertain attitude throughout."[68] By 1933 concerns about German militarism had reemerged as a factor in the mind of the general cinema audience.

A confluence of this new "anti-sentiment" and the incorporation of land and soil was John Ford's *Pilgrimage* (1933). I.A.R. Wylie's story of a rural Arkansas mother who loses her son in the war offered a means of linking the blasted warscape of the front with the mythic landscape of rural America. It was the second Wylie story Ford had adapted; the first, *Four Sons* (1928), was also set during the Great War. *Pilgrimage* is the story of Hannah Jessop of Three Cedars, Arkansas, who objects to her son Jim's romance with Mary, the girl from the farm down the road. Jim and Hannah have worked the farm since his father died when he was small. Hannah is a formidable figure and is determined to keep Mary and Jim from marrying. When the war breaks out she goes to the town draft board and offers her son for the army. He is drafted and goes to France. On his way to France his division makes a quick stop in Three Cedars and at the station Mary tells him she is pregnant. Refused permission to marry her, Jim goes to the front and as his regiment is waiting to go over the top shell explosions cause the trench to collapse and they are buried alive. On the same night Hannah is awakened by a storm and then Mary's father comes to her and asks her assistance in delivering Mary and Jim's baby. As little Jimmy grows up, he and his mother Mary are shunned publicly by Hannah, but she privately knits sweaters for the baby and watches him grow up. Ten years go by and the pilgrimage bill is passed by Congress that provides Gold Star Mothers with the opportunity to sail to France to visit the graves of their sons. Hannah is asked to go to see Jim's grave by the mayor and a woman representing a national Gold Star Mothers group. Hannah at first refuses but then agrees to go at the urging of the Mayor in order to "put Three Cedars on the map." As she is about to leave on the train Mary hands her flowers to put on Jim's grave. Later as she boards the ship in New York a woman whose son had no known grave gives her a plant to put in the cemetery. On her way over she meets other mothers from all parts of the US, a version of the melting-pot theme. In their Paris hotel one of the mothers breaks down when another mother begins playing "Dear Little Boy of Mine" on the piano. Another mother, a hillbilly from South Carolina, comforts her and says she lost three sons in the war. Hannah stands up and refuses to go to the cemetery because she "doesn't belong with the other mothers"; her son had not been good and "brought disgrace on us." Walking on a bridge over the Seine she sees a young American man, drunk and contemplating jumping. He has a fiancé his mother does not approve of and is going to have to go back to America without her. Hannah recognizes the situation as similar to her own and works to convince his mother not to make the mistake she did. The couple are united and Hannah goes to Jim's grave, lays Mary's flowers and the plant she was given, then lies down and asks Jim for forgiveness. The film ends with Hannah and Mary and little Jimmy reconciled.

The film offers a memory of the war that brings together questions of sacrifice and futility and focuses them on the impact of the war on a family. And it does this through the metaphorical vehicle of land and dirt. The link between America and Europe is made on these terms; Jim's grandfather's "own blood's in the land that's grown that corn" is echoed in the French General's speech at the Tomb of the Unknown Soldier: "We greet you on the soil ennobled by the blood of your sons." Significantly, the main character of the story, Hannah, is grappling with her fierce sense of certainty and her overwhelming guilt and regret. In that sense she is a Fordian character, finely drawn through her own tragic contradictions. She signs her son's death warrant by giving him up to the draft board because of her anger that he is disgracing the family through his romance with Mary. Paradoxically, it is through her idea of love and pride of family that she wants to protect him. The film tracks this inner struggle as she finally comes to realize that her love for her son and self-pride in family has resulted in her losing him forever.

Futility and sacrifice, the polarities of the American memory of the war, are cast against the deeper conflict between modern and traditional values reflected in and framed by Ford's depiction of family and his film style. The earth, plowed and tilled by generations, is contrasted with the blasted earth that buries Jim. The film opens with a straight-on shot of the farmhouse, and Jim and Hannah emerge to begin their morning chores. Hannah watches Jim as he goes out to the cornfield and begins to work. Ford frames Jim with his back to the camera, in much the same way as the returning soldier in Winslow Homer's 1865 painting *The Veteran in a New Field*.[69] While Jim is not yet a soldier, the association with the land and the position of Hannah as she watches him portend the ambivalent nature of the earth that is redolent in the Homer painting. The veteran, his back to the camera, is setting himself to the recycling of the soil from warscape into farmland, his blue Union coat lying cast off in the foreground behind him. The farm fields reference the places the battles of the Civil War and the Great War were fought and the scythe gives a metaphor of cutting the rows of corn like falling soldiers that calls up the violence of war. These are balanced with a sense of promise, albeit tainted, of swords into plowshares. In a reversal of Homer's veteran seeking regeneration, Jim applies himself to a task with which he is growing weary. Ford's use of this composition juxtaposed with Hannah's look foreshadows the events to come. The shot of Hannah watching him work sets out her deep commitment to family and the land. That same shot of Hannah looking comes again a short time later as Jim, finished with his work, leaves to go to see Mary.

Hannah's look is one of ownership; it is her hubris. She sees Jim as part of the land. Ford and cameraman George Schneiderman used sets rather than shooting the village on locations, which gives a sense of confinement to the land and the stifling effect of tradition. The first time we see Mary and Jim together they each directly address the camera, introducing modern love as sensual and of the earth while at the same time implicating the audience in their secret romance. They have to hide and their trysts are in the hayloft of her father's barn. Nothing belongs to them and the land is oppressive as they seek spaces out of the line of Hannah's purview. But escape is impossible. At dinner Hannah reads

FIGURE 2.4. *The Veteran in a New Field*, by Winslow Homer, 1865. Metropolitan Museum of Art, New York.

FIGURE 2.5. Ford's visual quote of Homer's *Veteran in a New Field* in *Pilgrimage* (John Ford, 1933). Digital frame enlargement.

from the Bible to Jim warning of "women's evil ways"; they each look directly into the camera, just as the lovers do, as she warns that Mary will "poison you against me." Such a strategy works to mix guilt with love and to depict Hannah as immovably wrongheaded. Later the conflict with tradition becomes explicit as Jim tells her land does not mean anything to him. She reprimands him, saying that his grandfather's blood is in their land and that his grandmother is lying under the apple tree. Land and soil here literally become the grounds for their conflict and for the terrible tragedy that befalls them both.

Jim, in France with his regiment, is buried before they are even able to get out of the trench. The burial fills all but one corner of the frame and is accompanied by the crashing sounds of the explosions. The next cut is to the Jessop farm in the middle of a storm; the sound of the shells and the artillery transmogrify into the sound of lightning and thunder and clattering of shutters slamming against the house. Hannah is jolted out of her sleep as if by the cannon's fire in a Griffithian metaphysical edit that links her spiritually with her son and with his death. The moment of retribution is tempered with regeneration: the storm becomes the soundtrack to the birth of Mary and Jim's son, Jimmy. Following this crucible moment the film sets out to regenerate the family and to bring Hannah to some reconciliation with her own conscience. By helping another mother avoid the loss of her son, and in asking for forgiveness from her son at his grave and from Mary and Jimmy when she returns to Three Cedars, Hannah achieves some absolution.

Wiley's story had appeared in the November 1932 edition of *American* magazine. Elliptically and in a series of remembrances she weaves her tale around the topical issue of the Gold Star Mothers. Ford's film, released in August of 1933, seems to have been the result of a decision by Fox to capitalize on the Gold Star Mother question. Fox had bought the rights to Wylie's story in 1931 as the first pilgrimages of Gold Star Mothers were taking place.[70] Wiley's choice of structuring the story through memories reinforces Lisa Budreau's assertion that the program indicated a deeper sense of the unresolved memory of the war by the 1930s. Similarly, Ford's and his production teams' choices also resonate with the open-ended character of the war's memory. This most sentimental of stories is rendered through the "anti-sentiment" that Watts noted in *What Price Glory*. Ford alternates the tragedy with comic interludes; the stubbornness of Hannah is at turns fearsome and laughable. The characters in the village are sympathetic, as when the mayor delivers the telegram notifying Hannah of Jim's death, but also self-serving, as when he tells Hannah that publicity of her going on the pilgrimage will be good for Three Cedars, Arkansas. Once in France, Ford alternates the melancholic scenes at the cemeteries and memorials with raucous humor where Hannah and her newfound friend Sally Hatfield from South Carolina shoot up a shooting gallery, at once invoking rube-in-the-city humor and also the legend of American country folk having dead aim.

The film's reception indicates a similar ambivalence in the memory of the war. *Film Daily* effused that it was "entertainment for any type of audience . . . painstakingly recorded against a beautiful background . . . the dialogue rings true."[71] *Motion Picture Herald* linked the film with Roosevelt's New Deal: "Fox is writing its own National Recovery Act with outstanding pictures like Pilgrimage." But a more circumspect review came from *Harrison's Reports* that commented on Fox's intention to road-show the film. "Pilgrimage a failure—only good for regular prices not roadshow." Again later in November *Harrison's* reiterated: "This picture flopped terribly as a Special. . . . It would have proved a good program picture but not a Special."

The film slotted into the gap between a war film and a woman's film. Fox's marketing department highlighted national press reviews that emphasized its appeal to women in their *Variety* press campaign for July 1933. "Women will love Pilgrimage," wrote the *New York Mirror*, while the *New York Evening Journal*'s Rose Pelwick observed, "Handkerchiefs were very much in evidence." Henrietta Crosman's performance was praised in all the review snippets in the advertisement. Yet the *Harrison's Report* warning gave a sense of how unsettling the subject matter was, weaving as it did the war memory into broader conflicts between traditional and modern concepts of motherhood, family, and society. In retrospect, by alternating between the melancholic and the raucous, Ford's "antisentiment" treatment of the subject matter looked forward to the kind of characterizations that underscored his status as "auteur." In 1988 Tag Gallagher wrote,

FIGURE 2.6. A Gold Star mother seeking redemption. Henrietta Crossman as Hannah Jessop in *Pilgrimage*. Digital frame enlargement.

with this little old lady is born the first "Fordian Hero," whom we will encounter in most subsequent Ford pictures in the guise of Will Rogers, Henry Fonda and John Wayne . . . whose judging, priesting, Christ-like interventions will momentarily but repeatedly redeem mankind from its myopic intolerance.[72]

Such subtleties are implicit in the film's contemporary reviewers because the background of the memory of the war was more contentious and acute in 1933 than 1988. Hence Fox's attempt to capitalize on the Gold Star Mother pilgrimages, while seeming to be on safe ground, in fact brought out the uncertainty and ambivalence of the memory of war. In 1933 and throughout the rest of the decade the question of the war as futile endeavor or noble sacrifice remained unresolved.

"LET YOUR RIFLES REST ON THE MUDDY FLOOR"

At the end of *The Fighting 69th* (William Keighly, 1940) Pat O'Brien as Father Duffy, looking slightly up, recites a prayer that contains the lines, "Here I beseech you the prayer of this America's lost generation. They loved life too. It was as sweet to them as to the living of today. They accepted privations, wounds and death that an ideal might live. Don't let it be forgotten, Father." As he speaks from the left of the frame, the ghostly images of soldiers of the 69th whose deaths are depicted in the film march by on the right. His words offer the salve of making sacred the term the Lost Generation. Associated with Gertrude Stein and Hemingway in the late '20s, the phrase here is populist, a unifying term rather than one of bitterness and despair. Making concrete the work of the entire film as a memorial, positioned between O'Brien and the soldiers are the monument and statue to Father Duffy that stand in Times Square. The film, released in January of 1940, certainly belongs to the category of Hollywood World War I films such as *Sergeant York* (Howard Hawks, 1941) that are less concerned with memorializing than with gearing up for World War II. Jeanine Basinger has rightly called the film "a transition film in a brink-of-war time slot."[73] The film, made after the German invasion of Poland in September 1939, anticipates the generic ingredients of the World War II combat film while at the same time building on previous Warner scripts such as the tough gangster and the pious priest (James Cagney and Pat O'Brien) of *Angels With Dirty Faces* (Michael Curtiz, 1938).

However, its redemption narrative, making the sullen and misfit Jerry Plunkett (Cagney) into an honorable member of the Fighting 69th, is also built upon the motif of the earth that has characterized war in the ground films since *The Lost Battalion*. Like that film, *The Fighting 69th* focuses on a well-known New York regiment and actual figures such as Major "Wild Bill" Donavan, Father Francis D. Murphy, and the poet Joyce Kilmer. It emphasizes the all-walks-of-life makeup of the characters, including the Jewish soldier Mischa Moskowitz (Sam Cohen), who joins up as "Mike Murphy." And as with *The Lost Battalion*, the main regeneration narrative focuses on fictional characters, in this case Plunkett. Plunkett brags throughout training camp that he doesn't need training, he just wants to fight, and he looks forward to getting medals and the glory when he comes home. Once at the front line, though, he panics and fires a flare that reveals his company's position to German artillery. The command post takes a direct hit and nineteen men are buried alive, which—adding fact to the fictional narrative—actually happened. The earth here becomes the basis, the beginning of Plunkett's regeneration, and with it the re-sacralization of the soil, which re-ennobles the purpose of the war. The questions and debates concerning noble sacrifice or futility no longer characterize the memory of the American experience of the war. Instead, in looking forward as the (dead) soldiers do toward what by 1940 was an inevitable if uncertain future, the uncertainty unifies the memory. The soldiers pull one of the survivors from the earth, enacting a rebirth, a resurrection. Father Duffy, held by the feet "like a tourist kissing the blarney stone," is lowered into the caved-in dugout. He calls out to any survivors, but there are none. The frame is filled dark with earth and the camera is positioned in the cave from the viewpoint of the now-buried soldiers. From the other side we hear Father Duffy give the last rites in Latin as the crumbling soil pulses out toward the camera like lifeblood.

The rejuvenation of nature continues in the next scene at the site where they were buried as the poet Joyce Kilmer (Jeffrey Lynn) recites a section of his poem "The Wood at Rouge Bouquet." Kilmer's reputation as a poet had been established with his poem "Trees," which had by 1918 become a favorite nationwide since its publication in 1913 in *Poetry: A Magazine of Verse*. Kilmer's poetic style drew on a spiritual relationship with nature. The lines from "The Wood at Rouge Bouquet" recited in the film connect the earth with heaven

> Slumber well where the shell screamed and fell.
> Let your rifles rest on the muddy floor,

You will not need them any more.
Danger's past;
Now at last,
Go to sleep!"
And up to Heaven's doorway floats,
From the wood called Rouge Bouquet
A delicate cloud of bugle notes
That softly say:
"Farewell!
Comrades true, born anew, peace to you!
Your souls shall be where the heroes are
And your memory shine like the morning-star.
Brave and dear,
Shield us here.
Farewell!"

Recasting dirt as the lower earthly end of a vertical trajectory, the origins of a journey heavenward, the poem reinforces the film's effort to literally upend the horizontal diegeses of *The Big Parade, What Price Glory, All Quiet on the Western Front*, and *Journey's End*. Hannah Jessop lying horizontally on Jim's grave asks *him* for forgiveness, as she does Mary and Jimmy later, *not* God. These soldiers leave their rifles "on the muddy floor" and rise up to "where the heroes are." Their memory, no longer compromised by questions of futility or the betrayal of commanders and political leaders, shines "like the morning star." This is the "geometry of remembrance," the horizontal and contemplative rising to heroic sacrifices and eternal rest.[74] By contrast, in *What Price Glory* the question of the existence of the soul remains unanswered. Jim in *The Big Parade* has no expectations of a heavenly afterlife; Quirt and Flagg know they are "just dirt."

Keighley's *Fighting 69th* reverts to the vertical. Plunkett's regeneration, which begins with his experience of being partially buried with his comrade because of his own cowardice, continues, as he is condemned to a firing squad for a further loss of nerve that costs lives. Father Duffy continues to believe in him, to persuade him to lose his fear by placing his soul into the hands of God. A German barrage damages the building where Plunkett is being held. He leaves, but instead of deserting he goes up to the line and, after blowing holes in the German wire to relieve his comrades, he throws himself on a grenade to protect the sergeant "Big Mike" (Alan Hale), who has been his nemesis throughout the film. In his death scene he tells Father Duffy "I've been talking to your boss." His sacrifice has become noble and his regeneration complete; he tells Duffy "I'm ready." The ascension of the sinner is complete. The myth of the fallen soldier reified in the film's closing mobile tableau accompanied by Father Duffy's prayer.

The apparent symmetry between *The Lost Battalion* and *The Fighting 69th* is striking, but not wholly consistent. Both films seek to capitalize on well-known events, a means of minimizing the risk of production costs, but the earlier film was in essence a production independent of major studio backing and distribution. *The Fighting 69th* was a well-funded, star-studded production helmed by the safe hands of a veteran director. The use of actual historical figures as a means of encasing the films in "history" differs in that *The Lost Battalion* worked to exploit not only the story of the Lost Battalion but also the debates about the repatriation of the dead that had emerged by 1919. By 1940 these questions had been, if not resolved, at least relegated to minor importance in the face of the continuing effects of the Great Depression and the start of another European war. The memorial function of the cutting between home and front that culminates in the image of the graves in France in *The Lost Battalion* instigates a horizontal movement that contrasts with the overt vertical geometry of the final scene in *The Fighting 69th*. While *The Fighting 69th* expounds a message of peace, in invoking the more traditional vertical, heaven/earth structure of memory it falls fully within the myth of the fallen. These soldiers, literally resurrected at the end of the film, unlike Paul Bäumer and his comrades, do not look back to the camera to accuse, but instead look away and forward. They continue the advance, their deaths justified. They are not continuing an advance because it is their job, like Quirt and Flagg, but because it is their (now) eternal duty. The film eschews futility and embraces noble sacrifice in the name of peace.

Throughout the films explored here the geometric axis of memory played out cinematically through the framing of landscape and the movement of the camera across and through those landscapes, from Edenic to blasted, drawing on pre-war visual traditions, in painting and theatre. Further, the films articulated the cross-currents of the memory of the war metaphorically, and at times literally, through land, soil, and dirt. From the sacred soil of the final scene in *The Four Horsemen of the Apocalypse*, through the vernacular dirt of *What Price Glory* and *The Big Parade*, and the sublime, electric earth of *All Quiet on the Western Front* and *Journey's End*, to Hannah's search for absolution as she lay horizontal on Jim's grave, these films track a memory of the Great War that bends to the horizontal.

Films that dealt with the war on the ground in the interwar period necessarily engaged with the questions of futility and righteous cause.

Their tendency to the horizontal lay partly in the paradox of aesthetic demands made of the war film that emphasize realism and entertainment. Most of these films attempted to balance their obbligato of melancholy with comic scenes and/or romance. The range from tragedy to comedy was a criterion of entertainment and artistic quality that consistently appeared in the marketing campaigns and in the films' receptions. The cinematic range of the war on the ground was circumscribed by the shape of the land; the demands of realism required claustrophobic framing, worm's-eye views of blasted landscapes and, with the coming of sound, the incessant, rhythmic booming of explosions and gunfire. The visual and sound scapes of Hollywood's Great War were troglodyte, enclosed. Those shifts in Hollywood's construction of the war were responsive to the discursive currents of memory across the 1920s and '30s, but they were only one aspect of the Great War in Hollywood memory. While tanks and radio technology figure somewhat in most of these films, it was the war-in-the-air films that hinged on the modern technology and combined them with the heroics of flight. It is to this cinematic engagement with progress and modernity via the memory of the Great War that we now turn.

Chapter 3

THE WAR IN THE AIR

> To those young warriors of the sky, whose wings are folded about them forever, the picture is reverently dedicated.
> —John Monk Saunders's dedication
> at the beginning of *Wings* (1927)

William Wellman's 1927 film *Wings* was marketed as a memorial at its very first screening. The world premier was held in San Antonio, Texas, close to Fort Sam Houston, where the aerial sequences and the reenactment of the Saint-Mihiel advance were filmed. The event raised $6000 to the memory of the "dead heroes of the Second Division."[1] Throughout the two years of its road-show run, where it was screened with a full orchestra at prestige city theatres across the US, the publicity consistently marketed the film as a tribute. *Paramount Around the World*, Paramount's international in-house publication, offered stories of famous war aces and peacetime aviators endorsing the film. French ace René Fonck on his visit to New York claimed to have seen the film three times, while the cross-Atlantic flyers Dieudonné Costes and Joseph Le Brix proclaimed the film "technically brilliant."[2] The combination of veteran flyers and record-setting aviators emphasized the film's dual role as memorial and as harbinger of the modern epoch to come. Their endorsement of the film's realism was tinged with the memory of the war while simultaneously celebrating the film, and aviation in general, as technological marvels. Implicit also in these celebrity airmen from all nations was the promise of continued peace and a reminder of the purpose of the war. Paramount produced a six-sheet poster advertising *Wings* as an "Aces of All Nations Drama" and recommended it as "truly voicing the spirit of internationalism." Famous aviators' attendance at screenings underscored this forward- and backward-looking trope, the memorial function and the promise of progress and internationalism that *Wings* initiated. Added to this was a dimension that was trumpeted as the film's unique quality, the visceral thrill of the aerial scenes. Paramount publicity ran snippets of newspaper reviews of the Los Angeles opening that underscored the film's affective qualities. "The most thrilling motion picture scenes ever taken," proclaimed the *Evening Herald*, while the *Los Angeles Times* wrote "a startling blending of almost bewildering effects. . . . The war is the background but though there has been war picture after war picture *Wings* is bound by the character of its aerial panorama to be reckoned a novelty." The *Illustrated Daily News* stated simply, "The picture's immensity leaves the spectator awed."[3] Such a combination of memory and vision in the film's reception had the effect of recasting the memory of the war as tragic but purposeful, replacing futility and dirt with the spectacle of flight and the sensation of combat in the air.

Its status as a memorial was also built into the film itself. It opens with the Paramount mountain, the clouds moving behind it. The horizon is low and the mountain rising up draws the eye upward. The marker of the brand with a predominant sky, albeit incidental, rhymes with the film's predominant narrative space, the heavens. The clouds begin to dominate as the mountain fades to reveal a phantom ride on the wing of a biplane, its view framed by ailerons, a pilot's view. In the distance another biplane comes into frame and dives toward the camera and then, coming to a stop, it rotates up as if on an axis and, its engine pointing directly upward, the bottom of the fuselage and the wings form a cross. The title *Wings* appears precisely within the boundary of the upturned wing. It gives way to a background of moving clouds as the credits appear. "Story by John Monk Saunders, Screenplay by Hope Loring and Louis Lighton, Editor in chief E. Lloyd Sheldon." That text gives way to "Photographed by Harry Perry," then two suspended wings and, beneath, "Titles by Julian Johnson." The clouds disappear and a traditional title card with black background gives the names of the players: Clara Bow (Mary Preston), Charles Rogers (Jack Powell), Richard Arlen (David Armstrong), and Jobyna Ralston (Sylvia Lewis). A title appears: "On 12 June, 1927, Charles A. Lindbergh paid simple tribute to those who fell in the war." Lindbergh's words follow: "'In that time' he said 'feats were performed and deeds accomplished which were far greater than any peace accomplishments of aviation.'" Then the dedication, written by John Monk Saunders, appears against a background of the ancient statue *Winged Victory of Samothrace*: "To those young warriors of the sky, whose wings are folded about them forever, the picture is reverently dedicated." The statue towers over a cross made of a broken four-blade propeller, the horizon at the bottom of the frame almost out of sight, the sky dominant.

Everything about these opening titles works on a vertical axis, a geometry of memoria that contrasts with the horizontal movement of the war in the ground. The Paramount logo, the anonymous pilot's view, the airplane that descends toward the camera and then points up, leading the eye heavenward, all assert the film's verticality, promising that its narrative will climb and fall, offering the thrill of flight and the pathos of war. The placement of the viewing point in the cockpit draws an equivalence with the cinema seat, the audience strapped in and ready for the climbing and diving sensations that follow. The ascendant theme is made more reverent in the invocation given by Lindbergh. His flight from New York to Paris on May 20, 1927, only three months before the release of *Wings*, had made him the personification of heroic endeavor. He represented a release from the downward pull of the memory of the war on the ground. Historian Robert Wohl points out that Lindbergh's image was burnished by poets as the redemptive force of a vision of a new age, opposed to the dreams of old men. The poet Edna Stimson proclaimed him "the embodiment of all we've prayed America might be."[4] As Wohl notes, the imagery that poets contributing to the volume *The Spirit of St. Louis: One Hundred Poems*, published in that same year, was consistent in its emphasis on the upward trajectory. Lines such as "A lad with wings to dare had faith to rise"[5] and "Adventuring with purpose high and free"[6] were an answer to "a faithless generation [who had] asked a sign" from an earth where "there were no more giants."[7] Writing four years later, Frederick Lewis Allen saw Lindbergh as "a modern Galahad for a generation who had foresworn Galahads" and he cited "the disappointing aftermath of the war" as a weight that Lindbergh had thrown off.[8]

The upward vision of his invocation combines memory with progress. Tempered by the tribute to the flyers of the war, it is a humble acknowledgment but also a hint of endorsement of the myth of war as the supreme laboratory for progress and modernity. The combination of memory and progress follows in Saunders's epitaph emblazoned over *Winged Victory*, a relic of forward movement, the sacrifice of the propeller cross against the boundless background of the sky. *Winged Victory* here resonates with Filippo Tommaso Marinetti's 1909 hymn to speed in the *Manifesto of Futurism*: "We affirm that the world's magnificence has been enriched by a new beauty: the beauty of speed . . . a roaring car that seems to ride on grapeshot is more beautiful than the Victory of Samothrace."[9] Such a background for the film's dedication enhances its paradoxical function as a memorial that looks to the future.

As the film's story opens, the first titles further develop the upward viewing trajectory. "A small town—1917—youth and the dreams of youth" appears against a background of three clusters of castle turrets that take the shape of arrows pointing toward the sky. The camera opens directly above a young man sleeping face down on the grass. Then, awakening, he turns over as if to leave the downward gaze behind. He looks up and, stretching as he awakes, opens his whole body to the sky. He raises his knees up to his shoulders in a thinly veiled erotic offering that equates visceral sensation and abandon with the heavens. "Jack Powell had always longed to fly . . . in every daydream he heard the whir of propellers." Jack Powell, his first name an endearment, his last a name consonant with power, looks up and the picture cuts to an airplane moving through the clouds. In a clear Marinetti-esque link between speed, automobiles, and flight, the camera then takes us to his car that he is stripping down, in which "he has left the ground several times." Finally the link with the erotic/romantic dreams and the machine are underscored by the introduction of Mary Preston (Clara Bow) peeping through lingerie hanging on a washing line and then jumping over the next-door fence to help him "soup up" his car. He tells her it will fly like a shooting star and in response she paints a logo that will be his mascot on his plane later and finally the real shooting star to which he and Mary look up toward at the very end of the film—a look upward and away from war and death.

With this vertical geometry the film inaugurates the war-in-the-air cycle of films and sets itself out as distinct from *The Big Parade* and *What Price Glory*, the two main successful war pictures of the previous two years from MGM and Fox, respectively. From the outset the two protagonists, Jack and David, seek to be aviators, an intent introduced through a shot of the Aviation Examining Station door, "a door that only the bravest of the brave dared open—a path of glory mounting toward the stars," a restatement of what Linda R. Robertson has characterized as the "dream of American air power." This vision was a fantasy of a combination of industrial power and American exceptionalism that would result in an airborne solution to "breaking the stalemate on the ground and turn the tide of war with a vast aerial armada of American-built planes."[10] Robertson connects the origins of the American dream of civilized warfare to this confidence in aviation, and to an abiding thread in the American memory of the Great War. Across the 1920s and into the 1930s that thread continued to weave its way through American "expectations about future warfare" and "the engineered vision of warfare in the sky."[11] It is a vision that links the memory of the past that points to the future, via a combination of technological advancement, noble gallantry, and sacrifice. It is distinct from the memory of the war on the ground in its emphasis on the vertical, a "mounting toward the stars." This chapter will use that tension between commemoration and celebration, melancholy and thrill to explore that trajectory of the war's memory via the war-in-the-air films made by the Hollywood studios in the interwar period.

WINGS, "APOSTLES OF A NEW ERA"

The story of *Wings* is about two boys from the same town, Jack Powell (Charles Rogers) and David Armstrong (Richard Arlen), who join the US Army Air Corps when America enters the war. They are both in love with the same woman, Sylvia Lewis (Jobyna Ralston). David and Sylvia are both from wealthy families. Jack is the middle-class "all-American boy," introduced first gazing at the sky and dreaming of flying. The girl next door, played by Clara Bow, is Mary Preston, who helps him to strip down his Model A Ford and make it a "hot rod." While the film makes it clear through their interaction over the car that Mary is in love with him, Jack's desires are aimed at Sylvia. In the following scene, David and Sylvia are shown swinging slowly together, a genteel anticipation of the flying acrobatics seen later and a clear contrast to the modern, machine-fueled enthusiasm of Jack. David and Sylvia are of the same class, and the film signals early on that this is a tradition that will be forever changed by the war. At the front, the two rivals become friends and an effective fighting team, although Jack remains blissfully unaware of the genuine relationship between David and Sylvia. However, while Sylvia remains waiting at home, Mary joins the Red Cross and becomes an ambulance driver at the front. During a leave in Paris, Jack and David drink their stress away. In a scene that features camera acrobatics and point-of-view subjective shots to render Jack's drunkenness and "interiority," Mary finds Jack about to go to bed with a French woman, Celeste, and rescues him, only to be accused of fraternizing immorally with the soldiers and sent home. Back at the front, Jack fights with David over a picture Sylvia has given him, but before they can resolve this they are called to action. David is shot down and Jack believes he is dead. David has survived his crash and steals a German airplane to try to make it back across enemy lines. Jack, bereft at the loss of his friend and feeling guilty for not having made it up with him, goes out on patrol looking for vengeance. He spots the German plane David is flying and shoots it down despite David's attempts to wave to him for recognition. When Jack lands beside the crash site in order to take a trophy insignia from the plane, he realizes what he has done. In the next scene Jack is back home, his hair now silvering at the temples. He confronts David's parents, who know the story, and he apologizes. At his house he sees Mary waiting for him and realizes she has loved him all along. He mentions that there was a "girl" in Paris and she forgives him. She says, "What happens from now on is all that matters, isn't it dear?" He puts his coat over her shoulders and they look up as a shooting star crosses the night sky.

Compared to *The Big Parade* and *What Price Glory*, both of which indicate a watershed in Hollywood's reworking of the male adventure plot in the service of "the decline in the taste for sentiment," *Wings* seems to be a step backward.[12] While the film *What Price Glory* softened the hard-boiled language of the play, it retained some of its cynicism in Flagg's comments on the useless slaughter, and while *The Big Parade* centered on the romance of Jim and Melisande, it was Jim's bitterness following his experiences at the front that gave the last scene its power. By contrast, *Wings*' depiction of Jack as unselfconsciously innocent and forthright seems drawn directly, from the tradition of boy's adventure stories, as Lea Jacobs points out.[13] Throughout the romance plot Jack remains unaware, both of David and Sylvia's love for each other and of Mary's love for him. His low position in the hierarchy of knowledge is central to the film's melodramatic rubric. He is watched over by Mary, whose idea it is to have the shooting star as his logo and who rescues (and preserves) his innocence in the Folies Bergère scene, and by David and Sylvia who, secure in their own class and their love for each other, allow Jack to believe Sylvia is in love with him.

The anagnorisis occurs when Jack recognizes that it is David he has killed, reads Sylvia's letter that she is in love with David, and finally realizes that Mary has been his true love all along. David and Sylvia, the moneyed class, are relegated to the past; David's final image is a combination of talismans in his grieving parents' home: the Gold Star in their window, his photograph on their mantelpiece, and the teddy-bear good-luck charm that Jack returns to them. Sylvia is left forlorn in the swing where she and David were first introduced. In contrast, Mary makes sacrifices to protect Jack's innocence in a gesture that seems designed to set Jack up as a symbol of American youth and at the same time trades on Clara Bow's image as the modern "It" girl, comfortable with her sexuality. Back

FIGURE 3.1. "Looking up": Charles Rogers as Jack Powell in *Wings* (William A. Wellman, 1927). Digital frame enlargement.

home "a man returning where a boy went away," as the titles claim, Jack remains clueless about Mary's actions to save his virtue by sacrificing her own reputation. In this way the film preserves Jack's innocence in spite of his wartime experience. He and Mary, as they gaze upward, are the heteronormative representatives of hope for the future.

The vertical language that John Monk Saunders uses in *Wings*' dedication to "the warriors of the sky," like the energetic wave of Viquesney's mass-produced sculpture *The Spirit of the American Doughboy*, is a language of hope. As in the barbed wire the doughboy is walking over, in *Wings*' preface there is a dialogic relationship with the horizontal. While Saunders distinguishes the flyers from the prosaic "soldier" and conjures the poetic eternal warriors, "whose wings are folded about them forever," death vies with eternity. The last phrase hovers between memory and progress, between the downward pull of memory and the upward trajectory of the promise of technology, all part of the lexicon that flying, and the war in the air specifically, had provoked.

The vertical/horizontal geometry is emphatic in the temporal relevance of Lindbergh's achievements and the continued and changing memory of the war through veterans' groups such as the American Legion. Following Lindbergh's transatlantic flight, and the subsequent release of *Wings*, the summer of 1927 had been redolent with the vertical language of the courage of aviators, civilian and military, while the horizontal implications were played as a countermelody in a minor key. In September of that year the American Legion held its ninth annual convention in Paris. In "They'll Be Glad To See You," a brief open letter to the Legionnaires in the September issue of *The American Legion Monthly*, Charles Lindbergh mixed the traditional with the modern by expressing the hope that "men who have been through the mill of war . . . return as apostles of a new era of aerial accomplishment in the land that produced the first airplane."[14] Here Lindbergh couches the veterans' sacrifice during the war as the necessary antecedent to his own accomplishment, making them the harbingers of the future. By contrast, in covering the legionnaires' pilgrimage, Wythe Williams of the *New York Times* called up another memory of the war. Williams had been a front-line reporter for the *Times* during the war and, writing in September of 1927, he noticed that the schedule of veteran visits to memorial sites did not include the grave of Quentin Roosevelt. The youngest son of President Theodore Roosevelt, Quentin had been killed flying over the German lines in July of 1918. His death at the time had been world news. Williams laments the fact that the Legion Convention program omitted a visit to the grave, pointing out that French veterans had made a pilgrimage there on Bastille Day two years before. His regret was as much for the fading memory of the American/French alliance: "In a small flag hole at the head of the grave stand two flags tattered and stained by the rain and time: the Tricolor and the Stars and Stripes." He reports that he had to be taken to the grave by French farmers, who pointed to the stone slab covering and told him "we have hope in that inscription, we pray." Williams waits to reveal whose grave it is until the last sentence, which starts with the inscription on the stone: "'He has outsoared the shadows of our night' this dead boy's father wrote, and beside this just his name—Quentin Roosevelt."[15] The reference is a resurrection, a reminder that while Lindbergh is an invocation to the future, in Quentin Roosevelt there was a past sacrifice, a metonym of American youth that also pointed to the future. Saunders's language of verticality is also tempered with a downward reflection. Here hope and memory are explicitly connected with aviation, and give purpose through progress by calling up past sacrifices.

MEMORY AND TECHNOLOGY

Lindbergh and Roosevelt as flyers were, in different ways, human symbols of the promise of technology, one looking forward, the other a reminder of its emergence during the war. In that sense they were avatars of what Jay Winter has called "heroic verticality" in the geometry of the war's memory. Of all the technologies of the war, it was aviation that emerged antiseptic, clean and resonant with older conceptions of chivalry and honor. Aviation was the military's, and moreover the American military's, answer to the mud and trenches, the stasis of a war of attrition. In the air was mobility, unfettered by barbed wire and dirt. Wellman sets out the vertical aesthetic by introducing Jack and David's war experience through a panoramic shot of the battlefields of France in a cinematic diptych. On the ground are the troops moving up to the front, a shot reminiscent of Vidor's rendition of Nevinson's *The Road from Arras to Bapaume*, but superimposed above the horizon are scenes of the mayhem of No Man's Land. Emphasizing the downward trajectory of the land war, the scene is prefaced with a title that is imposed over a swirling whirlpool of water: "Like a mighty maelstrom of destruction, the war now drew into its center the power and pride of all the earth." The diptych, rather than being static, transforms from columns of men marching toward the horizon flown over by planes to the sky and is then filled with a montage of No Man's Land, men falling, their movement halted. The shot suggests that on the horizon for these ground troops lies dirt and death, and in the process it sets up the boundless and clean skies that are the background for the dogfights and aerial combat that form the central vertical aesthetic of the film. This war will be seen from above and won in the clouds.

Wings was developed from an original story by John Monk Saunders, who had been a flying instructor during the war. He already had screenwriting credit on two films when his unfinished story was bought by Jesse Lasky at Famous Players-Lasky (later to become Paramount Studios). Saunders had been writing for popular magazines such as *Liberty* and *Cosmopolitan* and was an editor of *American Magazine*. Lasky was looking for a prestige feature to rival *The Big Parade*, which had been great box office for MGM in 1925. That film and the success of Fox's *What Price Glory* had demonstrated that audiences were receptive to "World War" films and themes that highlighted the tragedy of war. While Saunders had trained as a pursuit pilot, he remained in the States as a flying instructor at Bolling Field in Washington, DC, during the war. After the war he spent two years as a Rhodes scholar at Oxford, from 1919 to 1921. There he met and heard stories from veteran English pilots, from whom he claimed to get most of his material.[16]

The story fit into the Paramount category of "Show World Specials," the top budget category for the company. In fact, this film exceeded the usual $500,000 budget for this category by a considerable margin. The costs for the film were, according to the "Comparison of Estimate with Actual Cost Sheet," $1,972,086.66.[17] It was also accompanied by the "Magnascope" technology that blew up the cinema image during the aerial battle sequences from approximately 18'×24' to 22'×38'. This had the effect of filling the entire proscenium arch area when shown in large theatres.[18]

Wings' cinematography made lasting innovations in the aerial combat sequences. The importance attached to getting the realism of aerial battle was recognized by line producer Lucien Hubbard and director Wellman, who had been a decorated fighter pilot during the war with the Lafayette Flying Corps. The preparations made by director of photography Harry Perry, ASC, were extensive and included development of specific camera platforms and mounts on the airplanes. Perry was an experienced cameraman and was particularly adept at filming westerns. The industry preference for this type of exterior camera work was the Akeley "pancake camera" invented by the naturalist and taxidermist Carl Ethan Akeley.[19] Perry was an expert in the use of this camera and the Akeley was his choice for the aerial combat sequences.[20] The camera was designed to capture the movement of wildlife and had two innovations, the focal plane shutter with 230-degree opening and a gyroscopic system at the base of the camera that allowed smooth panning and tilting. The shutter served the purpose of reducing the blurring effect when the camera was moved or when photographing moving objects, while the gyroscope acted to smooth out the pans and tilts, minimizing shaking and fixing the image. The camera mounts were based on the machine gun mounts that had been employed during the war. One was set up in the back "observer's seat" of the airplanes and functioned exactly for the camera as it had for the Parabellum machine gun used early in the war by the German air service.[21] Perry told *American Cinematographer* in 1926:

> While on the picture I personally supervised over 200 motor driven cameras on airplanes, working out exposures and filters used on

each shot before it went into the air and, besides this, the other cinematographers and myself had nearly 300 hours of work in the air which involved the hardest kind of work and quite a few escapes from serious accidents.[22]

The number of camera operators and assistants matched the scale of the picture. These included top cinematographers from the other studios such as E. Burton Steene, who had been at MGM before coming to Paramount and who later contributed to the action sequences in Howard Hughes's *Hell's Angels* (1930) at RKO. Perry brought in his older brother, Paul Perry, ASC, who had been at Universal. Faxon M. Dean, ASC, had been a Pathé newsreel cameraman in the teens and worked for a number of studios in the 1920s, including MGM, Tiffany-Stahl, and Warners/First National. Along with Wellman, both Dean and Steene had been combat flyers during the war, which lent considerable first-hand experience in the design and execution of the combat scenes. This fact, along with the flying experience of Saunders, would figure markedly in the film's advertising and in its critical reception, highlighting the realism of the flying sequences and citing their experience as a mark of authenticity.

It was Wellman and editor-in-chief E. Lloyd Sheldon, with help from producer Hubbard, who culled the 300 hours of footage to put together a legible and narratively relevant set of aerial combat sequences. Their effectiveness in placing the spectator "in the pilot's seat" was emphasized in the *Literary Digest*'s review of the film's critical reception. One clear trope in this was the testimony of experts and veterans who had been directly involved in the air war. R. Sidney Bowen Jr., editor of *Aviation* magazine, wrote,

> to the airmen who were over there it is like living the old days over again . . . he experiences the old kick of half fright, half exultation, and grips the arms of his seat in suspense just as much as the novice who is sitting next to him and learning all about the art of aerial warfare for the first time.[23]

The review from the *New York Morning Telegraph* built upon the "learning experience" of the spectator:

> The spectator is shot from his chair into the heart of the howling heavens. An enemy plane crashes in his very face. . . . He drives his own ship into the midst of the fray in such realistic manner that an

involuntary tightening of muscle accompanies each burst of flame from the guns of his adversary.[24]

The effect was achieved through a strategy of editing operating along an axis of alternation between the pilots' and the weapons' view and that of the spectator. To this end, cameras mounted in the placements where guns and bombs were let fly (either in the belly of the Gotha bomber or on the machine gun mounts) had their reverse in the cameras positioned at the top of the cockpit facing the pilot and observer. Both main actors, Charles Rogers and Richard Arlen, flew their planes and operated the camera as they performed pre-rehearsed gestures, while the safety pilot in the rear seat ducked down out of shot.[25] The battle sequences then alternate between the "vision" of the weapon and the psychological realism of the expressions of the faces of the pilots and actors. The spectator is given alternately the distant observer's view, the combatant's view, and then another, more intimate view of the emotional and—when they are wounded or killed—physical shape of the characters. Added to this was the blown-up effect of the Magnascope of these scenes, which was, for its time, and by contemporary accounts, effective.

The overall design of these scenes was to produce sensory impact. The reviewers strove to render the experience in words the "old kick of half fear half exultation" or the sensation of "muscles tightening." These affective responses were central to the way cinema aesthetics had developed in mainstream Hollywood through the effective combination of visual techniques and characterization within a legible narrative structure. The employment of the aeronautic, ballistic, and mechanical technologies associated with the aerial combat of the war enabled the film to adhere to "realism," and in large part define the cinematic visual lexicon of the air war. In that regard, the film provided moving images for a popular memory of the Great War, one that both incorporated and yet differed from the infantry war of trenches and stalemate. However, in its strategy for affecting audiences, it also wrapped the memory of the war in the traditions of a medium rooted in the fairground attraction and in the interior "psychological realism" of the Hollywood narrative style.

The thrills of the aerial sequences are coupled with the emotional impact of David's death and Jack's return. The thrills are also not inconsequential. They combine the spectator's thrills with the character's traumas, bringing realism on two levels: the affective combination of sensation and emotion. The psychological realism, predicated on plausible cause, operates on the assumption of a delayed impact on the characters.

Jack's love of speed, his joy in flying, is tempered by the tragedy of killing his friend. The drunken Paris scene depends on a widely accepted notion of the need to assuage the stresses of combat through carefree behavior—sex and alcohol. But it is in Jack's graying temples at the end of the film that there is a hint of a more lasting impact, one that audiences would recognize from the traditions of cinema and theatre: the premature gray signifies a trauma. At the end of the film Mary glances at Jack's hair when she holds him, and for a fleeting moment she gives an expression of understanding. And she reminds him "I saw the war too Jack." This delayed response, this writing on the body the traumas of the past, increasingly became the subject of Saunders's subsequent films that took the air war as their setting or background.

By contrast, *Hell's Angels*, Howard Hughes's extravagantly expensive production of 1930, eschewed such detailed character motivation and the nuances of the psychological impact of war in favor of the technological spectacle of aerial combat. The background to the production is well known. According to Rudy Behlmer, the idea for the film was sparked by director/screenwriter Marshall Neilan, who suggested Hughes make a film that would "glorify and perpetuate the exploits of the Allied and German airmen of the World War."[26] Hughes spent record amounts of money on getting the aerial combat scenes using authentic World War I-era planes. The production employed the techniques of aerial filming that had been pioneered by Wellman and his team for *Wings*, with Harry Perry again heading up the camera team. The Zeppelin battle scenes were staged with models. The original story was sketched out by Neilan with Harry Behn, who had done continuity for *The Big Parade*. Although the first version was completed in March of 1929, it was silent apart from synchronized sound effects. Following a lukewarm reception at a test screening, Hughes decided to reshoot the film using the new technology of sound. The new version was scripted by John Moncure March and the dialogue scenes directed by James Whale. The original aerial scenes were kept and re-edited to fit with the new story line.

The film tells the story of three Oxford students who spend a summer in Germany before the war: two Englishmen, Roy and Monte Rutledge (James Hall and Ben Lyon), and their German friend, Karl Armstedt (John Darrow). During the summer, Monte gets caught having an affair with a baroness and is challenged to a duel. He leaves for England and his brother stands in for him and is wounded. Back at Oxford, war breaks out and Karl goes back to Germany. Roy is in love with Helen (Jean Harlow), who is fickle and has an affair with Monte. In a Zeppelin raid, Karl is bombardier and purposely drops the bombs in the Thames rather than on Trafalgar Square. In trying to escape the British planes sent up to defend the city, the Zeppelin commander orders Karl's bombardier capsule, which dangles from the Zeppelin, to be cut loose. Monte and Roy, flying in the same plane as pilot and gunner, are shot down by the Zeppelin, but another British pilot brings the Zeppelin down by flying his plane into it and bringing it crashing down in flames. Later Monte and Roy are at the front with a squadron of fighters, who are suffering appalling casualty rates at the hands of Baron von Richthofen's Flying Circus. At dinner in the mess hall the commander comes in and reads the roster for the following day's mission. Monte's name is called and in a passionate declaration of futility reminiscent of the crazed lieutenant in *What Price Glory* he refuses to go, calling the whole enterprise murder. Later, when the commander asks for volunteers to fly a captured Gotha bomber over the German lines to destroy an ammunition dump, Monte and Roy volunteer to go. That evening, before the mission, Monte and Roy find Helen—who has volunteered as a canteen worker—with another officer in a private booth at an estaminet. Helen is drunk and tells Roy to leave her alone, that she never loved him. Monte takes Roy to another estaminet, where they drink with prostitutes, and Monte, drunk, tries to get out of the mission, but Roy insists. They manage to bomb the German ammunition dump but are shot down as they try to return. Captured by a German commandant, they are told they will be shot unless they reveal where and when the big push will come. Monte wants to tell but Roy manages to shoot him before he does and then, refusing to divulge the information, is himself shot by a firing squad, his final line "I'm right behind you Monte."

Neilan's initial intent to glorify the airmen remains intact through all of the rewrites. *Hell's Angels* never descends to futility. Although it maintains heroic verticality throughout, it all but dispenses with any overt function as memorial in favor of sensation.[27] It does this on two levels: the thrill of the aerial combat scenes and the titillation of the scenes of sexual promiscuity, prostitution, and the display of Jean Harlow's body. The intention, as with *Wings*, was toward an affective "realism" by depicting both the life-and-death intensity of the pilot's experiences and the release of those tensions through abandonment of peacetime propriety via sex and alcohol. A revealing indication of the affective impact of one of the aerial combat scenes lies in an often-quoted 1936 article by the young Alfred Hitchcock in the British magazine *Picturegoer* entitled "Why 'Thrillers' Thrive." Hitchcock uses a scene from *Hell's Angels* to describe this exactly:

the British pilot decides to crash his plane into the envelope of the Zeppelin to destroy it, even though this means inevitable death to himself.

We see his face—grim, tense, even horror stricken—as his plane swoops down. Then we are transferred to the pilot's seat, and it is we who are hurtling to death at ninety miles an hour; and at the moment of impact—and blackout—a palpable shudder runs through the audience.

That is good cinema.[28]

While Hitchcock endorses the "shot–reverse shot" strategy that places the audience in the pilot's seat, and he does refer to the *British* pilot, his emphasis is its affective power rather than any memorial function in making the audience feel the experience of the pilots of the war.

Film Daily's recommendation to exhibitors on the film's release, six years before Hitchcock wrote, similarly saw its main appeal as sensation. After praising the aerial combat scenes as the film's main attraction, the review commented that "the love theme, which ends early in the story, is not missed because the events transpiring are so awe-inspiring that they minimize a conventional treatment of the subject." It goes on to

FIGURE 3.2. Behind-the-pilot shot from *Hell's Angels* (Howard Hughes, 1930). Digital frame enlargement.

emphasize the impact of the risqué storyline and Jean Harlow specifically: "Jean Harlow as fickle lady has plenty of s.a. and good looks."[29]

The Hays Office was similarly impressed with the aerial footage but predicted that the scenes with Harlow and most of the scenes in the estaminets, which depict prostitution fairly unambiguously, would meet with resistance from state boards and international censors. The script does not seem to have undergone the kind of pre-production vetting that was more or less the norm with the major studios, and the responses of the Hays Office were based on pre-screenings by Hughes's Caddo company. Following initial recommendations of cuts, James Fisher of the Hays Office wrote further suggestions that were wholly concerned with the scenes that depicted sexual situations. Of particular concern was Harlow's "very daring gown."[30] Predictably, Daniel A. Lord, Jesuit priest and writer, who was at the time working with the Hays Office on the new production code, wrote to Arthur H. DeBra at the Hays Office, "The aviation shots are marvelous and hold a real thrill . . . the morals of large parts of the story are atrocious." Lord objected to the costume and to the character of Helen: "The girl is a thorough rotter. Her conduct throughout can be justified only on the ground of straight lust. In her there is no question of war reaction or desire for freedom of the self-expression idea. She is just out for a good time, says it and acts it."[31]

The very problems that Lord identifies in the film are the attributes that Sidne Silverman, in his *Variety* review of the opening screening at Grauman's Chinese Theatre on May 27, 1930, saw as essential to its success: "'Hell's Angels' has an 'if' about it. And that 'if' is the censors. If any other screen in the country flashes Howard Hughes's air film the way it opened on the Coast 'Angels' is a cinch." Silverman took aim at the censors: "The picture is to the brim with sex. It won't teach the modern youngsters anything, but it will certainly give 'em an idea of themselves in action. So the censors will get a kick out of this stuff and cut it before anyone else can sit in."[32] The overarching significance of these responses is that they privilege sensation over any attempt at engaging with the memory of the war. In fact, Lord's letter highlights just that when stating Harlow's character Helen's behavior cannot be justified by "war reaction." In pointing to her scenes as not teaching "modern youngsters anything" Silverman also recognizes a "wise" youth audience that does not require the pressures of wartime to make sense of, and justify, her behavior.

Generally war films have a unique relationship with history in their veracity of mise-en-scène and the larger narrative of the specific war the film is set in.³³ Adherence to realism in commercial mainstream films requires advisors and equipment from the military, which can leave the filmmaker vulnerable to influences from the military sources that she has used. *Hell's Angels* offers a counterexample in that Hughes, using his own vast wealth, did not use the resources of the US military. The film referred to a number of real events, such as the reference to Richthofen's Flying Circus, which built upon the widely known exploits of the German war ace. According to *Variety* the plane ramming the Zeppelin was drawn from an episode where a French pilot had done the same thing over Paris. The behavior of the flyers while on the ground was lesser known but had been the source of stories Lewis Milestone had told Hughes. Nevertheless, *Hell's Angels* operates on an assumption that the deeds of airmen during the war were heroic and trades in broad-stroke stereotypes of the German military. Certainly *Wings* is not overly critical of the United States Army Air Corps, and the intertwined male adventure and romance plots serve to give Mary's experiences at the front, Jack's suffering, and David's death a sense of purpose. In *Hell's Angels* the romance plot is hardly developed beyond Roy's discovery that Helen does not recognize his noble intentions and that his brother Monte has no genuine sense of moral duty. In some ways both of these characters exhibit a modern response to an idea of futility. Helen refutes propriety while Monte calls out the commander and his colleagues as dupes complicit in wholesale murder. Yet neither Helen nor Monte needs the pressures of war for their hedonism; it's a built-in character flaw. The individual experience of battle is not limited to the main character but is as acutely expressed in minor characters such as Karl via his point of view through the bombsight and the unnamed British pilot who rams the Zeppelin, and with the flyers who are attacking and defending Monte and Roy as they fly back in the German Gotha from their bombing raid. Such distancing effects, the result of multiple reshoots and a connecting story built upon erotic situations not always justified by "war reaction," have the effect of pulling the story away from the original "glorifying" intent that Neilan set out. This does not necessarily preclude an interpretation of anti-war sentiment. Karl's diversion of the bombs, Helen's declaration that she wants to live, and more emphatically Monte's desire to live and to proclaim the unending missions as nothing more than murder, all point to a more downbeat assessment of the war. Yet these were not the primary impressions of the reviewers at the time; their preoccupation was almost wholly with the film's affective sensations.

Chapter 3

MELANCHOLY AND THRILL

Given that Hughes's production team consisted of some veterans who in one way or another were aware of the destruction and havoc the war experience had wrought, the theme of futility, if not obvious, was present in the film's production. James Whale, a veteran of the British Army during the war, had just come from directing successful runs in London and Broadway of *Journey's End*. Lewis Milestone, who had already worked with Hughes and was friendly with him, had made *All Quiet on the Western Front* while Hughes's team was reshooting *Hell's Angels* and they were in regular contact. It is slightly ironic that John Monk Saunders, who had not been to France during the war, wrote a number of air-war films that increasingly dealt expressly with the tragedy of loss, the futility of the war, and the psychological damage it inflicted on the participants. This downward trajectory, a realignment of the vertical geometry of *Wings*, manifested itself in his subsequent scripts for *The Legion of the Condemned* (1928), *The Dawn Patrol* (1930), *The Last Flight* (1931), *Ace of Aces* (1933), and *The Eagle and the Hawk* (1933). Saunders's interest in the tragic themes of the air war had been shaped not only by his experiences at Oxford but also by conversations with Irvin S. Cobb, a writer and journalist who had covered the war for the *Saturday Evening Post*. Saunders recounted that Cobb had told him of a night he had spent with a combat squadron of the Royal Flying Corps. "He was impressed by the gallant manner in which each of these young, inexperienced and untrained pilots flew out in the morning to face almost certain death. . . . Between themselves and death these young British flyers hung up an alcoholic curtain of laughter, song and card playing."[34] Saunders had developed this theme somewhat through the tragic death of David in *Wings* and in the now-lost *Legion of the Condemned*, a film of a squadron of disillusioned volunteer flyers in pursuit of death. *The Legion of the Condemned* was fairly well reviewed but it had fewer aerial combat scenes, with some of the footage shot for *Wings* recycled. It was with *The Dawn Patrol* these themes of duty and futility came together with the added spectacle of scenes of aerial combat.[35]

The Dawn Patrol is the story of the 59th Squadron of the Royal Flying Corps and their experiences in 1915. Major Brand (Neil Hamilton) is the commander; he is tied to the desk and is increasingly frustrated with having to send inexperienced flyers to their deaths on dangerous missions. He drinks to relieve his stress. Dick Courtney (Richard Barthelmess) and Douglas Scott (Douglas Fairbanks Jr.) are his best pilots, close friends who went to school together back in England. When an ace German pilot drops a pair of boots on their airfield as a challenge, Courtney and Scott disobey Brand's orders not to retaliate, fly to the German airfield, and bomb and strafe it. On the way back they are shot down but they survive. Later Scott is brought down and Courtney, thinking he is dead, drinks with the captured German pilot who did it. He is confronted by one of his own pilots, who accuses him of betraying Scott's memory. Courtney for a moment loses his composure and angrily says he will never forget Scott. Immediately afterward Scott comes in laden with bottles and they all drink with the German flyer. These scenes, and the antagonism with Major Brand, set up the film's underlying melancholic tone. That tone is intensified when Brand is transferred to the main headquarters and in a gesture of revenge he appoints Courtney to replace him. Courtney is then chained to the desk while he sends inexperienced flyers on missions now led by Scott. Courtney drinks heavily as he rails at the orders from high command over the phone but perseveres in his duty to carry them out. When Scott's younger brother appears as one of the replacements, Courtney has no choice but to send him up. He is killed and Scott blames Courtney. Brand visits the squadron with secret orders to destroy a German ammunition store deep behind German lines in order to help stop the upcoming German advance. The only chance of getting through is one plane flying low to avoid detection. Courtney cannot go himself and is forced to ask for volunteers. Scott steps forward. Courtney visits Scott in his room before he is to take off and proceeds to get him drunk. When he has passed out Courtney goes on the mission and, although successful, is killed. The final scene is of Scott, now the commander, announcing the 59th Squadron has received special mention . . . and then giving them the orders for another mission. The war goes on.

In July of 1930, just over a month after the premiere of *Hell's Angels* at Grauman's Chinese Theatre in Hollywood, Howard Hughes, through his Caddo Company, instigated a lawsuit aimed at First National Pictures and the director of *The Dawn Patrol*, Howard Hawks. He did this in conjunction with the London-based Gainsborough company, which owned the rights to *Journey's End*, which had premiered the previous April. They sought to prevent them from the continued public exhibition of their upcoming film because it "reproduces, appropriates or colorably imitates" scenes in *Hell's Angels* and *Journey's End*, which they claimed was the basis for the film's plot. The different claims are striking in their illustration of the treatment of the war's memory in each film. In his deposition Hughes states that from the beginning his intent was to depict "for the public the *most thrilling* air scenes in air battles, maneuvers and formations that experienced and veteran aviators could possibly produce, and that expert motion picture and aerial technicians could devise."[36] Throughout his ten-page deposition he reiterates the size and extent of the production and its creation of these air combat scenes in a "new and unique manner." The goal was to make "the greatest aviation picture in the history of motion pictures."[37] His main points of contention were that the techniques of filming the aerial combat scenes he had developed had been copied by Hawks's team and that they had also included a climactic scene similar to that of *Hell's Angels*, a single-plane mission to bomb a German ammunitions dump. He stated that he had had separate conversations both with John Monk Saunders and with Howard Hawks in the previous year where they discussed the story of *Hell's Angels*. Throughout his deposition Hughes stressed the spectacle and thrill of the aerial battles. He made no mention of the film as a tribute to the flyers of the war.

The plaintiffs also deployed James Moncure March, who had reworked the screenplay and dialogue for *Hell's Angels* when Hughes remade it with sound and had adapted the play *Journey's End* for the screen. In his deposition March recounted similarities in the script with *Journey's End*. His main contention was that both were "'intimate' stories of the World War which limit themselves to an exhaustive study of a few intimately connected major characters."[38] He pointed out that in both films the major dramatic conflicts in character take place not on the battlefield but within the confined space of their living quarters. He went on to draw attention to the fact that the characters in both films (and in the play) "represent the highest English tradition and are marked by the unaffected, almost casual conduct of the English gentleman at war."[39] While in both play and film all of the characters were undergoing the same "intense, nervous strain," it was only the central character who displayed it through angry outbursts and heavy drinking. In spite of this, the main character does not lose his sense of duty, and when confronted with a new recruit with whom he has a connection in civilian life, he treats him the same as the other recruits and reluctantly sends him on a dangerous assignments from which he is not expected to return.

March's testimony for the similarities between *The Dawn Patrol* and *Hell's Angels* and *Journey's End* was countered by Charles Graham Baker, the production executive of First National. Baker was responsible for stories, plays, and source material owned by First National. A former newspaper editor, he had worked in the film industry since 1915 as a writer and producer for most of the major studios. He was involved with popular successes such as Al Jolson's second sound film, *The Singing Fool* (1928), as well as *Pioneer Trails* (1923), and to support his expertise in flying films he also listed his work on the production of *The Air Circus* (1928). Also directed by Hawks, this was a comedy about a youth who wants to learn to fly to honor his brother, who was killed in the skies over France during the war. At the outset of his deposition Baker pointed to *Wings*, *The Legion of the Condemned*, *What Price Glory*, and *Lilac Time* (George Fitzmaurice,1928) as films that predated *Journey's End*'s appearance as either a play or a film in the United States. In terms of characters, he saw nothing original about dramas built around scenes that take place outside the action such as in airdromes (*Lilac Time*), or comic waiters or subalterns or drinking sessions before and after the action where characters have been killed. In short, the "pressure cooker" story device of placing the characters in one space and having them react to the actions that have taken place outside was not new. He focused on *Lilac Time* and *What Price Glory*, where characters break down under the strain of fighting. He quoted the distraught officer's speech to Captain Flagg at the height of the battle when he pleads "What price glory now?!" He countered March's contention that the stiff upper lip English gentleman at war originated with *Journey's End*. Again he pointed to *Lilac Time* as an example of a story that incorporated a Royal Flying Corps squadron in France with the main action set in their headquarters. The film starred Gary Cooper and Colleen Moore and was an attempt to exploit the public interest in aviation and the air war sparked by *Wings*. Moore plays a French farm girl who falls in love with the new replacement, Cooper, who is shot down but lives. The film culminates in her searching through the hospitals until they are reunited.

Hughes lost the lawsuit but March's testimony is revealing in that his objections are neatly divided between the two films; one is on the question of thrills, while the other is on *The Dawn Patrol*'s similarity to *Journey's End*'s tragic, melancholic tone and its depiction of nerve-shattered commanders. Hughes's intent on thrill-making in *Hell's Angels* drove the Caddo Company to litigation in order to protect the large investment they had made. While his film had a rapturous reception at its premiere on May 27 in Los Angeles and in New York, *The Dawn Patrol* premiered six weeks later on July 10 and was scheduled for general release in August. Hughes and his staff were still making adjustments at this time and would not release *Hell's Angels* until November. The *Variety* review of the premiere spelled out the basis for his concern: "What counts against 'Hell's Angels' ever getting its investment back is that it is following so much footage of the same type, notably 'Wings' and possibly 'Flight'. Had 'Angels' been turned loose when 'Wings' was it assuredly would have gotten as much money."⁴⁰ *The Dawn Patrol*, with its comparable aerial combat footage, would be another predecessor to steal Hughes's thunder.

The *Variety* review had little to say about the depiction of war strain on the pilots in its review of *Hell's Angels*. But its review of *The Dawn Patrol* might have been used as evidence in the lawsuit in support of Gainsborough's claim: "'Dawn Patrol' in tone and tempo is 'Journey's End' applied to the Royal Flying Corps." The review listed the characters both films had in common, the "neurotic young man who can't conquer his imagination," the "Cockney enlisted men," the "philosophical middle aged adjutant," and the "courageous boy commander," and noted the theme of futile outrage and "curtain of bitterness" at the "blundering" high command. Finally it stated the obvious: *Journey's End* "is in the trenches. 'Dawn Patrol' is in the skies."⁴¹

For all of *The Dawn Patrol*'s similarities with *Journey's End*, however, the reviewer approved of the aerial combat scenes and Hawks's intelligent handling of the subject matter. The film's realism was less assured and the reviewer left that judgment to "aviators and persons familiar with the mess of 12 years ago," an assessment that gives some perspective on the impact of the pacifist trend of that year. Unlike *Hell's Angels*, *The Dawn Patrol* links the sensations and tension of the combat scenes with their impact on the psychological state of the characters, a technique more in line with Milestone's *All Quiet on the Western Front*, albeit dwelling more on the interaction of the characters than on the experiences of one character. In this way *The Dawn Patrol* signaled a turn in the air-war cycle toward the psychological impact and, with the attention on the stresses of combat and the loss of friends, hewed closer to a horizontal geometry in its representation of the air war.

"I GIVE YOU WAR!"

It is notable that this move toward the "interior" states of characters and their response to the pressures of combat had an underpinning of cost-cutting. As the impact of the Depression hit the studios the scenes shot for *Wings*, *Hell's Angels*, and *The Dawn Patrol* were reused in other films of the air-war cycle and the subsequent aviation cycle of the mid- to late 1930s.⁴² It follows that John Monk Saunders would make use of this trend with scripts and stories for a series of air-war films that explored the psychological damage the air war had wrought. *The Last Flight* (1931), *The Eagle and the Hawk* (1933), and *Ace of Aces* (1933) each took the pressures and strains of air combat as their central motivating premise. *The Last Flight* is not really an air-combat film, but deals exclusively with the exploits of four flyers in Paris following the armistice, and in that sense is a returning veteran film, preoccupied with the problems of reintegration in peacetime. The other two explore the war's impact during the war. *Ace of Aces* is a story of an artist whose girlfriend urges him to join up against his principles of peace. Played by Richard Dix, the artist reluctantly becomes a pilot and then loses his pacifist sensibilities and becomes a cold-blooded killer.

The Eagle and the Hawk focuses on the stress of air combat on American flyers who flew for the RFC before the United States entered the war. The three main characters are a cross-section of white America, and are introduced in opening emblematic vignettes, a technique fairly common in studio pictures of this period. The main character, Jerry Young, played by Fredric March, is from the moneyed class, and is introduced playing polo and smiling. Henry Crocker (Cary Grant) is a construction foreman. His vignette illustrates his no-nonsense combativeness as he punches a workman who tries to push him over. Mike Richards (Jack Oakie) is shown in a bowler hat sitting in a city café; he is a boulevardier and the film's comic relief. In the film's opening scene Young has to choose which of his recruit team will be pilots and which will be observers. He passes over Henry Crocker and leaves him behind, thus creating bitterness between them. When Young and Richards arrive at the front, each flies observation missions with an observer/photographer in the seat behind him. Young loses his observer on his first mission and is deeply disturbed by the sight of the young man's body being pulled from the cockpit. The excitement and quest for adventure has turned sour. Young has lost four more observers by the time Crocker finally arrives at the base. He is paired with Young as an observer but while they make a good team his resentment remains.

Young proves to be such an effective airman that he is cited by the top brass as a "shining example" to the new pilots. He makes a speech to the new arrivals where he reluctantly tells them they are fighting "for humanity and the preservation of civilization," and just as he has finished it a bomb hits the headquarters. A beam kills one of the young recruits and Young cradles his head in his arms as he dies. Distraught, Young is given ten days' leave back to England. In London he finds the people oblivious to the horrors he has witnessed. At a party in a wealthy townhouse he is introduced to a young boy no more than eight years old. The child is filled with the glory and gore of the romance of war. As he asks about burning crashes, Young becomes more uncomfortable and excuses himself. He is watched by a glamorous woman, played by Carol Lombard, referred to only as "The Beautiful Lady." She follows him to his taxi, where they talk and then stop to drink champagne in the park. He thanks her for being kind to him and she responds, "I want to be kind." The suggestion is that they spend the night together.

While Young is away, Crocker asks not to be paired him with again because he is cracking up. Crocker flies with Richards and, returning from a mission, Richards is mortally wounded but safely lands the plane. Young, arriving back in time to see them pull Richards's body from the plane, blames Crocker for his death. He refuses to fly with Crocker again and on the next mission loses another young observer. He is awarded yet another medal and it pushes him over the edge. At a party held in his honor he is urged to give a toast. He stands up and referring to his medals he cries: "They're all chunks of torn flesh, and broken bones and blood . . . and for what?!" He holds his glass to the camera and shouts "I give you war!" He leaves the party, goes up to his room, and in a remarkable use of mise-en-scène looks at a door that has been blocked by two planks of wood in the shape of a tilted cross; his eyes then move toward the pistol in his holster hanging on the wall. He grabs it, moves out of frame and shoots himself. Crocker follows him and, finding him dead, puts his lifeless body into the airplane and takes him up. Once in the air he machine guns holes in the wings, shoots Young to destroy the evidence of his suicide, and puts the plane into a dive; they both die, thus preserving Young's reputation. The final shot is of a memorial plaque with the inscription "Captain H.J. Young who gallantly gave his life in Aerial Combat to save the world for Democracy."

The film featured a few scenes of flying but the main focus was on the dissolution of Young and on Frederic March's intense portrayal of psychological breakdown. His descent is unremitting with only the comedy playing of Jack Oakie as Richards and the "Beautiful Lady" scene to alleviate it. The memorial placed at the end of the film, rather than the dedication at the beginning as was the case with *Wings*, completes the irony. By 1933 the Wilsonian concept of saving democracy had become a painful memory and appealed to the emerging isolationist sensibilities. That had also been overridden by the veterans' Bonus March on Washington, DC, in 1932, the Hoovervilles, and the amalgamation of the veteran and the unemployed generally in Roosevelt's "Forgotten Man" presidential campaign speech of April 1932.

Still, these were quite heavy themes for a feature, and the reception of the film illustrates the point. Mordaunt Hall of the *New York Times* saw the depiction of stress and breakdown as a "vivid and impressive account of the effect of battles in the clouds upon an American ace." He found it "refreshing to see a story done as well as this, for in so many instances the producers would have insisted on a happy ending."[43] *Film Daily* also advised their exhibitors that this was a unique "war drama of the air" with "realistic action, powerfully gripping story and a smashing climax that sends you out thinking seriously about the futility of war."[44] Both Hall and *Film Daily* praised March's performance as powerful and, for Hall, realistic. However, *Variety* saw the film as another in what had become "the same old yarn of the man who gets fed up on the uselessness of war" while noting that the film's value was in the "deftness with which it has been developed than to any basic interest."[45] The reviewer was Epes Winthrop Sargent (whose moniker was "Chicot" or "Chic"), the veteran film and vaudeville critic who had written about the film industry from the production and story creation end as well as exhibition since the teens. In Sargent's view, the only thing unique about the film was the downbeat ending. Referring to what had become a trope since the "What price glory now?!" speech, he noted the bitter toast following the dinner "indulges in much the same tirade as has been written in other similar stories." Yet he too praised the final scene where "the element of novelty enters the story." The scene was "neatly turned, is unexpected and comes at a point which gives impetus to an idea which seems to be closing in with 'just another' tag." Still, Sargent was sensitive to the broader preference of cinema audiences for lighter fare and felt that the film would not do more than ordinary business. His assessment is revealing about the ebb and flow of the broader state of the public memory of the war: "No war is calculated to be a knock out just now," a clear reference to the already rising concerns about the prospects of another war as well as the more dominant domestic issues brought on by the Great Depression.[46]

It is worth exploring for a moment the way these reviews invoke a discourse of realism. In different ways both Hall and *Film Daily* praise the film for its realistic depiction of Young's psychological breakdown, focusing primarily on March's performance. *Film Daily*, the shortest review, sees March's performance as "simply immense . . . his greatest performance." While the review opens with effusive praise for the film's realistic action, it devotes most of the space to March's performance, which, given the relatively few dogfight scenes, suggests that the realism lies in his portrayal of a psychological breakdown. Mordaunt Hall goes into more detail about what he means by the film's "praiseworthy sense of realism." He points to the plausibility of the character's actions. "Every experience of Jerry Young (Mr. March) is set forth as it might have happened." In the next sentence he provides a more specific clue: "The girl who meets him and is impersonated by Carole Lombard does not appear until the picture is halfway through and after a sequence that takes place in London, she is not heard from again." The turn to the thinly veiled one-night stand is a reference to what the Jesuit Priest Daniel A. Lord had named a "war reaction," that is, an allowable instance of extra-marital sex because of the extraordinary circumstances of wartime. Hall's notion of realism as including the sexual behavior of soldiers chimes with the inclusion of such scenes in *What Price Glory, The Big Parade, Wings, Hell's Angels, All Quiet on the Western Front*, and oblique references to sex with women in *The Dawn Patrol* and *Journey's End*. In those films as in this one, the "realism" is structured in part by the presence and absence of women. Traditional romance is purposely cast aside in a classical narrative style predicated on plausible motivations. The institutional misogyny of this system is apparent in Sargent's opening to his review: "Strictly a formula story . . . with a laboriously dragged in romantic bit to get a feminine star's name on the program. But it takes more than 50 or 60 feet of sex stuff to make love interest. It might have been better left out." Sargent's review, which reverses itself in the last paragraphs by praising the film's unique and plausible ending, assesses its appeal by drawing it precisely down gender lines: "Men will probably go for the story and many women will appreciate the psychology."

Sargent's gender bifurcation of the film's appeal illustrates the multi-layered texture and liminal nature of the memory of the war by 1933. Rather vaguely, Sargent divides the appeal between the "story" and the "psychology." Presumably the "story" is the representation of men valiantly facing the strain of war and the comradeship that emerges while women viewers will appreciate the pathos of Young's experience. Put more directly, his heteronormative breakdown of the film's appeal lines up with the characters themselves. Men will identify with the male group, if not with Young, while women would observe his breakdown with sympathy, in the same way that "The Beautiful Lady" does. The way the film complicates Sargent's categories, however, shows more directly the horizontal direction of its rendering of the memory of the war. While there is no sustained love interest with women in the film, his relationship with Crocker, while superficially homosocial, does operate as the main narrative goal of coupling. Yet women are present in the film from the moment they arrive at the base in France. Most of this is expressed through the Jack Oakie character Mike Richards with comic scenes based on his Rabelaisian appetites for food and sex. The first scene at the base in France opens with

Richards reading a copy of a pin-up magazine called *Femmes du Soir*. Later his relationship with Fifi the café matron, whom he calls Fanny, is implied as more than casual. At breakfast before they go out on patrol he tells her "You may be Fifi to the rest of the world, but you're nothing but Fanny to me." According to the PCA correspondence, Mike's lines were, for the most part, left in the script, with certain objections coming from specific regions following the film's release on May 17, 1933.[47] The more serious relationship between Jerry Young and The Beautiful Lady, however, was subject to considerable cuts. In the first version submitted to James Wingate of the Hays Office the relationship between Jerry and The Beautiful Lady was unambiguously sexual. The scene included Lombard asking him "Your place or mine" with the couple returning to his hotel and Jerry waking up, reaching over to an empty space in the bed, and then finding a note on the pillow. The back-and-forth between the Hays Office and Paramount shows that Wingate warned against this scene. The first response, dated February 6, 1933, asked that they remove Young finding the note on his pillow from the morning-after scene.[48] On April 9, after viewing the film, Wingate asked for re-edits to the morning-after scene to remove him reaching over to find her gone. (The film was re-released in 1939 and subject to more cuts, most of them focused on this scene and also with the removal of "Your place or mine.") What was left in allowed a fairly unambiguous interpretation that Mordaunt Hall reads as evidence of the film's realism. At the end of his review Sargent also finds a place for this scene as part of the film's realism in terms of motivation. The interlude with The Beautiful Lady exists in the storyline to demonstrate how incurable is Young's damaged psyche: "he comes back to the lines still shaken." For Sargent realism lies in the plausible motivation and the building of character, while for Hall the realism is more closely connected to authentic, historically accurate responses to the continued stress of battle.

The erotic energies in the film at the level of the script and its reception fuel the downward trajectory toward the ending of death for the two main characters. The film signals that theme from the moment that the squadron's logo on their planes is shown to be a death figure holding a scythe. There are also literal signposts along the way of crosses, which appear to signify at once rescue, salvation, sacrifice, and finally the cross of the cemetery that is simply death. After the loss of his fifth observer, Jerry walks with his commander in front of the hospital with a prominent red cross in the background. He tells him he had imagined he would be fighting alone and not being responsible for other men: "I didn't expect to be a chauffeur for the graveyard." At his moment of deciding to commit suicide it is the haphazard cross of wood blocking a door that seals his decision.

The overlaying of signifiers becomes a central trope in the film, a palimpsest that undercuts any single meaning. The merging of erotic and romantic imagery operates uniquely in the lighting that links The Beautiful Lady, the young blond observer who falls out of Young's plane, and the corpse of the German ace Voss. All three are lit with a luminescence that overlays eros and thanatos in a manner that fuses and confuses their significance. They are all three blond, and the Lady is surrounded in light that seems to emanate from within, a dialectic between sacred pity and erotic contemplation. The young blond observer is lit from above, his youth emphasized in his open and somewhat feminine features that contrast with Young's dark and troubled countenance. He is lit in this way that singles him out and prefigures his death, representative of the endlessness of the cycle of killing. The dead ace Voss, in a pieta pose, once again blond, lit from above, lies beside his crashed plane, his chest exposed and the bullet holes clearly visible like Christ's wounds. His body prompts Young to comment on the waste of his youth. The Beautiful Lady offering her body as a sacrifice is further equated through lighting with the young observer and the ace, evoking equivalence between the "fallen" woman and the fallen soldier.

The film's use of these dissonant combinations is in the service of depicting Young's perception of the amoral world the war has brought. His disillusionment and eventual bitterness comes as his sense of purpose unravels, his responsibility for the observers he loses haunting him. These events and the moral structure he brought to the war motivate his behavior. Frederic March's performance of this dissolution, picked up by the reviewers, demonstrates that the film presents his performance through the eyes of the other characters—his commander, the young observers for whom he is held up as a "shining example," The Beautiful Lady—but more consistently through Crocker. The male coupling and their double suicide plays out like a dark version of one of the screwball comedies Grant and March would become known for. It is through Crocker's eyes that Young's psychological traumas are exhibited. The relationship between the two men undergoes a change in a pivotal scene that is shown from Crocker's perspective. He is awoken by Young talking and muttering in his sleep. He is reliving the dogfights and the loss of his observers in his dreams; he repeats their names along with "I lost him . . . Kids . . . little boys . . . I can't stand it . . . I'm going to stop the whole rotten mess." He sits up, still dreaming, and the camera closes

FIGURE 3.3. "I'm going to stop the whole rotten mess." Frederic March and Cary Grant in *The Eagle and the Hawk* (Stuart Walker, 1933). Paramount/Photofest. © Paramount.

in on his face as the tempo of his dream builds up to the point where Crocker socks him and knocks him out. When a young observer comes in to the room Crocker says it was his nightmare and that Young is sound asleep.

In Young's final speech he brings out the trope of body and machine that has run through the aerial war films since *Wings*. The songs the pilots sing underpin his speech about medals being blood and torn flesh. In the film these are not fully recognizable, but they are similar to the bitter satire of "Stand to Your Glasses Steady," whose refrain rhymes "The world is a world full of lies" with "Hurrah for the last man to die" sung in *The Dawn Patrol*, or "Pilot's Lament," in which a pilot who has crashed asks his comrades to "Take the joystick from out of my brain / Take the rudder from out of my kidneys / And assemble the whole thing again." Here the vertical heroics and glorious sacrifice for the future are leveled by the theme of futility and the irony of a celebration in a senseless situation.

The sacrifice theme has been fused with technology in an obscene reversal of transubstantiation. The machine has become the body of the sacrificed airman.

RETOOLING

The Eagle and the Hawk, while not the last of the World War I aviation cycle, does provide and endpoint to its downward trajectory. As indicated by Sargent's review, the shape of the air-war story had become "tired." His perception that the futility narrative had run its course is borne out in the continued production of civilian aviation films. Richard Barthelmess starred in the William Wellman–directed *Central Airport* (1933), and John Ford had made *Air Mail* the year before; both featured characters who were barnstormers whose maverick attitudes toward flying were coming up against the increasingly regulated aviation industry. Their backstory of having flown in the war was either explicit or implicit. In 1938 Clark Gable starred in Victor Fleming's *Test Pilot*, which continued the romance of flying and its dangers in the civilian air industry. The theme of unbearable stress and psychological disintegration becomes part of the motivation for these characters' maverick behavior. The conflict is derived from these characters' willingness, or not, to give in to the professionalization of the private air industry. The futility of war was no longer a central theme but a character motivation.

How well embedded this function of the war experience had become is evident in *Death in the Air* (1936), a B feature directed by veteran silent director Elmer Clifton. Produced by Fanchon Royer, one of the few women producers of the era, the film was an aviation mystery. The Goering-Gage Aviation company has had a number of unexplained accidents and the US Department of Commerce becomes concerned. The inspector brings a US military test pilot, Jerry Blackwood, to investigate. They learn from a dying passenger that the accidents have actually been the work of a mysterious flyer in a plane marked by a black X painted on its fuselage, which has been bringing the planes down. The company hires a psychiatrist, who determines that the mysterious pilot is probably a psychotic veteran pilot of the war. They find out that there are five veteran flying aces from the war living in the area, which looks to be southern California. Jerry brings the five ex-aces together as a ploy to determine which of them might be "Pilot X." The five pilots represent Germany, Britain, France, Canada, and the US. Jerry takes them into the air to try to find the mysterious flyer.

The French and German aces are killed by Pilot X. The mysterious killer then paints an X on the Canadian ace's plane and Jerry Blackwood, the young test pilot, mistaking him for Pilot X, shoots him down. That leaves the British and the American. The paint used on the Canadian's plane is found in the American's locker and he is taken away. The British pilot has a breakdown and takes the heroine, Jerry's love interest Helen Gage, the daughter of the owner of Goering-Gage Aviation, into the air. His plane is disabled by Pilot X. Jerry then shoots down Pilot X, who he discovers is the co-owner of Goering-Gage, Carl Goering. He had been an American flyer during the war who deserted and then flew with the Germans. Jerry and Helen then discover their love for each other.

It is a budget feature and the seams of the cheap production values are apparent. But the script's motivating forces behind Pilot X and evidenced in the British ace's breakdown are psychological damage due to their war experience. As a B film, its setup of motivations is economical and based around the introduction of each ace. In the first scene the aces are talking about who was the best ace of the war, with each claiming a compatriot; notably, the German names Baron von Richthofen. The co-owner of the company, who turns out to be Pilot X, is prophetically named Carl Goering, and while he is a melodramatic villain in that he was a deserter, his revenge has no obvious motivation other than the psychotic effects of war trauma. In the psychiatrist's words, "It is a direct result of the war." The symptoms, however, are most fully articulated by the British ace, Roland Saunders. After the Pilot X has killed the first three aces, Saunders has a breakdown and shouts maniacally, "Of course I'm a killer, We're all killers . . . innocent lives on our bloody hands!" Apart from the ham-fisted nationalism of having a German named Goering as the villain, the film treats the veteran flyers as relics from the past while the new couple, as well as the new kind of expert, the psychiatrist, are inhabitants of the future, of progress, and a thinly veiled representative of the new, well organized, technically advanced military-industrial complex. The film trades on the horizontal geometry of the war's memory for its motivations as a means of sealing it off and consigning it to history—a past from which the progressive future is released.

In 1938, Warner's decision to remake *The Dawn Patrol* was, as mentioned earlier, to capitalize on the renewed interest in the potential for a new war. Hal Wallis wrote to Jack Warner, "I think it would bring us a fortune now when the whole world is talking and thinking war and rearmament."[49] However, *Variety* demonstrated an apparent continued resonance of the theme of futility: "It comes along as a timely, gripping preachment against the futility of war."⁵⁰ Yet the main appeal of the film for the reviewer was its "red corpuscled . . . contribution to the aviation cycle." The reference was to Errol Flynn; the review lauds his performance as Courtney as having added "heavily to his popularity as a he-man star." The review accurately reports that film is unique from previous air war films in its depiction of the incompetence of the "brass hats." The futility narrative is less pacifist and more a critique of out-of-touch and out-of-control commanders. But *Variety*'s review takes as read the subtle shifts in emphasis from the 1930 Howard Hawks version. The new version refers to "nobody knowing what it's all about" but the reference to the real problem is clear in Phipps's speech. If peace comes, then it will last only "till another bunch of criminals sitting at a table decide to start another war and then we go at it again." With Hitler's Germany flexing its muscles by annexing Austria in March 1938, while the script was being revised by Seton I. Miller and Dan Totheroe, both of whom had adapted the original, the reference to criminals was clear.

Not picking up on the reference to a rearming Germany, the review focused on the performances of Flynn and David Niven as Lt. Scott. The strength of these two outweighed the fact that there were no women in the film at all. In John Monk Saunders's original story, and in the Hawks version, the rift between Courtney and Scott had its origins in their competition over a woman in Paris, which Courtney had won. This was removed for the remake. It is revealing, though, that the absence of women, or love interest, is directly connected to the film's adherence to realism: "In this and in the sad ending, producers have kept to realism at the sacrifice of a sugar coated, implausible ending."⁵¹ Once again realism is dependent in part on the presence and absence of women. The love interest is made up for in the eyes of the reviewer by the "friendships developed by the aviators." In Saunders's versions of realism throughout his flying films he includes women. In *Wings* the triadic relationship between Jack, David, and Sylvia is at the center of the tragedy. I will outline in the next chapter that the part of Mary was fleshed out and developed specifically for Bow by scriptwriting team Hope Loring and Louis Lighton. Saunders's films, *Wings* included, as well as *The Eagle and the Hawk* and *The Last Flight*—which I deal with in chapter 5—depend in different ways and degrees on idealized, indeed blonde, women as apparitions that make up a romantic triad that leads ultimately to the death of at least one of the male protagonists. The complete exclusion of women in *The Dawn Patrol* remake seems to redirect Saunders's horizontal trajectory back toward a vertical heroic narrative of sacrifice for the group of fellow flyers, caught up not so much in a hopeless and meaningless war as in the indifference and callousness of their superiors. In the next chapter this presence and absence of women is considered from the perspective of another production cycle that reversed the gender polarities and focused on women as nurses at the front.

Chapter 4

FORBIDDEN ZONES

Women, Vernacular, and "War as it really is"

The success of *All Quiet on the Western Front* and its message of the pity of war added a tragic dimension to the war film and signaled a departure from its roots in the male adventure story. The adaptation of the popular novel was in part due to the appearance in the late '20s of successful literary works that contributed to a shift in the geometry of the popular memory of the Great War from vertical to horizontal, from a heroic endeavor to an effort of senseless slaughter and futility. These included Hemingway's *The Sun Also Rises* and *A Farewell to Arms*, the British war poets, and the popular productions in London and on Broadway of R.C. Sherriff's play *Journey's End*. The success of these works drew the attention of Carl Laemmle Jr. and Robert North, who produced film adaptations of *All Quiet on the Western Front* and *Journey's End*, respectively. *All Quiet*'s popularity, alongside the cultural resonance of R.C. Sherriff's *Journey's End*, in turn prompted an undertone of melancholy that also began to appear in war-aviation films penned by John Monk Saunders such as *The Dawn Patrol* and *The Eagle and the Hawk* and predominated throughout the 1930s.

In these anti-war films, the role of women at the front was as supporting characters, or in the case of *Journey's End* simply a photograph pinned on a wooden post. In Budd Boetticher's oft-quoted words, "What counts is what the heroine provokes, or what she represents"; women, that is, provided motivation for the male characters and acted as ciphers for articulating the soldier's stunted desires and fears.[1] Yet coincident with men's anti-war literature of the late 1920s and early '30s, women's actual experiences at the front as nurses had been the subject of an emerging body of literature and popular magazine stories. Mary Borden's memoir *The Forbidden Zone*, which appeared in 1929, was followed by *Not So Quiet:*

Stepdaughters of War by Evadne Price (pseudonymously as Helen Zenna Smith) in 1930, and then in 1933 by Vera Brittain's *Testament of Youth*. Perhaps most telling of the ideological dynamics that accompanied women's accounts of the war was the republication in 1934 of Ellen LaMotte's graphic and unflinching account, *The Backwash of War: The Human Wreckage of the Battlefield as Witnessed by an American Hospital Nurse*, banned when originally published in 1916.[2] While women working as nurses had been a staple in films with war settings since the beginnings of narrative film, the early 1930s saw a short cycle of films that placed women at the center of the war film. One of the first of these was *War Nurse* (1930), produced at MGM and directed by Edgar Selwyn. The film was an adaptation of a set of serial stories for *Cosmopolitan* magazine, the full title of which was "War Nurse: The True Story of Women who Lived, Loved and Suffered on the Western Front," drawn from the anonymous memoirs of an American woman who had served at the front and ghostwritten by Rebecca West. Another, a year later, was *The Mad Parade*, a film distributed by Paramount and directed by William Beaudine. The two films did unremarkable business and their critical reception ranged from lukewarm to outright hostile. Yet this cycle is an illuminating instance of the Hollywood system's negotiation with the evolving public memories of the Great War. Both films were attempts to capitalize on a perceived public interest in women who had worked at the front, and in highlighting the traumas of war. They were also efforts to widen the appeal of the war film to women audiences. They drew attention to women's agency, their experiences, and their ability to deal with male weaknesses, both physical and sexual, and in the process they offered a new, witty, and dynamic perspective on desire at the front that had remained underexplored in the male adventure film.

Drawn from women's memoirs, these films centered, albeit differently, on the intersection between eros and thanatos familiar in the male war films but previously absent from fictionalized female war experiences. Consequently, the stories provided distinct challenges as well as opportunities for scriptwriters. They faced the same censorship problems the male war films had with depicting graphic violence, death, and injury along with explicit references to the participant's sexual tensions but also, crucially, unlike the male war narrative, they were centered around the question of women's desire. The scriptwriters' and scenarists' solutions in the male war films of using vernacular gesture and slang and an emphasis on the violence and pity of war, which had worked well in conveying a sense of "realism," were less successful in this war-nurse cycle. But despite its lack of success, this vernacular, spoken and enacted by women, offered a means by which the social, sexual, and physical conflicts and disruptions brought about by the world war as experienced by women could be expressed. More importantly, the resulting realism was often achieved through the efforts of women scriptwriters, whose incorporation of vernacular language and gesture had been fully developed in the characters of the gold-digger and the flapper in the 1920s.

The short war-women cycle of 1930–31 was based on assumptions within the industry of audience taste preferences and, moreover, gave women scriptwriters a rare opportunity to offer a more gender-nuanced account of women's war experiences. Simply put, the challenge of fulfilling audience and critical expectations of war-realism in a way that would pass censors was met by incorporating the snappy, wisecracking characters that had been the stock-in-trade of writers such as Anita Loos, Hope Loring, and Ethel Doherty and screen stars such as Clara Bow, Evelyn Brent, and stage star June Walker. The development of that process throughout the '20s and early '30s—indicating as it does a subtle but important and lasting shift from elevated rhetoric to low-down cynicism—is the subject of this chapter.

FROM ROMANTIC TO VERNACULAR

"His love asks to wipe away her tears—a little part of the young love that will soothe the wounds of war."
—Title card from *The Girl Who Stayed at Home*
(D.W. Griffith, 1919)[3]

BABS: Sure, and it's a great war, if you don't weaken!
JOY: Or when you do!
—Dialogue from *War Nurse*, 1930[4]

The above intertitle of Griffith's film and the dialogue from *War Nurse* are a general illustration of the trajectory of language, from romantic to vernacular, that characterized women's roles in war films across the 1920s. Griffith's ornate prose gives way to the type of worldly exchange between Babs and Joy in MGM's film *War Nurse* a decade later. During this period, Hollywood scripts that employed the Western Front as a background show a growing recognition and accommodation of the social changes wrought by the Great War. The nostalgic sentimentality of a woman's role in war as keeper of the hearth and home by 1930 had been challenged, though by no means replaced, by modern representations of women and their wartime experiences. The overlap here between characterizations of "modern" and "traditional" is evident in the language employed by title and scriptwriters, and in the performances of women in war films of the '20s and '30s.

The Girl Who Stayed at Home offers an example of how the overlap played out. The film was built in part on the tensions between traditional and modern representations of women cast in a war setting through its use of language in the titles and in the gestures of the actors.[5] The title card quoted above comes toward the end of the film at the culmination of the film's main romance plot between Atoline France (Carol Dempster) and American Lieutenant Ralph Gray (Richard Barthelmess). Griffith's treatment of war and women outlined the sacrifice of the anguish of waiting at home, grief, and the healing power of tears and love. He contrasted this traditional couple with the verbal and gestural vernacular of a "modern" couple, Ralph's ne'er-do-well brother James "Oily Jim" Grey (Robert Harron) and Cutie Beautiful (Clarine Seymour), a dancer in a New York café. Played as comic relief, James's ultimate transformation from a slacker into a hero is set up by his louche slouch and Cutie's flapper behavior and dress, and they both are represented through the vernacular language employed in the titles. As Jim is about to leave for the front Cutie confesses to flirting with other men. His response: "Look at me—thirty-one janes." She promises "I'll be so straight." Griffith casts the modern and traditional love plots as high and low, the romantic ideal versus a sexualised quotidian, a poetic against a vernacular.

The film's lukewarm reception indicates a rejection of the baroque language of the titles. "The Screen" column of the *New York Times* complained "Why does Mr. Griffith, who can make such eloquent, intelligible pictures, go to such pains to spell everything out? . . . Certainly his text is unnecessary and frequently mars the artistry of his pictures."[6] *Variety*'s Patsy Smith in her film fashion column "Among the Women" extends "The Screen's" frustration with the highbrow language of the titles to the depiction of the two women:

> The title of the latest Griffith release "The Girl Who Stayed at Home" suggested much in the way of a strong story. One thought of the many types of women who stayed at home, but after witnessing the picture were disappointed to find the title had sort of been "pinned" on a familiar Griffith war story theme.[7]

Smith reserved her praise for Seymour; "this little party has a gushy, mushy part which she handles so sincerely even those of the stony hearts and the tightly laced in laughter were inclined to smile indulgently at her enthusiasm." Smith's reference to the "many types of women who stayed at home" becomes more clear as she outlines the broad-based appeal of Seymour's performance of the flapper through a detailed description of her dresses. "As for dressing Miss Seymour was true to her type—short narrow frocks, picturesquely arranged dark locks and cheeky little draped turbans."[8]

The general drift of the reviews of the film move from impatience with the high-flown romance to an embrace of the down-to-earth modern couple. As the *New York Times* pointed out, Griffith films can sometimes be "disappointing because we have come to expect so much from him."[9] But all of the critics seem to be pointing to the passé sentimental depictions of "pure love." For these critics Griffith's effort to appeal to more "modern" sensibilities with Cutie seem to have had the effect of highlighting and undermining the sentimental and florid language of Atoline and Ralph. By the time of the film's release, similar upbeat depictions of romance with a dependence on a modernized vernacular language were already becoming established as a norm in characterization. This was true particularly for scenarist Anita Loos, who was establishing her career in contrasting staid, pious (often older) men with the modern wisecracking woman. She wrote in her 1920 book *How to Write Photoplays*,

> There are some things which cannot be expressed in pantomime. For this reason we advise you to use explanatory sub-titles with as clever and forceful wording as possible whenever the action necessitates explanation.[10]

Loos is here emphasizing the importance of the kind of rhythmic use of language that she excelled in to bring over a story. Her work with Constance Talmadge throughout the late teens and early twenties in films with provocative titles such as *The Virtuous Vamp* (1919) and *The Love Expert* (1920) established Talmadge as a light comedienne where the titles were foregrounded as part of the films' attractions. *Wid's Daily* noted that *The Virtuous Vamp*'s titles were "unusually good."[11] They liked the titles of another Loos-penned effort, *In Search of a Sinner*, enough to highlight an excerpt on the front page of the February 24, 1920, edition: "Said the modern St Anthony: 'I'm above temptation!' Replied the up-to-date enchantress: 'Well, stoop a little stupid!'"[12] The "up-to-date enchantress" is central to the comic conflict between modern and traditional, as is the underlying arch treatment of masculine desire. The comic deflation of putting on airs, and moreover of male behavior as staid and entitled, anticipates and contributes to a sensibility of "realism" through humor. The natural dialect, in Loos's wry hands, brings the "high hat" attitudes crashing to ground level. *Wid's Daily*'s endorsement was aimed directly at exhibitors as a quality that would result in profitable box office.

Loos's snappy and sharply aimed dialogue exemplifies the developing and changing idea of what constituted realism in the following decade. These were recognizably real characters who spoke a language of the present, the up-to-date.

Vernacular language and slang, in particular with its double entendre and use of euphemism, was a source for scriptwriters to input a realism drawn from everyday, censorable language, not only that associated with the military but also that of the street. This was particularly useful when depicting the moral compromises and transgressions that accompanied the all-male environment of the army and their behavior with women—both at the front and at home. Such uses of language and the actions and situations they referred to continued to be a focal point of concern for the Hays Office. Given such censoring limitations, realism in the depiction of the horrors of modern warfare resided in part in the tough language used to describe and convey the war experience. This became more acute with the coming of sound, with the use of effects such as explosions and the moaning and cries of the hurt and dying and with spoken dialect and slang. The role that vernacular language played in the ensuing cycle of war films was central in rendering war realistically and hinged on the axis of two discursive realms, the cynical and the erotic. Cynical language was used to express a resignation to the futility of the experience and to mask the trauma of having witnessed and participated in abject horrors. Connected to this as a motivating factor was an emphasis on the erotic charge of the repression and release nature of existence in the front lines. Men thrown together at the front developed attachments to each other and then, when on leave, attachments to prostitutes in estaminets and relationships with women in the villages just behind the lines, and of course with nurses and women volunteers in the field hospitals when wounded. Both cynicism and eros were constructed by a regulating propriety in the use of language. Dependence on vernacular allowed these rules to be bent and shaped to the extraordinary nature of the events the men and women at the front were undergoing. Consequently the front and the environments surrounding it were a "forbidden zone" where the term was polysemic, forbidden in terms of both the threat of death and the promise of escape from moral strictures. In this environment, straight-talking vernacular was a coping mechanism. For scriptwriters it provided a technique of realism and, at the same time, a means of sidestepping censorship.

Such a combination of the cynical and the erotic lent itself well to the developing mode of scriptwriting and the Hollywood "formula," which, as Ruth Vasey has outlined, required "plausible deniability" of any treatment of socially or morally sensitive scenes.[13] The incorporation of vernacular language, particularly once sound film became the norm, provided a brand identity of American films that in turn fed into more widely circulating images of Americanism that looked to the various regions of the US like modernization and internationally, to mainly European cultures, like modernization and Americanization. More critically, the use of vernacular as a means of double-coding "adult" themes offered a means by which the social, sexual, and physical conflicts and disruptions brought about by the Great War as experienced by women could be expressed. These strategies, as we will see, became more transparent in the production and reception of films featuring women in major supporting roles such as Clara Bow's Mary in *Wings* or in the short-lived cycle of films, such as *War Nurse* and *The Mad Parade*, that placed women at the center of war films' narratives.

HOPE LORING AND *WINGS*

Wings illustrates the input of the scriptwriting team of Hope Loring and Louis Lighton, who deliberately incorporated the flapper persona of Clara Bow as a means of ensuring a broader audience for such a big-budget feature. The move made sense, as she had been something of a sensation since 1925 when *Motion Picture Classics* featured her on the cover describing her as having "something vital and compelling. . . . She is Young America rampant, the symbol of flapperdom." While the incongruity between the flapper image and the girl-next-door role raised some consternation among critics after the film's release, it was her name that topped the bill of this prestige feature.

Though the story was John Monk Saunders's, the writing team of Loring and Lighton provided the detailed characterization and boosted Bow's role as Mary. Over the previous three years Loring had worked regularly with B.P. Schulberg in developing Bow's career as he loaned her out to other companies. Loring, along with her husband, Louis Lighton, had worked on the script for *Helen's Babies* for Principal Pictures (William Seiter) and *This Woman* (Phil Rosen) for Warner Bros., both in 1924. These were small parts for Bow but significant in that they mixed an innocence with a vitality and knowingness that became central to her image. Loring and Lighton had recently written screenplays for two hit features for her, *It* (released February 19, 1927) and *Children of Divorce* (released April 2, 1927), before working on *Wings*.

In *It* Loring's success lay in incorporating Bow's acting business, which combined a gestural vernacular with the linguistic vernacular in the use of her natural Brooklyn accent, witticisms, and double entendres in the titles. Their story for *It* was based on an Elinor Glyn article and tied in with Bow's persona both on and off screen.[14] Bow's specific embodiment of the flapper offered a demonstration of the efficacy of female characters incorporating vernacular, both in performance and dialogue, for lending a realism and "up-to-dateness." It was an image that held an attraction for female audiences, presaged the coming of sound, and was to achieve a fuller—and aesthetically significant—effect in the war-nurse film cycle.

Loring's influence is evident in the first scene, which features Jack and Mary with an introductory shot of Mary peeping from under underwear hanging on a clothesline, a motif taken directly from the introduction of Betty Lou in *It*. While the film was lauded by the critics and eventually won the first Academy Award for Best Picture, some critics voiced concern over the Bow character. *The Film Spectator* wrote, "That excellent little actress, Clara Bow, manages only to be a nuisance. There was no story reason for taking her to France. The flutter of a skirt has no place among whirring propellers." The sequence where Mary, who has volunteered as an ambulance driver at the front, finds Jack drunk in the Folies Bergère in Paris was judged to be expendable:

> when the characters are in France I would have shown the girls only in the opening and closing sequences, and I would have injected nothing to distract the audience's attention from the serious business of war. . . . that Paramount did not know what to do with such a story is shown by the fact that it does nothing to clear the reputation of Clara Bow who was sent home from France in disgrace.[15]

However, the following passage suggests that there was a realism to the scene that countered more traditional depictions of the war as a tragic but cathartic experience: "The drunk sequence should never have been shot. I know that our fine boys who went to France did such things, for I saw much of it myself, but it should not have been dragged into a picture to which it contributes nothing whatever." The drunk scene he is referring to is the scene of Mary in Paris looking for Jack because his squad has been called back for the big push. She finds him in the Folies Bergère, drinking with his comrades and women who are coded as sexually available, if not prostitutes. In order to keep Jack from "going upstairs" with one of the women, she trades her Red Cross uniform for the glittering sequins dress of a Folies Bergère dancer.[16] In the process, she masquerades as offering a different kind of "service," sexual rather than medical. The template for the new realism of *What Price Glory* and *The Big Parade* is augmented here by the visual vernacular of the Flapper. The vulgar language of Quirt and Flagg and the innocent promiscuity of Marguerite are given a distinctly American spin through Bow's masquerade as seductress. This is the star turn for Bow in Loring and Leighton's screenplay, one that reprises the scene in *It* when she alters an old dress to look like a ball gown. It has the effect of casting a light on a side of the war that did not mesh so easily with the *Film Spectator*'s romantic view of the war experience.

Saunders's story was published as a novel to tie in with the films' road-show release. A comparison illustrates the impact Loring's script and Bow's performance made on the finished film. Both include the "Cinderella" sequence where the French powder room attendant tells her to put on the sequins dress to get Jack back. However, the film makes more of the conflict between Mary and her French competition through the animated bubbles that Jack sees in his drunken haze. Mary shakes her dress, which produces the "bubbles" that draw his attention, but it is the tears in her eyes that persuade Jack to choose her over the French woman. In the novel, he passes out and the other woman leaves in disgust; it does not include Mary being caught in the compromised situation in Jack's hotel room and sent home in disgrace. The differences are significant. The established literary character of the "flapper/innocent" maintained some stability in novel form, but within Hollywood's production system it was undergoing a subtle change.

By working Bow's flapper persona into a character who is essentially a suburban girl-next-door type, Loring was able not only to bring on board Bow's sizable audience (which attracted both genders), but also to enhance the film's "realism" along the lines of vernacular and vulgarity. In fact, the film version emphasizes the situation in the Folies Bergère through a set of reaction shots of Bow/Mary that show she understands what is happening. On her approach to the table, Mary sees David with a woman on his lap. The woman whispers in his ear; there's a reaction shot of Bow, who shakes her head with tears in her eyes; they then stand up and David looks at Jack and says "All set?" Jack responds with "OK." In the film this is an echo of their ritual before taking off into battle. It

FIGURE 4.1. Mary rescues Jack at the end of the Folies Bergère scene in *Wings*. Paramount/Photofest. © Paramount.

makes a clear equivalence between combat and sex, and of course, disturbingly, between the airplane and women's bodies. In the book this is rendered through the double entendre banter between the boys:

> "Violets, who'll buy my violets . . ."
> One of the fliers, persuaded by a girl, rose from the table.
> "Ready to take off?" someone said.
> "All set?"
> "Keep her nose on the horizon and don't skid on your turns."[17]

Replacing the banter in the title cards between the men with the visual vernacular as performed by Bow displaces the censorable material through the series of reaction shots. Bow's persona in other films worked to give this scene plausibility. Mary, as written by Saunders, does not fully comprehend the codes; but Clara Bow, the flapper from Brooklyn, does. *Photoplay*'s two-paragraph review stated the same contradictory view as the *Film Spectator*: "A great war spectacle of the air. Thrilling airplane fights and manoeuvres in and above the clouds. Unfortunately the story is weakly built and, with the exception of several touching scenes, misses conviction." The last sentences point to the problem and demonstrate the contradiction faced by scriptwriters in this period: "Clara Bow, as the girl, is too sophisticated for the part. By all means see Wings."[18]

For these critics, Bow's incarnation as girl-next-door/Red Cross ambulance driver is a mask discarded in this scene for the image of the flapper and her own persona as "American youth rampant" in order to save Jack. Jack sees the "true" Mary/Clara through her genuine tears, distinct from the bubbles of the sequins on her dress, which qualify his lust by mobilizing his empathy. Through the haze of alcohol, he finds the love for her that he will finally recognize at the film's end, only to pass out in the hotel bedroom. In writing the scene this way Loring has effectively brought out Bow's star persona, the modern sophisticated woman whose knowledge of the world rescues Jack's innocence in these matters. The sentimentality of the scene, as Lea Jacobs suggests, "almost returns it to the realm of boys' fiction," but the war setting, the theme of prostitution, and the wider star persona of Clara Bow prevent that.[19] The critic's disapproval of Bow's "sophistication" highlights a contradictory criterion for realism when women are placed at or near the front. Jack's innocence, in terms of the horrors and trauma of warfare, of killing, is lost, but sanctified through the comradeship of his fellow airmen and the myth of chivalry among the flyers on both sides. Vulgarity and vernacular as a technique of achieving realism offer a further means of displacing the horrors of the front. Once women enter the "forbidden zone" the result is a heteronormative erotic charge. Consequently, the use of vernacular becomes both necessary for producers and problematic for critics and the Hayes Office. The production and reception of the war-women cycle that followed with the coming of sound brought these erotic tensions into high relief.

"WHAT EVERY FLAPPER IS TALKING ABOUT"

As we have seen throughout, the war film affords the opportunity to depict sexual behavior, if not outright prostitution. The Folies Bergère scene in Wings references a demimonde common in US cities and displaces it onto Paris. To put it directly, Jack and his drunken comrades are negotiating with the women for sex and it is the war context that justifies it. The scene's vernacular language, gestures, and double entendres have their origins in the pre-war demimonde culture of red-light districts or "vice resorts." The impact of the wartime mobilization of troops on vernacular language in the post-war decade, particularly that relating to heterosexual relations, was profound. Recent scholarship on the social history of sexuality in the US during and after World War I suggests that male troops emerged from their experience in the service with a sense of masculine entitlement. The wartime propaganda that demonized and dehumanized women in the interest of containing the spread of venereal disease among the troops "fostered an extreme misogyny."[20] While the War Department conjoined with pre-war reforms in efforts to make the new popular public spaces of entertainment such as amusement parks, movie theatres, and dance halls more socially respectable, a side effect was that men talked about the women who frequented them in demeaning and objectifying terms. This was couched in the vernacular that had arisen in saloon back rooms. Mara Keire has argued that the regulation of these areas in 1917–18, prompted by the Commission on Training Camp Activities and its anti-venereal disease propaganda aimed at the newly mobilized troops, initiated a change in the language used in the negotiations between men and women for sex, from a more-or-less equal status where women did their own negotiating to one that depended on male go-betweens who would identify "available" women for customers.

> Unlike later obscene exchanges during the First World War, sporting women were "bitches" and "bums," and only on rare occasion were they fetishized body parts. "Cocksucker," a common epithet, was obscene, but it was also active: it defined people, who were as often female as male, by what they did. As an insult it reviled agents, not objects.[21]

Working from the reports of vice investigators in the Northeast who recorded conversations in saloon back rooms before and during the mobilization of troops during the war, Keire noted a change where "sporting" women became identifiable in terms of their body parts. "Where once women interacted directly with men, one subject to another, in the venues of the new popular culture the enforced distance between men and women meant that men as subjects talked together about objects—women."[22]

The language was a vernacular of the street that operated in euphemisms and insults. Prior to the crackdown on "vice resorts," women to some extent controlled the business relationship and insulting a "john" about the size of his penis or his ability to perform was a means of closing the deal. In this pre-war context women were able to use vernacular as a means of maintaining some control over the negotiations. "Both men and women indiscriminately embroidered their conversations with epithets, applying them equally to both sexes."²³ In *Wings* David is prompted to "go upstairs" when the woman he is with whispers in his ear. Mary competes in the negotiations for Jack with her dress and the tears that produce the bubbles. Her masquerade enables her to maintain control; the romance plot requires that the tears provoke genuine empathy. In constructing the scene as both realistic and romantic, Loring employs a negotiation form without a middleman that harks back to pre-war conditions,.

How did the vernacular of the demimonde find its way into common usage and thereby into the entertainment culture of theatre, vaudeville, and film? H.L. Mencken offered an explanation in 1919. Blaming the Comstock Postal Act of 1873, which criminalized the circulation by post of erotica, contraceptives, information relating to abortion, and even reference to sexual behavior in private letters, Mencken wrote in *The American Language*, "to this day the effects of that old reign of terror are still visible. We yet use *toilet* and *public comfort station* in place of better terms, and such idiotic forms as *red-light district*, *disorderly-house*, *blood-poison*, *social-evil*, *social disease* and *white slave* ostensibly conceal what every flapper is talking about."²⁴ In drawing attention to these euphemisms and their use by women, Mencken is referring to his own 1915 definition of the flapper as a woman who is "impossible to shock," knows "dark secrets," lives in an "age of knowledge," and is "opposed to the double standard of morality."²⁵ Mencken's description of women understanding the codes of vernacular language as well as its inbuilt iniquities outlines the kind of antagonistic characters that Loos and Loring specialized in. Their wisecracks and snappy one-liners offered a counter that satirized patriarchs and sugar daddies and demonstrated a willingness and ability to negotiate the stark terms of their heteronormative culture with humor. This form of "realism" removes the veil of propriety to reveal the actual and often brutal terms of relationships where women's bodies were the object of exchange.

WAR NURSE

Character types such as Lorelei Lee from *Gentlemen Prefer Blondes* (1928) and Bow's Mary and their understanding and use of vernacular found their way into the women-centered war films *War Nurse* (1930) and *The Mad Parade* (1931). *War Nurse* was a prestige MGM production, and producer

Irving Thalberg's approach was to bring the language of the flapper to the story and combine it with the gritty realism of the war pictures. This is reflected in his choice of screenwriters Becky Gardiner and Joe Farnham. Gardiner was a staff writer for MGM who had worked on, among other things, the 1926 Paramount adaptation of *The Great Gatsby* (Herbert Brenon) as well as the Norma Shearer vehicle *A Free Soul* (Clarence Brown, 1931). Farnham, known for his humorous titles in the silent era, had a long list of credits and had won the first and only Academy award for title writing. His work on *The Big Parade* made him a logical choice for *War Nurse*. The director was the established Broadway theatre producer Edgar Selwyn. This was his second effort at film directing and he brought in June Walker, who had played Lorelei Lee in his successful stage production of Anita Loos's *Gentlemen Prefer Blondes*.

War Nurse begins with a written prologue that sets out the story out as a tribute and memorial to those who "volunteered for nursing duty in France untrained, unorganised, unrelated to the vast army of nurses sent out by government authorities or under the banner of the Red Cross." In this way it announces the "forbidden zones" with which this story of the trials and tribulations of a group of volunteer nurses at the front will deal.[26] The dangers they faced were not only the constant shelling and being surrounded by the wounded and dying but also having to deal with the unwanted attentions of sex-obsessed soldiers, the threat of pregnancy, and duplicitous boyfriends. The film's main character is Barbara or "Babs" (Walker), a well-to-do and world-wise New Yorker who volunteers for the Nurse Corps while on holiday with friend Rosalie (Marie Provost) in Paris just as the war breaks out. They are joined by a school teacher from Kansas (Helen Jerome Eddy), Cushie (Zasu Pitts) from an undisclosed rural area, and Joy (Anita Page), a young American ingénue who has come straight from a French convent school.

The film opens with a montage of actual footage from the war with a trumpet sounding over explosions and images of men marching. It then fades to a number of American women in a Paris hotel dressed in formal attire, drinking cocktails and reading a newspaper with the headline "Ypres Battle resumed: Frantic Need for Nurses." Much of the wisecracking goes on between the New Yorkers Rosalie and Babs:

BABS: "It's a fine break for us. In Paris on a vacation and some sorehead starts a war."
ROSALIE: "Right I could have had plenty of war back home in New York—with father and dear old aunt Fanny."

FIGURE 4.2. From left to right: Cushie (Zasu Pitts), Rosalie (Marie Provost), Joy (Anita Page), Helen (Martha Sleeper), and Babs (June Walker) wisecracking in *War Nurse* (Edgar Selwyn, 1930).

Much of the banter centers around the equivalence between war and marriage:

> BABS: "I've just signed up for the war"
> ROSALIE: "What are you getting married?"

The quips set them out as innocents who romanticize the war as a means of meeting men.

> ROSALIE: "Imagine moonlit nights in no mans land"
> BABS: "With five-million men out there that's our place darling."[27]

The film quashes these romantic notions within a structure that gives an edge to their street language but also parallels the trope "war makes boys into men." However, in reversing genders, the trope becomes unstable in that it illuminates the equivalence between visual and linguistic segmentations of the female body with the violent segmentation of the wounded male body. In the dialogue and in the "shot–reverse shot" structure, the female body is objectified or cut up. In an early script version, Wally (Robert Montgomery) had a line, "I can't remember her name, but say, a dame with ankles like that doesn't need a name," which was changed by Gardiner to "I can't just remember her name."[28] This is built into the dialogue as a foil to the women's banter, which reclaims their subjectivity through humor. It is this equivalence that provokes the nurses' euphemistic language, as a means of engagement with the men in the first instance and then as a displacement for the traumatizing effect of nursing wounded and dying men. The overall strategy of the dialogue and scene structure alternates between eros and thanatos, and ultimately between life and death.

The early scenes relay the privations of the front and the molding of the group into effective nurses. They subdue shell-shocked soldiers and remove metal from eyes, and their response is humor. Babs: "I've washed so many naked men that I'm ready to go live with the Eskimos—they only wash once a year." The alternation between flirting and wisecracking and the death and destruction the war brings in to the hospital is central to the film's depiction of the sexual dynamics between the nurses and the soldiers. The first time Wally meets Babs he asks her what he should call her. She replies "Call me anything you like but make it a long-distance call." But the underlying stress that the war setting brings is called up immediately when he asks about his friend who was brought in the previous night—she tells him he died an hour ago. There follows a silence punctuated by explosions as they turn their backs on each other. He then recovers and brazenly asks her if she ever goes out nights and she says she does. "You're just the kind mother used to make," he says, to which she responds, "Yes, but not the kind you make." As Wally leaves the scene the senior surgeon comes in and asks Babs to assist in taking shrapnel out of a man's eyes. He takes her into a ward full of moaning and dying men that we see in long shot and then a close-up of the man screaming as the doctor removes the bandages while Babs assists. We then see Kansas watch a man die and then clear his bed, a task she has become used to. The alternating structure, punctuated by the soundtrack, moves from dialogue to noise. The banter is foregrounded, which contrasts with the guttural sounds of men in pain in the ward scene and the background noise of explosions. The rhythm and buildup between these two thematic poles was seen by scriptwriter Becky Gardiner as central to the film's affective structure. In her notes to Thalberg on the script submitted by Joe Farnham, she requested they replace the line "Today I took a bandage off a man and looked into his eyes and saw right down his throat" with "I have been watching men cut to pieces all day, held them while they screamed with pain, watched them die." Gardiner wrote "If we say that the girls suffered all these things on the first day, we are left with a sense of nothing to build on."[29]

The relationship between Babs and Wally is articulated through the alternation between the desire and fear, sex and death, that the extremes of their situation demand. The constant presence of death lends sexual urgency to the romance plot. In the dialogue for their cycling-in-the-country scene, Wally tells her, "This is the last time I'll ever ask you to be careful" as they pull away on bicycles. Babs replies, "And it's the last time I will be." Gardiner wrote: "There is a double meaning and a 'come hither' in this which I think should be the note of all Babs' and Wally's scenes together."[30] Euphemism and double entendre, the coded language of sexual negotiations, were intended to characterize their romance.

The other nurses offer different versions of negotiating desire with propriety, their naïveté leading them to destruction. Anita Page's character, Joy, is the "innocent" in the film's seduction plot. She falls in love with a wounded pilot, Robin, who later promises to marry her. Unlike Babs and Rosalie, she is not wise to the dangers of duplicitous soldiers; she sleeps with him, finds out he is already married, and later realizes she is pregnant with his child.

During a bombardment there is a scene that articulates the futility of war but in terms that illustrate the raw sexual dynamic the war has brought about:

> BABS: "We do all this to patch the poor things up and what for? Just so they can go back and get wounded again."
> CUSHIE: ". . . They used to talk about what they'd do when the war was over."
> ROSALIE: "Now all they talk about is women."
> BABS: ". . . Seems to be the only thing the men are interested in . . . even the youngsters all say they'll die before they've ever lived."

Betraying her lack of sophistication and setting her up for her later "fall," Joy says "Well, it makes me awfully nervous that they all want to look at you and touch you." Finally the frustration and the grisly realities are summed up by Babs with a quip that in its turn works to objectify men's body parts: "Anything with two legs and a whole face will look like a scene from *Three Weeks* to me."

Gardiner's insistence on this reversal of the usual terms of objectification is evident in her notes to Thalberg. Her intention of reversing the power relationships is clear throughout these notes. Her original version had Robin, on his deathbed, call Joy, who is pregnant with his child, "Mummie!" To which she responds "Yes Robin, I'm here." Joy becomes his mother as he dies, a trope that punctuates the film's power reversals. Complaining about this scene's elimination, she wrote, "This was eliminated and I like Joy, who is carrying Robin's child, now pretending to be his mother in order to comfort him."[31] She also found the characterization of the women with terms of endearment problematic; in a scene where Kansas comforts Joy after she has found out Robin is married, her dialogue "poor child" had been changed to "poor kiddie." Gardiner objected to Thalberg: "I have an obsessive personal aversion to the word 'kiddie.'"[32] Thalberg listened and the final film cut the line altogether.

The film, and the evidence of what was left out, demonstrates that the trend toward "emotionally restrained" male adventure films marked by *What Price Glory* and *The Big Parade* has had a further augmentation by Gardiner through its focus on women's war experience. Norbert Lusk in *Screen in Review* noted, "The story shows the psychological and physical effects of war upon a group of young women volunteers from civil life who are doing their duty as nurses behind the firing line. It is an earnest, conscientious effort to reveal another side of war and it succeeds, even though the result is uneven."[33] Lusk noted the realism in Walker's acting: "Her casual speech is natural and devoid of accent. It would fit any American character, Miss Walker's great skill is found in being casual and keenly expressive at the same time." In many ways this is the same solution to the depiction of "war as war is" through vernacular and depiction of the consequences of modern warfare. The emotional restraint serves as a setup for the release of frustration by some characters; the wisecracking vernacular of characters in its understatement underscores this realism and the sexual dynamic overlaps with the pessimistic depiction of the war. It is not a case of simple role reversal, however. The sexual dynamic of the wisecracks between the nurses carries the recognition of the consequences, not so much of moral transgression, but of the moral strictures of their civilian life. This is the sacrifice that Clara Bow's character, Mary, makes in *Wings*. Similarly, Joy's pregnancy means she will be sent home by the Nurse Corps. The wisecracks put things into perspective. When Joy finds out that Robin, the father of her baby, is already married, it prompts the Zasu Pitts character, Cushie, to remark, "I warned them against aviators, they're too flighty. I prefer something close to earth." To which Babs replies, "Yeah, a worm."

Joy is transferred to the hospital in Paris and in her off hours takes to drinking and flirting with soldiers in bars, and to convey that, there is short a scene similar to that of the Folies Bergère scene in *Wings*. Her pregnancy is discovered and she is told she is to be sent home. Realizing she can't go home in "her condition," she runs away back to the front and Babs and her comrades. Babs agrees to help cover for her and let her attend to the wounded there until she has the baby. As Mary rescued the "innocent" Jack from the MPs, Babs works to help Joy avoid social and institutional censure. Implicit here is that the war's exceptional circumstances have changed the moral landscape. Unlike Jack, however, for whom the experience of war provides absolution and the only sacrifice is Mary's reputation, the resolution of Joy's predicament is death. She resumes her duties in the front-line hospital. Robin, the father, is brought in, mortally wounded, and confesses his love for her. They recite the Lord's Prayer together and when they get to "thy will be done on earth." he dies; they never get to the "heaven" part. She then quickly recovers her composure and, in an echo of Kansas's earlier acceptance of the death all around them, calls the orderly over and says "You can have this bed." But the shelling becomes more intense and, unable to suppress her fear any longer, Joy screams "Guns! All these Guns! Is there no end to it?!" Babs takes her out of the ward and calms her down with the phrase "It's a great war if you don't weaken," to which Joy replies "Or if you do." The line was meant by Gardiner to be threaded throughout the film as a kind of coping mantra that Babs and Rosalie say to each other. Gardiner noted its importance in setting up the final scene with Joy and Babs. Gardiner was not happy it had been deleted in the earlier scenes, "As we repeat it later it seems to me a fairly funny gag as the girls' point of view in summing up the war." In the final cut it only occurs between Joy and Babs, and as Gardiner predicted, it has lost the impact of showing that now Joy is in on the joke and her loss of innocence is really a gain in understanding and knowledge.

Joy's final scene is her death, having given birth. The previous scene with Babs has been leading up to this equivalence between women giving life and men dealing death, as Joy says, "Never mind me. They're too busy with death to be bothered with life." Her last words to Babs while she holds her newborn son are: "It's a whole new world for my little boy . . . a wonderful world. . . ." The line here is as it appeared in the rewrite, which had removed the first line of the original: "He doesn't know, so he'll never be afraid." Gardiner's notes show she wanted to keep the first line; since it is spoken by Joy it implies an ambivalence the rewrite was glossing over. "I am sure that the first line of this speech is all important and as it is the big scene of the picture we could surely take time for one more line. The wonder in Joy's soul is that there would be anyone in the world who would never have to know the corroding, horribly accumulating fear that all those who lived through the war had suffered." The implication is that the wonder is in Joy's soul, not in Babs's or the others'. The scene draws out the conflicting discourses in the memory of the war, one as noble sacrifice, the other as futility, but retains an ambiguity that the script's formula for plausible deniability afforded.

Given the broadly fatalistic attitude of Babs and the others, the film implausibly ends with Wally returning to Babs at the end of the war, having been shot down and taken prisoner. They are brought together over the baby, who Babs has taken on; they agreed to marry and take the baby, now named Wally, home. The sentimental ending, given the transgressions the film allows, was certainly required even in the pre-code period and has its antecedents in *The Big Parade* and *What Price Glory*. The Stallings/Anderson films, as Jacobs points out, resolve the pessimistic depictions and predicaments of the war with more sentimental endings than the play *What Price Glory?* However, as with *Wings*, there was some resistance by critics to similar strategies in *War Nurse*. The reviewer for the *Film Spectator* literally divides the good and bad parts of the film between sound and image. Praise came for director Edgar Selwyn and cameraman Charles Rosher: "In two or three shots . . . (Selwyn) groups a number of nurses in a highly artistic manner, and Charles Rosher, the veteran cameraman . . . brings them to life on the screen that will delight those who appreciate artistic photographic creations. . . . Every thrill, every bit of drama in the picture is contributed by the camera with the result that what we see on the screen is a motion picture that rises to the heights only in those scenes that are devoid of dialogue." The dialogue of Gardiner and Farnham receives particular criticism: "I don't think even the greatest pessimist will be prepared for the torrent of jabbering that flows over War Nurse and engulfs its virtues . . . they chatter so continuously that all of our attention is devoted to hearing what is said, leaving none for contemplation of the real meaning of what we see."[34]

While in many ways a swipe at sound cinema in general, the review does present a resistance to women wisecracking that resonates with the objections by critics to the Folies Bergère sequence in *Wings*. Given

Thalberg's strategy of previewing, it is unlikely that the dialogue was seen by test audiences in the unfavorable light that this critic suggests, and while the film was not a blockbuster, it did respectable business. However, it is harder to dismiss the underlying assumption that war-realism properly resides within the realm of the masculine. In fact, the use of vernacular in dialogue was something that the studios were striving for. MGM alone brought out East Coast playwrights, novelists, and journalists such as Maxwell Anderson, Ben Hecht, and Charles MacArthur. Famously, not all of them worked out, but the team of Hecht and MacArthur's stock-in-trade was snappy one-liners. Only one woman, Dorothy Parker, came from this draft of famous wordsmiths. *War Nurse*, if nothing else, suggests how well integrated this style had become among the staff writers at MGM before this illustrious migration and how central women scriptwriters were to the system.

Another factor in the realistic depiction of the war lay in the rendering of the damage to the male body. There are a number of films from both the silent and sound period that are concerned with returning soldiers wounded physically or psychologically. Amnesia, shell shock, amputations, facial disfigurement, tics, mistaken identity, and the reincorporation into civilian life served as character motivations throughout the twenties and thirties. A number of high-profile films, including *The Big Parade*, deal with the reluctance of soldiers to come home and the theme that the work for which they were trained has left them ill-prepared for anything else. *War Nurse*, like *Wings*, draws attention to this meditation on masculinity and arguably uses it to raise in addition the issue of the kind of restraints placed on women. Mary in *Wings* shrugs off the damage to her reputation so readily that one critic added that the consequences of this were implausibly ignored.[35] *War Nurse* takes this further and brings a number of issues to bear on the platoon of nurses, ranging from what is expected of them in their relations with soldiers who "may not live before they die," through the shame of pregnancy and scandal on returning home, to the fate of the plain woman from Kansas who contracts syphilis while on R and R in Paris. In the end she is killed while on an impossible mission to administer to a wounded soldier in No Man's Land. It seems that the formula for realism Stallings and Anderson developed with the film version of *What Price Glory* that combined vernacular with graphic depiction was built upon by Loring and Gardiner. By incorporating the already well-developed vernacular associated with the flapper they were able to create women characters who through slang could articulate their desire while retaining an emotional distance and thereby demonstrate the moral and psychological conflicts they endured. The exception taken to their banter by critics who suggested it detracted from the sanctity of the image concurs with broader shifts in the language of the memory of the Great War by 1930, as represented by *All Quiet on the Western Front* and *Journey's End*. Those films had introduced a new reverence for (male) sacrifice that found little room for humor. The fact that it was women's banter generated considerable critical animosity and prompted accusations of irreverence that had not been the case with the earlier male-centered films *What Price Glory* and *The Big Parade*. For those critics *War Nurse* violated the sanctity of war as a realm of masculine sacrifice.

THE MAD PARADE

Where *War Nurse* provides a resolution that returns Babs to a traditional family structure, *The Mad Parade* dispenses with this resolution altogether and replaces it with death and the sacrifice usually accorded to male fallen soldiers. The film began as a project for Dorothy Arzner with Jean Arthur, Ruth Chatterton, and Fay Wray. It originated from a story for Paramount entitled "Women Like Men" by Gertrude Orr and Doris Malloy, who also wrote the script, and it was meant to have an all-female cast. In the event, Arzner and cast were reassigned and the project was downgraded and shot by B studio Liberty pictures under the direction of William Beaudine, with a new cast headed by Evelyn Brent. *The Mad Parade* is the story of volunteer canteen workers, and sometimes nurses, located near the front. Evelyn Brent plays Monica Dale, the "sergeant" who has been at the front too long and has made a choice to "live now." She is in love with Tony, an officer and the boyfriend of her co-worker Janice Lee (June Clyde), and has been having an affair with him. Prudence, nickname Snoop, another co-worker, threatens to tell the head of the canteen, Mrs. Betty Schuyler, about the affair and get Monica sent home. On their way to meet the hospital train to pick up wounded they are shelled and one of their group, Dorothy, is struck by shrapnel. The group finds a shelter in a trench dugout and Dorothy is set out on the table and dies in Monica's arms. Janice confronts Monica and Monica replies: "All right I'm rotten, and so is this, the whole Mad Parade—It'll never be over for Tony, he's just like me." This is overheard by Snoop, who chides Monica. As Snoop then exits to a smaller room in the dugout Monica picks up a grenade and throws it into the room; it explodes and kills her. When Mrs. Schuyler comes in to discover Snoop is dead she asks if it was an accident. In a gesture of reconciliation Janice covers for Monica and says she didn't see what happened. They then come under friendly fire and draw lots to see who will go across No Man's Land to stop the artillery. Janice gets the short straw but Monica goes in her place, to redeem both herself and Tony. She succeeds but dies. As male hands cover her face, a male voice says: "Boy, that dame had plenty of guts." And another replies, "I'll say she did."

As with *War Nurse*, *The Mad Parade* sets out the "forbidden zone" of the front at the level of gender, but takes this a step further in that not only are social mores abandoned but gender is blurred, albeit through humor and double entendre: the first line the wisecracking Lil (Lilyan Tashman) says when woken up is "For cryin' out loud, how d'ya expect a guy to get any sleep around here?" Monica's role seems to reprise the role of Stanhope in *Journey's End*, articulating a deep cynicism but continuing to carry out her duty no matter how mad the parade. While *War Nurse* draws attention to this meditation on masculinity and arguably uses this to raise the issue of the kind of restraints placed on women that the war is loosening,

FIGURE 4.3. Monica (Evelyn Brent) dies in No Man's Land in *The Mad Parade* (William Beaudine, 1931). Digital frame enlargement.

The Mad Parade dispenses with this and merges desire and cynicism within the character of Monica, who can masquerade as a woman in a cocktail dress or a man in a uniform. Her journey to stop the artillery seeks to de-gender the geography of the front and draw another emphasis to "No Man's Land." She is punished for her transgression but it is her choice, driven by two related motivations: the sacrifice of her love/desire for Tony and the inability to ever return to the old life, represented by home.

Monica's punishment comes ultimately from a deeper cultural force than her own voluntary sacrifice. The film was subject to considerable augmentation by the Hayes Office, which, having seen the finished picture on May 7, 1931, objected to the use of "damns" and "hells," to the sarcastic references to the YMCA and to the implicit slur on the Red Cross. Liberty Productions agreed to these changes and to making ambiguous Monica's relationship with Tony by removing lines referring to them spending the night together and omitting a scene between them where the shadow of a bedpost is cast in the background. The effect of the cuts emphasizes Monica's moral transgressions by undermining the motivations behind them; when she first appears in a cocktail dress after a night out her relationship with Tony is only briefly mentioned, giving the sense that she is actually indiscriminate in her pursuit of pleasure, sex, and escape.

The critical response to *The Mad Parade* draws this out: *Film Daily* was not impressed, declaring it a "Drab and Heavy drama. . . . Weak entertainment without a man in the cast."[36] It highlighted its futility message: "Apparently the idea back of this story was to do a female Journey's End" and complained that "the constant bickering amongst the principals (was) somewhat wearing." Mordaunt Hall of the *New York Times* titled his review "Snarling Beauties" and called it "disappointing" with "artificial characters." However, he linked realism with language by observing that director Beaudine "started off with the thought of making this a true picture of the war, with no prettiness in the conversation between the girls." Praising the performances, he found the film an affront to the women who had actually served. "It is a picture which will exasperate those valiant girls and women who wore uniforms in France."[37]

The Mad Parade differs from *War Nurse* in that it seeks to render women with agency driven by the trauma of war into oblivion, rather than concern for propriety, absolution, and regeneration. Stallings and Anderson's formula for realism of combining vernacular language with graphic depiction in *What Price Glory* was taken up by Orr and Malloy with different results. Like Gardiner and Farnham with *War Nurse*, they extended that formula to include the vernacular associated with the flapper and the

Brooklyn girl to produce emotional restraint and level the field of negotiations for sex. Monica and Lil both perform the cynical/desiring body with language and gesture that challenged gender boundaries. Lil refers to herself as a "guy" while Monica draws an equivalence between her and Tony saying "I do my job—like a man," a theme reflected in the film's original title, "Women Like Men." But where *War Nurse* gives Babs a route home through family, Monica is irredeemably scarred by her experiences of the trauma of war, just as Tony is. Their shared experience makes them compatible and justifies their illicit relationship. When threatened with being sent home because of her behavior, Monica replies, "What will I do in the States?"

The exceptions to the women's banter taken by critics who suggest that it detracts from the sanctity of the image of war's sacrifice reprise the critical responses to *War Nurse* and are another indication of the broader shifts in the language of gender and the negotiation of desire and sex. The vernacular language the women employ in both films seeks to redress the imbalance incurred by the objectification of women through their body parts. While I am not suggesting this was a conscious move by the scriptwriters, it does act as an indication of the way that this vernacular, with its origins in the demimonde, moved into more common usage. The obscene language of objectification in the red-light districts was an actual consequence of the demonization of women by the VD propaganda used by the Commission on Training Camp Activities. If, as Keire suggests, this had an impact on the language used to identify and objectify women who attended more innocuous leisure activities such as the cinema, the appearance of these films over a decade later is evidence of its assimilation into the mainstream.

Related to the linguistic dissection of the female body is the objectification of male body parts that comes with the experience of seeing the male body blown apart, and with the task of putting it back together. These countercurrents, both the engagement with objectifying language and the experience of treating male bodies in segments as a medical procedure, center on gender in a fashion that qualifies the broader shifts in the language of the cinematic memory of the Great War by 1930 and the release of *All Quiet on the Western Front* and *Journey's End*. While those films represent a tipping point in that memory as futile and tragic, the inclusion of women at the front has unintended consequences for that memory. Monica has succumbed to the temptations to "live a little" and is unrepentant, and Orr and Malloy are careful to outline the motivations, although able only to do it through spoken language. Monica explains to her superior Betty why they are not "women anymore. . . . You don't suppose I can go through it, living in mud, smelling the dead, and still come out of it like I was?" Dropping her cynical veneer, she explains, "Betty, I kissed a man once, he was dying. I'll never forget the sight, just a thing with two blind eyes. He was off his nut and thought I was his wife. I kissed him and heard the rattle." Monica, like Babs, has become the observer and objectifier, a position ordinarily occupied by men. The wounded she has tended to have become "things." Unlike Babs, though, her claim of being as good as a man, and the film's theme of "women like men," has the effect of placing her in the position of having been both object of desire and subject of the traumas of war, witnessing the blowing apart of male bodies, a position from which there is no return. In drawing an equivalence between herself and Tony, they merge genders; they are no longer man and woman but traumatized comrades, a condition that she offers to Tony's fiancé, Janet, as a rationalization. Her relationship with Tony was not love; she swears to Janet that he really loves her before she goes out across No Man's Land to her death. Just before she makes her sacrifice, her parallel with Tony is complete when she finally kills Snoop with the hand grenade. It is her ultimate transgression—she has become a killer, but unlike Tony she has killed not the enemy but a comrade, for which there is no absolution.

The war-nurse cycle, although short-lived, illustrates the war as a gender "forbidden zone" that exposes the contradictions within traditional social structures and boundaries through the formula of combining cynicism with desire through the vernacular of wisecracking but noble women. The war setting provided the extraordinary situation that enabled apparent redirections or reordering of gender relations that were prominent in broader social discourses about marriage, extramarital relations, and sexual conduct in 1930 and the onset of the Great Depression. Yet what may be more remarkable is how these films track a dynamic in the language of gender relations that had been profoundly altered by mass mobilization, the demonization of women through VD propaganda, and the liminal spaces of entertainment where cinemas and the demimonde existed in close proximity. It was the work of women scriptwriters such as Loos, Loring, Gardiner, Malloy, and Orr that offered forms of slang and vernacular, rooted in that very demimonde, that countered the male objectification of women as body parts with wit and repartee and in the process exposed an aspect of the memory of the war that challenged more dominant discourses concerning women's role in the conflict.

PART II

Nostos: Home

Chapter 5

VETERANS

"Sweet jangled bells, out of tune"

In the American popular imagination, Great War veterans were carriers of the effects of the new modernity the war had brought into being.[1] They could be the victorious embodiment of the new America as a global powerhouse, the soldiers who brought peace to Europe. At the same time they could be infected with the lax morals and decadence of the old world and harboring the disease of revolution—either political or social, or both. As the Jazz Age gave way to the Great Depression the veteran acted as an undertone, at times an unwelcome relic of the past, at others a poignant reminder of social responsibility, but always the cipher around which competing discourses for the memory of the war and the state of the nation coalesced. The veteran then represented, or at least referred to, a force that was bringing about changes across the social fabric of American life. In 1930, Frederick Lewis Allen noted, "It was impossible for this generation to return unchanged. . . . Their torn nerves craved the anodynes of speed, excitement, and passion. They found themselves expected to . . . accept the moral dicta of elders . . . living in a Polyanna of rosy ideals which the war had killed for them."[2] The potent imagery, the fluidity of characteristics, and the range of behaviors that were associated with the public profile of veterans throughout the interwar period featured in the popular press, theatre, and literature were added to and shaped by the Hollywood narrative style. The forces of change the veteran character represented fit well with the Hollywood narrative style, which in many ways symbolized those changes and profited from the stories and stars that relayed them. Just how neat a fit can be seen in a review of William Dieterle's *The Last Flight* (1931) in the Chicago Tribune. "Mae Tineé" lauded the story of four aviators and a single lady, Nikki, who drink their way through Paris, for its modern feel: "There's a vague, eerie Alice in Wonderlandish unreality about its biting reality which makes the picture different from anything seen before."[3] The oxymoron offers a clue into the meanings that veteran characters could convey, the reality of war experience on one hand, and on the other the surreality of their charming yet aberrant behavior. Although the film culminates in a romantic coupling, the story of four cracked pilots following an ethereal and enigmatic woman through post-war Paris was slightly outside the norm. Their "unreal" behavior was motivated, and at the same time legitimized, by their "real" experiences in the air at the front. The article also illustrated the degree to which this behavior could be infectious. Referring to the aviators as "jangled bells, out of tune," it assured the readers they will "take them to their hearts." In the process, the article illustrated the broader the traumatic impact of the war had on civilians. Nikki's behavior was also a "tragedy of war's aftermath," as was that of another character, Frink, who is described as "a sort of a rotter of a journalist—I guess war made HIM that way too." Frink and Nikki have not seen combat but they, too, are shaped by the war. In attributing these civilian characters' behavior to war experience, the article illustrates how any number of characteristics can be made plausible simply by invoking the war. This chapter explores the way veteran characters fit into the classical Hollywood style and how they presented timely opportunities for scriptwriters as a means of conveying a modern sensibility to breathe life into and refresh dependable storylines. At the same time, as relics of the war, the veteran characters literally embodied varying versions of the war's memory as they played out across the interwar period.

CHARACTERIZATION

Veteran characters from the Great War held the potential for mystery, pity, and fear, depending on their response to their experience of the hyper-stimulus and trauma of total modern war. Consequently, the celluloid life of Great War veterans was marked by a shift toward a recognition of the internal strife and social problems they faced that had by the mid-1920s become the prevailing theme in public discourse about their actual experience.[4] These evolving characterizations, developed in response to the changing complexion of veterans' issues in the political and social realm, coincided with the establishment of the classical style of narration by the Hollywood studios. Well established by 1919, it emphasized clarity of storytelling through a character's traits and individual agency.

Bordwell, Staiger, and Thompson point to the multiple-reel feature as an important impetus, which by 1920 was the central part of the film program. Complex characterizations with plausible motivations and relationships with other characters were necessary to "sustain a multiple-reel film" and ensure audience comprehension.[5] In their 1920 book *How to Write Photoplays*, Anita Loos and John Emerson stressed the importance of providing the character with instantly recognizable traits. They suggest this comes through action: "A good method is to introduce important characters with some characteristic incident—the miser stoops to pick up a penny, the bully kicks a street urchin, and so forth."[6] In his 1913 manual *The Technique of the Photoplay*, Epes Winthrop Sargent also emphasized the importance of setting up characters economically:

> Each time a new character comes upon the screen there is a certain mental relaxation on the grip of the plot while the identity of the newcomer is determined. Take advantage of that lapse to get the introduction over with and then when the essential action comes there is no drop in the interest, no matter how momentary.[7]

By including a war veteran in their screenplay, scriptwriters had a ready-made condensed characterization that set up a wide choice of motivations. Veterans can behave in a heroic or villainous manner or act as a supporting character; they can behave erratically, and the fact that they have been to the front provides an open basis for motivation that scriptwriters can build on. Veteran characters' behavior in films between the wars varies greatly; however, the key to their modernizing effect was that they tended to refer directly or indirectly to the prevailing popular conversation about returning soldiers as a social and cultural concern.

The final scenes of Frank Borzage's *Humoresque* (1920) offer an early post-war example of using the veteran to provide motivation for the scene's dynamic interaction between the characters and bring the narrative to a conclusion. In the final scene, the main character, Leon Kantor, a promising concert violinist, returns from the war with a paralyzed arm. He is listless and apathetic until he is visited by his love interest, a singer, Gina Berg. As she leaves the room he sees her silhouette collapse behind a curtained glass door and jumps up from his chair to scoop her in his arms. He has been miraculously cured by his love for her. The war, his experience, and his "cure," however implausible, serve to resolve the film's primary theme of mother-love by transferring it, through his love for Gina, to the heterosexual couple.

First published in *Cosmopolitan* in 1919, Fannie Hurst's novella *Humoresque* was the tale of an immigrant Jewish family, the Kantors, and their rise from the Lower East Side tenements. Mama Kantor nurtures her son Leon's talent and he becomes a virtuoso violinist, playing concert tours in America and all over Europe, giving the family to the means to move into high society. The Great War hovers over the plot, and Hurst infused the story with war metaphors describing conditions in the tenements of the Bowery as "Every Man's Land" and the inhabitants as "a reeking march of humanity and humidity." Her story ended with Leon leaving for the front in France, forsaking a lucrative concert series to join the Army and promising to meet Gina again when he returns. Hurst incorporated the war to provide the story's sweet and tragic ending. Before he leaves his mother asks him to play Dvořák's *Humoresque* one last time for her.[8] Afterwards, at the request of his sister, he plays a "new song"; Gina sings the words, and as she does Hurst describes "her glance mistily off, the beautiful, the heroic, the lyrical prophecy of a soldier-poet and a poet soldier." The lines are from American poet Alan Seeger's poem "I Have a Rendezvous with Death":

> But I've a rendezvous with death
> On some scarred slope of battered hill
> When spring comes round again this year
> And the first meadow-flowers appear

After he has gone, the story ends with his mother holding his first violin, "cracked of back and solitary string," and ends with a repetition of the same four lines.

The poem was well known to audiences and critics in 1920, as was Seeger himself, who was killed fighting with the French Foreign Legion in the Battle of the Somme on July 4, 1916. Seeger's poetry collection *Poems*, published immediately after his death by Scribner's, was the fourth-best-selling non-fiction book of 1917. Seeger had been promoted by the press, particularly the *New York Times*, as an American war poet along the lines of Britain's Rupert Brooke. "I Have a Rendezvous with Death" embodied the kind of romantic poet-warrior sentiment that became a central emotive touchstone in the run up to the United States' involvement in the war. Hurst's post-war use of it capitalizes on the image of the "self-sacrificing hero" that Seeger had come to represent, and to signal Leon's certain death.[9] Enshrining the mother-son relationship through death in this way maintained the story's theme of the rise from the tenements of the Jewish family through the efforts of a mother's love for her son.

For the film, scriptwriter Frances Marion and director Borzage added the scene where Leon returns a wounded veteran and is cured by Gina. This had the effect of updating Hurst's story to ameliorate the "mother-love" angle. Hervé Dumont's account of the film's production states the first version of the new ending had Leon returning home having lost his hand. Both Adolph Zukor, head of Paramount-Artcraft, and William Randolph Hearst, whose Cosmopolitan company made the film, were unhappy with the gritty depiction of tenement life and with the ending. Borzage and Marion reworked the ending so that Leon is suffering from war neurosis, which has presented as the paralysis of his arm.[10] Having Leon suffer from shell shock had the effect of building on the realism of the earlier scenes. In the finished film Leon has suffered shrapnel in his arm but there is an ambiguity that the titles explain: "Months of suffering had driven the daylight from the mind of Leon Kantor. And groping in the darkness, he struggled against that all destroying—Fear. Fear that he could never use his wounded arm again." When Gina asks the doctor if he will recover, he replies, "Not in his present state of mind." The change of emphasis from physical injury to neurosis is significant. While ascribing an implausible action that seems to break the classical dictates, Leon's "cure," when looked at closer, is made somewhat believable through its attribution to his war experience.

Seventeen years later, in *How to Write and Sell Film Stories*, Marion explained that motivation can be slight and rendered in broad strokes: "motivation seldom needs to be shown in great detail. Give a suggestion of it and, if it is at all reasonable, the audience will accept the idea and carry it to its logical conclusion."[11] Leon's motivation here is somewhat open in that within the moral universe of the story it is the strength and purity of his love for Gina that provides him with the ability, a "terrific effort" in the words of the doctor, to take her in his arms as she falls. Such a melodramatic trope was common in stories published in women's magazines like *Cosmopolitan*. But there is also a clear reference here to the medical condition of shell shock, or war neurosis, that was broadly understood to exist, as were cures for those maladies through catharsis of the kind the film reenacts. Popular (and obviously vague) understandings of the symptoms of war neuroses were along these lines. Marion's advice concurs with that of the earlier script advisors to roll up the motivations within the character's traits; hence, the behavior of Leon becomes plausible because of his status as a war veteran.

Marion's advice goes on further: "Once an audience has accepted a motive, it will accept almost any act, no matter how far it deviates from the normal, if it rises consistently from that motive."[12] Explanations for

Leon's action in the film's ending are multiple and folded into one another. The most obvious is his love for Gina as catharsis—a jolt that revives the dormant nerves in his arm. It also chimes with a more forensic explanation of cure through catharsis, an appeal to activity that was prevalent in the immediate post-war popular discourse concerning neuroses. News reports, such as that in the January 2, 1921, *New York Times* story about the opening of a new hospital in Perryville, Maryland, for veterans with war neurosis, outline the dynamics of symptom and cure for these men: "the basis for whom is an emotional factor buried in their unconscious mind . . . they have lost confidence. . . . Patients are therefore encouraged to indulge in various forms of activity provided for them." The article goes on to outline the path of finding the buried emotional factor through lengthy talking therapy, a combination of psychoanalytic and behavioral therapy that does with some degree of accuracy account for the medical approach at the time in the U.S.[13] However, in Marion's phrase, "a suggestion" that alludes to these explanations was enough in the case of *Humoresque* to be convincing to contemporary audiences.

TEMPORALITY AND THE VETERAN

The veteran also embodies time and veteran characters often work as a means of conveying its passage. The veteran's status as having been to war not only brings to the narrative a set of culturally resonant character traits; it also conveys recognizable references to both historical and story time. A veteran of a particular war, like the historical figure in a biopic, denotes the historical period of the narrative. The return of Ashley Wilkes from the war in *Gone with the Wind* (Victor Fleming, 1939) denotes the time period as later in the Civil War, after Gettysburg. At the beginning of *The Last Flight* the cuts from the crash following a dogfight to the hospital clock's minute hand approaching 11 a.m. and then to the two wounded pilots links the historical time with their experience and sets out the cause of the mental state of the characters that will be developed in the rest of the film. The veteran therefore offers the potential to build into the narrative a temporal marker and to establish a historical setting and time that enables scriptwriters to embed the narration within a clear temporal progression without drawing its mechanics to the audience's attention. Leon's return in *Humoresque* after the armistice in November 1918 offers an early example of the use of the veteran and time in two ways: to ensure suspense and to clearly demarcate the passing of time. Leon's announcement that he has enlisted provides a deadline for the romance plot with Gina. He will leave, possibly never to return, setting out the anticipation that the couple may or may not be able to express their feelings.

The suspense in the farewell scene is further enhanced by the deadline of the departure of the ferry to take Leon to his post. Borzage and Marion kept close to the theme of mother-love even up to this scene, where Mama Kantor asks Leon to play *Humoresque* before he goes. While he is playing there are cuts to Abram Kantor holding his watch, his gestures emphasizing the scene's urgency. Gina then asks Leon to play "I Have a rendezvous . . .". His mother asks what "rondy-voo" means and Leon says it means an engagement, "doesn't it Gina?" and he looks off camera. In another tactic of delay, the next shot is of his mother looking on and *then* to Gina, who nods yes. Looking at Gina, Leon says he hopes he has an engagement with her and she responds in kind, and he sets out another deadline by saying "In the Spring?" Then his father, still looking at his watch, reminds him that he has "fifteen minutes to make the ferry." Here the deadline is a local device that functions to create suspense in establishing the romantic relationship and to set up the return, both motivated by the temporal dictates of the process of enlistment-departure-return implicit in veteran characters.

The passage of time between his departure and return is also expressed in an ellipsis; the length of time of the war itself is enough of an indication of how much time has elapsed. In the case of other examples such as Tom Powers's brother Mike in *The Public Enemy* (Wellman, 1931) or Tom Holmes in *Heroes for Sale* (Wellman, 1933), specific time is not strictly necessary; it is enough to have gone to the front. In *Humoresque*, however, an expository inter-title marks the passing of time and indicates Leon's imminent return: "There passed agonizing months of waiting. . . . Then a cablegram told that Leon was on his way home." In this case, the narration of the film, however briefly, is made transparent as it functions to set up the shock that his mother and father experience when the soldier that comes to their house is not Leon but a friend who tells them Leon has been wounded.

In other films in the 1920s and the early sound period of the 1930s, ellipses, or indications of duration, through the off-screen experience of the veteran and the invocation of the War are handled differently. Two film versions of *Smilin' Through*, the 1922 Norma Talmadge Production for First National and the 1932 MGM version starring Norma Shearer, both directed by Sidney Franklin, offer an insight into the way that characterization of the veteran developed in relation to their experience as an off-screen traumatic event or experience.[14] The films were adapted from a 1919 play written by Jane Cowl and Jane Murfin under the pseudonym

Allan Langdon Martin. The play had been a profitable hit on Broadway that year, running five months from December 1919 to May 1920. Murfin and Cowl, under the same pseudonym, had already mined the war as a profitable subject in 1917 with their play *Lilac Time*, which First National adapted in 1928. The play *Smilin' Through* was meant to capitalize on the popular interest in spiritualism that had gained traction in the immediate post-war years. Its success attracted Joseph Schenck's interest as a vehicle for his then wife Norma Talmadge and, under the aegis of her film company, he bought the rights to the play for $75,000.[15]

The story is set on the English country estate of John Carteret, who communicates daily with his dead wife Moonyeen, murdered on their wedding day, and longs to rejoin her in the spirit world. His life is changed when he takes in his niece Kathleen after his wife's sister and her husband die leaving her orphaned. Kathleen has grown up to look exactly like Moonyeen. Their life is disrupted by the appearance of Kenneth Wayne, an American visitor and heir to the adjoining estate. He has come to join the British Army but before he goes off he and Kathleen fall in love. The problem lies in the fact that Kenneth's father is Jeremiah Wayne, the man who murdered Moonyeen and toward whom John Carteret holds an eternal grudge. In the play and in the 1922 film the ghosts of Kathleen's and Kenneth's mothers inform us that John has maintained his bitterness for 50 years. The murder of Moonyeen is told in a flashback in Act II of the play and in the middle of the film. (Talmadge played both Kathleen and Moonyeen, while Harrison Ford took the roles of Jeremiah and Kenneth.) John refuses to allow Kathleen to see Kenneth, but their love is inevitable and she waits for him as he goes off to fight for the British Army for four years. In the meantime, John's communications with Moonyeen cease because of the hatred he holds in his heart. After the war, Kenneth returns, wounded in the leg, crippled, and shell-shocked, and he refuses to see Kathleen. Finally John, through the admonitions of his close friend Dr. Owen, recognizes Kenneth's sacrifice and forgives him. In the final scene John dies at the domino table in the garden and then joins Moonyeen in the spiritual world while Kenneth relents and reunites with Kathleen.

THE MODERN COUPLE IN *SMILIN' THROUGH*

The story of *Smilin' Through* presented some challenges in temporal structure. The murder of Moonyeen, the traumatic moment for John, takes place 50 years before the main action of the play. Further, the four years of the war pass as an ellipsis toward the end of the play. The play was constructed in three acts with a prologue. The program indicates the temporal structure as Prologue: Outside the Gate; Act I: The Carteret Garden, 1914; Act II: The Same, Fifty Years Before; Act III: The Same, 1919. In both play and film the costumes of the ghosts, the wedding party, and the makeup of John at different ages contribute to providing a clear indication of the period and the passage of time. The structure as laid out in the play demonstrates that the story hinges on time rather than place, and specifically historically significant time in Acts I and III. In adapting the play for the film, the 1922 version stayed close to the play in terms of structure, but the alterations came in characterization to fit the star persona of Talmadge and had a broader dynamic range between pathos and bathos. The role of Kathleen in the film became more modern; Talmadge was known for her modern, flapper-type roles, where Moonyeen's and Kathleen's "Irishness" was emphasized in the play. The role of Willie, Kathleen's suitor, was played more comically in the play by Glenn Hunter. In addition, the film introduced a younger sister for Kathleen, a character not in the play. The other roles in the film, however, remained unchanged.

The double roles of Moonyeen/Kathleen and to a lesser extent Jeremiah/Kenneth offered a meaty role for the star. These roles were played by co-author Jane Cowl and Orme Caldara in the Broadway play. The doubling motif continued on a more subtle level with the temporal structure defining character motivation. John and Kenneth suffer from originary traumas that both affect their behavior and at the same time account for it. John's trauma is acted out in the flashback of Act II, while it is an indication of the effectiveness of the shorthand of characterization of the veteran that Kenneth's trauma is referred to by his wounded body and mind. He merely steps into the frame or onto the stage on crutches. In order to rid themselves of the mental states brought on by their trauma, both are dependent on the "family" of Kathleen, John's friend Dr. Owen, and Moonyeen. The doubling further extends to the women's treatment of two traumatized males—one traumatized by murder, the other by war.

The temporal plot structure of the play and the 1922 film drew on the conventions of each medium to clearly indicate the time shifts. The original play production at the Broadhurst Theatre in New York did this through the printed program, while the film relied on inter-titles. They both also built into these the cues for these shifts. In the play, John sits down to recount to Kathleen the murder of Moonyeen on their wedding day at the end of Act I, allowing time for scene and costume changes for

Act II. The film does this through cues of time shifts in the combination of titles and costume. The temporal structure also provided character motivation and emphasized the curative powers of women and love amid the fantasy of the Victorian English rural idyll, invoking a sensate nostalgia. By 1931 the hint of dissatisfaction with this kind of ghostly whimsy, apparent in the *Film Daily* critique in 1922 that "movie folk don't understand the idea of presenting spirits of dead people on the screen and may be inclined to laugh at the idea,"[16] became more prominent. The shift toward "realism" in war films, marked by *What Price Glory, Journey's End,* and *All Quiet on the Western Front,* played a part in this shift, but also was part of a broader trend in what Lea Jacobs has called a "decline of sentiment" where "A new note was struck in *Greed* (Von Stroheim, 1924) and the naturalist-inspired films that followed . . . and *A Woman of Paris* (Charles Chaplin, 1923) and the sophisticated comedies . . . [that were] providing the modernist underpinnings of a contemporary cinema."[17] The temporal structure of the Talmadge film maintained the play's flavor of nostalgia and from the evidence of its reception ran counter to taste preferences for less sentimental fare. The fan magazine *Photoplay* called the film "Reminiscent of a gorgeous valentine—one of those ornate celluloid and lace creations that remained in the drug store window year after year because no one in town had enough money to buy it." While the review was favorable, praising its "real feeling" and "enchanting beauty," the emphasis on its depiction of the past and the spiritualist overtones relegated it to the realms of a pleasant but lightweight confection.

Kenneth's and Kathleen's characters were reworked in the 1932 version and the temporality inherent in the send-off to the front and the veterans' return was given a sensual urgency that had the effect of modernizing their relationship. Scriptwriter John Balderston, brought in to polish the script for the 1932 version, had a grasp of changes in audience expectation and taste across the previous decade. He had performed similar script doctor duties on Universal's recent successes *Frankenstein* and *Dracula* and was brought in as part of Irving Thalberg's process of tightening up scripts by working with a number of writers drafting and fine-tuning.[18] As a war reporter on the Western Front for the McClure Newspaper Syndicate, Balderston had witnessed the horrific consequences of the war first hand, and he brought this experience to *Smilin' Through*.[19] In detailed script notes Balderston outlined what he saw as the sentimentality problem:

> This play 'dates' remorselessly, but the theme is eternal. The public will always love romances in old gardens, youth parted by war,

FIGURE 5.1. Frederic March as Kenneth and Norma Shearer as Kathleen in *Smilin' Through* (Sidney Franklin, 1932). Author's collection.

ghosts of lovers holding out to the survivors threats of eternal separations . . . But current distrust of false sentimentality, current cynicism, the recent education of millions to expect better dramatic as well as technical mechanics, and plausibility, in their entertainment, mean that, when you present this picture, you will find audiences *hoping* that you are going to give them beauty, glamour, romance, but far more critical than even a few years ago; far more ready to resent cheap hokum and false laughs of a kind they would condone in other pictures, but not in this one; ready to grant you your ghosts, your old fashioned tale, and to rejoice in them, provided you furnish a story they can believe and accept.[20]

Balderston built his advice on the necessity of creating plausibility in character motivations, which in turn hinged on historical accuracy. These, he argued, would provide a structure of "bones" to "this mass of jelly." He went on to outline in twenty-two pages of notes how to go about building plausibility into the emotions, and placing the experience of war at the center. For example, he drew attention to costume and pointed to the experiences of women volunteers on the home front and criticized the use of glamorous costumes for Shearer: "No woman of her sort would have bought new clothes during the war." He applauded the use of the sound of thundering guns in France to drive home Kathleen's anxiety. Using the veteran's connotation of historical time, he called for a montage that might indicate that Kenneth's return, along with that of other returning soldiers, happens at a time that closely follows the armistice. Throughout the twenty-two pages he continued to stress the need to pay close attention to a realistic experience and plausible behavior that audiences would accept. He was specific about the motivations for the behavior of Kenneth; in the final scenes he argued the need to be explicit:

> As indicated in the stage direction (Kenneth) has the abnormal hatred of shell-shocked patients of being cross-examined. Since Owen is a doctor and knows this, he does not ask questions, and when we cut to the scene where Owen is trying to make him walk, we still do not know how he feels about Kathleen and why he does not want to see her. . . . Accordingly it is right that when he collapses, he should break out . . . and pour forth in one speech the fact that he loves her too much to burden her with a wreck like himself, that he's no good, that he wishes he had been killed so that he could have died the man she loved. This does more than merely furnish a good climax to the scene with the crutches. It motivates Ken's behavior, and wins him the pity, approbation and respect of the audience. And it gets over a big difficulty, to the advantage of the scene, and especially of the woman's part.[21]

Balderston incorporated widely held assumptions about shell shock and the instability of veterans while at the same time using the formula that intertwines that discourse with the romance plot. The real cure for both John and Kenneth lies in the love of Moonyeen and Kathleen, respectively. However, the bones of the structure lay in providing plausible motivations so that, in Balderston's words, the audience will go out of the cinema saying "how much more charming [it was] than this modern stuff and why can't we have more of what we used to love so much?"[22] Balderston recognized that the key to achieving a lasting after-image of the pastoral shimmer of the past was in setting it against the sound of the guns in France, the drab home front with (slightly) muted styles and fashions, the goodbyes of lovers on the train platforms, and the tangible consequences of war on the male body and mind when they returned. He also understood the paradox of providing a veiled reference to changes in courtship and "modern" romance. As Kenneth is about to depart for the front, they rework the "we may never have this chance again" scenario that was critical in the romance plots of war films throughout the 1920s:

> KENNETH: Oh, darling, I love you so.
> KATHLEEN: Is that all?
> KENNETH: All?
> KATHLEEN: Don't you want me, too? I want you. I'm not ashamed to say it. I'm yours. You're mine. I want that to be true, before you go.

This dialogue was not a part of the original play or the 1922 film. It played to Norma Shearer's star persona in previous films that had been associated with progressive attitudes toward sex, such as *The Divorcée* (Robert Z. Leonard, 1930), *A Free Soul* (Clarence Brown, 1931), and the adaptation of Eugene O'Neill's *Strange Interlude* (Robert Z. Leonard) released immediately prior to *Smilin' Through* in July 1932. The dialogue was central to the project of de-sentimentalizing the story, and the war setting made this possible. Kathleen/Shearer can express her sexual desire because of the duress of the times, the urgency of the moment, the deadline of Kenneth's train leaving. This sensuality in the modern romance plot offers a further contrast with the spiritual romance of Moonyeen and John fifty years before. Kathleen's and Kenneth's is a love with a real external deadline, while John and Moonyeen's deadline rests solely upon when he will recognize that his bitterness and hatred are the obstacle to their eternal happiness. One is spiritual, the other corporeal, and the hard deadlines of train departures and the threat to Kenneth's body and mind prompt physical desire. These are examples of the temporal structure embedded in the wartime romance and the return of the veteran that ably aids the construction of the seamless narration of the classical style and ameliorates the sentimentality of the original story.

SHELL SHOCK, "THE ART THAT CONCEALS ART"

Balderston's commentary is instructive for understanding the role that popular perceptions of shell shock played in establishing a final barrier to the romance plot and giving it a harder, more realist, edge. He recommended that Kenneth's condition be introduced gradually:

> After the war, as we learn—not all at once—but little by little, in the right way, in the right place and at the right time—Ken returns shell shocked. He thinks he's no good, unworthy of her, and he tells Dr Owen so in a heart-broken outburst when Owen convinces him that his inability to walk without crutches, although he is perfectly sound, is due to lack of guts.[23]

Balderston's commentary is evidence of the degree to which a medical understanding of war neurosis, or shell shock, had entered into public discourse by 1932. The plight of veterans had been a leading story in the press since the soldiers' return in 1919, from the legislative wrangle over compensation to the more personal stories of homeless veterans. His description of Kenneth's feelings of unworthiness and cathartic outburst and their gradual introduction traces war neuroses' pathology and guides the rhythm of the plot in the final scenes, providing the problem for which the romance is the cure. On this level it is hardly any different from Leon's cure "by true love" in *Humoresque*, but Balderston is aware of the changes in public understanding by 1932 and also—and they are connected—the need to qualify sentimentality. In the final act of the 1919 play, after John has relented and apologized to Kenneth, leaving the way open for his marriage to Kathleen, Dr. Owen confronts Kenneth about his state of mind:

> KENNETH: But it's too late now—I'm not fit—
> OWEN: Not fit my eye! You talk just like all shell-shockers! Why inside of thirty days, with your mind full of happiness, you'll be playing cricket!
> KENNETH: But, doctor!
> OWEN: I'm your doctor and I KNOW.[24]

Balderston, too, assumes the cause of shell shock is tied to lack of confidence. But the problem he identifies is less the accuracy of the etiology of war neurosis than the glib and sentimental nature of love as the "cure." "All lavender and old lace stories can be called 'dull' but they can make millions, if done with the art that conceals art." What he calls the "real sophistication" of the picture lies in the importance of the depiction of "real" war and its effects:

> We had much trouble over this, and I think we solved it. The retired doctor getting his commission in the R.A.M.C. as a dugout, the other old man jealous because too far gone even to be a dugout,

Kathleen jumping into the canteen in her village, Willie turning up with his commission and going out to fight, the dramatic values in the love story of the boy Ken going off into the furnace and the girl's fear, heightened by the thudding of the guns in France, which leads her to cry out for thirty-six hours of love with him—all this is not a motion picture war, but the real war, as it affected the lives of people like this. We haven't twenty lines directly about the war in the film but we show how the war affects, as it did and it must, the lives and actions of everyone of our characters—and there isn't one conventional 'war shot' with the exception of the returning soldiers; the curse is taken off that by Ken returning—alone.[25]

The "realism" lies in depicting war's effects rather than showing war scenes, the breaking up of an old friendship over outdated notions of national identity and fading masculinity, the rejection of old moral strictures in the form of release of the desire for "thirty-six hours of love." Even the one shot that explicitly depicts soldiers is qualified by Kenneth's solitary return. The war's "real effects," represented most patently by Kenneth's neuroses, modernize the story.

The tone of Balderston's recommendations in February of 1932 is followed through in the subsequent drafts, particularly around the depiction of Kenneth's physical and mental state when he returns. In the script dated June 7, Kenneth's return at the station is, as Balderston suggested, alone. The directions read:

> We now see the soldier is not Kenneth but a cheery-looking young Cockney private. He turns from depositing the suitcase, moves to the open door of carriage, and puts up a hand to assist someone from the train. And now Ken comes into view. He walks on crutches, descends painfully, assisted by his kindly orderly. His face is drawn and wan. His eyes sunken. There is a set hopelessness about his expression. But interest shows in his eyes as he strives to peer through the darkness about him. This place has meant so much.[26]

The realism, which counters the sentiment, lies in the emphasis on the performance and gesture in the depiction of Ken's thoughts. In the play, Kenneth's return takes place in John's garden. Immediately prior to bringing Kenneth to him, Dr. Owen reads John a letter from the hospital surgeon: "His wound has caused a limp which will be with him always. His greatest trouble now is depression—like most shell-shocked victims—He believes he is a big useless wreckage." The evolving versions of the script for the 1932 film illustrate the gradual move toward showing his neuroses rather than telling it. Two early versions by James Fagan in May and June have Kenneth's condition explained by the orderly, the "cheery Cockney," now called Bates: "shell shock—that's wot's the matter with 'im. Thinks he's a gonner—no good—a burden to everyone. They're all alike them shell shockers. Too bloody 'umble—as yer might say, beggin' yer pardon sir." A later version of Kenneth's return had him emerging from the train following a conversation between two amputees and the depiction of a "basket case":

> STATION, MEDIUM SHOT: Door from one of the coaches. Five or six ambulance attendants, Dr. Owen and Dr. Jordan are gathered at the door. Silently a large basket is carried out from the coach. MOVE FORWARD and see that the basket contains a badly mutilated soldier who should not, however, in the least resemble Kenneth. Two or three of the ambulance attendants turn away their faces at the sight. Owen steps forward and greets the man.
> OWEN: I'm Dr. Owen. We're very proud to have you in our hospital.[27]

The graphic nature of the scene, meant to delineate Dr. Owen's benevolence, was deleted from the final shooting script, as was the orderly's explanation.

In his earlier summary Balderston emphasized the necessity of having Kenneth's outburst take place prior to his meeting with Kathleen, a temporal order that would increase the suspense of the scene, create motivation for Kenneth's behavior, and generate audience sympathy for Kathleen. Balderston's version has Kenneth in a separate scene trying to learn to walk in Dr. Owen's office. The rewritten scene incorporated symptoms of shell shock, his cathartic "pouring forth," his feelings of worthlessness, as motivating factors that win him "the pity, approbation and respect of the audience." Its function in the plot is even more economical in that it sets up the final scene with Kathleen in a way that garners her all of the audience's sympathy. She finds Kenneth in his father's derelict house about to leave for America without seeing her. He sits down, hiding his wounded legs, and acts as if he has lost interest, first pleasant and then cruel as he speaks of their past together as long ago, their love simply a wartime peccadillo. Devastated, she finally runs out. The audience and Kenneth *know* that he is shell-shocked and wounded but Kathleen does not. Balderston points out "the whole scene is thrown to the girl. We feel for her and with her as she proceeds on her false assumptions and undergoes her humiliations. . . . I stress this point, as I think it very important for the star and indeed for the whole dramatic value of the situation." She leaves in tears, which in turn places the onus on John to forgive Kenneth, a sentimental engine for the plot that Balderston has worked to ameliorate through the depiction of the "real" effects of the war. As in *Humoresque*, the love of the woman is the cure, but this has had the effect of incorporating a realistic portrayal of the symptoms of war neuroses within a dynamic of plausible motivation and character interaction. The result is a "modernizing" effect.

While the film's "sophistication" lay in the retooling of sexual mores brought about by the separation of the lovers by war, its "realism" lay in the depiction of Kenneth's shell shock through Fredric March's performance. The term "shell shock" is not mentioned in the final film. Instead, the script direction describes his expression as a faded smile that grows bitter when alone; he is "vexed and nervous" and makes "impatient movements." When questioned, he responds with the temperamental outburst of a shell-shocked man. The symptoms of shell shock are written on his body and his manner rather than explained by another character.

In the scene of Kenneth's return at the station in the final cut of the film, he is gradually revealed emerging from the back of the train after other wounded soldiers, one blinded, have stepped off. The camera closes in on his darting eyes as he looks quickly around, his face in a grim set expression. Once he has gotten off the train and irritably answered Dr. Owen's questions, we see his whole body from behind in medium-long shot as he tries to descend the station stairs on his own, his legs dragging, and falls. That is where he makes his "heart-broken" outburst to Dr. Owen. His overall manner is one of mercurial mood shifts; his face at one moment is apparently pleasant but when he is alone his expression darkens, displayed in close up.

March's performance was praised in the press. Edwin Schallert of the *Los Angeles Times* commented, "the best interpretation because it is so well shaded. He makes a marked differentiation between the two characters that he plays, which are somewhat a la Jekyll and Hyde."[28] The reference to the Robert Louis Stevenson classic regards the two roles he plays, Jeremy and Kenneth, but it also draws attention to March's portrayal of mental instability in Kenneth as veteran, his "before and after," which he presented again in *The Eagle and the Hawk* one year later, and it adverts to March's leading role in *Dr. Jekyll and Mr. Hyde* for Paramount the previous year. He won an Oscar for that performance and was on his way to establishing an "actorly" star persona that emphasized his abilities and his range as a performer. (He would later play other veteran characters in *The Dark Angel* (1935), also directed by Sidney Franklin, and William Wyler's 1946 film *The Best Years of Our Lives*.) Schallert's equation of the two roles also applies to the change in Kenneth, from enthusiastic suitor to embittered and shell-shocked veteran. Kenneth and Kathleen are a modern couple representative of the ordeals of the new twentieth century. They have supplanted the "lavender and lace" of John and Moonyeen and counteracted their whimsicality and nostalgia with an energy born out of conflict and, once Kenneth is in the healing arms of Kathleen, a faith in the future.

PERFORMING SHELL SHOCK

The war, its effects, its consequences, and the modernizing discourses associated with it coincided with deeper social issues in the 1932 *Smilin' Through* that were less evident in the earlier film version or the play. Kathleen's declaration of desire, "I *want* you," resonated with the changing and contested moral discourses surrounding marriage and sexuality. The empathetic approach of Dr. Owen offered a vague glimpse of a more enlightened understanding of war neurosis.

Similarly, shell shock begets another social consequence named in the title of the 1932 RKO film *A Bill of Divorcement*, an adaptation of British author Clemence Dane's 1921 play that dealt with the rights of women in divorce legislation in the UK. There, the war had accelerated an already rising divorce rate that was at the center of public debate on the changing attitudes to marriage throughout the 1920s and '30s.[29] Dane's play was written in support of proposed changes to the law that gave women the right to divorce on the same grounds as men. In her playbook, Dane's direction sets this out explicitly: "The audience is asked to imagine that the recommendations of the *Majority Report of the Royal Commission on Divorce v. Matrimonial Causes* have become the law of the land." Set in 1933, fourteen years into the future, the play conjures a situation where divorce, initiated by the wife of a shell-shocked veteran in this case, was sanctioned by law according to those recommendations. It was an optimistic reckoning, since the divorce laws in England did not fully accommodate the Report's findings until the late 1930s.[30] An ardent supporter of reform, Dane built her play around the issue of divorce by reason of insanity. The play's device of incorporating shell shock afforded her the opportunity to

FIGURE 5.2. Katherine Hepburn and John Barrymore in *A Bill of Divorcement* (George Cukor, 1932). RKO Radio Pictures/Photofest. © RKO Radio Pictures.

set out a balanced case by invoking sympathy for the afflicted husband while exploring the social disapproval and emotional turmoil that women faced when initiating divorce proceedings.

Set in the English countryside on Christmas Day, 1933, the play tells the story of the return, after 15 years in an asylum, of a shell-shocked veteran named Hilary Fairfield to his wife Margaret and their daughter, Sydney. Margaret was only seventeen when she married Hilary as he went off to war in 1915, and he has never seen his daughter, born while he was at the front. Having apparently suddenly become well, he returns just as Margaret is about to remarry, having divorced him by reason of insanity through recently passed divorce legislation. Her fiancé, Gray Meredith, is a few years older than her. Sydney is seventeen and in love with the local Rector's son, Kit Pumphrey. Her Aunt Hester, Hilary's sister, described in the stage directions as "one of those twitching, high minded, elderly ladies in black," lives with them in the Fairfield family home. She is against the divorce and remarriage and refers to it as a "deadly sin." When Hilary returns he cannot understand that he fought for a "law making machine that I've called my country" and now finds himself divorced. He seesaws back and forth between reason and rage and is finally convinced that Margaret would be happier with Gray. However, his side of the family holds the deeper secret of insanity, which has emerged because of his shell shock. Because of the threat of passing on insanity to her children, Sydney breaks her engagement with Kit and chooses to spend her life taking care of her father.

The play opened at St. Martin's Theatre in London's West End on March 14, 1921. It struck a chord with post-war English theatregoers with its subject of reform and its direct reference to the ravages of the war. The run lasted through 401 performances. During that run, the play was brought across the Atlantic by American producer Charles Dillingham and English actor and real-life wounded veteran Allan Pollack, who took the role of Hilary Fairfield. They brought in Basil Dean, who had designed the London production, and gave the role of Sydney to rising Broadway star Katharine Cornell. They opened at the George M. Cohan theatre on October 10, 1921, to uniformly positive reviews. Critics highlighted Cornell's nuanced performance as in rendering Sydney's transformation from confident ingénue to self-sacrificing daughter, which was, according to B.F. of the *New York Tribune*, "in turn rebellious, melting, sullen, vivacious, sympathetic and heroic."[31] Her long Broadway career had its basis in part in her success in this role.

Divorce as an issue carried different meanings with New York audiences and in the play's reception. Seeking to reassure, the *Tribune* implored, "erase from the tablets of memory the words of doom about British divorce laws, the relation of Church and State and other matters alien to our ears. The essence of the drama is a potent infusion of love and duty."[32] Instead of the treatise on women's rights, the main critical focus was on the veteran status of Pollack as Hilary. Pollack had left a promising career on the American stage in 1914 to enlist in the British Army and was wounded in 1916: part of his jaw was shot away. He had spent three years recuperating in hospital. The *New York Telegraph* review noted his performance as well as his veteran status:

> The enthusiasm which greeted him was not by any means solely a personal tribute to the returned war hero but a recognition as well of his masterful interpretation of the role of Hilary, the shell shocked British officer . . . it required all the art which he brought back unimpaired by his long absence to do it justice.[33]

Kenneth Macgowan, drama theorist, theatre critic for the *New York Globe*, and later Hollywood film producer, outlined the tensions in Pollack's performance between the "command of his art" and his real-life trauma: "Perhaps his voice is too bell-like in the strange risings and fallings in its inflections, but that is, I imagine, a defensible symptom of a mind that quavers on the edge of the pit." At the time of writing his review Macgowan was in the process of writing the first of his drama theory books, *Theatre of Tomorrow*, where he called for "an intense inner vision of spiritual reality which will push the selective process so far that to call the result realism will be an absurdity."[34] Pollack's performance of shell shock proffered an extraordinary example of Macgowan's prescription for a new drama that reaches beyond a surface realism down into "those deep and vigorous and eternal processes of the human soul which the psychology of Freud and Jung has given us through study of the unconscious, striking to the heart of emotion and linking our commonest life today with the emanations of the primitive racial mind."[35] Recourse to primitivism, faux Darwinism, and Freudian topographies of the psyche was indeed fashionable in 1921, and while he does not explicitly reference shell shock, the link with his description of Pollack's performance as a "defensible symptom of a mind that quavers on the edge of the pit" is an hint of Macgowan's ideas that modern acting should be a process of uncovering or revealing inner states. That the veteran as a figure is central to that theory is illustrated by his focus on Pollack's conflation of real experience with characterization in playing the shell-shocked Hilary.

Pollack's performance and the critics' praise would not have escaped David O. Selznick's notice when he first saw the play at the Cohan. While it was not until 1931 that he bought the rights for it as his first film in his new position as producer for RKO studios, he had long wanted to make a film of the play. In his words, the problem was that he "could never sell it to my bosses, because of the insanity angle which was supposed to be taboo for pictures."[36] The emphasis on Pollack as veteran in the Broadway version had overridden the issue on the stage but required a different solution ten years later. In his new role in charge of production at RKO, Selznick devised the film as a highbrow effort with Barrymore and Billie Burke, leading lights of the American stage, and directed by recently arrived stage director George Cukor. He sought to exploit the patina of quality and prestige that its theatrical origins would provide, which was duly picked up in the reviews.[37] It was also the screen launch of stage ingénue Katherine Hepburn, who had the role of Antiope in the revival of Julian F. Thompson's 1924 comedy *The Warrior's Husband*. Launching an unknown was a strategy that Selznick got from the play's effect on Cornell's career ten years earlier, and he was looking to find new stars for the RKO roster.[38] It was Hepburn's first film, and the stage direction for Sydney in the play reads like a recipe for Hepburn's star persona as it developed in the ensuing decade: "Her manner is brisk and decided. She is very sure of herself, but when she loses her temper . . . she loses her aplomb and reveals the schoolgirl."[39]

The play and the film depend upon Hilary's veteran status and the actor's performance of his mental instability, which is the threat of madness about to erupt. The stage direction for his entrance describes him as "a big fresh-coloured man with gray hair and bowed shoulders. In speech and movements he is quick and jerky, inclined to be boisterous, but pathetically easy to check. This he knows himself, and he has, indeed, an air of being always in rebellion against his own habit of obedience."[40] They indicate a tension within the character, a conflict between an impulse to resist and an impulse to comply with external forces and relationships. Dane could be describing the aggression symptoms that psychiatrist Abram Kardiner noticed were common in his extensive study of U.S. war veterans undertaken in the 1920s and '30s:

> This feature of aggressiveness and violence is present in every traumatic neurosis. . . . One does not find it in the physioneuroses of peacetime. . . . [It] is not deliberate or premeditated. . . . His aggression is always impulsive; nor is it capable of being long sustained.

Entirely episodic, it often alternates with moods of extreme tenderness. One never finds the aggressiveness and the impulsive violence without reactions of tenderness.[41]

Kardiner noted that these aggressive episodes, accompanied by moments of compassion, resulted in inhibitions in their "relations with the outer world," and Dane's characterization of Hilary demonstrates a similar dynamic of social paralysis.

These characteristics are present in Hilary's first appearance at the house. Margaret, his now ex-wife, is at the Christmas Day service with her fiancé, while Sydney, his daughter, is at home, having just been told by her Aunt Hester that there is insanity in the family and that her father's had only been brought on by shell shock. Hilary (Barrymore) enters the common room through the French window from the garden. The stage instructions are deliberate and detailed:

He comes in, treading softly, his bright eyes dancing with excitement, like a child getting ready to spring a surprise on somebody. Something in the fashion of the empty room (for he does not see Sydney crouching in the cushions) disconcerts him. He hesitates. The happy little smile fades. His eye wanders from one object to another and he moves about, recognising a picture here, fingering there an unfamiliar hanging, as it were losing himself a dozen times in his progress around the room. He comes to a stand at last before the fire-place, warming his hands.[42]

Danes's understanding of the effect of the inner conflicts is demonstrated in these specific directions where gestures are central to conveying the complexity of Hilary's thought processes.

In most of the biographical works on both Cukor and Hepburn there is an anecdote about the filming of this scene, told to illustrate the generosity of the seasoned and respected actor John Barrymore toward the young Hepburn in her first film. In the first take, Barrymore went through the scene rather perfunctorily, and when he had finished he noticed that even though Hepburn was not in the shot she had been emoting in character with tears in her eyes. He noticed her dedication and went over to her, cupped her face in his hands, and asked Cukor to do another take. This time he was transformed: the power of the actor was revealed as he brought the character of Hilary to life in the second take.[43] The story is relevant to this exploration of the veteran characterization in Hollywood, as it helps to outline the intersection between Barrymore's acting style and popular conceptions of shell shock and insanity more broadly.

The accounts of this episode do not extend to a description of Barrymore's technique, but the performance is recorded, and through that it is possible to see the nuances in gesture and bits of business he employs. Like the shell-shocked soldiers Kardiner observed, he evinces an inner conflict between exuberance and anger, between intensity and repression. This expresses itself first in his body and costume as he walks through the threshold of the French window, in a trench coat bound around him to suggest simultaneously the uniform of an officer and the straitjacket of the asylum. He is holding his hat in both hands at his waist with the manner of a man walking into a dream. As he wanders through the room his face is open and bright, but then as he stops the smile fades to an expression of contemplation, perhaps trying to remember what the familiarity of the room should prompt, or trying to banish troubling thoughts or obsessions. His expression moves between these two poles as he traverses the room. The shots alternate between him and Sydney, as she watches him. The shots are not quite point-of-view. In a marked difference from the play, rather than watching from the fixed position of "crouching in the cushions" of the sofa, she shifts her position. She is shown looking first through the stair banisters decorated with Christmas pine foliage and then through the branches of a flower arrangement on the table. In the scene both of the actors move, he according to the stage directions of the play, she to get a better view of him. (Cukor's approach to the film was to employ a combination of moving camera and actor movement to give the film a dynamic dimension to counter the one-room confines of the play.) He shuffles across the room, bumping against a chair inadvertently, and then to the mantelpiece, his back to the camera. The expression in his shoulders and gait is somewhere between a childish slouch and world-weary slump. When Sydney breaks the silence and asks him "What are you looking for?" he turns around and his expression is bright again as he thinks she is his wife, Margaret, or "Meg" as he calls her. She says she is not Meg and he slightly recoils, his expression one of catching himself. She asks, "Where have you come from?" His face darkens into a depth not yet shown; his eyes dart, caught up in a dark memory. "That place" he responds.

Through his gesture and expression Barrymore sets out the conflict within his character and also provides a sense of warning, in tandem with Sydney's expression of fascination bordering on horror, and later Margaret's genuine fear, that he could go much farther. All of this falls within the kind of characterization techniques of the classical model that Anita Loos and Frances Marion would recognize as presenting traits that will be worked through in the narrative, offering a transparent reading of Hilary as returning veteran. In this case the actor's business gives the character depth, evoking at once sympathy and apprehension.

Barrymore was seen at the time as having helped originate the deeper expressive "realism" that Macgowan was calling for. Barrymore's signal stage achievements, the ones on which his reputation rested, were his portrayal of Richard III in 1920 and Hamlet in 1922–25. The roles signaled a shift in his acting style from what some critics had described as a convincing but at times limited range. Much of this critique centered on his voice.[44] His preparation for both Shakespeare roles was extensive and his work with Margaret Carrington on his vocal technique brought a depth to his range and to the uniquely modern characterizations, particularly in his portrayal of Hamlet. There are two elements to this that are relevant to the portrayal of Hilary, and particularly his introductory scene. The first is Barrymore's *range* of movement, both in his body and in his eyes and facial expression. The second is in the modulation of his voice, a fact noted in Alexander Woolcott's review of his Richard III as "rich, full and flexible." [45] In the *New York Times* review of *Hamlet* James Corbin heard "deep tones" prevail: "Very rarely did the speech quicken or the voice rise to the pitch of drama, but when this happened the effect was electric." And his overall summation was as if he, too, had read Kardiner's study 20 years before it was published: "Even as his will struggles impotently to master his external environment, perform the duty enjoined on him by supernatural authority, so his spirit struggles against the overbrooding cloud of melancholy."[46] His rendering of Hilary demonstrates some of this range; his voice modulates between anger and tenderness, his body between youthful hope and dark despair, sometimes exuberant, sometimes pleading, sometimes explosive with anger. Barrymore's techniques, as the critics describe them, align closely with the broader cultural understanding of war neuroses.

Not surprisingly, he brings some of this to his performance of Hilary. Throughout the film Barrymore adopts a slouch, a sense of the weight of unimaginable dreams and events on his shoulders, one that takes Clemence Dane's original direction of "bowed shoulders" and lends it psychological detail. From his first appearance Hilary brings with him the quality that Leon and Kenneth bring after they have been to the front, the bodily marker of a traumatic time indelibly stamped on their psyche. His voice and body render his inner conflicts such that his movement is shuffling and at times absent minded. In his first scene he moves across the room to his bookshelf and bumps into a chair, not fully aware of the space around him. Recalling another scene from another film, *Dinner at Eight* (Cukor, 1933), Cukor noted that Barrymore was very creative in the detail of his characters and he gave him latitude to do so. His character in that film is a failed actor who ultimately takes his own life. Directing the suicide scene, Cukor told him that his character had "'always bungled everything and now some awful indignity should happen to him.' Then Jack walked across the room again . . . right in the middle of the carpet was a stool and he tripped on it—an awful middleaged, ungraceful sprawl which was so sad and so marvellous in the picture."[47] The connection between his benchmark performance of *Hamlet* and these conflicted characters lies in the development of his range of vocal inflections and bodily movement that belie the internal struggle over their "overbrooding sense of melancholy." [47] While almost a decade had elapsed between his *Hamlet* and the filming of *A Bill of Divorcement*, Barrymore's performance of Hilary's symptoms of shell shock and "insanity" offered an additional means of modernizing the social issues with which it was attempting to grapple.

Within the norms of the classical model it is the job of the script to invest these characters with plausible motivations through their immersion in, and recourse to, contemporary discourse, medical and social in the case of veterans, or at least to contain them within the dictates of clear storytelling. The "insanity angle" that Selznick cites as a reason for his difficulty in selling *A Bill of Divorcement* to the studios was ultimately overridden by what he saw in the play as the utility of the star-making role of Sydney that had been "road tested" on Broadway. The force of Selznick's power at RKO was such that he was able to green-light the film, but not without some important changes to Dane's play that subtly reoriented the role of Sydney. For Broadway playgoers in 1922 the issue of divorce was of lesser importance than Hilary's shell shock, the issue of inherited insanity, and the mercurial performance of Katharine Cornell. Along the same lines, Hepburn's performance in the film presents her as a modern woman who locks horns with her Aunt Hester, is protective of her mother, and ultimately makes the "responsible" decision to avoid marriage and look after her father. In the Dane play the ambiguities around inherited insanity and shell shock are overridden by the plea for fairer divorce laws. In the film those conflicts are brought to the fore and center on Sydney's resolution. Her realization that her father's insanity is hereditary and "brought on" by shell shock is entwined with her status as a modern woman. Assertive and intelligent but "wild" and irreverent in her aunt's eyes, she declares, "It's against my principles to kneel down and declare I'm a miserable sinner. I'm not miserable and I'm not a sinner."

The main conflict in the film becomes Sydney's decision to negotiate with the past that both her father and her aunt represent. Her "wildness," i.e., her modernness, is explicitly presented as a symptom of her own predisposition to the family disease. Her mother tells her, "You get so excited . . . you remind me . . . your father was so excitable." One reading might be to see this as a means of containing the modern woman within the patriarchal family home. Yet her decision to break her engagement to Kit and take care of her father places her on an equal footing with him. Where the film differs from the play in this regard is in the final scenes. In the play, Sydney overhears her mother telling Gray she cannot go with him but must stay with her ex-husband, Hilary, because if he's left alone "he'll go mad again" and "I've got to do what's right." She interrupts them and tells her mother to go with Gray—"Father—He's my job, not yours." The active decision is Sydney's, for which she is later berated by her father: "It's your damn clever doing that she went. D'you think I can't hate you?" In the film it is Hilary who overhears Margaret declare to Gray that she is "losing all she has" in losing him. The action that spurs Sydney to make her mother go with Gray is instigated by Hilary when he *feigns* anger and tells Sydney to get them out of his house, threatening to kill Gray. After they leave, Sydney realizes that he really loves her mother, but he says "she only pitied me, she loves him." Yet the Dane play ends on a note of supplication. After she has told her father that she is clever, can paint, write, and act, and that she will make him proud of her, Aunt Hester responds "She's like the rest of the young women. Hard as nails!" To which Sydney objects with the final line of the play "I'm not hard. I'm not hard." By contrast, the film ends on a note of reconciliation and healing. Hilary says, "We'll have a good time together somehow won't we?"—lines spoken by Sydney in the play. At that moment Kit whistles outside the window, but without responding Sydney shuts the curtains and goes to the piano, signaling her rejection of marriage and children in favor of self-sacrificial singlehood. She plays an unfinished sonata her father had written and it triggers a memory in him. She plays some endings she has tried and then he sits down and completes it and the film ends. The ending does wrap Sydney back into the arms of her father, but within a cooperative therapist/patient relationship in which she holds the power. Thus shell shock/insanity has had the effect of "modernizing" their relationship. Through a kind of music therapy she sets him on a road to recovery, and in the process reworks the play's tract on English divorce law toward a generational reconciliation. Crucially, also, the star persona of Hepburn as a modern, independent, and capable woman gets its initial definition in the role of Sydney and continues into her next films, *Christopher Strong* (Dorothy Arzner, 1933) and *Little Women* (George Cukor, 1933). It is the modern Sydney that is the template for this star persona—played out against the figure of the veteran, relic of the past, an embodiment of the memory and ravages of the Great War.

WASHOUTS: IMPOTENCE IN *THE LAST FLIGHT*

Early in *A Bill of Divorcement* Sydney, exasperated with her mother attributing her mistakes to the war, declares: "It's extraordinary to me—whenever you middle-aged people want to excuse yourselves for anything that you've done that you know you oughtn't have done, you say it was the war." By 1932 this line's implications had acquired an almost ubiquitous familiarity, nowhere more so than in the new American writing of F. Scott Fitzgerald and Ernest Hemingway. The central figures Jay Gatsby in *The Great Gatsby* (1925) and Jake Barnes in *The Sun Also Rises* (1926) were veterans dealing either directly or indirectly with their wartime experiences. As early as 1927, in their monthly memo to the heads of the studios, the Hays Office pronounced Hemingway's novel unacceptable as a film project because of the central theme of impotence.[49] The tale of the wounded and castrated veteran Jake Barnes's adventures in Paris and Spain had been a literary and popular success and the Hays Office was aware of the attraction popular novels held for the studios. Even more tempting was a story that held a sexual secret, in this case impotence, and the novel's reputation for hard boiled language fell into the already successful production trend of realist films centering on the consequences of war such as *The Big Parade* and *What Price Glory*. The trope of veterans traveling Europe's bars as a palliative for their war experiences, and as a further consequence of the war, would have seemed an ideal prestige project for a studio such as MGM or Paramount.[50]

The problems *The Sun Also Rises* posed for producers and their team of scriptwriters were not unique. Taste preferences, market assumptions, and financial considerations were as much a challenge in studio decision-making as the reports and restrictions from the Hays Office—in fact, those three concerns took precedence by and large, and the Hays Office was often ignored where possible. However, the challenge for the scriptwriters was to negotiate the subject matter of impotence in such a way as to provide plausible motivations for the character's actions. Jake Barnes's adventures proved difficult to render under the studio system because the central conflict was internal within Jake, whose consistent drinking and relative inaction left little room for heroics and resolution through action. More critically, the returning veteran, and the attendant symptoms of this archetype, had not yet been fully developed in terms of explicit delineations of the causes for their behavior. While alluded to in the conflicts that arise in films such as *Humoresque* and both versions of *Smilin' Through*, impotence was a symptom of the traumatized veteran that was not explicitly discussed in most public forums. And as with other symptoms entailing sexual (dys)function or sexuality, displacement strategies were used for talking around these topics. Conrad Aiken's review of the novel in the *New York Herald Tribune*, October 31, 1927, referred to the "sordidness" of the situation.[51] In cinema, as in theatre and literature, while ultimately displaced and usually resolved, the symptoms of trauma were written on the body. Barrymore's physical performance of Hilary and March's darting eyes in *Smilin' Through* provide plausible physical manifestations of war neuroses that were not possible with Jake Barnes. His impotence *was* his motivation.

Solutions to the adaptation of *The Sun Also Rises* were not forthcoming, and for some time the studios heeded the warning of the Hays Office: an adaptation of the novel did not appear from a Hollywood studio until Henry King's 1957 version for 20th Century-Fox. However, in *The Last Flight* (1931), John Monk Saunders found a means of writing around the psychological and physical problems suffered by veterans by displacing the impotence theme through an allusive slang. The movie was an adaptation of Saunders's ten popular "Nikki and Her War Birds" stories published in the magazine *Liberty* from November 1930 to April 1931. Suspiciously similar to *The Sun Also Rises*, the stories featured four ex-aviators infatuated with a woman who joined them as they traversed bars in Paris and Lisbon trying to drink to erase their symptoms of war trauma and impotence. Yet the stories provided an acceptable solution by resetting the narrative problem from avoiding discussions of impotence to rekindling desire in the main character as an indication of what his underlying problem had been.[52]

In the words of one of the four protagonists, Shep Lambert, the object is to "get tight"; when he is asked "What then?" his response is "Stay tight." He is accompanied by his pilot, Cary Lockwood, whose hands have been badly burned bringing his plane down and in the process saving

Shep's life. The two other damaged flyers joining them are "Bronko" Bill Talbot, an all-American football star, and Francis "The Washout." In Paris they meet a single rich American woman named Nikki whom they "adopt" and who accompanies them, and is the center of their attentions, as they drink their way through the bars, nightclubs, and cafés of Paris. There is a burgeoning relationship between Nikki and Cary that takes the form of an initial antagonism. Cary, who is sensitive about his burned hands, is not quite as far gone as his comrades and he takes umbrage to Nikki's curiosity about his scars. Nikki follows Cary when he goes to the Paris cemetery Père Lachaise to visit a pilot friend of his who is buried there. He shows Nikki the tomb of the famed couple Héloïse and Abelard. However, again Nikki inadvertently hurts his feelings and he leaves Paris for Lisbon. She and the rest of the group follow him, and while they are there Shep is stabbed in a fight by a Portugese man who in turn is shot by Francis, "The Washout." Francis slips away "swift as a cat" and disappears from the story. Shep dies of his wound. Later, at the bullfights, Bill is gored trying to tackle a bull and they leave him in the hospital. Cary and Nikki travel back to Paris and it is implied that he is helped on the road to recovery from what is clearly impotence as well as burns by their blossoming romance.

1930 had been a good year for Saunders with the successes of *The Dawn Patrol* and the Nikki stories in *Liberty*. His turn to the aftereffects of the war had a particular logic. In many ways, his adaptation of the stories to *The Last Flight* made a sequel to *The Dawn Patrol* in that it served as a follow-up vehicle for Richard Barthlemess, and the importance of his involvement was reflected in his salary, which was the lion's share of the budget for the film. A central pillar in Barthelmess's star persona was well established through veteran roles such as the disfigured soldier in the film version of Arthur Wing Pinero's *The Enchanted Cottage* (John S. Robertson, 1924) and the wounded boxer veteran in *The Patent Leather Kid* (Alfred Santell, 1927). Barthelmess had had good success with *The Dawn Patrol* and further developed his association with the pity of war in the role of the troubled aviator who ends up in command, sending inexperienced boys to their deaths and drinking constantly to dull his senses. While the Nikki stories relay the war experiences of the flyers through the dialogue, recounting them as memories, *The Last Flight* built on the previous films by opening with dogfight sequences to reprise the context of the main characters' war experiences. Cary (Barthlemess) and Shep (David Manners, who had played Lt. Raleigh in *Journey's End*) are shot down, but Cary manages to bring the plane into a crash landing by holding on to the burning controls with his hands. Badly burned, his hands are the outside evidence of the psychological scars he bears.

The stories had appeared every Friday in *Liberty* and became "well-loved" among the readers. In letters to Saunders via the magazine, readers wrote in to the column "Vox Pop" to express their admiration, with a few mentioning the desire to see them made into a film. These letters give a good indication of the appeal of the stories at the time and their context within the developing public debate about the fate of the veterans. Reader George M. Ord wrote to *Liberty*,

> I was with these boys at the front, in Paris, and in the billets after the war. If our people could only understand your Nikki stories what a difference it would make to these men. Many of them could be rehabilitated. They ought to be. They are brave, loveable, true soldiers—the debris of war. They ought to be in the hospital with many Nikkis for nurses.[53]

The veteran here is the focus for current debates about the role, and failure, of social institutions in their care and treatment while presaging positions directly critical of President Herbert Hoover's administration and the failure of government generally. In fact, the film fit quite neatly into the developing Depression-era house style at Warner Bros. In this sense *The Last Flight* has the anti-sentimentality and the sense of social exposé of that style and, like other early '30s returning-veteran films, operates on the displacement of those anxieties onto the minds and bodies of veterans, albeit in this case outside of the United States. The veteran "back home" later became the more explicit representative of the "forgotten man" in Warner films as diverse as *I Am a Fugitive From a Chain Gang* (Mervyn LeRoy, 1932) and *Gold Diggers of 1933* (Mervyn LeRoy, 1933), or the exposé on drug use by veterans in *Heroes for Sale* (William Wellman, 1933), which also starred Barthelmess.

Where these later films deal more or less explicitly with the social neglect of veterans, the Nikki stories and their film adaptation operate within a system of displacement and fetishization of the traumas experienced by these flyers. The working title of the film during the script phase had been "Spent Bullets," an explicit reference to the impact of their war experience on their bodies and minds. The sequence that follows the aerial combat acts as a prologue to the film, providing motivation for the flyers' behavior. Cary Lockwood (Barthelmess) and Shep Lambert (Manners) are examined and released by their Army physician. As the doctor watches them leave, he states to his colleague that they will be unable to fly in civilian life. His description incorporates the popular discourse concerning war neurosis. The fact that they have plummeted 6,000 meters is like "dropping a fine Swiss watch on the pavement. Shattered, both of them. Their nervous systems are deranged, brittle." The reference to the "wounded mind" draws on the earlier conceptions of shell shock and shell concussion cases by the British military in 1915, which stipulated that the problems be directly related to action with the enemy.[54] The metaphor of the body as broken machinery then sharpens to the technology of war: "They're like projectiles hurled at the enemy. They've described a perfect high arching trajectory. Now they've fallen back to earth, cooled off, useless." His use of ballistics language as a metaphor for their shattered minds ends in a condemnation, which sets out the impotence theme that permeates the stories and the film and at the same time offers the displacement mechanism through which it can be both shown and finally resolved. His prognosis is grim: "I hate to think of what may become of them."

Before they leave, the doctor skirts the issue of their mental state as if it were unspeakable, and instead Cary and Shep are given specific advice about how to deal with their physical wounds. Cary is recommended a series of exercises, while Shep is told that his facial tic will subside eventually. Later we see the other two characters are given only symptoms; Bill is at times unusually aggressive, while Francis "The Washout" is constantly falling asleep and keeps a watch that chimes every fifteen minutes to keep him awake. Apart from Cary, all of these characters, including Shep, demonstrate symptoms that indicate irreparable psychological damage, but no outward physical damage to the body. The symptoms rehearse the medical debates during the war itself concerning shell shock; in a crude sense, the hero, Cary, is recoverable because his wound is physical, and he is troubled. Like Kenneth in *Smilin' Through*, he "lacks confidence." In his letter, George Ord gives voice to this assumption: "Shep and Bill are fortunate, the pity is they could not have finished it on the front. God knows what will happen to 'The Washout'—jail, the penitentiary, or the gutter."[55]

The novel's and the film's signifying systems work to displace the flyers' impotence onto symptoms written on their bodies. Saunders himself sets out the psychological dynamics of his characters in the publicity material for the movie. He refers to "the energy" that veterans contain, using the hyperbolic metaphors of bodily sensation:

> He is still vibrant with surging nervous energy. Something in him clamors for wild action for speed, for anything but humdrum. There

is something in the bearing and in the eye of an ex-airman which is instantly recognizable to others of his kind. Only those who have gone through the soul shattering experience can see beneath the exterior of an ostensibly able bodied and normal man, and glimpse the tense spirit within.[56]

"Tense spirit" and "surging nervous energy" operate as plausible motivations for the behavior of the characters, a displacement that holds the solution to the representation, and resolution, of impotence in the film. Saunders's explanation incorporates a kind of crude topography of surface and interior, where only one who has undergone trauma can truly understand the turmoil inside the veteran flyer. Only they can read the damage in each other that the apparently calm surface hides. They each understand and share the tension between their headlong rush to oblivion, their need for comradeship, and their desire for Nikki. The resolution of those tensions depends, in both the stories and the film, on Nikki and on Cary.

Nikki is the genius loci of the film, acting as guide to, as well as object of, the flyers' displaced, and impotent, desires. Empathy for the shell-shocked pilots is channeled through her knowing reference to her body and theirs. With its allusive language about bodily functions and direct references to body parts, the film is suffused with corporeality. Throughout, Nikki herself is alluded to as a victim of trauma at the hands of her mother, the symptoms of which are written on her body. "I know I'm not good looking," she says, and when asked about her crooked tooth, she says it helps because when she is kissed too hard her lip bleeds, "So now I don't let anyone kiss me." (In the film this line is altered: "I don't let anyone kiss me . . . hard.") When asked about her nicotine-stained teeth, she responds that they are not: "When I was a little girl . . . I was very ill once and those are fever stains." When asked what was wrong with her, she responds, "My mother was a Christian Scientist and she wouldn't tell me."[57] In *Single Lady*, Saunders's novelization of the stories, her eyes are described as "unnaturally large and black and blind; like the eyes in heads of girls painted by Marie Laurencin. They looked as though they had been treated with belladonna; the pupils were so dilated as to blot out the irises almost."[58]

In adapting the Nikki stories for the screen, Saunders used the same strategy of displacement onto the various signs of the dismemberment and bodily segmentation of Nikki. In the film she is introduced holding a set of teeth in her champagne glass, then later the boys follow her up to her hotel room and at various moments comment on her skin, her neck, her back, her legs, her toes, and so forth. These are paralleled by the

FIGURE 5.3. David Manners (Shep), Helen Chandler (Nikki), Richard Barthelmess (Cary), John Mack Brown (Bill), and Elliot Nugent (Francis) in *The Last Flight* (William Dieterle, 1931). Warner Bros./Photofest. © Warner Bros.

segmentation of the male bodies through the physical manifestations of traumas of the war; Cary's hands, Shep's facial tic, The Washout's doziness, and Bill's manic enthusiasm. At the same time Saunders incorporates nonsensical language to demonstrate the cynical worldview of both the flyers and Nikki. Closed to the outside world, they inhabit their own milieu where no one says what they mean and everyone knows what they mean when they say it. The Hays Office notes registered concerns about using euphemisms for going to the toilet, such as "going for a Chinese singing lesson" or "going to shave a horse," although these were kept in the final version.[59] For the most part the film transcribes the stories with much of the original banter and slightly risqué activity intact. However, there are significant variances. In the film, the four ex-aviators are joined by a reporter, "Frink," who had not fought in the war. Frink's attempts to force himself on Nikki, unrestrained by propriety and driven by an overactive libido, function to underline the displaced desire Cary and the other veterans have for her.

Another particular deviation from the original story lies in the characterization of Francis, "The Washout." In the final film script the character is one-dimensional and his killing of Frink implies that his future lies, as Ord fears, in the criminal underworld. In the stories and novel his character is more fully articulated. His drowsiness is not due to some nondescript trauma; it is due to the fact that he takes drugs and frequents secret midnight parties that feature a thinly veiled form of S&M, where participation is a lottery. In the novel his trauma of the war is given full articulation: his loss of his companion transformed him. Shep imitates The Washout's lisp as he relays the story to Nikki. When asked where he goes at night by a suspicious Bill, the narrator fills in the details:

> There was a strange group of people, men and women who met secretly at night somewhere in the Bois de Boulogne. The exact spot and the hour remained a secret until the last minute when the word passed around.... Shortly before the appointed time, taxi cabs could be seen to leave various smart hotels headed in a mutual direction. The cabs would arrive almost simultaneously at the prearranged spot in the bois. Lights were turned off. Mysterious figures debouched from the tonneaus and flitted into darkness.
> Bill wanted to know what happened then.
> "Brother" said Shep "it ain't no church social".
> It was understood that whoever embarked upon these midnight excursions was morally emancipated and committed to any consequences.[60]

The Washout's character was altered in the script, clearly deemed unsuitable, before it was passed to the Hays Office. In fact, in the final cut his nickname The Washout is only obliquely referenced and not explicitly directed at Francis, although the banter about his chiming watch immediately precedes the use of the term. The slang term "washout" gained currency during the war; it meant someone who was useless or unsuccessful and explicitly referred to a person who was dropped from a course of training. However, its use by Saunders also obliquely refers to potency and, within post-war masculinity discourse, is a reference to Francis's homosexuality, "morally emancipated and committed to any consequences." Saunders's homophobic rendering of Francis as unrecoverable "other" fits within the period's dominant heteronormative discourse and he would have certainly been aware of D.H. Lawrence's use of the term in his poem "Pansies" (1929): "now it's a country of ... young washouts pretending to be in love with death."⁶¹ Francis's aberrant sexuality in the stories is pathologized and criminalized, but crucially his behavior is justified through his war experience. This is written onto his "yellow eyes," where there is a glimpse of "murder."

In all of the manifestations of the narrative, salvation is possible only for Cary, and only in the resolution of heterosexual coupling with Nikki. However, the stories give a greater latitude to Nikki's agency. There and in the novel *Single Lady*, it is Nikki's internal thoughts as she enters the Père Lachaise cemetery with Cary that express, almost word for word, the "spent bullets" speech that the doctor gives at the beginning of the film. In the novel Nikki's thoughts function to give voice to her empathy with them, something the film displays through the allusive language games that she plays with them. It is not until the end of the film, when the rest of the flyers are dead or gone, and she gives Cary the heart-shaped stone she saved from the tomb of Héloïse and Abelard, that Nikki shows a more normative love for Cary. Saunders's experience as a film scriptwriter enabled him to understand the need to establish character motivation early when he gave these lines to the doctor at the beginning of the film. Setting out the pathology of the flyers' neuroses at the outset, and having it delivered by the authoritative voice of the doctor, provides the motivations for their behavior and simultaneously engenders pity for them. The *Variety* review approved of this change:

> It opens with a thrill and a tear to suit the femmes, who see Barthelmess and David Manners coming down in a plane and then in a hospital. Before the picture unwinds much further the two are grown into four, all as handsome, shattered airmen wandering aimlessly against life in sensitive and temperamental progress.⁶²

The appeal of the stories, as shown in the letters to *Liberty* and in subsequent reviews of the film, lay in the playful use of the allusive slang and the odd humor. *Film Daily* called it "charming" and "whimsical."⁶³ The *New York Times* critic Mordaunt Hall devoted one and three-quarters columns to the film. He offered a sympathetic bemusement in watching the characters descend into oblivion: "It is an interesting and occasionally brilliant attempt to reflect the post-war psychology of four wounded American aviators." He cited the "curious dialogue and the mad cap doings of the four men and the girl . . . [which] cause one to imagine that the minds of the characters are unhinged," and goes on to list each character by their symptom. He also notes a similarity that Nikki shares with them in this respect.[64] Like the group of ex-flyers, Nikki does demonstrate, through nonsensical phrases of displacement, symptoms of her own traumas. She is in Paris alone because she is running away from the vaguely referenced problems with her mother. She tells a story in the film of how her mother bought shoes that were too small for her and therefore her feet are misshapen. Later, as she goes to run after Cary, who is going to the Père Lachaise, she returns to change her shoes because she "runs faster in red ones."

This use of language as a displacement strategy between characters operates to highlight Cary's and her salvation with each other in that they are, at pivotal moments, able to drop the façade of wordplay. The crucial scene of the film in this respect takes place in the Père Lachaise cemetery, at the grave of Héloïse and Abelard. Cary relates their story, one of lovers united forever in death through Abelard's castration, though the language he uses is oblique rather than allusive: "He gained a footing in a certain household as tutor to a maiden called Héloïse. And employed his unlimited opportunities for the purpose of—Well, betrayal. Not, however, unmixed with real love. He carried her off to Brittany." Saunders, the seasoned scriptwriter, employs the vague term "betrayal" while in the novel he uses the more direct "seduction." Describing the castration as "*the* most brutal punishment" in the film is made more explicit by Nikki's knowing response "Oh dear." In the novel the phrase is "the most brutal mutilation." In an earlier draft of the script Cary's full line ended with "There was left for him only the life of a monk," but this was taken out at the suggestion of John V. Wilson in his notes on the script for the PCA.[65] The film also omits the letter Héloïse wrote to Abelard that is the heart of the legend, which in the novel Cary refers to as "the most beautiful letter there is going."[66] In both cases the allusive language of the banter with the others gives way, in this their private moment, to less oblique references in the telling of the castration tale, which itself alludes transparently to the desensitizing effects of his war trauma.

The castration/impotence theme of the magazine stories, the novel, and the film highlights the way that specific patterns of motivation for characters work within the parameters of recognized public discourse. Yet "Nikki and Her War Birds," *Single Lady,* and *The Last Flight* are explicit attempts to capitalize not only on the burgeoning image of the veteran as forgotten man, but also on the more sensational subject matter of the aberrant activity of damaged men. The *Variety* review of the film noted this and praised William Dieterle's first effort as a director for "keeping the shell-shocked side of the permanently wounded airmen continuously before the audience."⁶⁷ In the process the figure of the veteran, and the medical discourses embodied therein, becomes the justification, at the level of the script, for varied forms of "aberrant" behavior including the fetishization of women and the thinly veiled displacement of impotence onto the physical symptoms of tics, drowsiness, and incessant drinking. While the characterization of Francis as "sexually aberrant" is all but dropped in the film, the residue of this remains in his justified criminalization; it is then a short step to Paul Muni's character in *Scarface* (Howard Hawks, 1932) but an even shorter and more explicit one to Warner's *I Am a Fugitive from a Chain Gang* (1932).⁶⁸

The film was not a complete success at the box office in spite of favorable reviews from the trades. But it is unique in that it stands as one of the few films of this period driven solely by traumatized characters, Nikki as well as the flyers. The "touch" of the war here lies not only in character motivation but in what Mordaunt Hall referred to as the film's "wild and irrational" character. If nothing else, it demonstrates that veteran characters' backgrounds offered broad, wide-ranging, and yet plausible sets of behaviors that were able to drive the narrative in new ways, lending it a sense of "the modern" in revealing at times the otherwise unspeakable.

NETWORK OF THE LIVING DEAD: GRAND HOTEL

A much more successful film, also driven by traumatized characters, was MGM's *Grand Hotel*, released in November 1932. Directed by Edmund Goulding and produced by Irving Thalberg, the film adaptation of Vicki Baum's play, in turn adapted from her novel, followed the comings and goings of the denizens of the Grand Hotel in Weimar Berlin. Where *The Last Flight* sets out the war explicitly as the primary motivating force for the characters' odd behavior, *Grand Hotel*, saturated with the effects of the war, suppresses it. Yet each of the main characters is driven by circumstances that are directly or indirectly the result of its devastating consequences. The film follows six characters whose lives intersect in the Grand Hotel. Baron Felix von Geigern is an aristocrat and war veteran whose family has fallen on hard times, and he has resorted to being a jewel thief. Grusinskaya is an aging prima ballerina from Czarist Russia whose world has collapsed because of the revolution and whose career is on the slide. General Director Preysing is a business owner who is desperately trying to rescue the family firm through a merger with a company in

Manchester. While not stated, it is probable that the business problems are a consequence of Germany's defeat or of the reticence of a British company to do business with a German one. Flaemmchen is a working woman struggling in a post-war economy who sometimes poses nude for magazines to earn extra money and acts as a stenographer and personal secretary (with all that that implies) to rich men. Otto Kringelein is a former accountant with Preysing's firm who has a terminal disease and has decided to live out the last few weeks of his life in high style. Finally, there is Doctor Otternschlag, a veteran surgeon whose face has been half blown away by a grenade, who seems to live at the hotel. Played in the film by MGM stalwart star Lewis Stone, the Doctor is the only character who outwardly wears on his body the impact of the war.

The story revolves around the Baron, who links all of the other characters. He is not what he seems. His position as a Baron is a cover for the fact that he is a thief, broke and desperate for money. He is kind to Kringelein and offers to show him the luxuries of the kind of lifestyle he can no longer afford. His intentions are not honorable, as he knows that Kringelein is carrying thousands of marks in his pocketbook. Further, as a jewel thief, he is initially interested in Grusinskaya's pearls, which she is known to travel with. He takes pity on Flaemmchen, whom he first meets on the fifth-floor lounge, and strikes up a conversation. Throughout the conversation, he offers a gentlemanly counterbalance to Preysing, the dishonest businessman who has hired her services. Even here, though his first encounter with Flaemmchen is flirtatious, it is clear he is not above paying for her services as well. His only straight connection is with the Doctor, with whom he has the unspoken camaraderie of veterans. The Doctor knows he is an aristocrat fallen on hard times—and a thief.

The Baron breaks into Grusinskaya's room to steal her pearls; she returns unexpectedly, so he hides. He sees that she is going to take poison and stops her. They fall in love and he spends the night in her room; admitting he is a thief, he returns the stolen pearls. He then promises to accompany her to Vienna but will not allow her to pay. The following day he takes Kringelein out to buy new clothes, then he takes him motoring, to a boxing match, and finally out flying, all with every intention of robbing him. While at the bar in the hotel, he tells Flaemmchen he is in love with someone else, and witnesses Kringelein telling Preysing what he thinks of him. At a card game in Kringelein's room, Kringelein stakes the Baron but he loses all his money to Kringelein who, with beginner's luck, takes all the winnings of the evening. Kringelein, over-excited, falls ill, and Doctor Otternschlag helps him into bed. The Baron finds Kringelein's pocketbook with all his money in it and takes it. Kringelein wakes up and panics; the Baron has a change of heart and says he has found it and returns the money. Later, with nowhere to turn, the Baron breaks into Preysing's room to rob him. Preysing, about to sleep with Flaemmchen for money, hears him, catches him with his wallet, and beats him to death with the telephone. Flaemmchen runs to Kringelein's room and agrees to accompany him to Paris in the last weeks of his life. Grusinskaya keeps calling the Baron's room but finally leaves, convinced by her manager that he will meet her later. The last line of the film is given to the doctor, who walks toward the hotel's revolving door: "Grand Hotel. Always the same. People come, people go. Nothing ever happens."

This kind of narrative structure was relatively new in Hollywood. Rather than one protagonist pursuing narrative goals with the aid of helpers, or multiple protagonists pursuing the same goal, *Grand Hotel* has multiple protagonists pursuing different goals. This "network" narrative was an innovation that other studios followed, and it reemerges in various manifestations up to the present day.[69] That type of structure depends on rapid and economical characterizations; the character's type indicates early what their narrative goals are and how they pursue them. Preysing is a desperate man who is trying to save his company and ultimately lies to do it. Played by Wallace Beery, his characteristic largesse is incorporated to emphasize Preysing's brutish manner. Flaemmchen is a "stenographer"; she will sleep with her clients for a price but ultimately seeks a better life. Kringelein has a time limit: he wants to live before he dies. Grusinskaya is struggling with her professional decline. The war has affected all of them but it is most clearly evident in the two identified veterans, the Baron and the Doctor. The network structure allows a broader view of characters who are all linked by their shared historical moment and space: Weimar Berlin. The war in this way acts as an underlying motivating factor in the characters' behavior. Unlike the Baron, who seems on the surface to display none of the behavior of a traumatized veteran, the Doctor's horrific facial scarring, like his listless and cynical demeanor, exudes the traumatic impact of the war.

The Doctor, like Nikki in *The Last Flight*, acts as a genius loci, a guide to the other characters and a means of articulating the underlying numb hopelessness they are struggling with. In an early assessment of the playscript, translator Arthur Hanko wrote notes for the director indicating the central importance of the role:

> Must be given by a really first rate actor, because this part has to carry the most important accentuations of the closing scenes of the

acts of this play. He has to maintain a certain weird rigidity, but without the usual stage-diabolism. A halo of coldness and aloofness must surround him.[70]

Otternschlag was to float above the action, avoiding where possible direct interaction with the other characters. This is nowhere more evident than in an early scene at the hotel lobby desk. The Doctor approaches each concierge asking if there are any messages, and in each case the response is no. As he does this, the camera follows him from its position at the center of the circular desk behind the staff. As he passes from one attendant to the next he walks behind the Baron, who is talking to Grusinskaya's ballet master, Pimenov. In an early version of the script Pimenov is to be heard commenting on the various hotel characters "The war dropped them here and forgot them." To which the Baron replies "I was in the war." In the final version of the film it is only the Baron's response that is heard. A small change, but it is enough to provide motivation for the Baron's later actions as well as explain his camaraderie with the Doctor.

The war, then, sits within the characters, submerged into and blending with their varied motivations. Irving Thalberg had seen the play and was attracted to its structure and pace and the interaction between the characters. In the script conference notes he called it "full of life," "a painted carpet upon which figures walk. Audiences love these things if they are properly done."[71] The play had opened with alternating spotlights on each of the characters in phone booths as they spoke. The technique had the effect of introducing the characters quickly and effectively, and Thalberg wanted to employ that in the film. In a script conference held on December 26, 1931, director Edmund Goulding notes that Lewis Stone, who played the Doctor, wanted to know why the Baron had to be identified as a thief from the beginning. Thalberg responded, "it is a story with so many characters and people—the more we understand—each motive—that great drama is involved."[72] The network structure is maintained through the urgency and significance of each protagonist's goal.

The innovation that the film is most known for is going against received industry wisdom by casting A-list stars in all of the main roles. Greta Garbo played Grusinskaya; John Barrymore, the Baron; Lionel Barrymore, Kringelein; Joan Crawford, Flaemmchen; Wallace Beery, Presying; and Lewis Stone, the Doctor. Thalberg noted that it was a "lousy story" about "lousy people" and it was this lousiness that attracted him: "The audience love our characters," as they connect with real people. By casting stars in these roles he had touchable, "realist" characters played

FIGURE 5.4. From left to right: Lewis Stone (Doctor Otternschlag), Lionel Barrymore (Kringelein), and John Barrymore (Baron Geigern) in *Grand Hotel* (Edmund Goulding, 1932). Digital frame enlargement.

by unreachable stars. Using the scene toward the end of the film where the staff are discussing the murder, Thalberg saw the potential in that it would connect with audiences. The staff talk of the guests as the fan magazines spoke of stars; Thalberg saw the potential in their response: "Aha, this is like my life."[73]

Throughout the script conferences Thalberg maintained his insistence on preserving the lighthearted veneer of the play, which he felt depended on sympathy for the Baron. While he, Goulding, and producer Paul Bern employ the network structure, there is still a clear sense of character hierarchy. Preysing is the villain of the piece, offsetting the Baron and reminding each character, apart from Grusinskaya, of the consequences of having no money and the harsh realities outside the hotel. For Thalberg, the critical relationship was that of the Baron and Grusinskaya, and in discussing the final scene where she leaves, not knowing he has died, he explained that he wanted to sustain that feeling with her and that the audience had to believe their love was true.

> I'm certain of this that the greatest and most important thing is the Baron's constant buoyancy that he has over her to make her

feel assured of his ultimate success [in getting the money to go to Vienna] that he'll be there [at the station]. . . . The fact that as he's lying dead and we know it she goes out confident [in her] belief. . . . We can't lose that mood of hers in the play of this terribly dejected creature who went around saying how terrible life is and then completely changes. It was so beautiful.[74]

Similarly with Kringelein, the Baron's relationship is one of tenderness; his gentlemanly nature doesn't allow him to take Kringelein's pocketbook when he has passed out. Thalberg again wanted to keep sympathy with the Baron through these gestures. He liked the way they provided a tension between "suspense and hope": "You get suspense against hope, against hope that when he tries to steal Kringelein's money you don't blame him." He wanted the audience on the side of the Baron, sympathetic, but also with Kringelein. The Baron, his relationship with Grusinskaya, and his empathy for both Kringelein and for Flaemmchen in their conflict with Preysing, enacts audience empathy through romance and compassion. The Doctor, rarely mentioned in the script conferences, is given none of these detailed motivations, not evincing feeling or empathy in the audience. Instead he is the center of the film's vapid modernity, while the others are enacting emotions and desires that will prove ultimately fruitless. Like Grusinskaya's buoyancy, any sense of empathetic engagement the Doctor may show for the Baron or Kringelein is fleeting; it will deflate. Thalberg's idea of maintaining audience sympathy for the Baron is striking in its contrast with the Doctor's visible invisibility. It points to an aesthetic that disavows, but needs, the Doctor for sophistication and affected ennui in order to sustain a feeling of optimism that barely outlasts the end of the film. Each character exits through the revolving door to their darker futures, preceded by the Baron's departure in a hearse.

The network structure in the hotel was complemented by the circularity of the Cedric Gibbons film set. It provided a visual motif for the circulating stories that intersect at given points. The circularity also reinforces the endlessness of drama that goes on in hotels, and the Doctor's positioning in the lobby highlights his centrality. He was described by the MGM reader Clare Peeler, who reviewed the play for Thalberg, as being "terribly scarred in the war and between morphine and cynicism leads a half-dead life."[75] This followed through to the publicity: "The Doctor, wounded in the war, affected with insurable [sic] soul-sickness, watched his fellow guests in the Grand Hotel with morbid interest. Too weary for emotional experiences himself, he enjoys those of the people whom he

FIGURE 5.5. Circular motif in Cedric Gibbons's set for the lobby of *Grand Hotel* underpins the downward spiral of the various characters' stories. MGM/Photofest. © MGM.

watched and listened to in the Grand Hotel. Tragedy and comedy passed before him as if the hotel lobby were a stage."[76] Within the broad circle of the hotel there are smaller circles: the hallways, the reception desk, and of course the revolving door. The Doctor's morphine addiction is not evident in the film apart from the moment when he gives Kringelein an injection when he has collapsed after the card game in his hotel room. In the novel the morphine addiction is one of the Doctor's main characteristics. But, as in the film, a critical point in this regard is his treatment of Kringelein. The injection he gives Kringelein comes from the little black satchel he carries with him. In the novel, once Kringelein is asleep, the Doctor uses the revolving door metaphor when he tells the Baron, "Just sit in the Lounge and watch the revolving door . . . you'd think it was crazed. In and out. In and out . . . suppose you come in through the revolving door you want to be sure you can get out again." He plays with the syringe. "You must be able to die when it suits you . . . I am a living suicide. . . . One of these days I shall take ten of these ampules and inject them into my veins, then I shall be a living suicide no longer."[77] The Doctor's nihilistic ennui is glossed in the film but not completely absent. Instead of being verbalized, the Doctor's mental state is relayed through makeup, costume, and figure of movement. At times he floats around the periphery of the scenes where other characters are the main focus. At the beginning of the film he hears Kringelein pleading with the snobbish concierge for a suitable room. He literally floats above the flowing movement of people in and out of the revolving door, across the lobby floor, and at the bar. His dead glass eye and distorted ear guide the network structure, focusing on important narrative moments in each character's progression. Rather than excise the Doctor to tell an entertaining story, Thalberg and Goulding reinforce his centrality visually. The effect is like water flowing down a drain, reinforced by the emphasis on the Doctor's proclamation of "always the same" as he sits observing an endless and purposeless whirling universe. He is a dead calm center, shaped by the war which, as a deep motivating vortex, guides the characters' behavior and directs their intersecting narrative lines ever downward.

CONCLUSION: MODERN SENTIMENT

Grand Hotel inverts John Balderston's directions for modernizing the story of *Smilin' Through*. Instead of filtering an old-fashioned story through the modern problems that washed up on the waves of post-war attitudes toward marriage, sexuality, mental illness, and enablement, Thalberg and Goulding work into Baum's modern story their own understanding of audiences' hopes and anticipations: filmgoers left having seen a nihilistic tale with "beauty, glamour, (and) romance" told with well-known stars, Cedric Gibbons's design, and the choreography of the camera and editing by William H. Daniels and Blanche Sewell, respectively. Maintaining buoyancy through the exotically modern mise-en-scène and the enigmatic Doctor Otternschlag allowed them to avoid the "cheap hokum and false laughs" Balderston cautioned against.

Such a strategy in *Grand Hotel* incorporated romance and sentimentality as a leavening device rather than a transcendent power: the characters disappear out of the revolving door at the end of the film to be replaced by a young American couple in motoring leathers and with attitude. They could be introducing a screwball comedy. The romance dissipates with the Doctor's wry comment that "nothing ever happens."

The veteran characters in *Humoresque*, both versions of *Smilin' Through*, *A Bill of Divorcement*, *The Last Flight*, and *Grand Hotel* demonstrate variant strategies of character motivation across the period between 1921 and 1932. I have tried through these six examples to illustrate the classical systems' dynamic relationship with the shifting public attitudes and discourses that surrounded the veteran. Lea Jacobs has argued that during the 1920s, with the rise of the new American literary voice, the studios were responding to broader shifts in taste preferences, away from sentiment. She has noted that, rather than being completely suppressed, sentiment persisted within a dynamic with emerging modern sensibilities such as those represented by the naturalism of von Stroheim's *Greed* (1924) and the sophisticated comedy of Chaplin's *A Woman of Paris* (1923).[78] These six films, where the veteran plays a critical role in framing sentiment through a modernizing effect, offer some support for that argument. The veteran as a character in a system dependent on plausible motivations, combined with the popularity of stories set around the war and its consequences, enabled a balance between sentiment and the "real" problems made manifest by it. The veteran character allowed a flexibility and latitude for scriptwriters that helped solve the problem of how to make a sentimental story current. What is evident in these examples is that those motivations have a historical specificity. In *Humoresque* the cure for neurosis lay in the purity and intensity of the love between Leon and Gina, a current popular assumption at the time. It was a sentimental ending added to a "realist" depiction of life in the Jewish tenements of the Lower East Side. In the first version of *Smilin' Through* the treatment depended upon the star persona of Norma Talmadge as flapper. A decade later, the second version incorporated the send-off as a means of allowing Norma Shearer to build on her already existing persona of a woman with desire. At the same time, the depiction of Kenneth's return allowed more sophisticated references to the pathologies of shell shock as they were known at the time. Both of these factors modernized what script consultant John Balderston had called a "remorselessly dated" story. In this way the treatment made the story relevant and up-to-date for contemporary audiences through reference to the plight of veterans, which had reached a peak with the Bonus March in 1932. *A Bill of Divorcement* refocused a tract protesting British marriage legislation onto the relationship between a daughter and her shell-shocked father with the effect of her rejecting marriage, a characteristic that became a central pillar in the construction of Katherine Hepburn's star persona. Barrymore's depiction of "insanity brought on by shell-shock" drew on his background in performing inner conflict that had a basis in a popularized perception of Freudian theory. Finally, two films—*The Last Flight* and *Grand Hotel*—offered innovations through style and characterization that in different ways responded to the prevailing drift of taste preferences from the sentimental by invoking characters and settings imbued with the ennui of the Lost Generation. Each of these offers evidence, through the roles of the veteran characters and their desires and motivations, of the ebb and flow of the memory of the war, and a contribution to innovations within the classical system.

Chapter 6

WAR RELIC AND FORGOTTEN MAN

Richard Barthelmess as Celluloid Veteran

The hero thought the heroine as lovely
as could be
And she as much as told him there
was none so nice as he
And though she had a crooked nose
And couldn't crash in beauty shows
And he was shell shocked—all this
goes
To cheer up you and me
—Rose Pelswick, Review of *The Enchanted Cottage*,
NY Evening Journal, 14 April 1924

At the end of the picture, I am certain you will not feel that Tom has lived in vain, as after all, in the story we are doing nothing but telling the life of Christ, a man who lived and died for the people but they never realized it until centuries after he was gone.
—Memo from Darryl Zanuck to William Wellman
on the ending of *Heroes for Sale*, March 8, 1933

Warner Brother's producer Darryl Zanuck's comparison of the character Tom Holmes with Christ in *Heroes for Sale* (1933) provides an insight into how the characterization of the veteran in Hollywood feature films had developed in the fifteen years since the armistice. Those years laid the foundations for the cultural commemoration of the returning veteran in the United States. Tensions between modern and traditional efforts to imagine the veteran's experience during and after the war generally played out across art and literature and were often divided along the lines of elite and popular forms. The returning veteran was an embodiment of those competing discourses, each seeking to make sense of the war. At times of commemoration the veteran was a relic of the past to be honored and feted, but during periods of social unrest the veteran became an unwelcome reminder of the war's cost and a threat to the social order, a forgotten man. Through fiction films and newsreels, the Hollywood industry's status as an aesthetic, commercial, and social phenomenon offered a significant contribution to the cultural construction of the veteran. The veteran as a character offered a means through which reliable storylines could be brought up to date, and social issues such as disability, marriage and sex, and the deprivations brought about by the Depression could be explored—and exploited. Film actors could demonstrate their talents through the wide emotional and psychological range these characters demanded. Fredric March, John Barrymore, Lewis Stone, and Richard Barthelmess had played veteran characters and enhanced their reputations. This chapter will look at how the veteran character helped to shape Richard Barthelmess's star persona through connecting the type of roles he played in his early career with his portrayal of veterans of the Great War.

Tying the veteran as martyr to the Depression allowed Zanuck to put a topical spin on previous depictions of the veteran as pitiable-but-noble that had held sway throughout the 1920s. Zanuck's choice for the role of Tom was veteran actor Richard Barthelmess, a star of the silent era of the 1920s. Barthelmess had made the transition to sound through his depictions of war-torn characters, most notably as Captain Dick Courtney in *The Dawn Patrol* (1930) and as Cary Lockwood in *The Last Flight* (1931). Zanuck's casting of Barthelmess drew on his star persona that had been built on "b'gosh" roles of boyhood innocence lost, most notably in D.W. Griffith's *Way Down East* (1920) and Henry King's *Tol'able David* (1921).[1] The boy-into-man roles he had become known for also included a number of returning war veteran scenarios such as John S. Robinson's *The Enchanted Cottage* (1924) and Alfred Santell's *The Patent Leather Kid* (1927). In veteran films and the aviation cycle he played characters for whom the traumas of war were central motivating forces. His role in *The Last Flight* as Lockwood, a traumatized airman who, along with his three comrades, instead of going home goes to Paris to drink, acted as a quasi-sequel to *The Dawn Patrol*. His persona as the conscientious hero led quite easily from the troubled aviator in *The Dawn Patrol*, who sends inexperienced boys to their deaths and drinks constantly to dull his senses, to the rudderless veteran on a never-ending binge in post-war Europe. Barthelmess's career, from his portrayal of a wounded flyer in *The Enchanted Cottage*, through his role as a cowardly boxer who finds his courage on the field of battle in *The Patent Leather Kid*, to the reformed addict in *Heroes for Sale*, illustrates the role of the star system and its attendant fan culture in the construction and development of the returning veteran as a persistent after-image of the war.

THE VETERAN AND THE SOCIAL PROBLEM FILM

Throughout the 1920s and early '30s, Hollywood's treatment of the returning veteran orbited around a theme of sacrifice, at times incorporating "traditional" reverence and "civilian debt" themes that had been associated with Civil War veterans[2] and with British litanies of remembrance post-1918.[3] At other times the representation of the veteran in Hollywood narratives diverged toward a more modern mode that, as in *Heroes for Sale*, explicitly attached the veteran to social and political upheaval. The latter was particularly true of Darryl F. Zanuck's approach at Warner Brothers. Zanuck had taken charge of Warner's production schedule in 1930 as the effects of the Depression were being felt across the industry. He developed a distinct and economic house style that adopted "a bleaker, darker world view [that featured] fast-paced, fast talking, socially sensitive (if not downright exploitative) treatments of contemporary stiffs and lowlifes, of society's losers and victims."[4]

By 1932 it had become clear that public opinion was swinging toward presidential candidate Franklin D. Roosevelt, and Zanuck's production decisions began to reflect this. The veteran was pivotal in his strategy of aligning the studio's product to Roosevelt's New Deal. *I Am a Fugitive from a Chain Gang* (1932) was based on a true story of a returning veteran conned into committing a crime and sentenced to hard labor on a Georgia chain gang. The film was tough and uncompromising, ending with the main character (James Allen) disappearing into the night hiding from the authorities. The "Forgotten Man" finale of *Gold Diggers of 1933* was a Busby Berkeley spectacle that linked the returning soldier with the legions of unemployed men on American streets. In both cases, as in *Heroes for Sale*, the veteran stood in for what Roosevelt referred to in his 1932 "Forgotten Man" radio address as "the forgotten . . . indispensable units of economic power, for plans like those of 1917 that build from the bottom up and not from the top down, that put their faith once more in the forgotten man at the bottom of the economic pyramid."

The story of *Heroes for Sale* was inspired by the sentiments in Roosevelt's speech. Barthelmess plays Tom Holmes, a wounded veteran whose heroics have been unfairly claimed by his cowardly friend Roger. Because of the pain of his wounds he becomes addicted to morphine and, once this has become known, is fired from his job at Roger's father's bank. He kicks his habit, marries Ruth (Loretta Young) and, while working at an industrial laundry, gets his fellow workers to invest in a machine to decrease their workload invented by his German communist friend Max (Robert Barratt). At Tom's instigation the workers club together to pay to get Max's invention patented. However, the benevolent laundry owner dies of a heart attack, and after the company is taken over most of the workers lose their jobs. While Tom tries to stop the workers from rioting, Ruth is killed in the violence and he is arrested as an agitator. After his release he uses the money he has made on the patent to continue the soup kitchen where he first found help. Under the scrutiny of the "Red Squad" he is forced to leave town and he goes off into the night, leaving his son, Bill, with Ruth's best friend, Mary. The final scene depicts Bill and Mary looking at a plaque commemorating him. She tells him that his father has "given everything, taken nothing." In the final shot of the film the camera moves into a close-up as the boy says "I want to be just like my Dad."

This final shot completes the work of the film, and the intention of Zanuck, which is to enshrine Tom as a memory. Like Allen at the end of *I Am a Fugitive from a Chain Gang*, Tom is not dead but wandering the countryside under cover, a haunting reminder of the consequences of the Depression. Warner Bros. under Zanuck in this period offers a rare transparent example of the interplay between social and political events and conscious aesthetic choices within a popular culture industry. Crucially, as with all commercial film production, Zanuck's use of the veteran in these films was designed with an eye on the box office rather than altruism. Zanuck's method for the social problem film cycle at Warner's was an emphasis on what he called "headline" stories that had hard-hitting and topical resonance.[5] This set Warner apart from the other major studios, while the "documentary" production techniques they employed aided in reducing production budgets, which had become necessary with the downturn in the economy. Zanuck also reduced costs by setting *Heroes for Sale* primarily in the city, where the action could be shot on permanent sets and in the rooms of small apartments, plus he used cheaper contract players in supporting roles.

FIGURE 6.1. Richard Barthelmess in *Heroes for Sale* (William A. Wellman, 1932). Warner Bros./Photofest. © Warner Bros.

Zanuck's method incorporated an economical approach to building the careers of contract players into stars. Typecasting actors on much smaller salaries, like James Cagney and Edward G. Robinson in gangster roles in *The Public Enemy* (William A. Wellman, 1931) and *Little Caesar* (Mervyn LeRoy, 1931), avoided the considerable cost of an established star.[6] However, economies of this kind were not possible with an established star like Barthelmess, whose salary of $125,000 per picture was the film's most significant expense. Consequently, when devising a project for such an expensive star, it was important to cut costs elsewhere. Stories like *Heroes for Sale*, which had the topical working title of *Bread Line*, sprang from the newspaper headlines and originated in-house, were more desirable than expensive adaptations of successful novels or plays.

Barthelmess's salary was based on his successes throughout the 1920s. Warner had taken up his contract when they acquired First National Pictures in 1928 and he had been a bankable star for them in

The Dawn Patrol, *The Last Flight*, and *The Cabin in the Cotton* (1932). In line with Zanuck's method, the genesis of *Heroes* lay in the search for a project for Barthelmess that used the characteristics of his persona, was generated within the studio, and had topical impact. According to Robert Lord, who wrote the script with Wilson Mizner, Zanuck was "stuck for a Barthelmess story." He and Mizner discussed possibilities for an afternoon but came up with nothing.

> The following morning we received a note from Mr. Zanuck telling us that he had the germ of an idea: 'A soldier who had distinguished himself in the American Army in France gets caught in the depression and ends up in the bonus army.' . . . it was a very timely theme because the newspapers were full of accounts of the bonus army which was marching on Washington.[7]

Zanuck's preferred theme of Christ-like sacrifice fit well with Barthelmess's star persona as a decent guy caught up in forces beyond his control. The story allowed a "bleak" journalistic exposé of injustice replete with "low-lifes and stiffs," with Barthelmess providing the redemptive note of the suffering, righteous veteran. This type of narrative conflict was Barthelmess's stock-in-trade and had been a feature of *The Dawn Patrol*, where his character, Dick Courtney, is torn between his conscience and his orders to send young inexperienced flyers into certain death. Similarly, Cary Lockwood, his character in *The Last Flight*, is caught between his desire for Nikki, a wealthy American woman, and his camaraderie with his fellow traumatized airmen with whom he has decided to drink away his troubles in Paris and Lisbon. The trajectory of Barthelmess's career from the early 1920s demonstrates Zanuck's reasoning for tailoring the role of Tom Homes in *Heroes*, but also illustrates the development of veteran characters across the 1920s and early '30s.

A "WAR RELIC": *THE ENCHANTED COTTAGE*

Barthelmess's portrayals of veterans began with *For Valour* (Albert Parker, 1917), followed by D.W. Griffith's *The Girl Who Stayed at Home* (1919). He first attracted notice as the upright brother to Bobby Harron in this film, which depicted their ordeal as members of the "Lost Battalion." *The Film Daily* described it as "a transformation of Bobby (Harron) from a hollow chested youth to one of Uncle Sam's soldiers."⁸ The film's emphasis on transformation through battle from boy to man would be a theme that Barthelmess would assume following Harron's death in 1920. The next two Griffith films launched the two main trajectories of Barthelmess's star persona. His role as "The Yellow Man" in *Broken Blossoms* (1919) established his credentials as a quality versatile actor, while his portrayal of the young hero David in *Way Down East* (1920) set a template for the transformative boy-into-man roles that he would play throughout the decade.

In 1921 Barthelmess left Griffith to co-found Inspiration Pictures, where he starred in and produced *Tol'able David*, which won the *Photoplay* magazine Medal of Honor as best film of 1921. Adapted from the 1917 *Saturday Evening Post* short story by Joseph Hergesheimer, the film features Barthelmess as seventeen-year-old David, who proves himself by rescuing his girlfriend and her grandfather from their criminal cousins who have taken their farm over, crippled his older brother, and caused his father to die of a heart attack. *Photoplay* described his performance as touching "tragic heights" and said he "portrays the awkward mountain youth with exquisite pathos and whimsicality."⁹

Barthelmess's performance strategy in *Tol'able David* was to grow from carefree boy to responsible man, incorporating a combination of gestures and poses across the film. *Photoplay*'s review illustrates how his acting style informed the popular press's articulation of his developing star persona. His ability to move between "exquisite pathos" and "whimsicality" centered on his alternation between explosive and pathetic gestures at key moments, which complements the medium/medium-long shot/close-up alternation of the film's style. Such integration with camera placement and shot size is consistent with the classical style and industry practice at the time. Even in the medium and longer shots he tends to rely more on his eyes in his facial expressions. It has the effect of making his expressive range alternatively explosive and tentative which, while seeming at times stilted, lent itself well to the portrayal of pensive and righteously angry veterans.¹⁰

Star personas exist beyond the film text through their circulation in fan discourse, studio publicity, and critical reception. During the 1920s and '30s studio control of these was normally either actual or agreed in the sense that journalists and studio publicity departments cooperated in a reciprocal relationship. By 1924, Barthelmess's "sensitive boy" image was well established and provided a basis for a portrayal of the wounded and bitter veteran Oliver Bashforth in an adaptation of Sir Arthur Wing Pinero's 1921 play *The Enchanted Cottage*. In April 1923, the same time as

Barthelmess acquired the Pinero property during its run at the Ritz Theatre on Broadway, an article in *Picture Play* magazine appeared calling for a change in the adolescent roles in which he was being forced to appear. "Dick has almost outgrown his juvenile roles; he is quite capable of doing in his own way the sort of thing that made Valentino famous."[11]

Here Barthelmess is an individual within a system over which he has little control, which echoed the roles he had played up to this time. Yet as co-founder of Inspiration Pictures he had complete control over his choice of roles. The company distributed through First National Pictures, who handled the publicity for all his releases, and he had full knowledge of his film's publicity campaigns. The article functioned as pre-publicity for the film production of *The Enchanted Cottage* and his role as the wounded veteran Oliver Bashforth.

The Enchanted Cottage is a story of an embittered British veteran of the air war, Bashforth, whose body is shattered. His family is insensitive to his plight and he is pitied by his fiancée, who is in love with another but feels duty bound to marry him. He releases her from their commitment and goes to a rural village in the English countryside to hide away. He discovers that the cottage has a history of being let to honeymoon couples across the last three centuries and their ghosts contribute to its pastoral and healing atmosphere. He notices the kindness of a "plain" woman, Laura Cunningham (May McAvoy), and insensitively suggests they marry since no beautiful woman would have him. Her reaction makes him realize his mistake and helps him to find his own capacity for empathy. They begin to see the beauty in each other and, more crucially, themselves. Prompted by the care of the ghostly couples they shed their unsightly exteriors and become beautiful. Believing they have been "cured" they tell their friend the Major, who had been blinded in the war, that a wonderful transformation has happened. He understands and from their excitement can "see" their beauty. When Oliver's family arrives to visit, the Major is enlisted to tell them that Oliver is whole again. When the couple come down the stairs it is clear from his family's reaction that they have deluded themselves and they appear to themselves, and to the audience, once again as broken and ugly. After Oliver's family leaves the Major caresses Laura's face and says they have been the victims of an illusion. Overnight, however, Oliver goes to Laura and the ghosts visit them again, and they awaken in a shaded glen, transformed into their beautiful selves, self-sufficient and beyond the reach of the realities of the modern world.

The choice of adapting this play for the screen made sense as a calculated response to the limited success of Barthelmess's recent films, none of which had matched that of *Tol'able David*. The play's success in London and New York demonstrated the story's appeal and its fantasy element was promising for the medium of film. *New York Times* film critic Mordaunt Hall noted this in his review of the film, calling it "much more satisfying on screen than it was on the stage."[12] It also carried the cultural capital of being written by a famous English playwright. Pinero was known for having initiated "realism" at the turn of the century in the English theatre with plays such as *The Second Mrs. Tanqueray* (1893), a tragic woman-with-a-past drama in which, as a 1925 writer in the *New Republic* said, "the characters and their actions symbolize 'social changes.'"[13] While his reputation as an innovator had waned by the early 1920s, *The Enchanted Cottage* represented a departure for him. *New York Times* theatre critic John Corbin referred to the influence of J.M. Barrie in a piece entitled "Barrieized Pinero," writing, "Pinero has used the best form possible—phantasy—in treating his social theme. [His] experience in an ambulance service made him wish to persuade lovers, especially derelicts of the war that beauty is more than physical appearance."[14] Pinero had first-hand experience of maimed soldiers and the problems they faced and in this play he intended to directly address British post-war grief and anxiety around the disabled returning soldier.

While the play was written for a British theatre-going public, its theme of the physical and mental cost of the war bore relevance to debates concerning the treatment of returning veterans taking place in the US. Since 1919 veterans had faced the uncertainty of returning to civilian life and for the next five years struggled to find a "collective political voice."[15] Debates about the Adjusted Compensation Bill for veterans made headline news throughout the early 1920s. In 1924 the most influential veterans' group, the American Legion, negotiated a settlement that paid veterans compensation in bonds that would not mature until 1945. Later this agreement became the focus of veterans' unrest in the Bonus March of 1932. In April of 1923, during the play's run on Broadway, the plight of veterans became the centerpiece of an investigation into graft and the misappropriation of funds in the recently formed Veterans' Bureau by its head Charles R. Forbes. The suffering of wounded veterans was highlighted in this scandal by the exposure of corruption in the construction and operation of hospitals.

These high-profile issues playing out on the front pages of the press were accompanied by an increased public awareness of shell shock. "Popular journalism reflected, sometimes accurately, sometimes ineptly, the medical developments and the variety of military viewpoints. It dealt mainly with attitudes toward the shell-shocked soldier, speculations about cause, and methods of treatment." By the early 1920s journalists had generally accepted that soldiers suffering from shell shock were "ordinary people who fell ill in spite of themselves," not malingerers.[16] The language of psychoanalysis, albeit often a distorted and reductionist version, had entered the popular press via the topic of the shell-shocked soldier. The physical wounds and the bitterness of the character of Oliver Bashforth resonate with contemporary popular press constructions of veterans. Versions of these journalistic expressions reflecting medico-psychological discourse were evident in the reviews of the play and the film. When the 1922 London production of *The Enchanted Cottage* opened at the Duke of York's Theatre, the press reviews provided a cascade of adjectives that hovered between the physical and the psychological in their descriptions of the wounded veteran. Critics used terms such as "poor wreck," "his nerves wrong" (*The Times*), "pitiful victim," "maimed warrior" (*Daily Express*), and "nerve wracked recluse" (*Daily Telegraph*) in their summaries of the play's narrative.[17] A year later the Broadway reviewers carried on in the same way, describing the Bashforth character as a "broken war victim" (*The Telegram*). Arthur Roland in the *Official Metropolitan Guide* called him "bruised in mind and maimed in body."[18] *New York Times* drama critic John Corbin wrote of Bashforth as a "maimed and shellshocked soldier [who] has buried himself in a remote country village."[19] Each of these adjectives endows Bashforth with the stigmata of physical and mental disability that prevailed during the early 1920s.

Most telling is Corbin's description of him as a "maimed war relic." The use of the term "relic" demonstrates the way the veteran was objectified in popular discourse and acts as a reminder of the war. "Relic" used in this way conflates its reference to the body or remains of saints with an object of remembrance, a memorial. In conjoining the physical and mental, such phrases as "bruised in mind and maimed in body" imply abjectness; the veteran is an uncomfortable reminder of the past. This is borne out in Oliver's relationship with his family and his fiancée. He is an object of their pity and sense of duty. A central dynamic in the early stages of both play and film is that between his fiancée, Beatrice, and his sister, Ethel. He sees his fiancée's desire to partake in physical activity such as fox hunting with a suitor she clearly prefers, and he lets her go. Ethel offers a more persistent reminder of his loss of masculinity; she is uncompromising and insensitive in her disapproval, features reinforced in Florence Short's performance, which *Film Daily* labeled "mannish."[20] Pinero's critique of class indifference and family insensitivity sets up the couple's revelation in the last act. The play was consistent with Pinero's style of depicting "uncomfortable" references to social change: Bashforth's body and demeanor brought the war out of the past, disrupting their comfortable lives. While this prompted critical approval of the stage production, the advice to film exhibitors was more circumspect. Praising the acting of Barthelmess and May McAvoy in the role of Laura, *Film Daily* noted, "It touches on a subject more or less sordid and not a wholly pleasant theme," and in its overall assessment of the film it stated, "Very sincere effort to present a phase of life not often touched upon nor treated. Excellent human interest but do people want the unhappy side of life even with the splendid moral that this story holds?" The reference to "a phase of life not often touched" is a vague euphemism for the depiction of disability that would not go down well with audiences in neighborhood and small-town cinemas. The implication is that it is too highbrow. In *Moving Picture World* Laurence Reid put a more positive spin on the same assessment: "Should appeal with sensitive patrons everywhere."[21] In these assessments the veteran, for "the masses," is an unpleasant reminder of the past, and out of place within the modern entertainment space of the cinema.

In most of the reviews for the film the uncomfortable subject matter is displaced by praise for the performances of Barthelmess and McAvoy. Maurice Henle, syndicate writer for Newspaper Enterprise Association, praised Barthelmess's "change from a wrecked, broken up soldier to himself" as startlingly effective. Henle proclaimed Barthelmess's performance "Another Miracle Man," referencing Lon Chaney's performance as "The Frog" in George Loane Tucker's *The Miracle Man* (1919).[22] Louella Parsons employed the same strategy, pointing to the scene where he "rebels against his crippled, shrunken body" as "the finest thing he has ever done on the screen." [23] Both critics invoke pathos as a marker for quality and artistic merit. The film's theme of two characters made beautiful "through love's eyes," while bound up in a discourse of bodily perfection, endorses the transformation and the determination of the two to reject the discrimination of his upper-class family. Parsons sees that they have been "treated badly by fate." The returning veteran in this sense offers a marker for a shift toward social acceptance of the shell-shocked and the disabled, but one that seems reserved for more "discerning audiences" and not the usual film-going masses.

The scene Parsons refers to comes early in the film, where Oliver confronts himself in a mirror. His state of mind is emphasized by chiaroscuro lighting and the intertitle reads "You misshapen wreck—get away!" Exploding in anger, he throws his cane, shattering the glass. Barthelmess's performance style employs the range of gestures he used to

FIGURE 6.2. Richard Barthelmess and May McAvoy in *The Enchanted Cottage* (John S. Robertson, 1924). Author's collection.

build his character in *Tol'able David*. *The Enchanted Cottage*'s demand for a shift between broken war body and ideal body called for a different strategy, where his rage is turned inward and depended upon a full-body performance throughout. He outlined his approach to the role in the July 1924 issue of *Cinema Art*:

> In the first place I had to work on his face. . . . I had to create hollows under my eyes, drawn cheeks and the scrawny neck of a man whose nerves had been wearing him out. Finally I had to give the impression of his having been wounded . . . so I decided upon a crippled ankle, not because it was easiest to portray, but because it would lend itself to greater contrast when in part of the film Oliver believes himself to have regained his youth and vigor.[24]

While an accurate description of his method, it is also disingenuous, given that the two actors who had played Oliver, Owen Nares in London and Noel Tearle in New York, had also used the crippled ankle motif, with one leg drawn slightly up and the neck twisted distorting the facial expression. Appearing in *Cinema Art* almost three months following the original release date, this looks to have been a strategy to draw attention to the performance and away from a "phase of life not often touched"—that is, disability.

The phrase "derelicts of the war" has a connotation of the broken physical body but also of the abandoned and forsaken veteran. Declaring Oliver a "relic" marked him as an intrusion of the past; as "derelict" this takes on the added connotation of guilt, of civic responsibility and debt to the soldier's sacrifice. The English cottage and its characters act as a refuge from the twin amnesias of heedless modernity (his sister) and stifling tradition (his family), both overvaluing surface at the expense of spiritual beauty. In contrast, the Major is blind but "sees" and understands Oliver's and Laura's beauty as well as his own benevolent role, and the housekeeper, Mrs. Minnett, knows that their cure lies in the spiritual presence of the ghostly couples and the cottage itself. Hence, the village and its inhabitants offer an idealized space where the ravages of fate are accepted. Pinero's didactic blend of fantasy with "realism" proposes the benevolence of an ideal society in order to provide the environment for Oliver's self-realization. His bitterness and anger derive from an obsession with his own body; it is not until he is absolved of his solipsism through illusion that a love that is healthy, balanced, and virtually devoid of sexual desire can become his cure.

The film's second intertitle explicitly sets out the problem returning veterans faced: "In the Great War Oliver Bashforth, like many of his comrades, had found heroism a daily commonplace—but after came the real struggle—to fit a helpless body into a cruelly indifferent world." Yet the solution is through fantasy: the couple remain in the liminal space of the enchanted community, between worlds, between modernity and tradition, between desire and chastity, but also between the living and the dead.

The intertitle offers one indication of scriptwriter Josephine Lovett's attempt to bring home the topical nature of the film to US film audiences. An early version of the script introduced the characters Laura and Oliver on Armistice Day at the Tomb of the Unknown Soldier at Westminster. However, the first two shots are at the dedication of the Tomb of the Unknown Soldier in Arlington cemetery in Washington, DC. The script called for a montage of monuments representing the Allied powers. The script directions for the first shot are: "Open up on Unknown Warrior's grave at Arlington. . . . Facing it are two couples, one of wealth, position, breeding; one of toil, poverty, kindliness. The former placing a magnificent floral tribute, the latter laying a bouquet from the old farm soil. They rise and see each other." The next scene is a pantomime of the two couples "sharing the memories of their sons."[25] Following similar shots at the Arc de Triomphe in Paris and in Rome, the script introduces Laura and Oliver at Westminster, where they do not know each other. Laura, a governess, has with her a child who asks if his father is in the grave. Then a shot of Oliver limping toward the tomb is followed by the title "Oliver Bashforth seeks from a silent comrade the courage to 'carry on' . . . to keep a straight soul in a twisted body." The child then asks how his father and Laura's brother could be in the same grave. Oliver's title follows: "It is the best of all of us that lies there son. So your Miss Pennington is right." The scene's connection with the Unknown Soldier was intended to underscore the status of Oliver as not of this world: "the best of all of us" lies in the grave.[26]

The construction of monuments and the order of the ceremonies surrounding Armistice Day were high-profile issues in 1924. Commemorations provided platforms for veterans' groups and individuals to exercise their political voice. The money spent on the building of monuments to American servicemen in Europe by the American Battlefield Monument Commission, the pilgrimage of Gold Star mothers to Europe, and the Veterans Bureau scandal gave rise to a feeling among veterans that more attention was being paid to the dead than to the living. "Although Americans were united in their desire to pay tribute to those who fought and died, they could not agree on the precise nature and intent of Armistice Day rituals."[27] Published three months after the release of *The Enchanted Cottage*, veteran Laurence Stallings's autobiographical novel *Plumes* (1924) set its final chapter at the Arlington tomb on the Armistice Day of the burial of the bones of the Unknown Soldier. The novel charts the ordeal of returning veteran Richard Plume, who suffers extreme chronic pain from wounds received at Belleau Wood and endures the indignities of unemployment, poor pay, and an insensitive society. The final scene takes place at the open crypt. Richard, because of chronic pain in his leg, is unable to negotiate the steps and sits and watches his son and his veteran friend Gary walk up to the grave. In a scene similar to that of *The Enchanted Cottage* his son Dickie asks what the grave is for and Gary replies:

> "For a soldier to sleep in."
> "Why doesn't he sleep in his bed?" Dickie was puzzled.
> "General won't let him," Gary said solemnly.[28]

The bitter irony of Stallings's scene stands out against Oliver's sadness and indicates the work of the film to override the conflicts of the returning soldier that Stallings's novel seeks to expose.

FROM WAR RELIC TO FORGOTTEN MAN

The use of remembrance ceremony had the effect of equating Oliver with the venerable dead, adding a dimension to Barthelmess's persona that was latent in his boyish image. Through the reviews' emphasis on his performance of disability, Barthelmess emerged from *The Enchanted Cottage* with an idealized spiritual masculinity. An article in *Picture Play* by "psychoanalyst" Don Ryan offered a profile of Barthelmess's appeal to women as a screen lover:

> Barthelmess is the boy lover whom every woman has in the back of her head.... The woman fan who watches Dick Barthelmess enjoys a spiritual companionship. The physical cripple of *The Enchanted Cottage* steals into her heart divorced of the lame body, aflame with the flame of the spirit.[29]

Ryan contrasts Barthelmess's "spirituality" with Valentino's corporeal attractions. His description of Valentino feminizes him: "Valentino makes capital of his physical charms as any feminine vamp would do. He has a fine pair of legs, developed by dancing.... The women, God Bless them, want to see them."[30]

The comparison supports Miriam Hansen's reading of Valentino as a "figure and function of female spectatorship" who "provoked an almost hyperbolic display of patriarchal ideology."[31] The incipient racist and homophobic discourse in Ryan's comparison highlights how Barthelmess inhabited a "from-boy-to-man-through-conflict" narrative of heterosexual white masculinity, which sat easily within the predominant discourse of the heroic (white) soldier.[32] Both the spiritual, asexual masculinity and the hegemonic representation of the white soldier in memorial and commemorative culture was a comfortable fit with Barthelmess's boyish innocence that informed Zanuck's decision to construct the Christ-like sacrifice of Tom Holmes in *Heroes for Sale* for him.[33]

Barthelmess made nine more pictures for his company, none of which were remarkable box office, and he continued to attract mild criticism for not changing. His performance in the British colonial adventure *The White Black Sheep* (Sidney Olcott, 1926) was summed up by *Photoplay*: "Richard Barthelmess again plays the wondering boy who fights his way back for dear old England this time. Hokum."[34] In 1926 Barthelmess accepted a lucrative offer from First National Pictures of $375,000 for a three-films-a-year deal and closed Inspiration Pictures. His first was *The Patent Leather Kid* (1927), a big-budget feature designed as a road-show with live orchestral presentation and sound effects. The film was adapted by Adela Rogers St. Johns from a 1926 *Cosmopolitan* story by Robert Hughes about a boxer who was brave in the ring but a coward at the front. It centered on a romance between The Kid, a tough East Side boxer, and an equally tough wise-cracking dancer, Curley. When war breaks out she chides him for not joining up and then goes to the front, where she dances for the soldiers and works as a nurse. When he does join, the bravery he shows in the ring deserts him, but he finds his real courage on the battlefield avenging the death of his trainer, Jimmy "Puffy" Kinch. Wounded, he is declared a hopeless case by the surgeon, but Curley pleads with the doctor to save him. He survives but is paralyzed. Curley takes him outside to watch a parade of soldiers go by. As they hoist the flag and the band plays "The Star-Spangled Banner" he asks Curley to salute for him. Suddenly he moves his hands a little and then shakily stands up and salutes, and the film ends.

The East Side slang in the titles and the physical performance were a genuine departure from Barthelmess's usual range of country boy or highbrow aristocrat. It still drew on his naïve boy persona but added the theme of social regeneration. The Warner file notes for the publicity recommended tag lines such as "Over the Top with an East side Boxer. The Dramatic Story of the Regeneration of a Soul, with the War as a Background." As a counter to the spiritual nature of his persona, the publicity centered on his character as a street tough transformed: "The crowds hissed when his padded fists flew—He sneaked through battles a yellow slacker—yet he came back from the war a man."[35]

Barthelmess's performance is genuinely energetic. Again he employs the combination of intense facial expression with powerful upper-body movement in the scenes in the ring but contrasts those with a minimal stillness and vernacular "tough" gestures outside. On the battlefield he incorporates full-body gestures to mark his shift from cowering in a foxhole to expansive heroics. Director Alfred Santell's depiction of the underworld of 1917 New York set up the transformation where his wounds and the love of Curley make him a hero and a patriot. While Barthelmess's persona as boy-transformed-through-violence remained intact, the film inverted his role from country boy to city tough and from English gentry to American urban denizen. Lea Jacobs has traced the aesthetic lineage of anti-sentiment in "masculine" cycles of 1930s Hollywood films to developments in the 1920s. These include "films involving smuggling and urban crime."[36] *The Patent Leather Kid* demonstrates an attempt by First National to modernize Barthelmess's persona. Jacobs sees the emphasis on vernacular language, demonstrated in the Stallings/Anderson play *What Price Glory?* (1925) and in films like *Underworld* (1927), as signaling an incorporation of "what was understood to be a modern, terse and elliptical mode of narration."[37] The appeal of Hughes's story was partly in its evocation of city vernacular. Indeed, vernacular was central to the intertitles and to Barthelmess's performance. Mordaunt Hall of the *New York Times* wrote, "He makes the kid, what is colloquially termed hard boiled, without exaggerating the tendency to talk out of the side of his mouth."[38] Hall's review does not mention *Tol'able David*, which indicates the success of First National's revitalization of Barthelmess' career by hardening the boyish image, rather than discarding it.

The Patent Leather Kid shifted the "war-torn body" aspect of his persona from "war relic" in *The Enchanted Cottage* through the regenerated body of the Kid pointing to the "forgotten man" role in *Heroes for Sale*. It modernizes his earlier persona through its urban setting and by attaching war narratives to the boyhood-to-man trope.

Barthelmess's career at First National and then at Warner benefited from the choice of stories that worked off a modernizing motif. His roles in *The Dawn Patrol* and *The Last Flight* linked him specifically with the traumas of the battlefield and the mental anguish that followed. The residue of these roles of the veteran wrestling with internal forces shaped the later part of his career. Prior to the release of *Heroes for Sale* he played an airline pilot grounded because of a crash in *Central Airport* (1933). In this civilian aviation film Barthelmess plays Jim Blaine, quite plausibly a veteran whose restlessness is motivated by the guilt of the crash. Blaine is "decent guy" caught up in troubles that make him a social outcast. The patina of "guilt" that Barthelmess's characters bear became a part of his persona in the remainder of the '30s, notably his role in Howard Hawks's *Only Angels Have Wings* (1939). Neither of these roles has the specific connection to the war that *The Enchanted Cottage* and *Heroes for Sale* do; they simply play off an established and evolved role that incorporates narrative conflicts and behavioral patterns in the script that are more explicitly addressed in *Heroes for Sale* as indicative of the plight of veterans as the "forgotten men" of the Depression.

I have tried to point to some specific convergences between the evolving star image of Richard Barthelmess and the memorialization and regeneration of the veteran across the years 1924 to 1933. His persona in the sound period resonated with certain constructions of the veteran circulating in the popular press. The change from country boy to war relic to forgotten man made him an icon of boyish innocence profoundly affected by the physical and psychological traumas of the Great War. The veteran's image as "Forgotten Man" was manifest in the presidential campaign with Roosevelt's 1932 speech as a means of incorporating the wave of public sympathy with the veterans of the Bonus March. Zanuck understood the convergence of Barthelmess's persona with the veteran as it had been developing since *The Patent Leather Kid*. In a memo to director William Wellman during production of *Heroes for Sale* he emphasized the connection: "I thought Barthelmess very good in this stuff. . . . When you shoot the episode at the end of the picture I want a Roosevelt Speech."[39] The speech did not make it into the final picture but his explicit reference to it highlights the ways in which the Barthelmess's persona had explicitly been shaped by and in turn contributed to the construction of the veteran in Hollywood feature films up to then.

Chapter 7

THE AFTER-IMAGES

The behavior of veteran characters in Hollywood cinema in the 1920s and '30s, as we have seen, needed almost no other rationale than that they had been in the war. The causes of the whimsical double entendres in *The Last Flight*, Dr. Otternschlag's ennui in *Grand Hotel*, and the internal turmoil of Oliver Bashforth in *The Enchanted Cottage* were self-evident. The experience of war was sufficient and plausible motivation. Dr. Otternschlag's floating presence and disfigured face and Oliver's twisted body acted as physical manifestations of that experience, but in neither case was the character malevolent, just damaged. Francis "the Washout" in *The Last Flight* commits a killing, although justified, and disappears into the void, most likely to the criminal underworld. He has learned to kill in the war, a skill that is not legally useful in peacetime. Each of these characters is a discarded relic of the past.

The war as a factor also had the effect of modernizing character motivation, such as that of Norma Shearer's Kathleen in *Smilin' Through*, whose desire for Kenneth is physical as well as spiritual—and it is urgent. She is not willing to wait for marriage; Kenneth may not live through the war. The war-nurse cycle, albeit short-lived, recasts what Daniel Lord called "the war situation," where the conflict for the nurses is whether to "give in." The war as a setting enabled deeper questions about gender relations and women's sexual desire to be cast as a conflict between outmoded traditional and up-to-date modern behavior.

However, while the war's social impact augmented the conflict between traditional and modern as character motivation and narrative engine, its influence was not confined to films with war settings. The memory of the war is less evident, or indeed present by its absence, in certain film cycles of the period. The cycles also map across changes in taste preferences through the 1920s and '30s as in the trajectory of the geometry of memory from vertical to horizontal, the move from the heroic to reflections on the futility and waste of war, in the ground war and air war films. With Hughes's *Hell's Angels* the emphasis on the sensation of aerial combat scenes was a central attraction, and in that sense the aviation film defined and in turn was defined by the medium of cinema. On this level, war films traded in the extraordinary and the sensational much as did thriller melodramas, horror, the gangster film, comedy, and even the musical. Those apparently unrelated genres had at times some recourse or reference to the social impact of the war, whether as backstory or character behavior. While these were most clearly expressed in explicit references, particularly in terms of motivations of characters, the war also came through as a less direct factor in the aesthetic makeup of genres and styles. In this way the war's memory rides along in horror, for example, through its focus on the body, in the crime film in terms of the appearance of the remorseless killer, and in the social problem film in highlighting social injustices. This final chapter sets out to explore this after-image of the war in certain apparently unrelated genre films.

EXTRAORDINARY BODIES

The boundaries of horror overlap with other genres such as science fiction and earlier forms of sensational melodrama. While the term "horror" was used sporadically in the early period and through the teens, Gary D. Rhodes has noted that there is not an identifiable cycle of films that the contemporary trade press referred to as horror in that period. Instead there were a number of films that were "horror themed" that included reference to ghosts and dreams, as well as versions of well-known literary works such as Mary Shelley's *Frankenstein; or, the Modern Prometheus* and Robert Louis Stevenson's *The Strange Case of Dr. Jekyll and Mr. Hyde*.[1] The horror film as an industry category as such does not make an appearance until the success of German Expressionist films made in the early 1920s attracted the attention of the studios, and then, with the coming of sound, the horror cycle of 1931–36.[2] In both cases Universal Studios produced the successes that began the cycles. In the 1920s Lon Chaney starred in two big-budget productions, a rarity for Universal at that time: *The Hunchback of Notre Dame* (Wallace Worsley, 1923) and *The Phantom of the Opera* (Rupert Julian, 1925). With the arrival of sound, Universal produced the two definitive films, *Dracula* (Tod Browning, 1931) and *Frankenstein* (James Whale, 1931), that kicked off the cycle in the 1930s. None of these films have an explicit reference to the war. Instead they evince a sensibility in their depiction of the extraordinary body of the monster, in references to the supernatural, ghosts, and the undead, and the crises in discourses ranging from the moral to the medical and the legal that were in part accelerated by the effects and damages of the war.

Returning wounded veterans interrupted the normative social construction of disability in the US. The veterans who had been injured or permanently disabled during the war were "made that way" through their service to the country. Rather than being congenitally disabled the wounded veterans wore on their body their service and the debt owed to them by the nation. Rosemarie Garland Thomson points out that disability has traditionally been "Constructed as the embodiment of corporeal insufficiency . . . a repository for social anxieties about such troubling concerns as vulnerability, control and identity."[3] The world the veterans reentered was one where the able body was normative and the disabled body either invisible, exotic, or deviant. The bitterness at having become "other" is described in Laurence Stallings's novel *Plumes*. The main character, Richard, whose leg was shattered in France, is told by his cynical friend Gary, also a wounded veteran, "Here it is. You've lost youth. Not gradually with a compensating acquisition of age. Just plucked out of you raw and bleeding. . . . You think the war robbed you of it, when it only hastened it. Every one loses it, some not so soon as you. . . . You imagine there's no bitterness in the whole world like yours."[4] Gary's measure is the able-bodied; he does not mention Richard's disability, but Richard has crossed over into a world where his disability marks him, first as a veteran but also as disabled. Gary reminds him that with time everyone loses youth, but he also in this implies that eventually his veteran status will diminish against his disability. The world he has returned to is one where disability overrides his humanity and his body has become "extraordinary," bearing the stigmata of the effects of the war but also, in Thomson's phrase, that of "corporeal insufficiency."

The return of wounded veterans ultimately effected changes in the Federal Government's approach to all people with a disability. As a result of the US entering the war in April 1917, Congress enacted pieces of legislation that anticipated the return of wounded veterans. The first of these was the War Risk Insurance Act, which ensured a monthly income for servicemen who had been disabled in the war. Then in 1918 came the Soldier Rehabilitation Act, which committed to providing vocational training for disabled veterans. The move to provide vocational training was extended to all persons with a disability through the 1920 Civilian Vocational Rehabilitation Act.[5] As Martin F. Norden notes, however, this progressive move in legislation was not echoed in the main studio film production. "The movie industry expressed a strong interest in assimilating physically disabled people . . . but as a general rule it rarely presented such characters as healthy in mind and body with steady-state impairments."[6] Immediately post-war the disabled veteran and the legislation designed to rehabilitate raised awareness of society's treatment of all people with disabilities. Yet against this background emerges the work of Lon Chaney and his films that revolved around his performance, in Thomson's terms, of the extraordinary body.

The fact that the studios persisted in mainly negative representations owes something to the entertainment traditions in American culture based in sensation such as circuses, carnivals, and freak shows. These traditions, on the decline by the 1920s from their heyday in the nineteenth century, were being supplanted by cinema. The industry, however enlightened it may have tried to appear, paid attention to its roots in these sensation-based forms and to its audiences' preferences. The popularity of these forms in the previous century can be best understood through the methods of P.T. Barnum and his techniques of publicizing "curiosities" and "freaks" beginning with the opening in 1841 of his American Museum in New York City. Barnum often advertised his exhibits and "hoaxes" in the form of questions. In his exhibit titled "What Is It?" he displayed exotic, often fake "curiosities" and extraordinary bodies such as "Siamese twins" Chang and Eng, bearded ladies, and General Tom Thumb. Thomson sees these shows as coming about at a time in the development of the "new democratic polity" where the older perception of the abnormal body as a portent of divine wonder was being replaced by science and its move to categorize nature. The sublime, extraordinary body "began to be eroded by science . . . to be seen as an aberrant body that marked the borders between the normal and the pathological."[7] Barnum's American Museum burned down in 1865, but the entertainment form of the "freak show" expanded and remained popular in the US until 1940. Thomson provides a cogent account of how these were interpreted by the audiences who saw them. She explains their popularity by pointing out that they "challenged audiences not only to classify and explain what they saw but to relate the performance to themselves, to American individual and collective identity."[8] She points out that the new democratic polity of early nineteenth-century America was invested in the concept of the "common man," and along with it the older meaning of the "monstrous" or extraordinary body as a sign to be read remained resilient. Changes in this social formation "allowed the ancient practice of reading monstrous bodies to thrive."[9] By the mid-nineteenth century such an "egalitarian" sensibility was imperiled by increasing industrialization and the emergence of a new middle class with its attendant rationalism. The consequent insecurities, among the immigrant and working classes particularly, prompted fascination with the extraordinary body of the freak show. The professional culture of authority "threatened the common citizen's sense of mystery and autonomy . . . and pressed an insecure polity to invent a corporeal other."[10] Cinema's emergence was precisely within this environment of the sideshow and the fairground, and as it developed into a pervasive entertainment form by the 1920s it brought the audience of the fairground with it.

The end of the war saw a nexus between the returning wounded/maimed veteran, the legislation designed for wounded veterans then extended to include all people with disabilities, and the competing discourses concerning disability between scientific categorization that distanced the disabled body and the older resilient reading of the extraordinary body. This was all overlaid by the increasing expansion of the film industry. Narratives that explicitly refer to the disabled body in this period intersect with both the civilian disabled body and the disabled veteran and prompt stories that within the fantastic realm of the "gruesome thriller" depict the rational world of science, law, and medicine gone wrong. Turning the rational world upside down, challenging and blurring the normalizing categories of the body, was not only a quality of the freak show, it was also the basis for the André de Lorde plays of the Grand Guignol theatre in Paris at the end of the nineteenth century. Inspired by the work of Edgar Allan Poe, de Lorde's plays were built on rational science and law gone wrong, mad scientist characters, insane asylum settings, and the "extraordinary" bodies of the inmates, often accompanied by copious amounts of blood and gore. These plays push the boundaries of the apparent certainties of a rationally ordered world to their breaking point.[11] While the influence of the Grand Guignol on 1920s Hollywood films is indirect, mainly through its influence on German Expressionist films, it runs parallel with the sensational effect of the freak show in the US. These antecedents and the high-profile issue of state responsibility for the disabled prompted by the returning wounded veterans provide a background for the appearance in 1920 of a cycle of thriller melodramas marked by the popularity of Lon Chaney playing disabled, often malevolent characters. Those factors offer a perspective on Chaney's star persona as it developed across the period as an anomaly, in that it was based on an aberrant masculinity when compared to the athletic masculinity of Douglas Fairbanks or the exoticism of Rudolf Valentino.[12]

At the very beginning of Wallace Worsley's *The Penalty* (1920), the intertitle "A victim of the city traffic" follows the opening credits. The film, starring Lon Chaney, tells the story of Blizzard, an underworld king, who as a child was injured in a traffic accident. In the opening scene we learn that young Dr. Ferris (Charles Clary) has amputated his legs above the knee. The child overhears Ferris's senior physician say that he was wrong to do so and that he has "mangled this poor child for life." Dr. Ferris tells his mentor that there is another wound, a contusion at the base of the skull. So begins a set of motivating factors that drive the story of an amputee who becomes a ruthless lord of San Francisco's demimonde. Blizzard runs his empire from a sweatshop where he brutalizes his women workers, not allowing them to look at him. His rage at his condition has become a malevolent strength and he seeks vengeance on Dr. Ferris, who is now older, and whose daughter Barbara is a sculptor in the city and is engaged to marry Dr. Wilmot Allen (Kenneth Harlan). In a gesture of defiance against the larger social world from which he is excluded, he plans to loot the city by organizing a Bolshevik-type "Red" uprising as a diversion. In the meantime, Lichtenstein (Milton Ross), the head of the Federal Secret Service, sends Rose (Ethel Grey Terry) as an undercover agent to infiltrate Blizzard's operation. Blizzard reads in the newspaper that Barbara wants a model for a sculpture she is planning entitled *Satan After the Fall*. He becomes friends with her, planning to use her as bait to bring her father to his private operating theatre, where he will force him to transplant Barbara's fiancé's legs onto his and then marry her. He has also discovered that Rose is an undercover agent and threatens to kill her. In an early depiction of Stockholm syndrome, Rose falls in love with him. Rose helps him to bring Wilmot to Blizzard's house by impersonating Barbara's young assistant, Bubbles, and telling him she has gone to Blizzard's. Wilmot goes and is captured. Then Dr. Ferris arrives and Blizzard blackmails him into performing the operation. However, when Blizzard awakes, Dr. Wilmot has assisted Dr. Ferris in removing the pressure on Blizzard's brain that had been caused by the contusion he suffered in the accident in his youth. Blizzard is cured and he and Rose now have true love, but Blizzard's henchmen are afraid he will turn them in. While Rose and Blizzard are playing the piano, Frisco Pete shoots him. He tells Rose "Fate chained me to Evil—for that I must pay the Penalty." In the last scene Barbara unveils her bust of *Satan After the Fall* and tells her father, "All that's left of him. An evil mask of a great soul."

Blizzard's accident resonates with cinema audiences' experiences of the real dangers of modernity, of death and injury by accident, and his character evokes the myths of the damaged body as a sign of deviance. This is enhanced by his treatment of particular women he selects from his workforce who are forced consorts and, in an allegory of sexual dominance, are made to work the pedals of his piano as he plays while maniacally proclaiming his desire to "walk as men walk" and be "master of the city." His plan for a Bolshevik uprising was recognizable by audiences as a reference to the "Red Scare" of the previous year. As this film was released less than two years after the end of the Great War, these factors are related to the social and political changes that were being wrought as a result and yet they can also be traced more directly to fears and anxieties that pre-date the war.

For the sake of argument, US audiences may have seen the story as a veiled allegory for the effect the war was having on everyday life. One interpretation available at the time might go along the lines of attributing Blizzard's behavior to two medical conditions that were associated with returning veterans. The first would be the psychological ramifications of having lost limbs and thereby being socially stigmatized. This fits a profile of veterans who were disabled and were forced into crime by circumstances. The second would be the contusion, connecting to shell shock caused by damage to the spine and brain. The belief that actual damage to the nervous system caused neurosis was an early explanation for what is now known as post-traumatic stress disorder (PTSD). Either of these offers an explanation that audiences at the time would recognize. Crucially, however, the film itself makes no reference to the war and suggests that other factors may be more pertinent to the context of anxieties and fears that circulated at the time.

The Penalty was a breakthrough film for Chaney and, along with *The Miracle Man*, where he played a con man who impersonated a man with a disability, initiated a cycle of sensation melodramas that would become his specialty until his death in 1930. *The Shock* (Lambert Hillyer, 1923) and Tod Browning's *The Blackbird* (1926), *The Unknown* (1927), and *West of Zanzibar* (1928) are films where Chaney played disabled characters or characters that are impersonating disability. These films work this into their narratives in ways that use contemporary discourses concerning the interaction between the disabled body, the law, and medicine. *The Penalty* draws from sensation-based realism to construct a crime drama that seems to address the myths that at the time surrounded the medical profession and the disabled body. Similarly, *West of Zanzibar* features the combination of disability and revenge, while *The Unknown* and *The Blackbird* feature Chaney as a criminal who masquerades disability. Each in different ways plays out, and plays with, myths that attach the mark of the disabled body with evil and malevolence.

In his genealogy of the horror film, David J. Skal sees the Chaney cycle as one important precursor to the horror cycle of the 1930s initiated by the Universal classics *Frankenstein* (1931) and *Dracula* (1931). In building his case he points to the use of the disabled body as evidence of the impact of the Great War.[13] That connection draws attention to the broader historical factors that were at play during the 1920s. For instance, the actual narrative reason for Blizzard's condition and behavior, both mental and physical, is a traffic accident. Accidents were an all-too-common feature of everyday life of the teens and '20s. Train wrecks, automobile crashes, and industrial mishaps were tacitly accepted as a hazard of modern life. However, their consequences were far reaching and affected perceptions of law and medicine that intersected with the discourses concerning disability that are central to the Chaney films. The war's high profile in the public imagination during and following the war played a role in effecting the shifting perceptions of disability, but its impact on Hollywood production, and some sense of why Hollywood persisted in ambiguous if not negative treatment of disability, is better understood through this indirect route.

THE TRACES OF THE WAR IN THE CHANEY CYCLE

Skal's historical accounts of both the Chaney films and the key German Expressionist films of the 1920s identify as a consistent sub-theme the role that the Great War plays in explaining their social function and their role in collective memory.[14] They are seen as articulating the profound anxieties and traumas of the war through mechanisms of displacement and excess. Infused in their characterization, their camera angles and mise-en-scène are the traces of the traumatic fissures wrought on the collective body of the nation by the war. The symptoms of war neurosis can be found in the stiffened gait of the somnambulist Cesare in *The Cabinet of Dr. Caligari* (Robert Weine, 1920); the suppressed rage of disabled returning veterans is seen as implicit in the themes of amputations, disability, and madness in the Chaney oeuvre.

Skal is not alone in pointing to the war as a primary influence on the aesthetics of the horror film. Anton Kaes, in his landmark study of Weimar cinema, argues that the profound social and psychological impact of the Great War on film aesthetics produced a "shell shock cinema." He notes that while not all Weimar films of this period can be seen this way, there are key films that demonstrate that this cinema "focused on experiences of loss and grief [that] resonated against a background of shared memories."[15] Kaes is referring exclusively to the experiences of German audiences in the Weimar period and his study centers on that group's shared historical trauma. But he does point to shell shock cinema's aesthetic influence in Hollywood and its contribution "to an emergence of modernist film language that shaped the look of film noir [and] continues to inspire Hollywood's horror and science fiction movies today." He argues that these shell shock films "pushed the limits of visual culture" and were developed in response to the traumatized population in Germany.[16] The result was an indirect impact upon Hollywood production through the influence of the films themselves and émigré personnel such as Paul Leni, F.W. Murnau, and Karl Freund who worked in the studio system.

In outlining *The Penalty* (1920) as a "mutilation-revenge melodrama," Skal states, "Though its theme was veiled [the film] also spoke suggestively

FIGURE 7.1. Lon Chaney as Blizzard in *The Penalty* (Wallace Worsely, 1920). Goldwyn Pictures/Photofest. © Goldwyn Pictures.

of the impotent rage of maimed war veterans who were being assimilated back into society in unprecedented numbers."[17] He also identifies this connection in the productions for which Chaney is probably best remembered, *The Hunchback of Notre Dame* (1923) and *The Phantom of the Opera* (1925). Skal argues "both bore more than a passing resemblance to the faces of the *mutilés de guerre* that haunted Europe and America, with smashed features, missing noses and mouths full of broken teeth."[18] He illustrates this relationship with a 1924 etching entitled *Skingraft* from a portfolio by German artist Otto Dix and with a photograph of wounded French veterans published in *L'Illustration* on June 11, 1927. These are juxtaposed with a photograph of Chaney in his *Hunchback of Notre Dame* makeup in order to demonstrate the similarity and suggest possible sources directly rooted in the war. Like Dix, who served in the German army, the European émigrés to Hollywood in many instances had direct experience of the war or were influenced by and/or were a part of the art movements that arose directly from its carnage.

The relationship to the war Kaes sees in the aesthetics of Weimar Cinema is less clear in the case of Lon Chaney's movies and most particularly with his collaborations with Tod Browning. A number of these collaborations incorporate the lowbrow traditions of the freak show and the carnival as a central narrative and representational strategy. Skal has written on this tradition as it relates to the Browning/Chaney films and in Tod Browning's work over all.[19] In Skal's account, Browning's carnival background plays a central role in the themes of mutilation and freakery in his films. Similarly, Chaney's relationship to makeup is as rooted in the "reveal" aesthetics of the carnival sideshow as it is in the tradition of the theatre. The history and culture of the carnival sideshow rather acts as a backdrop to Skal's biographical approach. Along with Thomson, Robert Bogdan and Rachel Adams in separate studies have offered more comprehensive analyses of the sideshow. From 1840 the culture of the carnival and freak show was profoundly shaped by the industrialization of entertainment, a culture that Bogdan argues is central to what he calls "the manufacture of freaks."[20] Adams highlights the central importance of audiences in comprehending the narratives that surrounded the freak show performances. Like Thomson, she points out that the performances' meaning depends upon an understanding of the varied historical moments of the "audiences and the performers themselves." She also stresses the importance of nineteenth-century modernization as provoking specific narratives of "exotic places, miraculous events or horrifying accidents" in order to "give coherence to bodies that otherwise suggested an intolerable fragmentation and dissolution of meaning."[21] Arguably this is precisely what many of the Chaney films work to do in their employment of exotic settings and accidents in their depiction of damaged bodies. *The Penalty* and *The Shock*, for example, surround their disabled characters with explanatory narratives. Their sensation effect comes from the ineffable nature of the damaged body, made so because it embodies the contradictions inherent in the positivist ideologies of modern progress. His collaborations with Browning take this farther. In *The Unknown* and *The Blackbird*, the Chaney characters impersonate disability and create false histories, which the film's ultimate work is to reveal.

In the case of the United States, which constituted the primary audience of the Hollywood industry, the Browning/Chaney films' construction of meaning might be better illuminated when seen against the background of industrial modernization. The confluence of the returning veteran with the publicized rehabilitation legislation blurs the boundary between the disabled veteran and the disabled civilian. Coupled with competing interpretations of the disabled body mobilized by the freak show, the memory of the war becomes implicit in these films, or at least a *possible* interpretation. The civilian disabled body associated with the wounded veteran body in this way offers a latitude in interpretation. Put another way, the disabled veteran body and the disabled civilian body take on each other's residue so that the disabled body as played by Chaney, sympathetic or villainous, attenuates identification through the prominence in public discourse of disabled veterans' issues and subsequent legislation in 1920. While urban and rural American cinema audiences of the 1920s were no strangers to the ravages of railroad, traffic, and factory accidents on the human body and perhaps even inured to them, the issue of the disabled veteran gave a new perspective on disability. The sideshow attractions of amputees and medical curiosities addressed these anxieties and fears that accompanied everyday life in ways that drew attention to the genuine dangers of the workplace and public spaces such as trains and city streets, and to this can be added disabled veterans. The longer experience with the physical impact of modernization is germane to a more nuanced understanding of how the impact of the war on the body could provide perceptions of disability with a new kind of legitimization.

Given that these factors indicate a deeper set of historical forces at play, the connection between the Great War and the Chaney cycle of sensation films in the '20s (and then the horror cycle in the 1930s) is less direct than some historians suggest. In the United States there was certainly a general social anxiety around the results of mechanized warfare on the human body. At the end of the war and the beginning of the '20s, images and stories of the war in film, magazines, and newspapers continued to be pervasive. In 1931 Frederick Lewis Allen recalled the general currents of feelings:

> A whole generation had been infected by the eat drink-and-be-merry-for-tomorrow-we-die spirit which accompanied the departure of the soldiers to the training camps and the fighting front . . . some of them had acquired under the pressure of war-time conditions a new code which seemed to them quite defensible; millions of them had been provided with an emotional stimulant from which it was not easy to taper off. Their torn nerves craved anodynes of speed excitement and passion.[22]

But as Allen suggests, those anxieties ran across a range of social and moral issues, particularly those to do with sex. And the film industry duly responded with dramas of reckless youth like Cecil B. DeMille's *Manslaughter* (1922) or *A Society Scandal* (Alan Dwan, 1924). Read more closely, however, Allen sets out the war as a catalyst for mobilizing already-existing discourses concerning the effects of modern living. Here a whole generation is "infected" by those men and women who had seen the war and had returned refusing to settle to older ideals and mores. The war for this generation, even those who did not experience it, provided an augmented perspective from which to see the often-brutal terms on which modern life operated. Industrial accidents and the dangers of modern travel had been sources of increasing anxiety for decades. The always present and underlying threat of diseases had been made profoundly acute with the influenza epidemic of 1918. Threats from everyday life were seen more starkly, and the attitudes of war veterans offered a readily available attitude of affected "blasé" and thrill seeking. Seen in these contexts, the Chaney films of the 1920s that have disability and crime at their narrative center are examples that the war provided an enhanced perspective on these pervasive sets of shared experiences of trauma.

THE TRAUMAS OF MODERN LIFE

The Great War did not have the same qualitative impact in the United States that it had in Europe. Far fewer deaths and injuries were suffered by the US armed forces than by Europe's warring nations. Less than

120,000 US personnel lost their lives, compared to almost 1 million British, 1.7 million French, and 2.5 million Germans.[23] The intensity of the experiences of populations in Germany and Britain perhaps helps to explain the sophisticated aesthetic mechanisms of displacement in the German Expressionist films, for example, or in the somber realism of works such as British playwright R.F. Sherriff's *Journey's End* or the "existential dread" of J.B. Priestley's 1928 novel *Benighted*.[24] In the US, concerns over reintegration and employment raised by returning veterans were no doubt highly visible, but of a different order than those in Europe and Britain. In Britain disabled veterans were dependent on charities for assistance, while in Germany the returning soldier was dependent on the Weimar State. In both cases staggering war debts drove the policies.[25] On the other hand, US veterans returned to a booming economy but with high inflation and few employment opportunities. Veterans as a group were perceived by the public largely through a mixture of patriotic pride and political anxiety. Veterans' organizations like the American Legion received considerable attention from the press and were highly visible presences at local celebrations, parades, and commemorations. It is important to note also that veterans were at times imagined as being associated with potentially radical ideologies, particularly communism and anarchy. As Jennifer Keene suggests,

> Fears that exposure to postwar political upheavals sweeping through Germany and Russia might have radicalized returning servicemen led to government surveillance of them. . . . In addition Americans worried, as they have after all wars, whether men conditioned to kill could resume normal lives.[26]

Nevertheless, the most high-profile veterans' group, the American Legion, which led the move for better compensation, were consistently anti-Bolshevist and anti-immigration, at times resorting to vigilantism.[27] Such factors suggest a more complex picture of the war's effects on cinema culture in the US that extends beyond the representations of disabilities and deformities. Or, more accurately, those representations, particularly when applied to veterans, invariably overlapped with dominant perceptions during this period of disability as a representation of moral degeneracy.

In *The Penalty* Blizzard's plans to organize a Bolshevist rebellion piles onto his stigmata as amputee the sinister possibility of insurrection. In the 1913 Gouverneur Morris novel from which the film is drawn, this pathology of duplicity is apparent. Early in the novel Blizzard disguises himself as a down-at-heel organ grinder and from this position on the street is able to oversee his criminal undertakings and schemes:

> Passers were now more frequent. Some looked at him and continued to look after they had passed, others turned their eyes steadfastly away. Some pitied him because he was a cripple, others, upon suddenly discovering he had no legs, were shocked with a sudden indecent hatred of him. A lassie of the Salvation Army invited him to rise up and follow Christ; he retorted by urging her to lie down and take a rest.[28]

This scene does not appear in the film, but the passage describes accurately the regime of looking that the film constructs. The body of Chaney and the virtuosity of his performance is the central structuring object of the camera placement, mise-en-scène, and editing. This is set out in the opening shot of Dr. Ferris cleaning up after the operation, and then his look in the boy's direction motivates a short series of shots of that lead to an iris shot of the boy in his bed, preceded by the title informing us that he is "unconscious of his fate." The iris underscores the boy as the focus of the narrative. Later Blizzard is the object of artist Barbara Ferris's gaze as the model for her sculpture *Satan After the Fall*. Further, he is spied on by Rose, a secret service operative sent to uncover his plans. As if to underscore this structure, Blizzard intimidates the women who work for him and he forces them to avoid eye contact. Rose draws his admiration when he notes that she looks him in the eye. The film's narrative structure and subject/object strategy line up with the curious, the pitying, and the disgusted that Morris describes. In this way the film, through an emphasis on looking and watching that echoes public anxieties prompted by the disabled body, follows the novel in making the explicit connection with the amputated body as potentially politically dangerous. Laid bare is the disruption of the disabled body as evidence of the cost of progress and industry and the fallibility of medicine and science.

The impact of industrialization had rendered amputations and extreme bodily injury publicly visible over the last half of the nineteenth century and up until World War II. The returning disabled veteran entered a public space where the visibility of disability was both common and framed within what disability studies scholars have termed the moral model of disability. This model sees disability as the result of bad actions and as the sign of moral transgression. In effect, the disabled veteran's status as hero was threatened by this model, but also threatened it.

The visible evidence of accidents and deaths in the form of injured workers and destitute widows and orphans was considerable. The appearance in the public space of a disabled worker presented an image that contrasted with the dominant discourse of progress and freedom. Jason Witt's detailed history of the origins of tort law in the United States demonstrates the social disruption and anxiety resulting from such industrial accidents:

> In theory, American workers may have been free laborers. But they were also mangled and torn, disabled and killed at extraordinary rates. . . . By the last decade of the nineteenth century, industrial accidents stood as a vivid manifestation of the failures of industrial capitalism. The amputee workingman and the widowed working-class mother mocked the promises of the capitalist wage labor to deliver greater freedom and rising standards of living. Solutions to the accident problem were thus tightly bound up in the great political struggles of industrializing America.[29]

This high visibility of the human damage of industry and travel appears in Morris's novel. The setting is at a corner across from Washington Square in New York City. Having seen Blizzard begging in the street, Barbara Ferris asks the waif Bubbles if he knows who he is. Bubbles then lists the type of legless beggars that he knows in the street:

> 'There's a half a dozen in the city.' And he named them. 'Burbage: he's the real thing. Got his legs took off by a cannon ball in the wars. Prior: he ain't no 'count. Drunk an' fell under a elevated train. He ain't saved nothin' neither. He drinks *his*. Echmeyer: He's some Jew worth every cent of fifty thousand dollars; They calls him con-ge*yen*etul 'cause he was born with his legs lef' off him. Fun Barnheim: he's a German, went asleep in the shade of a steam roller and he never woke up till his legs were rolled out flat as a pair of pants that's bin ironed. Then there's Blizzard.'[30]

The novel instructs the reader in reading these characters through the moral model of disability. Bubbles' judgments are a set of interpretations and stereotypes of drunks and immigrants told in street vernacular. Burbage the soldier sits at the top of this hierarchy as "the real thing." Military service here is the only status that absolves the stigma of disability. However, each beggar is categorized by the cause of his disability. This, like the narratives that surround the freak show performers, serves to morally categorize their bodies. Blizzard's category, however, is determined only by a sense of fear, since as a street waif Bubbles knows the power that Blizzard wields in the city underworld. When asked by Barbara how he lost his legs, Bubbles replies: "Blizzard don't boast about it like the others. But he ain't no common beggar. He's a man."[31] So in this hierarchy even the soldier does not qualify. Blizzard's power rests, at this point in the story, with a mystery that will only be resolved through the revelation of the root causes of his behavior. An answer that can only come with the aid of Dr. Ferris, the agent of medical progress and compassion.

THE LIMITS OF MEDICINE

The dangers of railroads, which destroyed lives and mangled bodies, had long been a part of popular culture by the time of the Lon Chaney films of the 1920s. Popular songs such as "Asleep at the Switch" and "The Wreck of the Old 97" circulated widely in the form of sheet music and later, in the 1920s, as recordings.[32] Film and stage sensation melodramas featured train wrecks and accidents as narrative devices and as their central sensation scenes. Aldrich outlines the specificities of the anxieties generated by the railroads: "Modern writers on risks have stressed that public perceptions present more than simple accident probabilities. People especially fear risks that are unknown, involuntary, fatal, hard to control, catastrophic and new."[33]

In *The Penalty*'s first scene Dr. Ferris is told he has needlessly amputated the boy's limbs. Here the uncontrollable risks of the traffic accident intersect with fears of medical malpractice. Later in the film, and in the novel, Dr. Ferris's knowledge of the origins of Blizzard's mutilation ultimately gives him the power to make sense of Blizzard's body, and of his mind. In this sense he is enacting the medical model of disability, which seeks to cure or manage disability. Ferris knows that the contusion in Blizzard's skull is the cause of his criminal behavior and hence the film recuperates the fallibility of the medical profession through confidence in its progress.

Nevertheless, *The Penalty* depends to some degree on a deeper sense of mistrust of medicine. The war offered ample evidence of the limits of medical advances as wounded soldiers returned. But as with travel and industrial accidents, this was reified through discourses of social and scientific progress. The war was ratified as an unavoidable laboratory for the advancement of medical procedures, which produced innovations such as blood transfusions and plastic surgery. These positivist tracts countered the considerable impotence of the medical profession when faced with the injuries of modern warfare. In this and in other Chaney films such as *The Shock*, surgery is the miracle cure, performed by a talented surgeon. Both depict modern medicine as ultimately limitless, where the pursuit of knowledge and the process of experimentation lead to progress.

A further historical context is important here. The cinemas in which these films were shown were themselves sources of anxiety. The limits of medicine became devastatingly clear during the influenza epidemic of 1918, which resulted in over 670,000 deaths in the United States alone—a figure that dwarfs the mortality for US servicemen in the war.[34] The epidemic was also subsumed by the patriotic discourse of the war effort: "the flu seemed indistinguishable from the war, as it was enabled significantly by the global travel of military personnel, flourished among the very population that was dying on the battlefield and left similar carnage in its wake."[35] Across the short period of April 1918 to February 1919 the disease spread itself evenly across the rural and urban areas. Cinemas across the country were ordered closed, causing more than financial loss. Citing the deaths of prominent industry figures, *Moving Picture World* wrote, "The gloom that has overshadowed the industry has been made more intense by the ravages of the grim reaper."[36]

That the cinema was a place where disease can be caught and spread was a justification for movie theatres and the films themselves being regulated. This had been a persistent dynamic since the fixed-site cinema became prevalent in the early part of the first decade of the century. The flu epidemic was a dramatic instance of the dangers posed by simply going to the movies. Moreover, the epidemic had a lasting, yet unquantifiable effect that a loss of that magnitude had among the population. Such a significant event must be figured into the horizon of experience of US cinema audiences throughout the 1920s, a background to the first cycle of the horror-themed melodramas.

SHIFTING PERCEPTIONS

It may be that the impact of the war on the perception of disability is a more productive way of exploring the war's impact on cinema culture in the 1920s. Veterans returning home discovered the levels of marginalization the disabled in the previous decades had been living with. Philip K.

Longmore and David Goldberger, in their study of the League of the Physically Handicapped and that group's attempts to redirect public policy on disability during the Great Depression, have demonstrated the institutional discrimination that existed: "Recent scholarship has identified the early twentieth century as the moment when policy makers and health care, charity, social services and education professionals institutionalized the medical definition of disability that dominated public policy."[37] This took place against a background that is helpful in gaining a sense of the visibility and cultural construction of disability during the 1910s and '20s in the United States. Longmore and Goldberger point to instances of discrimination at that time. Courts upheld the rights of railroads and public transport to refuse service to disabled, a terrible irony given that the railroad companies were often responsible for their injuries. Some cities such as New York licensed "cripples" to beg, while Chicago law prohibited the disabled from appearing in the public space at all. The law read:

> No person who is diseased, maimed, mutilated or in any way deformed so as to be an unsightly and disgusting object or improper person to be allowed in or on the public ways or other public places in this city shall therein or thereupon expose himself to public view.[38]

The creation of the League of the Physically Handicapped took place in the early '30s, but there was a considerable set of developments that led to this. One important factor was the discourse on disability applied to the disabled veterans. The practice of medical rehabilitation was a new development for these soldiers, but the model had been based on the crippled children's hospital schools. The disabled veteran was emasculated by the attitudes that lay behind these institutions, which "insisted that manliness could (and would) not be achieved until [he] re-entered the workforce laboring as an able bodied person."[39] Bubble's declaration that Blizzard was "a man" gives evidence to the way that *The Penalty*'s narrative is working through this construction of disability. This is not to say that the film and the novel display particularly progressive attitudes. The character trait in the film that underscores Blizzard's masculinity is bound up in sado-masochism. The treatment of his workers and of Rose the undercover agent makes this clear. However, the agility and unfettered desire of Blizzard marks out his masculinity in spite of his disability. Further, his position as the king of the underworld of crime in San Francisco in the film, New York City in the novel, marks him as a successful if unscrupulous capitalist. Under the terms of the requirements for full citizenship he was "laboring as an able bodied person."[40]

Across the 1920s disabled veterans joined other veterans in their disgruntlement with government and with the institutional construction of them as dependents.[41] Their demands provoked cultural and public policy crises and gradual shifts in the way disability was perceived by government institutions as well as the general public. The civil service had opened job possibilities to disabled veterans only. This prompted protests and valid arguments by the civilian disabled, who made demands for inclusion that began to question the definitions of disability, debates that persist into the twenty-first century.[42]

Jennifer Keene's detailed study of the doughboy and the "remaking of America" points to the radicalization and demonization of the returning veteran that was the result of popular constructions. These had a considerable impact on public policy toward veterans. The formation of the American Legion and the debates that accompanied its lobbying for the treatment of veterans offer a rich field of evidence for how disability and veterans became discursively intertwined. This prevailed into the Second World War, and the strength of the anxieties that accompanied the veterans of the Great War had not really diminished. Of the hearings concerning the GI Bill in 1942, Keene writes:

> No one present at these hearings disputed the need to plan properly this time around for the ex-servicemen's return to society. What they were guarding against, however, depended on how one interpreted the previous twenty-four years. For some advocates, the revolutionary potential evident in soldier's demonstrations of 1919 and the Bonus March (1932) necessitated keeping as many veterans as possible off the streets. The type of law Congress passed, Colmery told the Senate subcommittee holding hearings, would determine if this veteran generation would be a 'force for good or evil in the years to come.'[43]

This characterization of the new veteran gives some sense of the trepidation that the doughboy veterans provoked in public policy. This also offers a backward glance at the characterization of veterans in 1920s and '30s Hollywood films as unstable character types. The gangster cycle of the Warner Studios demonstrate this, as do their "social problem" films such as *I Am a Fugitive from a Chain Gang* and *Heroes for Sale*.

The Chaney films, however, are responding less to the specific impact of the mutilations of mechanized warfare than to the comparatively longer history of the impact of industrialization on the human body. The effect of such widespread public experience of industrial mutilation is a two-way street. This can be seen in the attempts by cities such as Chicago to limit the visibility of the disabled, an effort in public erasure that demonstrates the ideological forces at play. The term "disgust," enshrined in a city ordinance, is driven by a discourse that links sanitation, public aesthetics, and the perfect body. However, its hidden discourse is the fact that a disabled worker was a publicly visible example of the cost of industrial capitalism and the indifference of large corporations to the welfare of their employees.

Chaney's crime thrillers such as *The Penalty* and *The Shock* indulge in an excessive display of the model of moral disability. In the case of *The Penalty* the film attaches a spectacular malevolence to the scar of disability, setting up expectations that are then given an unexpected twist. The real source of the evil is hidden and physiological: it is a contusion at the base of the skull. Further, the complexities of their motivational structures and their characterizations problematize simplistic prejudices based on physiognomic myths that equate disfigurement with evil or malevolent intent. For an audience that had experienced a level of collective trauma in the form of industrial accidents and a devastating influenza epidemic, the image of the returning veteran as unstable and potentially threatening merged with these broader discourses and myths. Yet the mechanisms by which the films bared the devices, however different, were a means of empathizing with the predominant characterization of "the cripple" that offered a counterweight, albeit inadequate, to the prevailing discourse on disability.

BENIGHTED

The original plays *The Enchanted Cottage* and *Smilin' Through* had recourse to a whimsical supernatural world as an antidote to the grief and loss brought about by the war. Pinero intended *The Enchanted Cottage* to offer the British public some relief, while Cowl and Murfin were more directly committed to the existence of an afterlife as a balm for those grieving the war dead. The Chaney cycle of thrillers, while not explicit in reference to the war, provided a direct engagement with the horrific impact of modernity, whether civilian or military, on the human body. The direct reference to the war and the spiritualist themes in the *The Enchanted Cottage* and *Smilin' Through* gave way in the Chaney films to the corporeal and the psychological. Rather than offering solace they display, or reveal, the mutilations of the body and the mind subsumed into already-existing anxieties about modern living. The Universal cycle of horror films that began in 1931 with Tod Browning's *Dracula* and James Whale's *Frankenstein* incorporated both trends but, as with Cheney's films, without direct reference to the war.

The memory of the war as a background in these films is implicit, as Skal demonstrates, and requires reading the war into the films via their historical moment. In these readings the characters, usually the monster, such as Frankenstein's Monster or Chaney's characters, are influenced in their performance and in their makeup by what the scriptwriters, actors, makeup crew, and/or filmmakers may have known of the impact of the war on (usually) male bodies. However, Anton Kaes's model of reading the impact of the war in Weimar cinema differs from Skal's in that his focus is on the unique experience of the German cinema-going public. Kaes employs "shell shock" in his concept of "shell shock cinema" in his analysis of the aesthetics of certain films in which he sees a displaced reenactment of the traumatized psyche of the German nation.[44] Skal, in reading Hollywood horror, employs a "return of the repressed" model, which sees sociocultural and psychological anxieties and taboos emerging in the uncanny atmosphere— the distorted, decaying, extraordinary bodies and performances of the monsters—that induces thrills in a culture where death and injury are hidden away. Kaes, however, sees in the German Expressionist films a different relationship to death in Weimar culture. He notes that the utter prevalence of death and injury suffered by the German population rendered the fantasy worlds of literature and cinema inadequate in providing metaphor, and coping mechanisms, for fears of mortality. He cites Freud's "Thoughts for the Times on War and Death," where Freud suggests that before the war the function of fiction had been to displace those fears. By the war's end there had been so many deaths that "we are forced to believe in it. People really die; and no longer one by one, but many, often tens of thousands, in a single day . . . death is no longer a chance event." Fiction's role had been altered by the war and no longer able to serve a denial of death. Death and mourning were a reality in post-war Germany, not a repressed fear to reemerge in fiction to effect thrill and sensation. Kaes instead points to the repressed as the German defeat in the war, not death and injury.[45] He also limits his analysis to the prestige products that German studios produced such as *Nosferatu*, *Metropolis*, and *The Cabinet of Dr. Caligari*, because they were meant for export and to demonstrate them as "masterworks from Germany and were hence specially motivated to tell stories that were specific to national history."[46] Reenacting "the shock of war and defeat" is of a different order, and serves a different function for German audiences, than monstrous metaphors in the characters of *Frankenstein*, or the dread in *Dracula*. In the Hollywood paradigm of sensation and thrill these allegories of death and injury remain somewhat undetermined, associated as much with the hurts of modernity generally as with the war in particular. Reading back into them, as Skal does, uses the war as a means of giving these fears a visual lexicon but they also, I suggest, stand in for longer historically persistent anxieties and risks.

The German émigré influence on the Hollywood system brought an aesthetic model that was fashioned through a form and style developed for reenacting the mental states of the traumatized German populace. The war in this way partially resides in the Hollywood horror films through the influence of the first wave of German émigré personnel, who shaped the silent horror cycles of the interwar period such as Paul Leni's films *The Cat and the Canary* (1927) or *The Man Who Laughs* (1928) and were ultimately embedded in the aesthetic norms of the horror genre when sound arrived. While the fantasy dreamscapes of the mise-en-scène alongside canted camera angles and expressive lighting in the horror cycles have their origins in the trauma aesthetics and reenactment of Weimar cinema, their function in the Hollywood films and for American audiences was in the more traditional mode of metaphor.

In *Frankenstein* that influence is evident in the script directions that Garrett Fort had made in the draft screenplay and in the decisions James Whale's team made in shooting the creation scenes that were inspired by Rotswang's laboratory in *Metropolis*.[47] However, James Whale also brought to his work in the Universal horror films a sense of black humor combined with pathos. Having directed the successful theatrical version of *Journey's End* and then the Tiffany/Gainsborough film, Whale provided another direct link with the war and Hollywood memory, one that is more closely associated with a British post-war sensibility. James Curtis, Whale's biographer, puts the link succinctly:

> Whale applied the themes of his earlier films and plays—human stories of war and doomed love—to his films of the supernatural, and where others regarded their monsters as menacing plot devices, Whale considered his as fully-dimensional characters and invested them with the complexities of human emotion.[48]

His monsters share some of the pathos with Oliver Bashforth in Pinero's *The Enchanted Cottage*. The image of Colin Clive as Stanhope sitting next to the unconscious Raleigh, who is paralyzed and dying, has its distorted echo in Clive's Dr. Frankenstein, who intently watches the hand of the monster for signs of life. It is worth recalling the critic Richard Watts, who saw in *Journey's End* a surprising British sentimentality that didn't hide behind the rough humor of what he saw as the equally surprising American lack of sentiment in *What Price Glory?*'s Flagg and Quirt. *Journey's End* instead was "frank in its appeal to pathos."[49] That sensibility pathos combined with dark humor and expressionist mise-en-scène and cinematography was a hallmark of Whale's work with not only *Frankenstein*, but also the *The Invisible Man* (1933) and *The Bride of Frankenstein* (1935).

There are two films in the Universal cycle of the early 1930s that take the war as a more explicit dynamic: *The Old Dark House* (James Whale, 1932) and *The Black Cat* (Edgar Ulmer, 1933). These two films provide an example of how repressed features of the war emerge as an "other" and specifically as a memory that has been transplanted from England in one and Europe in the other. *The Old Dark House* was James Whale's second film after the critical and commercial success of *Frankenstein*. The film was an adaptation of J.B. Priestley's second novel, *Benighted*, which had been published under that title in Britain in 1927 but as *The Old Dark House* in 1928 in the US. The change in title in the US brought expectations of a parody of "haunted house stories," which had been popular in theatre in the late nineteenth and early twentieth centuries and a staple of film since 1899.[50] The theme was perennially revisited in various genres throughout the 1920s, from D.W. Griffith's 1922 *One Exciting Night* to Paul Leni's 1927 *The Cat and the Canary*. James Curtis, in his detailed biography of Whale, noted that Priestley had intended the novel to be linked to the war and built the story around the veteran character Roger Penderel to "transmute the thriller into symbolical fiction with some psychological depth."[51] The film is undeniably English in its subtle wit and references to class and a dissolute aristocracy. It has fun with the conventions of the haunted house tradition but also attempts a social commentary on the malaise that Priestley saw in post-war Britain.

The Old Dark House is the story of five young people who are forced by a raging storm to stop and seek shelter in an old house inhabited by an ancient eccentric family, the Femms, and their servant, Morgan. The first of the people to arrive are a married couple, Philip and Margaret Waverton, played by Raymond Massey and Gloria Stuart, and their friend Roger Penderel, played by Melvyn Douglas. Both Philip and Roger are veterans

FIGURE 7.2. "Penderel didn't seem to have escaped the war yet." Melvyn Douglas as Roger Penderel and Brember Wills as Saul Femm in *The Old Dark House* (James Whale, 1932). Universal/Photofest. © Universal.

of the war. Having driven through the pouring rain, they are soaking wet as they knock on the door. It is answered by Morgan, the house servant, played by Boris Karloff wearing makeup that gives him a Neanderthal-like visage with a prominent cut on his nose. They are then greeted by Horace Femm, played in high camp by Ernest Thesiger. Soon his slightly deaf and unwelcoming sister, Rebecca, played by Eva Moore, meets them and tells them "there are no beds," which means they will spend the night gathered around the fire in the dining hall. Margaret asks if she can change into dryer clothes and Rebecca shows her to a room. As Margaret is changing, Rebecca tells her of the lusty parties that had been held there. She begins to rant about religion and says that the women who came wore fine silks but that they would rot. She then points to Margaret's dress and says it will rot, and then presses her finger on her chest and says "That's finer stuff, and it will rot too." After being given warnings about Morgan, who is dangerous when he is drunk, and hints of other more dangerous members of the family upstairs, they are joined by Sir William Porterhouse and his girlfriend, Gladys DuCane, played by Charles Laughton and Lilian Bond. Porterhouse is from Sheffield and is a self-made man, and Gladys is a chorus girl. Penderel and Gladys go out to his car to get some more whiskey. The front door closes on them, and so they sit in the car in the barn where they talk, drink, and end up falling in love. Meanwhile, the rest of the visitors are sitting around the fire with Horace Femm when the lights in the house go out. Rebecca tells Horace he must go upstairs to fetch the large lamp. Horace is unwilling to go because it is near the locked room where his pyromaniac brother, Saul, resides. Philip accompanies him and they hear a strange laugh from another bedroom. In the meantime, Margaret is left alone in the dining room, where she begins to make shadow animals in the light cast against the wall. Rebecca appears as a shadow beside her and frightens her. She goes to the door to find Penderel but is there found by Morgan, who is now drunk and chases her around the room. She runs upstairs and finds Philip with the lamp. Philip knocks Morgan unconscious; then he and Margaret go to investigate the sound and find 102-year-old Sir Roderick Femm (played by veteran stage actor Elspeth Dudgeon). Sir Roderick tells them that the house used to be a happy one filled with guests, but then two of his children died when they were twenty and then "madness came, we are all touched with it a little you see, except me, at least I don't think I am." Roderick warns them about Saul upstairs in the locked room who "just wants to destroy, kill . . ." He wants to make the house a "burnt offering." Roderick falls asleep and they go back downstairs and realize that Morgan has let Saul out. Morgan and Saul appear at the top of the stairs. Morgan comes down and Philip and Sir William struggle with him. Penderel puts Margaret and Gladys in a cupboard to be safe and goes to face Saul. They struggle and he knocks Penderel unconscious and then begins to set fire to the tapestries. Penderel awakes and goes upstairs. As he tries to stop Saul, they both fall through the balustrades; Saul is killed and Penderel is badly hurt. Morgan reappears and finds Gladys and Margaret coming out of the cupboard. He is obsessed with Margaret until she tells him Saul is lying hurt. Morgan goes to him and holds him in his arms, sobbing. Phillip and William reenter and Gladys goes to Penderel, thinking he is dead. She holds him and sees that he is still alive. The next morning, the storm has subsided and Philip and Margaret drive to get an ambulance for Penderel, who is still lying Pietà-like in Gladys's arms. He awakens and says "So I'm really dead and gone to heaven." Gladys says "No, it's morning and we've only just left that hell behind." Penderel asks her to marry him; they kiss and the film ends.

Priestley intended his novel *Benighted* as a metaphor for the impact of the war on British society, but the war had also been a formative experience to many in the production team and cast of the film. Priestley himself had served in the front lines from 1914 to 1918 and had been wounded, buried by a trench-mortar. Whale, too, had been at the front and a prisoner of war. R.C. Sherriff, who co-wrote the script and was the author of the play *Journey's End*, had been wounded at Passchendaele. Benn W. Levy, the other scriptwriter, served in the RAF at the end of the war. Charles Laughton (Sir William Porterhouse) had been gassed while serving. Raymond Massey (Philip Waverton) joined the Canadian Army in 1914 and was wounded in 1916. The subject matter of the film, the intent of Priestley to make the war the background to the film, the war experience of the production personnel, and the inclusion of veteran characters literally and metaphorically makes *The Old Dark House* distinctive as an example of how the memory of the war was woven through an otherwise unrelated film narrative.

Priestley's title, while ostensibly referring to the house and the strange Femm family, also refers to the dark past of the war and to the veteran Penderel, whom Priestly describes through Philip: "A queer youth!—Philip looked down on him from a great height. . . . Unlike him, Penderel didn't seem to have escaped the war yet, and every night with him was still the night before one moved up to the line."[52] Priestly saw the young people who come to the house as representative of the modern world, while the Femms and Morgan represented "various forms of post-war pessimism pretending to be people."[53] Whale brought the combination of pathos and dark humor that he had developed in *Frankenstein* and in the staging of *Journey's End* to *The Old Dark House*. As Carl Laemmle Jr. at Universal intended the film to be a Karloff star vehicle on the back of *Frankenstein*, his character, Morgan, has a similar although toned-down makeup. His face is distorted, with one eye drooping, mottled skin, and a cut over the nose; his dead stare and stalking hesitant gait are like those of the Monster. The themes of science gone amok, the hubris of Dr. Frankenstein only vaguely legible as a repressed war reference in *Frankenstein*, is explicit in *The Old Dark House*.

As with *Journey's End*, *The Old Dark House* takes place mainly in one area, with the feeling of dread created by the spaces referred to but not seen. At the outset the characters are driving through a fierce storm, the wheels spinning through clinging mud. Mud and dripping water so often associated with the front dominate this scene as Philip complains that the canvas top is dripping water down the back of his neck, Margaret is frustrated that they are lost, and Penderel is in the back of the car singing. Like the dugout in *Journey's End*, the relief of the hearth and warmth in the dining room of the Femm house is never really secure. Horace Femm is afraid the house will wash away, and the strange behavior of Rebecca and Morgan give little comfort to the wary guests. While Margaret has been taken away to change by Rebecca, Horace offers some gin to Penderel, who eagerly accepts. Horace raises his glass: "I will give you a toast that you will not appreciate, being young—I give you illusion." Penderel responds: "Illusion? Ha! I'm exactly the right age for that, Mr. Femm." Horace: "I presume you are one of the gentlemen slightly, shall we say, battered by the war." Penderel quickly responds, "Correct, Mr. Femm, War generation slightly soiled—a study in the bittersweet—the man with the twisted smile, and this, Mr. Femm, is exceedingly good gin." The list of descriptors delivered wryly recalls Priestley's own description of the dark humor in the British troops' song "Hanging on the Old Barbed Wire," which he described as "purely English, for it means that even that devilish enemy, that death trap, the wire has somehow been accepted, recognized and acknowledged almost with affection."[54] Later, as they are drinking in the car, Penderel tells Gladys of his fiancée, who married someone else while he was at the front, that she "had rather good judgment." Earlier Gladys describes him as not fitting into these times: "factories, cheap advertising, money grubbing . . . they make Mr. Penderel a kind of fish out of water." The Femm characters are objects of amusement for Penderel rather than threats. His relationship with his friends is also estranged. The horror of his experience has rendered him an outsider in the post-war world, a condition he manages "almost with affection." He describes his trouble as not "thinking enough things are worthwhile."

Priestley, as well as scriptwriters Sherriff and Levy, were certainly writing from experience. Priestley, however, felt little sense of attachment to his war years. He noted that, unlike writers and artists such as Hemingway and sculptor C.S. Jagger, who had been to the front and found they were "drifting away from reality" after the war, he had felt that "dream began . . . when the guns roared."[55] To Priestley's own memories of the war as a "vast piece of imbecility" should be added those of the production team of the film. James Curtis's account of the making of the film is of a happy set where the actors enjoyed the precise direction of Whale and particularly the way he and Ernest Thesiger worked on Benn Levy's lines with timing and gestures to achieve the effective combination of camp humor and dread that sets Whale's horror films apart. Whale's tendency to undermine expectations in ways that were both comic and unsettling brought out the depth that lurks in *Benighted* as well as the "Hanging on the Old Barbed Wire" type of black humor. The unlikely casting of the diminutive Brember Wills, another veteran both of the war and of the London stage, as the dangerous Saul Femm was both comic and deadly. Further, he cast Elspeth Dudgeon, a doyenne of the English theatre, as the ancient Sir Roderick Femm, a gender switch that was hidden from the audiences at the time: she is credited on the film as John Dudgeon.

Such playfulness permeates the film and gives it the gallows humor that Priestley builds into the novel, but in quite different ways. The fight between Saul and Penderel in the book is tense, with Saul unseen until he lunges at Penderel. Penderel's thoughts just prior to that indicate the intent of the novel, which is to find a resolution for him. He is waiting for Saul to descend on him:

> How queer it was that there was something inside you that could relish, grinning with irony, the most damnable situation you found yourself in, pointing out how damnable it was! He'd discovered that in France, when, as now, something in him was afraid and something else wasn't, something shook and something grinned. Some of the old faces came popping up, smiled, and were gone; fellows he thought he'd forgotten; a spectral parade.[56]

Later, just before his final fight with Saul, he experiences a cathartic moment, brought on by his situation and his meeting with Gladys:

> It seemed as if the corner were turned at last, and he had a flashing vision of life stretched widely and gloriously before him, the shining happy valley, lost for years and apparently gone forever, a dream bitterly cast off, until this strange night brought glimpse after glimpse of it through thinning mist, and now finally swung it into full view. Now he knew what it was like to be alive.[57]

Nowhere is the equivalence between the war veteran and the undead more evident than here. Like Priestley's own relationship with his experience, the war's nightmare was lifting; the irony, of course, is that in the book Saul kills Penderel. Whale and his team's choice of the small actor to play Saul is not simply playfulness for its own sake; the inner dialogue of Penderel in the book is replaced in the film by a drawn-out scene where Saul pulls a knife on Penderel and begins to cite the book of Samuel in the Bible and the story of Saul's jealousy of David, who has just slain Goliath.

(In a word, the biblical David, like Penderel, is a veteran.) The scene does not convey the war-related thoughts of Penderel as in the book, but it does give the sense of genuine dread. At first, because Wills is much smaller than Melvyn Douglas, who plays Penderel, he seems helpless, but then he becomes a genuine threat. In the initial version it was left ambiguous whether Penderel lived, but preview audiences found that ending too pessimistic and it was reworked so that Penderel survives and the film ends with him in the arms of Gladys and proposing marriage to her. Even here there is an explicit evocation of war imagery. Penderel, head bandaged and lying in her arms, evokes the depiction of the soldier as Christ-like in the arms of a Red Cross nurse as in A.E. Forenger's well-known 1918 poster "The Greatest Mother in the World,"[58] itself a reference to the Pietà.

The film's release was timed in late October, near Halloween but also in the run-up to Armistice Day. In fact, its run at the Theatre on Broadway was cut short to make room for Paramount's *A Farewell to Arms* (Frank Borzage, 1932). Even so, the explicit references to the war went unacknowledged in the reviews that appeared in the first week of November 1932. *New York Times* critic Mordaunt Hall praised the players and the atmosphere but found the story "disappointing and incomplete."[59] Abel Green in *Variety* called it "inane" but thought its "eeriness" and the presence of Boris Karloff would go over well in smaller theatres. He also heard derisive laughter in the Rialto at the romance of Penderel and Gladys.[60] Conversely, *Harrison's Reports* found their romance a "ray of sunshine" amid the tense atmosphere, which would "please the followers of horror melodramas."[61] None mentioned the war references, and even the Universal publicity department in their house magazine either did not or would not make the link when they ran an article praising the talents of Gloria Stuart in her first films, including *The Old Dark House*, on a page next to an article entitled "Armistice Day Suggestions." The advice to exhibitors about the best way to connect their theatres with Armistice Day was by booking *All Quiet on the Western Front*. The article began with the line "November the 11th for generations to come will be a day which will live in the memory of the American people."[62] For Universal publicity the memory of the war was an advertising opportunity. Trading on the memory of the war was acceptable with *All Quiet on the Western Front* but not with a horror film, no matter how prestigious that cycle may have been for Universal at the time. *Harrison's Reports* finished its review with the phrase "too horrible for children," and the implied specialist audience for the "horror melodrama" cycle had already begun to accrue the lowbrow aura it had by the late 1930s. However, all of the reviews identify

Penderel as the main character in the film, and the need for a revised ending gives some indication of audience empathy for that character. Sensation discourse was central to all film advertising, and particularly with horror, it overrode any other dramatic appeal the film may have had.

DEAD ALL THESE YEARS

If *The Old Dark House* brought Priestley's story of British post-war memory and malaise to the screen via metaphor and sensation, Edgar Ulmer's *The Black Cat* modernized the metaphor of the haunted house as the gothic expression of the past of the past via a version of German Expressionism for American audiences. Ulmer's film put the war more directly in the story as a causal motivator for the behavior of its two European veteran characters, using a mise-en-scène that stacked modernist architecture and décor on top of the brutal concrete of military fortifications, and on the slaughtered thousands that lay underfoot. Further, it put a young American couple on their honeymoon in Europe in direct danger from, quite literally, a European memory of the war, and it acted as a warning for what the future might hold.

Edgar Ulmer had been working in the Hollywood industry off and on since the early 1920s, as an art director at Universal and with F.W. Murnau on *Sunrise* (1927) at Fox. Back in Berlin he co-directed *Menschen am Sonntag* (*People on Sunday*, 1930) with future exile personnel Fred Zinnemann, Robert and Curt Siodmak, Billy Wilder, and Eugen Schüfftan. Returning to Hollywood and Universal, he wrote the story idea and directed *The Black Cat* in 1934. Though he was part of the original group of German émigré personnel in the 1920s, Ulmer is seen as belonging to the second wave, the exile community of German directors, who left Germany in the 1930s due to the rise of Hitler. Gurd Gemünden has pointed to the impact this had on Ulmer's films: "that foreground characters who are displaced and forever wandering about . . . the existential restlessness of the exile . . . marks the lives of the two antagonists of *The Black Cat*, Hjalmar Poelzig and Vitus Werdegast."[63] In the case of the German émigrés of the 1920s, the war in German national memory has a distinct bearing on their Hollywood films. *The Man Who Laughs* (1928), directed by Paul Leni, was drawn from a Victor Hugo story but employs the characteristics of mise-en-scène that he had employed in his earlier German films such as *Das Wachsfigurenkabinett* (1924), which was released in the US as *Waxworks* two years later. Expressionism as a response to the traumatic memory of the war in

Germany in the 1920s, once relocated into the Hollywood system, altered from the reenactment mode that Anton Kaes outlines in the films made in Germany. Like the Lon Chaney films, *The Man Who Laughs* and *The Cat and the Canary* were not recognized by contemporary critics, studio heads, or the general American public as anything other than horror or thriller melodramas. And yet the line of the influence of expressionism I have just outlined was in reality not quite so clear-cut. German filmmakers in Hollywood in the 1920s and '30s worked the range of Hollywood genres, and the influence of their political views waxed and waned with the dictates of the American market and taste preferences. Thomas Elsaesser's characterization of the émigré/exile in America is one of a conflation of two "national imaginaries," each bound by a set of shared cultural values. In this formulation those values undergo changes, and indeed are created to an extent, by the interaction with the other "national imaginary." Hence the German/Hollywood conflation produced film styles that, while holding to the classical Hollywood norms, economic constraints, and the restrictions of the Hays Office, had elements of both but were distinct from each. They should be seen as a set of "miscognition and recognition, across the gap that opens up between the two kinds of imaginary, represented by Europe's view of America and America's view of Europe."[64] In the 1930s exile personnel such as Fritz Lang, Billy Wilder, Ernst Lubitsch, and William Dieterle brought with them a political sensibility that was responding to the rise of Nazism and the failure of the Weimar republic. "Exile cinema tried to alert an American public to the internal and external threat of fascism and dictatorship."[65] At the same time they were subject to the dictates of Hollywood representations of Europe. Whale's gothic Welsh mansion in *The Old Dark House*, or Frankenstein's castle, and Dracula's resting ground in Transylvania were mainstays of Universal horror. Hence Ulmer's *The Black Cat* stands as a unique example of a combination of war memory and cautionary tale, wrapped in the generic cloth of the Universal horror cycle.

By any measure *The Black Cat* is an anomaly. Its narrative contains considerable implausible gaps and ellipses and the characters' motivations are not always clear, but the plot, the style of the camera work, and the set design pushed the boundaries of the horror genre significantly. The story is of an American newlywed couple, Peter and Joan Alison (David Manners and Julie Bishop, credited as Jacqueline Wells), on their honeymoon in Hungary. They find themselves on a bus with Vitus Werdegast (Bela Lugosi), driving in a storm through a World War I battlefield. Werdegast is a Hungarian veteran of the war and a psychiatrist who has returned after being imprisoned by the Russians for fifteen years. As they are making their way through the rain and muddy road, the bus driver tells them of the battle where bodies were "piled twelve deep" and the river below them was "swollen with blood," and up on the hill is "where engineer Poelzig now lives. . . . He built his home on its very foundation. Marmaros, the greatest graveyard in the world." As the driver speaks there is a close-up of Werdegast, who closes his eyes, remembering his experiences there. The bus crashes; the driver is killed and Joan is hurt. They go to Hjalmar Poelzig's (Boris Karloff) house. Werdegast gives Joan a narcotic to help her sleep. It transpires that Werdegast has returned to settle a score with Poelzig, who left him and his men to the Russians at the Marmaros battle. Worse still, Poelzig took Werdegast's wife with him, traveling around the world. Unbeknownst to Werdegast, Poelzig has killed her and embalmed her body, and then married their daughter, Karen. Poelzig takes Werdegast on a tour of the lower levels of the house, built on a huge gun emplacement, and points to the embalmed bodies of a number of women that are hanging in glass cases from the walls. Poelzig then shows Werdegast the body of his wife, and Werdegast is bent on revenge. Throughout, Werdegast and Poelzig vie with each other in strange ways, through verbal aggression and a chess match of death for the possession of Joan. Poelzig has his eye on Joan for a satanic ritual sacrifice and as he is talking to her Karen appears and interrupts them. He takes Karen away and kills her, but Joan can hear them. The film comes to a climax when Werdegast rescues Joan from being sacrificed and then captures Poelzig and proceeds to skin him alive with surgical instruments. Joan and Peter escape and Werdegast pulls a lever that ignites all of the unused explosives in the vaults below the house and destroys it.

Unsurprisingly, the memory of the war, filtered through the contemporary generic conventions of horror—though those are extended by this film—was virtually opaque for an American audience. As in *The Old Dark House*, the war is a motivating factor, but *The Black Cat* did not connect with reviewers with its incorporation of the memory of the war to convey a warning from fascist Europe. Unlike the whimsical and at times wistfully sad character of Penderel in *The Old Dark House*, the war has made Werdegast a creature of irrational vengeance, while Poelzig is a Satan-worshiping, serial-killing monster. The virtues of modernizing the gothic house story with Bauhaus architecture on top of the killing machine of the war that is in turn built upon a dungeon of torture, sacrifice, and surgical horror seem to have overwhelmed deeper anti-war or anti-fascist subtexts. Rather than the self-deprecating humor of the "the slightly

FIGURE 7.3. Caught in the mud at the site of the battle of Marmaros: "The greatest graveyard in the world." David Manners, Jacqueline Wells, and Bela Lugosi in *The Black Cat* (Edgar Ulmer, 1934). Universal/Photofest. © Universal.

soiled generation" exchange between Penderel and Horace Femm, Poelzig and Werdegast enact a humorless reunion of the "living dead." The intent is to convey a deep existential horror. Poelzig, in a long speech to Werdegast, says,

> You say your soul was killed, that you have been dead all these years. And what of me? Did we not both die here in Marmaros fifteen years ago? Are we any less victims of the war than those whose bodies were torn asunder? Are we not both the living dead?

The reviews of the film rarely mention the war beyond its function as draping the film with the atmosphere of death. *Variety* was not impressed and saw it as an unsuccessful attempt by Universal to combine their two big horror stars and called it a "clash of two eyebrow clinching nuts."[66] However, *Variety* also took the space to describe the film's setting as "a spooky manor built over the ruins of a world war fort where 10,000 soldiers drenched the valley in blood in a terrible military defeat caused by Karloff's treachery. That is told but not shown." While lamenting the prosaic exposition of the backstory, there is a clue to a certain expectation of pacifist messages in war subjects implicit here in the description of the "terrible military defeat." Further *Variety*, as did the Hays Office, found the Satanism and the skinning alive to be pushing the boundaries of taste and as "dubious showmanship." *Variety*'s lukewarm review did, however, predict it would do good business, and it did; it was also an indication of the trade press's expectation of quality from a cycle that was beginning to decline in popularity.

The exhibitor's journal *Film Daily*, however, focused on the sensation qualities: "For those who like their horror and chills in the movies, this one is a pippin." Disregarding the spurious link with the Edgar Allan Poe story, the word to exhibitors was "It carries a terrific air of weird unreality and impending calamity that will satisfy the most ardent thrill hunter."[67] The different orders of war memories between *The Old Dark House* and *The Black Cat* offer contrasting "national imaginaries" as they encountered American audiences. The conflation of national imaginaries in *The Black Cat*, filtered through lower budget restraints and at times narrative gaps, for modern scholars gives the film a uniquely modernist quality.[68] Yet Ulmer's "messy modernism," to use Gemünden's phrase, resulted in building upon the already-existing stereotypical othering of Eastern European and German characters. He notes that the film's ending, complete with a modernist altar for the satanic ritual, also included clear references to German and Austrian "decadent nobility." (In the script one couple attending the ritual bore the name of Goering.) However opaque, *The Black Cat* was a cautionary tale that used an Austro-German memory of the Great War as evidence of the damage that isolationist policy had done. It also pointed to future representations by outlining character traits for decadent Europeans and Nazis.

THEY GAVE THEM GUNS

In Armitage Trail's novel *Scarface*, Tony Guarino is a killer. But he learns to be a more efficient at his craft and acquires leadership skills on the Western Front. When the commander of his unit is killed, Tony takes command and his unit holds their position on the Western Front, surrounded. After pushing back German attacks from all sides, they are finally relieved by new forces as the enemy retreats. His new commander finds him wounded but the unit still intact. The commander is impressed with these qualities, but Tony has better uses for them when he returns home to Chicago. He becomes a new kind of gangster, more ruthless and aspirational than the old bosses. In Howard Hawks's film, the war episode is reduced to the X-shaped scar on Tony's face. In a telling, coarse gesture he boasts to Poppy, his boss Lovo's girlfriend, that he got it in the war. It marks him out as unpredictable, as it has the effect of standing in for deeper psychological wounds, and it also gives his behavior a probable cause. While in Trail's novel Tony was a violent psychopath before he went to war, in the film the war's impact, reduced to the scar on his face, is more ambiguous. In the novel his experiences there acted as his "finishing school" but his behavior was inherent, only enhanced by his war experiences. Hawks's version opens it up to broader interpretations, blurring the line between nurture and nature.

In the film *The Public Enemy*, Tom Powers (James Cagney) derides his shell-shocked brother Mike (Donald Cook) as a hypocrite when he refuses to drink the beer that Tom has brought for his welcome-home party. When Mike says the beer is tainted with the blood of those Tom has killed, Tom replies that killing was OK as long as he was in a uniform. Tommy is depicted as tough and amoral, but Wellman builds into the film a chilling scene of his policeman father beating him with a leather strap. As with Tony Camonte (his name changed from Guarino for the film), the source of Tom's behavior is made ambiguous and one of the key attractions of the film is how Tom alternates between tough-guy behavior and his loyalty to his friends and family. Other characters help delineate his character. His pal Matt Wood goes along with Tom but is there to highlight the consequences of Tom's bad choices when he is killed. Tom's brother Mike is straight and joins up in 1917 while Tom stays home. On his return he is visibly suffering from shell shock. When he throws the beer barrel against the wall his behavior is attributed to moral outrage and shell shock in equal measure. Mike's character falls in line with recognizable attitudes toward veterans at the time. He is troubled but he tries to improve himself through going to night school. When Tom offers him money he refuses it, a gesture resonant with the debates about adjusted compensation for veterans that had been ongoing throughout the 1920s and would culminate in the Bonus March in 1932.

The war and its effects as a backdrop to these films and in social problem films such *Heroes for Sale* and *I Am a Fugitive from a Chain Gang* continued to be an aesthetic option for scriptwriters and directors throughout the decade. Toward the end of MGM's *They Gave Him a Gun* (W.S. Van Dyke, 1937), Jimmy Davis (Franchot Tone) reflects on his choice of becoming a gangland killer. "While the other guys were off to college I was getting my own kind of diploma in France." A generic hybrid of the war film and the social problem film, *They Gave Him a Gun* ruminates on the socio/psychological impact of the war on young men. Fred P. Willis (Spencer Tracey), a carnival barker, meets Jimmy Davis at training camp on their way to the front. Fred sees Jimmy is from the country and not wise to the world and takes him under his wing. The first indication Fred gets that Jimmy might be enjoying killing is at target practice, where he proves to be an excellent marksman. "It ain't much fun only shootin' targets." At the front they are pinned down by a German machine gun in the blown-out roof of a house. Jimmy's squad is told to clear it. They go, but the rest of the squad are all killed and Jimmy ducks into a church screaming and frightened, thinking a German solider is about to shoot him. When he realizes the soldier is dead, he takes his rifle and moves into the steeple to gain a higher view of the machine-gun nest. As he shoots each German soldier he becomes ecstatic, an enthusiastic killer. Fred, from his cover on the ground, smiles at Jimmy's work, and does not see the darker side of his enjoyment of it. As the platoon moves forward a shell hits the steeple. Fred visits Jimmy in the field hospital but has a hard time getting past the tough but compassionate nurse Rose Duffy. He and Rose fall in love. Fred goes back to the line and is reported killed but has only been captured. After the war is over, Fred returns to his outfit. Just as they are about to be shipped home, Fred sees Jimmy, who tells him Rose and he are to be married, and that he would die if he couldn't be with her. Rose tells Fred she wants to be with him and would never have agreed to marry Jimmy had she known he was alive. But Fred pretends that he was trying to give her the brush-off and they part.

Ten years later, Fred owns a traveling circus and runs into Jimmy, who is now a gangster. Jimmy keeps his real line of work hidden from Rose, but Rose finds out Jimmy is going to commit a robbery with his gang and reports him to the police. He is caught and jailed, and rather than bail him out Rose tells him he has to tell the truth. He does, and while he is in prison his cellmate, another veteran, keeps hinting that Rose is seeing Fred while he's locked up. They escape and Jimmy makes his way to Fred's circus, where Rose is now working but remaining true to Jimmy. The police arrive and surround Jimmy, Fred, and Rose, who are in the circus trailer. Jimmy pulls a gun on Fred and threatens to kill them both, but Fred takes the gun away from him and Jimmy agrees to give himself up. As they emerge from the trailer Jimmy makes a suicidal run for it and is gunned down.

As a hybrid, the film attempts to present a pacifist message from the opening music, a martial but downbeat fanfare followed by a darkened strain of George M. Cohan's "Over There." The didactic tone of the film is introduced by an artillery piece turned to point straight at the audience/camera. A shell comes hurtling out of it and explodes to become the list of the cast. The titles are then spelled out by machine-gun shots that reference both the war and gangster cycles. In this way the film announces its somewhat muddled combination of anti-war and social problem themes. That lack of clarity was reflected in the reviews. *Variety* was not impressed; it declared the best chance this film had was its "anti-war preachment" and found the "attempt to suggest a psychological link between the World War and gangsterism in America" feeble. It said it was "fairly exciting" mainly because of the actors, but hindered by a "soggy" sentimentality.[69] *Film Daily*, on the other hand, thought it had "B.O. [box office] wallop." Eager to reassure exhibitors that the film was not overly moralizing, the reviewer found that the anti-war theme had been handled well through "dramatic action and story."[70] By this period the idea that war experience bred criminals had been filtered through events such as the Bonus March on Washington, the debates about compensation, and in 1937 a downturn in the economy that saw a rise in veteran unemployment. Throughout the decade the veteran on screen was a refraction of how the veteran was represented more widely. The veteran as "forgotten man" was conflated with all men suffering from the effects of the Depression, and—with the influence of veterans' groups, particularly the American Legion, and the high-profile political wrangling over reparations—veterans also conjured up suspicion of special-interest groups.[71]

These ambiguous assumptions about veterans ran in tandem with the changing shape of the memory of the war and its causes. By the mid-1930s suspicion of industrialists and bankers, who were blamed for the economic collapse of 1929, dovetailed with revisionist histories of the American involvement in the war, which suggested there had been a conspiracy by those in big business to get America into the war in order to maximize the profits they were already making in munitions manufacture and wartime support industries. The widely read *Road to War* by Walter Millis in 1935 and H.C. Englebrecht's *Merchants of War* a year earlier had depicted the American intervention as a tragic mistake and a result of industrialist conspiracy.[72] The opening montage of the film, created by Slavko Vorkapich, echoes this with a depiction of the manufacturing of weapons in detail, from steelworks to test firings. The first scene after the opening montage emphasizes the industrialized warfare motif by showing Fred and Jimmy in the mechanistic, anonymizing process of induction and training. Fred is given a hat that is too small for him; the implication is that it is he that must conform. Later he meets Jimmy standing in line; their individuality is subsumed into the military system. They have become cogs in the war machine, like the guns and cannon in the montage.

Yet by 1937 there was already a shift in public attitudes toward America's role in foreign affairs. The amendments to the Neutrality Acts of 1935–39, while limiting American support for any belligerent nation, indicated some changes in attitudes toward foreign policy, particularly in intellectual circles and on the left. *Variety*'s and *Film Daily*'s reviews are revealing in this context, not for how they differ but for their underlying continuity. *Variety*'s recommendation that the anti-war angle will be its best chance actually concurs with *Film Daily*'s praise for the film's cinematic, visual rendering of the anti-war aspect as insurance against exhibitors' resistance to didactic, overly wordy films. War as futility in films with war subjects had by this time become de rigueur for the studios. The impact of *All Quiet* had been that significant, but it was also an opportunity for productive ambiguity where anti-war sentiment could appeal to a wide range of the political spectrum, or at least not offend the majority of cinemagoers.

In the trade reviews the film's hybrid quality was problematic. *Film Daily*'s optimistic reading was not sugar-coated by *Motion Picture Herald*: "thoughts must have crept into the selling mind that it would not be easy for managers to sell the picture." The problem was one of generic identity; "it entails three separate and distinct stories . . . blended into an understandable whole. The first is a grimly realistic and frankly grisly war story. The second is stark gangster . . . yet separate and apart, the third is a human love story." The overt promoter's optimism of *Motion Picture Herald* presents this as a problem of "finding the audience that will understand and appreciate the picture." This in spite of noting that the romance section does not offer a "humanizing contrast" that will provide "a tension easing balance" with the other two elements.[73]

As it transpired, MGM's marketing department chose to emphasize the film's "thrills." However, *Motion Picture Herald*'s breakdown of the film articulates the extent to which the memory of the war had been distilled into categories that fit the requirements of an entertainment industry seeking broad, national appeal. Each section draws on pre-established aesthetic norms of representing the war and its after effects. The war section operates on the horizontality associated with *All Quiet on the Western Front* and *The Big Parade*. The gangster section invokes the link between war trauma and the social problems of the reintegrating veteran as in *Heroes for Sale*, while the romance plot, rooted in the gender dynamics that were introduced in the war-nurse cycle, traverses both. Each of these offers, at the end of the 1930s, an epitaph for the trajectory of the Hollywood memory of the war of the previous two decades.

The war scenes are definitively horizontal. The opening shot of the battle sequence is a worm's-eye view of a blasted tree, the sky filling up most of the frame and the dramatic music, more tragic than heroic, followed by a cut to empty sky in which a shell whistles and then explodes. Shots alternate between sky-dominant and dirt-filled frames, punctuated with explosions that obliterate the sightlines. The montage editing presents an indeterminate position between the lines, as with *All Quiet* and the final battle sequence in *The Big Parade*. There is a shot of a cemetery, and then of a solder being shot in the face and writhing on the ground, no doubt the source of the reviewer's comments as "grimly realistic." These shots are of anonymous soldiers caught up in a chaotic montage of the horror of war, after which come the first shots of Fred and Jimmy together orienting the viewer into the narrative space. As Jimmy's squad is ordered to take the machine-gun nest, the film returns to the primary narrative function of Fred looking and Jimmy acting. Significantly, Fred's view of Jimmy is investigative, but at this point partial. He does not see the psychopathic delight in killing, particularly when he shoots a German soldier trying to surrender. In this way the audience is privileged above Fred in the film's hierarchy of knowledge. Rather than heroic and vertical, as Fred initially believes, Jimmy's success at clearing the machine-gun nest is undercut for the audience by his behavior, and becomes the subject of Fred's investigation for the rest of the film.

The romance plot is introduced as Fred tries to visit Jimmy in the hospital. This plays out via the traditions established in the war-nurse films of the use of vernacular and wisecracking repartee between nurses and men, both patients and male doctors, as a mechanism for negotiating and containing the "forbidden zone" of women's desire. The "realism" in these films, as we have seen, centered on illicit or extramarital sexual behavior, coded through the language of vernacular and fenced in by the narrative resolutions of either marriage or death. As the film is post Production Code, the banter is now one-sided, with sexual innuendo absent but, tellingly, threatened physical abuse remaining. When Fred goes to the hospital to see Jimmy he meets Rose Duffy, the nurse at the registering table. She has already been established as a tough but compassionate professional. His character, a carnival barker, is tough talking, although played by Spencer Tracy; he is an everyman character, a "good Joe." He tries both vernacular language and gesture to get her to let him in to see Jimmy but she refuses. He later gets another nurse, who is also wise to his language and intent, to let him in and he hides while he watches Rose caringly attend to Jimmy. Their relationship is established when she drops into his vernacular:

> FRED: "Oh, you're one of those prohibition dames huh, that wants to vote. What you need is a bust in the eye."
> ROSE: "Hold everything, chest beater. If you think that kind of conversation is gonna make me drape myself around your thick neck you're pathetic. In my time I've had a heel mark on every vertebra and at this late date I'm not gonna collect anymore of them from a heel like you. You webfooted gutterpup."

Their banter, unsettling in its reference to violence, is central to drawing the distinction between Fred, the rough carnie, and Jimmy, the small-town naïf turned psychopathic killer. Rose Duffy, whose name is a conjunction of beauty with a reference to the popular wartime priest Father Duffy, takes the mantle of the nurturing nurse with Jimmy. When he is delirious he calls her "mom" and she calls him "boy." Fred watches this conversation and when he sees her he takes her hands and says "I been watchin' you hold a guy's life in them." The myth of the soldier born a man through warfare is underscored here with Fred acting, as he has throughout the film, as if he is Jimmy's father, and Rose his mother. To emphasize that nurturing relationship, she asks Fred, "Why do you slobs have to all look like kids when you're hurt?" The plot complication develops when Fred is thought to be dead and she agrees to marry Jimmy. The Oedipal scenario here is not a subtext; it is central to the film's resolution. Rose is fought over but ultimately she, like Babs in *War Nurse*, enters into her new relationship with Fred as an apparently equal partner. Bound by propriety, Rose remains faithful to Jimmy while he is in prison. What is important here is the comparison of her life with Jimmy, one of deception and excessive luxury, with a more equal partnership with Fred, where she helps make his circus business a success. Woven into the Oedipal frame is her maternal relationship with Jimmy, seemingly sexless, while desiring an adult relationship with Fred. Fred and Rose offer an image of the new, more equal couple that signals changes wrought in heterosexual relationships during the Depression.[74] This is not to suggest that the film is in any sense progressive in its gender politics; indeed, the type of relationship between Fred and Rose was already well established through screwball comedy, and while offering a modern version of couple-dom, it still denies Rose ultimate agency. The differences between the two relationships work to present two versions of veterans via the comparison of a healthy comradeship with an unhealthy, unresolved Oedipal one.

The hybrid formula's weaknesses were worked through more seamlessly in *The Roaring Twenties* (Raoul Walsh, 1939). In the two years since *They Gave Him a Gun* it had become clear that war in Europe was inevitable. When it was released in October 1939, the war in Europe had already begun, and *The Roaring Twenties*, framed as a memory by Mark Hellinger, who wrote the original story, is an endpiece to Hollywood's memory of the war in the interwar period. It opens with a message from Mark Hellinger, who drew from his experiences as a reporter in 1920s New York City during the height of prohibition and the gang culture and nightlife it enabled: "This film is a memory." To illustrate the import of this period the preface is followed by a montage of newsreel footage that reverses time from 1940 to 1918, passing through images of Roosevelt, Hitler, and Mussolini through Hoover and a destitute man eating soup and bread to Calvin Coolidge and finally Wilson and the war. The war is introduced by the image of a world exploding and then cut over a montage of No Man's Land in an attack, again shot from the ground, chaotic and smothering. The voiceover is rhetorical—"April 1918—almost a million American young men are engaged in a struggle which they have been told will make the world safe for democracy"—but also fits within the ambiguity that allows the phrase a wide interpretation, either isolationist or interventionist.

The story structure is similar to *They Gave Him a Gun*; the experience of the war affects the characters by enhancing their intrinsic qualities, which are fully expressed on their return home, held together by a romance plot. The main character, Eddie Bartlett (James Cagney), is generous, empathetic, and tough. George Hally (Humphrey Bogart) is the factory owner's son who is a psychopath, and Lloyd Hart (Jeffrey Lynn) is the honest college kid whom Eddie watches out for at the front, and is Eddie's lawyer as he rises to the top of the bootlegging world. He is watched over by Panama Smith (Gladys George), the brassy nightclub owner modeled on the real-life Texas Guinan. Instead of a love triangle, though, the film has Bartlett in love with a young nightclub singer, Jean Sherman (Priscilla Lane). But the modern couple is really formed with Lloyd and Jean, equals in the sense that they are both working in legitimate jobs, lawyer and singer, while Eddie is isolated because he is driven into the bootlegging business by the poor treatment he and the other veterans received on their return. He heroically gives up his quest for Jean and dies protecting her from Hally, and in the arms of Panama. He is an outsider, a relic of the past, both as gangster and bootlegger, but also because he had been to the front.

The success of the film lay mainly in its presentation as a memory, as kind of nostalgia for both that time and for the earlier gangster cycle. The *New York Times*' Frank Nugent, in a mainly negative review, noted,

> For here again we find the fighters of 1918–19 back from the war discovering they have lost their glory with the armistice, turning to bootlegging and highjacking and murder during the delirium of the speakeasy era, taking a licking in the stock market crash of '29, penning their farewell letters to the world in blood spilling from bullet wounds.[75]

Nugent's recount could also stand as shorthand for the memory script Hollywood studios worked to throughout the 1930s, with an added hint of impatience. The veteran as gangster, as unreliable and unstable, was by 1939 an old saw regardless of the moral divide of the characters. It had played out not only across a number of crime melodramas but, as we have seen, across the generic spectrum. The Great War and its social impact had become thoroughly embedded in the Hollywood production system. Its impact, whether implicit as in the horror film or explicit in social problem films, was manifest. Hollywood studio product was (and is) reactive to social trends and discourses. Warner had built a reputation through Zanuck with stories generated out of headlines, and continued to do so throughout the 1930s. Other studios such as MGM also produced films with the war as a backdrop, causal motivation if not a setting. For most of the twenty years since the armistice, the studios and their producers had found the war a convenient modernizing narrative device. MGM's *My Man Godfrey* (Gregory La Cava, 1936), for example, introduced the screwball couple, played by Carole Lombard and William Powell, through a "scavenger hunt" for a forgotten man. Lombard's character is a wealthy socialite at a party when they go to the "Hooverville" by the river in New York City, where she finds Powell, who through the course of the film makes her see the plight of those who have been dispossessed by the Depression economy and by association veterans. The coupledom that is forged out of their union is one that was more reciprocal than traditional marriage had been, and the war's impact was brought in to aid the causal motivation for that change. Beyond the war film, the war had been present through characters such as the veteran, the hobo, the flapper, the gangster, and monsters, through performances ranging from the stilted gait of Frankenstein's Monster to the traumatic neuroses of veterans, and through production values such as set design. The

Hollywood "formula" of plausible deniability and ambiguity in order to appeal to a broader range of tastes and political sensibilities was fully served by the war. Through these devices and storylines in this twenty-year period there lingered an after-image of the war through its effects and consequences as a reminder, often of different aspects and mobilizing diverse discourses, from the plight of veterans to pacifism and isolationism. By the outbreak of war in Europe in 1939 these topoi began to be eclipsed by more pressing concerns and a resulting change in audience taste patterns and preferences.

CODA: AFTER THE AFTER-IMAGE

The World War II film overshadowed the World War I film in subsequent years. Steven Trout credits the Vietnam War with revitalizing some of the questions about the purpose of war and its effects on those who fight and are involved in it that characterized the memory of the Great War in American culture between the wars.[76] Jay Winter places a time frame on cinematic representations of war. He sees the silent period as distinct by its ability to suggest and infer in ways that sound films and the spoken language cannot.[77] His second period runs from 1930 to 1970, with the 1930s marked as a moment when some of the few truly pacifist films were made (he cites *La Grande Illusion* of 1937 but I would also include *Journey's End* and *All Quiet on the Western Front* here). The period was also marked by the approaching war that was "unthinkable and around the corner", a phenomenon that is evident in *The Fighting 69th* (1940) and *Sergeant York* (1941). This period he sees as ending with what he calls the "Vietnam moment" is where the sensibilities of a more circumspect and resistant aesthetic came into play. Films that were critical of the war and drew attention to its effects on people's bodies, minds, and lives introduced a darker mode of representing war. We have seen here that a number of those aesthetic and representational strategies can be traced to the way that Hollywood remembered the war in the 1920s and '30s.

With some notable exceptions, there have been relatively few Hollywood films set in the 1914–18 war made in the post-war period or in Winter's third period from 1970 to the present. Yet the techniques of filming battle scenes as chaotic, with the trajectory toward the horizontal and the pitifully ironic, remain resilient. This is nowhere better exemplified than in Sam Fuller's *The Big Red One* (1980). The film opens in 1918 with a wooden crucifix in No Man's Land with Christ's eyes hollowed out as if he has been blinded or worse. The scenes are instances of futility. The opening has Lee Marvin as a private who stabs and kills a German soldier who is trying to surrender. He later finds out the war had been over for four hours. The rest of the film follows Marvin, now "The Sergeant," who leads a company as they go through the major engagements of the European theatre the First Division (The Big Red One) was involved in during World War II. In a pointed irony, the wooden crucifix appears again when the company is ambushed under those same hollow unseeing eyes that emphasize the desacralization of the soil where the crucifix stands, the same soil that was fought over in 1914–18. The last scene of the film takes place at the end of the war. Having been unable to save a starving boy from the death camp his division has liberated, The Sergeant is confronted by a German soldier, who is trying to surrender, and he stabs him. When his men tell him the war has been over for four hours, he works to save the German soldier's life. Yet there is no redemption or salvation here except coming out alive. The film ends with Private Zab (Robert Carradine), the pulp novelist, a thinly veiled version of Fuller, in a voice-over saying "Surviving is the only glory in war, if you know what I mean." This last scene is reminiscent of Paul Bäumer caught in a bombardment in a cemetery with the crosses and the coffins emerging from a desacralized earth. Fuller, a veteran who had seen and filmed the liberation of the concentration camps, filmed this last scene primarily in low angles, from the ground. There is no inclination to the verticality of hope in any sense of the endeavor of war. Fuller's interest, like that of Stallings and Vidor or Remarque and Milestone, was in those unfortunates who were caught up in it. The move from the Edenic to the blasted landscape, from the wonder of nature to the moonscape of human-inflicted suffering that Vidor and Milestone introduced into the Hollywood war film lexicon, remains intact in Terrence Malick's *The Thin Red Line* (1998). Stanley Kubrick's contrast between the troglodyte world of the trenches and the palatial abodes of the generals in *Paths of Glory* (1957) and his overriding sense of ironic futility in *Full Metal Jacket* (1987) owe something to Vidor, Walsh, Whale, and Milestone. So too does the devastation at the end of Oliver Stone's *Platoon* (1986) as Chris (Charlie Sheen) looks down at the corpses from the battle, a shot that is filled with profaned earth.

While few films take as their subject the American World War I veteran, there have been many films about veterans returning home across the post–World War II period. They range across territory similar to those of the '20s and '30s, from characters who are amnesiac such as Ronald Colman's character Charles Ranier/"Smithy" in *Random Harvest* (Mervyn

LeRoy, 1942) to Jake Gyllenhaal as Captain Colter Steven/Sean Fentress in *Source Code* (Duncan Jones, 2011). In both films, establishing the character's identity is the main goal of the narrative. Veterans as social problems continue to pervade Hollywood screens, offering scriptwriters a full range of plausible actions.

The challenges posed by total war to traditional gender, race, and class relations reemerge throughout the post-war Hollywood film, particularly post-1970. The racy banter of *M*A*S*H* (Robert Altman, 1970) owes something to the war-nurse cycle. While African American soldiers' experience in World War I was all but ignored by Hollywood at the time, films such as the Hughes Brothers' *Dead Presidents* (1995), which incorporates the veteran as social problem motif, draws on the tradition of *I Am a Fugitive from a Chain Gang* and *Heroes For Sale*. *Red Tails* (2012), directed by Anthony Hemingway and produced by George Lucas, is an account of the Tuskegee Airmen of World War II. The tropes of being ignored by superiors, and losing friends, while doubly intensified by the racial prejudice they experienced, draws on the conflicts laid out in *The Dawn Patrol* and *The Eagle and the Hawk*.

Lucas famously was inspired by Battle of Britain footage for the movement of the rebel fighters in *Star Wars*, a series of films that combine thrills and a fetishization of technology with a passing nod to the pity of war, similar to Howard Hughes's *Hell's Angels*. Steven Spielberg ventured onto the fields of the Great War with *War Horse* (2011), a film that imports the British memory of the Great War as catastrophic and futile via the novel (1982) and play (2007) by British author Michael Morpurgo. In the process Spielberg draws on a British memory of the war that Hollywood frequently turned to in films of the '20s and '30s. In some sense it is accurate to see Spielberg's *Saving Private Ryan* (1998) as working with the ground laid by *Wings* and *The Big Parade* in building the trauma of modern war into the characters.

Hollywood's contribution to the American memory of the Great War operated, as we have seen, along the terrain of the wider public discourses that characterized that memory across those decades. The studio system was, and is, reactive to events and the ebb and flow of discourses that informed the war's memory. It is clear that World War I has been somewhat overshadowed by World War II, Vietnam, and now the Gulf War and the wars in Iraq, Afghanistan, and Syria. These wars have prompted films that work through similar tropes to those that Hollywood developed in the years following the Great War: the pity of war, the isolation of the returning veteran, the social impact on relationships drawing attention to the plight of those who have suffered and are suffering. These and the trajectory from vertical to horizontal, from hope to loss, are woven into the fabric of a film aesthetic that is now central to contemporary cinematic treatments of war and its effects. In that sense, the Hollywood memory of the Great War that emerged in the interwar period endures.

NOTES

Introduction

1. Baum, *Grand Hotel*, 9.
2. Ibid., 13–14.
3. Balio, *Grand Design*, 88.
4. Kaes, *Shell Shock Cinema*, 2.
5. Ibid., 3.
6. Ibid., 5.
7. Ibid., 3.
8. Bordwell, Thompson, and Staiger, *The Classical Hollywood Cinema*, 92.
9. Thompson, *Exporting Entertainment*; Vasey, *The World According to Hollywood*.
10. Hansen, *Cinema and Experience*, 41.
11. Resina and Ingenschay, "Preface," xi–xii.
12. Ibid., xii.
13. McLoughlin, *Veteran Poetics*, 69.
14. Winter, *War Beyond Words*, 126–127.

Chapter 1

1. Winter, *War Beyond Words*, 144.
2. Chaplin, *My Autobiography*, 146.
3. Much has been written about this "slacker controversy." See Robinson, *Chaplin: His Life and Art*, 193–196; and Maland, *Chaplin and American Culture*, 35–37.
4. Reed, *The Chronicles of Charlie Chaplin*, vi–vii.
5. Robinson, *Chaplin: His Life and Art*, 253.
6. Carroll, *Comedy Incarnate*, 56.
7. Anonymous, "Sure Fire Timely Fun That Will Delight Any Audience," *Film Daily*, November 17, 1918, 32.
8. Sime Silverman, "Chaplin's Shoulder Arms," *Variety*, October 25, 1918, 36.
9. Delluc, *Charlot*, quoted in Robinson, *Chaplin: The Mirror of Opinion*, 43–44.
10. Brand, "How the 'Lost Battalion' Helped to Make History."
11. Slotkin, *Lost Battalions*, 342.
12. Anonymous, "Announce Names of Notables Selected to act as Judges of The Lost Battalion," *Motion Picture World*, June 28, 1919, 1961.

13. William J. Reilly, "Sell History in Lost Battalion," *Moving Picture World*, September 6, 1919, 1481.

14. Anonymous, "Historic War Episode Reenacted by Survivors: The Lost Battalion," *Wid's Daily*, July 6, 1919, 3.

15. Ibid.

16. Brand, "How the Lost Battalion Helped to Make History."

17. Quote from *Morning Telegraph* in advertisement for *The Lost Battalion* in *Moving Picture World*, August, 2, 1919, 641.

18. Anonymous, "Historic War Episode Reenacted by Survivors: The Lost Battalion," *Wid's Daily*, July 6, 1919, 3.

19. Service flags were window banners that families who had members in the service could display to demonstrate their commitment. By the summer of 1918, mourning the death of soldiers at the front became a topic of discussion where traditional mourning practices, i.e., the wearing of black, were deemed inappropriate. A gold star replaced the blue star on the service flag, signaling the loss of a loved one, which "reflects a need to see the loss in terms of preciousness and as a valuable contribution." This system of public display was gendered in that the black armband was favored by men while the gold star in the window was deemed more appropriate for women. See Budreau, *Bodies of War*, 96.

20. Budreau, *Bodies of War*, 73–81.

21. Miller, "Nature's History," 4.

22. Griffith's landscapes in his Civil War films included African Americans either as incorporated into an idealized rural setting as in *His Trust* and *His Trust Fulfilled* (1910) in the manner of Edward Bayer Bellevue's painting *The Lewis Homestead in Salem Virginia* (1855) or as threatening interlopers into an Edenic idyll as Gus and Silas Lynch (white actors in blackface) are in *The Birth of a Nation* (1915). See Williams, *Playing the Race Card*. Williams quotes Vachel Lindsay, who wrote that the final Reconstruction chapter of *The Birth of a Nation* was a "White Anglo Saxon Niagara" where "black men are quite literally wiped from the screen" (120). See also Jackson, "The Secret Life of Oscar Micheaux." See his analysis of the Gus and Flora scene, where he sets out that Flora is looking and is identified with the Edenic landscape which Gus, "a serpent in Eden," disrupts (222).

23. Mayer, *Stagestruck Filmmaker*, 125–126.

24. Merchant, *Reinventing Eden*.

25. Ibáñez, *The Four Horsemen of the Apocalypse*, 142.

26. In his research on Mathis's Valentino scripts Thomas Slater notes that Mathis refocused the film to highlight Julio's spiritual regeneration and thereby develop a more complex masculinity to his star persona. Mathis's note on her visual source for the final scene can be found in *The Four Horsemen of the Apocalypse*, screenplay, scene 738 (Archives—Museo Nazionale del Cinema di Torino). For this and other script references see Slater, "June Mathis's Valentino Scripts," 109.

27. Budreau, *Bodies of War*.

28. Ibid., 70

29. Ibid., 76–79.
30. Whitman, "One Million Dead," in *Specimen Days*, 98.

Chapter 2

1. Sandburg, "Grass."
2. Owen, "Spring Offensive."
3. See Knutson, "Hidden in Plain Sight." Knutson notes that O'Keeffe's series of abstract work were inspired by landscape sketches undertaken in Palo Duro Canyon, Texas, from 1915 to 1917, when the war and rotogravure images dominated the news. O'Keeffe's letters from the time note her interest in these images and reports from the front. Knutson suggests that this and the enlistment of her brother Alexis had a distinctive impact on her abstract landscapes both at the time and later in the 1928 painting *Abstraction—Alexis* for her brother, who was suffering from having been gassed. He died of influenza in 1930 (62–63). Claggett Wilson's work, drawn from his experiences at Belleau Wood as a marine, combined blasted figures and landscapes in his 1919 series of watercolors. David M. Lubin notes in his book *Grand Illusion* that Wilson's use of landscape in *First Attack on the Bois de Belleau* seems to prefigure Vidor's use of landscape and figures in the Belleau Wood sequence in *The Big Parade*, although he notes that these paintings were not circulated publicly until 1928.
4. Lubin, *Grand Illusions*, 186–187.
5. Laurence Stallings, "The Big Parade," *New Republic*, September 17, 1924, 66–69.
6. Vidor, *A Tree is a Tree*, 111.
7. Vidor returned to these themes as a means of developing the everyman-caught-up-in-larger-events theme in *The Crowd* (1928) and *Our Daily Bread* (1934). In these iterations the themes of steel and wheat offered two variants of settings, one urban, one rural.
8. Vidor, *On Film Making*, 108.
9. Stallings, memo to Irving Thalberg, "Original Story."
10. Vidor, *A Tree is a Tree*, 117.
11. Vidor, *A Tree is a Tree*, 120. The military advisers were probably drawing on their own experience in France in the Argonne, St. Mihiel sector near Verdun. The terrain there is more varied than that of the British Sector on the Somme, where the kind of straight roads that Nevinson depicts and Vidor was imagining are more prevalent.
12. Vidor, notes to assistant director David Howard.
13. Stallings, memo to Thalberg, 10.
14. Vidor, *A Tree is a Tree*, 114.
15. Fitzgerald, "Letter to Maxwell Perkins," 107.
16. Trout, *On the Battlefield of Memory*, 7.

17. Boyd, *Through the Wheat*, 267.
18. Ibid., 204.
19. Ibid., 207–208.
20. Vidor, *A Tree is a Tree*, 115–116.
21. Boyd, *Through the Wheat*, 251.
22. Ibid.
23. Ibid., 269–270.
24. In the original version of the film the red cross on the ambulance was colored red.
25. Vidor, Director's personal notes on *The Big Parade*.
26. Jacobs, "Men Without Women," 309.
27. Stallings, "The Big Parade."
28. Stallings and Anderson, promptbook for *What Price Glory*.
29. Jacobs, "Men Without Women," 314.
30. Ibid., 311–312.
31. Lubin, *Grand Illusions*, 173. See also Trout, *On the Battlefield of Memory*, 158–175.
32. Lubin, *Grand Illusions*. David Lubin describes *The Machine Gunner* as "A portrait of pragmatic bravery . . . It glamourizes its subject by eschewing glamour." 174.
33. Trout, *On the Battlefield of Memory*, 170.
34. For example, on July 27, 1926, according to *The Film Daily*, The American Legion was able to include "150 stars" to take part in their patriotic show held at the Olympic Auditorium downtown Los Angeles while Louis B. Mayer provided them with support staff from his studio. See Anonymous, "Stars Aid Legion Show," *Film Daily*, July 27, 1928, 2. In November of the same year the wryly named "Phil M. Daly" reported in *Film Daily* that Universal and Famous Players, the production wing of the Paramount corporation, had supplied free films to the American Legion post in Hollywood, Florida, while the Hollywood cinema there was being repaired because of storm damage. See Phil M. Daly, "And That's That," *Film Daily*, November 1, 1926, 1. The Legion in various areas of the country also owned and operated film theatres, which were often called "Legion theatres," and lobbied for Sunday opening times in a number of areas. See Anonymous, "Sunday Shows Up at Wayland," *Film Daily*, December 22, 1926, 2. They were also incorporated into advertising and promotion of films at the local level, mobilizing veterans for parades and exhibitions of their war relics before the premieres of films. See Anonymous, "Behind the Front," Exploit-O-Grams, *Film Daily*, July 16, 1926, 3, and "The Unknown Soldier," Exploit-O-Grams, *Film Daily*, August 6, 1926, 8.
35. Budreau, *Bodies of War*, 142.
36. Cooper, "Maybe Your Old Buddy Fights in Films."
37. Harding, "What Price Censorship."
38. Sherwood, "EXTRA! Hollywood Declares War!" 38.
39. Hall, "The Screen: A Lost Chance."

40. Ibid. It is interesting to note that this film received a withering reception in Britain, with the critics citing sentimentality as a particularly American characteristic. See Christine Gledhill's incisive analysis of how this equation of sentiment functioned in the British critical establishment's linking it to melodrama and carrying a "working class or feminised attribution" as opposed to a sense of "naturalism" and "class inflected undemonstrativeness." Gledhill, *Reframing British Cinema*, 132.

41. Anonymous, "The Unknown Soldier at the Rivoli," *Film Daily*, June 16, 1926, 7.

42. Trout, *On the Battlefield of Memory*, 109.

43. Ibid., 131–133. As an example of the instability of the dominant unifying intent of the Tomb of the Unknown Soldier, Trout points to Harlem Renaissance poet James Weldon Johnson's 1930 poem "Saint Peter Relates an Incident of the Resurrection Day." In that poem as the "Great Roll" is called the Ku Klux Klan leads the way to rescuing the Unknown Soldier from his tomb. The soldier that emerges from the tomb and goes on to heaven is a "tall black soldier-angel marching alone."

44. Mosse, *Fallen Soldiers*, 91–92.

45. Stallings, memo to Thalberg, 13.

46. Kaes, *Shell Shock Cinema*, 212.

47. Winter, *War Beyond Words*, 89.

48. McGuire, "Filtering and Interpreting The Great War," 670–671.

49. Michael T. Isenberg notes that while the film was ambiguous in its antiwar message by focusing specifically on the German experience of the war, it lined up with the American Government's line that the German people had been unscrupulously led. Isenberg, *War on Film*, 138.

50. Gunning, "Landscape and the Fantasy of Moving Pictures," 36–37.

51. Ibid.

52. Black, "The German Veteran Speaks," 67.

53. Louella Parsons, *Los Angeles Examiner*, quoted in advertisement for *All Quiet on the Western Front*, *Variety*, April 30, 1930.

54. Llewellyn Miller, *Los Angeles Record*, quoted in advertisement for *All Quiet on the Western Front*, *Variety*, April 30, 1930.

55. Sime Silverman, "All Quiet on the Western Front," *Variety*, May 7, 1930, 21.

56. Ibid.

57. Robinett, "The Narrative Shape of Traumatic Experience." In this article Robinett refers to the fade-to-black links between scenes in Milestone's film as a cinematic device equivalent to Remarque's use of "abruptly shifting tenses" and "intrusive memories and traumatic experiences" (305).

58. Curtis, *James Whale*. Curtis records that Pearson, who had been directing films in the UK since the teens, was so concerned about Whale's understated approach that he gave him a copy of *Pudovkin on Film Technique* (100).

59. Curtis, *James Whale*, 94.

60. Pare Lorentz, *Judge Magazine*, quoted in advertisement for *Journey's End* in *Film Daily*, Friday, May 16, 1930 6–7.

61. Harry Evans, *Life Magazine,* quoted in advertisement for *Journey's End* in *Film Daily,* Friday, May 16, 1930, 6–7.

62. Author uncited, *The New Yorker,* quoted in advertisement for *Journey's End* in *Film Daily,* Friday, May 16, 1930, 6–7.

63. In their 1937 follow-up to their landmark study *Middletown,* Robert and Helen Merrill Lynd reported a male graduate from "X State College" complaining about its conservatism. "They take Dos Passos off the shelves so you won't get polluted." The Lynds recorded rumors that the local Daughters of the American Revolution had "blocked the staging of Journey's End by the college dramatic group." Lynd and Lynd, *Middletown in Transition,* 216.

64. Richard Watts Jr., "Our Ways, Their Ways and a Play: Inevitable Comparisons of What Price Glory to Journey's End," *Herald Tribune,* reprinted in *Boston Transcript,* November 9, 1929.

65. Jacobs, *The Decline of Sentiment,* 179.

66. Anonymous, "Beyond Victory," *Film Daily,* April 12, 1931, 32.

67. Anonymous, "Beyond Victory," *Variety,* April 8, 1931, 19.

68. Anonymous, "Private Jones," *Variety,* March 28, 1933, 15.

69. McBride notes that Ford had grown up near Prout's Neck in Maine, where Homer painted, and he claimed that as a boy he had visited him in his studio and watched him paint. McBride, *Searching for John Ford,* 39.

70. Within the subsequent two years the pilgrimages had become a kind of show piece for an official memorialization of the fallen soldiers. They demonstrated the work of the American Battlefield Monuments Commission in displaying the grandeur of the monuments and cemeteries built in France. The War Department saw it as a way of showing compassion and care for the fallen and their families. At the same time, veterans' groups such as the American Legion saw the pilgrimage program as keeping the memory of their service during the war in the public imagination. For women's groups the program represented a significant success and a fortifying of a political voice. Budreau, *Bodies of War,* 239–240.

71. Anonymous, "Pilgrimage," Film Daily, July 17, 1933, 7.

72. Gallagher, *John Ford,* 94.

73. Basinger, *The World War II Combat Film,* 94.

74. Winter, *War Beyond Words,* 144.

Chapter 3

1. Anonymous, "$6000 in San Antonio," *Variety,* June 1, 1927, 13.

2. Anonymous, "Fonck, World's Greatest War Aviator Has Seen Wings Three Times," *Paramount Around the World,* March 1, 1928, 24.

3. Anonymous, "And Now the Triumph of 'Wings' in Los Angeles, The City Where Motion Pictures Are Made," *Paramount Around the World,* April 2, 1928, 22.

4. Stimson, "Lindberg. May 1927," quoted in Wohl, *The Spectacle of Flight*, 32.
5. Haley, "A Faithless Generation Asked a Sign," quoted in Wohl, *The Spectacle of Flight*, 32.
6. Cripps, "To C.A.L." quoted in Wohl, *The Spectacle of Flight*, 1.
7. Haley, "A Faithless Generation Asked a Sign," quoted in Wohl, *The Spectacle of Flight*, 31.
8. Allen, *Only Yesterday*, 220.
9. Marinetti, "The Founding and Manifesto of Futurism," 19.
10. Robertson, *The Dream of Civilized Warfare*, x.
11. Ibid., xi.
12. Jacobs, *The Decline of Sentiment*, 179.
13. Ibid., 130–131.
14. Lindbergh, "They'll Be Glad To See You."
15. Williams, "Eaglet Grave Lies Out of Legion Path."
16. Saunders, "Deposition: August 1930." Saunders gave his biography for a deposition in a lawsuit against Howard Hawks and Warner Brothers by Howard Hughes for similarities to his film *Hell's Angels*.
17. Anonymous, "Comparison of Estimate With Actual Cost."
18. Jeff Cohen, "Of Magnascope and Vitalite."
19. Alvey, "The Cinema as Taxidermy," 26.
20. Turner, "Wings—Epic of the Air," 36.
21. Funderburk, *The Early Birds of War*, 44.
22. Turner, "Wings—Epic of the Air," 37.
23. Anonymous, "Personal Glimpses: When War-planes Flame and Audiences Gasp," *Literary Digest*, November 12, 1927, 36.
24. Ibid., 38.
25. Wellman, *The Man and His Wings*, 120.
26. Behlmer, "World War One Aviation Films," 420. According to Robert Wohl, Hughes had also been discussing the air war with Lewis Milestone, who had been with the US Army Signal Corps during the war. Wohl, *The Spectacle of Flight*, 123.
27. For a discussion of the divergent approaches to representing war in *Hell's Angels* and in *All Quiet on the Western Front*, see Baird, "Hell's Angels Above the Western Front."
28. Hitchcock, "Why 'Thrillers' Thrive."
29. Anonymous, "Hell's Angels," *Film Daily*, August 24, 1930, 10. Note: "s.a." means "sex appeal."
30. Fisher, memorandum re: Hell's Angels.
31. Lord, letter to Arthur H. DeBra.
32. Sidne Silverman, "Hell's Angels," *Variety*, June 4, 1930, 25.
33. Andrew Fiala has outlined two broad types of "realism" that are unique to the war film: one that is based on the individual's experience and one that offers a broader, more general view of the collective experience of the battlefield and the

war. Both of these he sees as subjective and prefers the term "representational realism." Fiala makes the point that "Hollywood films are often firmly grounded in the events, places and individuals of actual history," which leaves them bound to a tightly constrained verisimilitude. Fiala, "General Patton and Private Ryan," 338.

34. *The Caddo Company, Inc., a corporation, Plaintiff vs. First National Pictures, Inc., a corporation, et al.*, affidavit from John Monk Saunders, 1–2. (This is also reprinted in Behlmer, *Inside Warner Bros.*, 338–340.)

35. A number of sources have pointed out that *The Dawn Patrol* was written in large part by Howard Hawks, who later claimed authorship, and that he had Saunders put his name to it because of his reputation with aviation pictures.

36. *The Caddo Company, Inc., a corporation, Plaintiff vs. First National Pictures, Inc., a corporation, et al.*, affidavit from Howard Hughes, 2.

37. Ibid., 3.

38. *The Caddo Company, Inc., a corporation, Plaintiff vs. First National Pictures, Inc., a corporation, et al.*, affidavit from Joseph Moncure March, 2.

39. Ibid., 2.

40. Silverman, "Hell's Angels." *Flight* was a 1929 Columbia film directed by Frank Capra. Advertised as "the first all-talkie aviation epic," it was the story of Marine fliers in Nicaragua.

41. Anonymous, "The Dawn Patrol," *Variety*, July 16, 1930, 15.

42. Rudy Behlmer, "Deja View." In fact the 1938 remake of *The Dawn Patrol* used virtually all of the flying footage from the original film. As Behlmer notes, "Hal Wallis wrote to Jack Warner: 'By using our exterior shots from Dawn Patrol, and just remaking the interiors, which consist almost entirely of little headquarters shack, we should be able to remake the picture for a 'a quarter' . . . and I think it would bring us a fortune now when the whole world is talking and thinking war and rearmament." 131.

43. Mordaunt Hall, "The Screen: Frederic March, Jack Oakie and Sir Guy Standing in a Drama of World War Air Fighting," *New York Times*, May 13, 1933.

44. Anonymous, "The Eagle and the Hawk," *Film Daily*, May 6, 1933, 4.

45. "Chic" (Epes Winthrop Sargent), "Eagle and the Hawk," *Variety*, May 16, 1933, 21.

46. Epes Winthrop Sargent was the author of influential works in the film industry during the teens: *The Technique of the Photoplay* and *Picture Theatre Advertising*. With the director of Publix Theatre Managers Training school, John F. Barry, he co-wrote *Building Theatre Patronage: Management and Merchandising*.

47. For example, in July 1933 the "nothing but Fanny to me" line was objected to by the board of censors in Alberta, Canada. James Wingate of Hays Office, letter to Harold Hurley.

48. Wingate of Hays Office to Harold Hurley.

49. Behlmer, "Deja View," 131.

50. Wear, "Film Reviews: Dawn Patrol," *Variety*, December 14, 1938, 14.

51. Ibid.

Chapter 4

1. Boetticher, "Entretien avec Budd Boetticher."
2. Borden, *The Forbidden Zone*; LaMotte, *The Backwash of War*; Mortimer, *A Green Tent in Flanders*.
3. Title card from *The Girl Who Stayed at Home* (D.W. Griffith, 1919).
4. Gardiner, "Notes on War Nurse to Mr Thalberg," scene 199, 17.
5. The film's structure operates on a more broad inscription of the modern/traditional conflict. Atoline's father is in fact a Confederate veteran who has moved back to the family chateau in France, as he cannot abide the defeat. His transformation comes when his land is liberated by the US army from the Germans, his daughter saved, and he consigns his treasured Confederate flag to the trash heap and salutes the Stars and Stripes.
6. Anonymous, "The Screen," *New York Times*, March 24, 1919.
7. Patsy Smith, "Among the Women," *Variety*, March 28, 1919, 90.
8. Ibid.
9. Anonymous, "The Screen."
10. Emerson and Loos, *How to Write Photoplays*, 35.
11. Anonymous, "A Humdinger of a Comedy: The Virtuous Vamp," *Wid's Daily*, November 30, 1919, 23.
12. Anonymous, untitled, *Wid's Daily*, February 24, 1920, 1.
13. Vasey, *The World According to Hollywood*, 21.
14. In his biography of Clara Bow, David Stenn writes that Schulberg brought Loring and Lighton in to rewrite the story Elinor Glyn had written "and devise one for Clara incorporating the 'It' concept." Stenn, *Clara Bow*, 82.
15. Anonymous, "'Wings' A Truly Great Picture," *Film Spectator*, March 3, 1927, 7.
16. The act of "going upstairs" with women in bars and estaminets behind the lines attracted concern in the PCA reports on a number of scripts of war films during this period.
17. Saunders, *Wings*, 156.
18. Anonymous, "The Shadow Stage," *Photoplay*, September 1927, 52.
19. Jacobs, *The Decline of Sentiment*, 131.
20. Keire, "Swearing Allegiance," 248.
21. Ibid., 255.
22. Ibid., 261.
23. Ibid., 255.
24. Mencken, *The American Language*, 127.
25. Mencken, "The Flapper."
26. Aware of the sensitivities of the representation of its emblem in film, care was taken to distance the story from any association with the Red Cross. This was not wholly successful, though, as in a letter to Col. Jason S. Joy the legal advisor to the Red Cross, H.J. Hughes, noted that *War Nurse* "did not merit our

criticism as it affects any Red Cross material. . . . However a number of exhibitors throughout the country engaged in a misuse of the emblem in advertising this film." Hughes, letter to Col. Jason S. Joy.

27. These lines are from the final script version and are in the finished film.

28. The Turner/MGM script collection at the Margaret Herrick Library contains script notes by Gardiner to Thalberg. These notes give an insight into the changes Gardiner made to the dialogue. Gardiner, "Notes on War Nurse," scene 49, 5.

29. Gardiner, "Notes on War Nurse," scene 39, 4.

30. Gardiner, "Notes on War Nurse," scene 58, 7.

31. Gardiner, "Notes on War Nurse," scene 193, 15.

32. Gardiner, "Notes on War Nurse," scene 155, 14.

33. Norbert Lusk, "Screen in Review," *Photoplay*, November 8, 1930, 64.

34. Anonymous, "Becky and Joe Were Told to Write Dialogue, and Certainly Wrote It," *Film Spectator*, November 8, 1930, 8.

35. Anonymous, "'Wings' A Truly Great Picture," *Film Spectator*, March 3, 1927.

36. Anonymous, "The Mad Parade," *Film Daily*, September 20, 1931, 10.

37. Mordaunt Hall, "The Screen," *New York Times*, September 27, 1931.

Chapter 5

1. In this case, the predominant image of the veteran was white and male. The African American veteran did also resonate with the possibility of change and with anxieties and fear. These, however, had a specific resonance that was suppressed, or at the very least negotiated through mintrelsy, in Hollywood configurations of veterans and the experiences of soldiers in the war.

2. Allen, *Only Yesterday*, 94–95.

3. Mae Tinée, "Nikki Charms Her Flock of Warbirds," *Chicago Tribune*, September 19, 1931.

4. Keene, *Doughboys*, 161–178.

5. In their 1985 study on the development of the classical Hollywood cinema, Bordwell, Staiger, and Thompson outline how scriptwriting how-to manuals recommend devices and techniques where character traits provide motivation for their behavior and interaction with other characters in the story. Bordwell, Thompson, and Staiger, *The Classical Hollywood Cinema*, 180.

6. Emerson and Loos, *How to Write Photoplays*, 65.

7. Sargent, *The Technique of the Photoplay*, 100–101.

8. The film does not indicate which part of the Humoresque Opus 101 he is meant to be playing. An educated guess based on its popularity at the time would be No. 7.

9. Miller, "'An American Soldier Poet,'" 29.

10. Dumont, *Frank Borzage*, 74.

11. Marion, *How to Write and Sell Film Stories*, 93.

12. Ibid., 94.

13. Anonymous, "Snug Harbor for the Shell Shocked," *New York Times*, January 2, 1921.

14. The play was adapted for the screen once more as a musical by MGM in 1941, directed by Frank Borzage and starring Jeanette MacDonald and Brian Aherne.

15. Anonymous, "The Best Picture Norma Has Had in a Long Time," *Film Daily*, March 5, 1922, 2.

16. Ibid.

17. Jacobs, *The Decline of Sentiment*, 273.

18. The film's writing credits list screenplay by Ernest Vadja and Claudine West with dialogue by Donald Ogden Stewart and James Bernard Fagan. However, the script history held in the MGM script files dates the script work beginning with continuity by Frances Marion throughout June 1931; John Meehan worked on the continuity from August to November of 1931, Claudine West worked on it through December, John Balderston was brought in in February 1932, then West in March again along with Vajda and some pencil notes from playwright Edward Childs Carpenter. Throughout May and June, Fagan reworked some of the dialogue, then in July John Ogden Stewart worked on the scene at the train platform where Kenneth returns from the front, then later that same month Meehan returned to polish some more before shooting.

19. Morsberger, Lesser, and Clark, "John Balderston," 25.

20. Balderston, "Valedictory Memo," part 1, 1.

21. Ibid., part 3, 10.

22. Ibid., part 1, 1.

23. Ibid., part 2, 4.

24. Martin, *Smilin' Through*, 94.

25. Balderston, "Valedictory Memo," part 1, 4.

26. Fagan, *Smilin' Through* Shooting Script, June 7, 1932, 124–125.

27. Stewart, *Smilin' Through* Shooting Script, July 13, 1932, 123.

28. E. Schallert, "Ideal Romance Wins the Tear," *Los Angeles Times*, September 8, 1932.

29. Cameron, "Irreconcilable Differences," 477–478.

30. Ibid., 480–481.

31. B.F., "Love and Duty Play is Presented at Cohan Theatre," *New York Tribune*, October 12, 1921.

32. B.F., "Love and Duty Play is Presented at Cohan Theatre," *New York Tribune*, October 12, 1921.

33. T.H. Lewis, "Pollack Returns to Cohan Theatre," *Morning Telegraph*, March 11, 1921.

34. Macgowan, *Theatre of Tomorrow*, 221.

35. Ibid.

36. Selznick, *Memo from David O. Selznick*, 45.

37. Mordaunt Hall, "The Screen is Indebted to the Stage," *New York Times*, October 9, 1932.

38. Selznick recalled, "I went through one of those searches for a new girl that drive everybody crazy because we needed new stars at RKO, and because I was convinced that the story would be more moving and believable if it was played by a girl that hadn't previously been identified with other parts. Furthermore, the role had made great stars on the stage, such as Katherine Cornell." Selznick, *Memo from David O. Selznick*, 45.

39. Danes, *A Bill of Divorcement*, 4.

40. Ibid., 30.

41. Kardiner, *The Traumatic Neuroses of War*, 97.

42. Danes, *A Bill of Divorcement*.

43. Overstreet, "George Cukor," 17–18.

44. Morrison, "The Voice Teacher as Shakespearean Collaborator," 132.

45. Alexander Woolcott, "Second Thoughts on First Nights," *New York Times*, March 21, 1920.

46. John Corbin, "The Play: A New Hamlet," *New York Times*, November 17, 1922.

47. Overstreet, "George Cukor," 24.

48. Morrison, "The Voice Teacher as Shakespearean Collaborator," 152–153.

49. Joy, Memo to Heads of Studios.

50. By contrast, the reviews in the literary magazines of the day did not generally shy away from referring to Jake's impotence. Allen Tate, in his review of the novel for *The Nation*, accused Hemingway of betraying the "interior machinery of his hard-boiled attitude: 'It's awfully easy to be hard-boiled about everything in the daytime but at night it is another thing,' says Jake, the sexually impotent, musing on the futile accessibility of Brett. The history of his sentimentality is complete." See Lynn, *Hemingway*, 331.

51. Lynn, *Hemingway*, 330.

52. This did not go unnoticed by Hemingway and his editor Maxwell Perkins. In a letter dated August, 1931, Hemingway wrote to his lawyer, Maurice Speiser, to express concern that Saunders's story would detract from negotiations with studios for the rights to *The Sun Also Rises*. Referring to *The Last Flight*, he wrote, "Film is made from stories by John Monk Saunders which appeared last year in *Liberty*. They were inspired by Sun Also, at least readers kept writing into the magazine to ask why they had paid J.M.S. to write the Sun Also." See Jividin, "Power of Attorney," 25.

53. George M. Ord, in "Letters from Readers," *Liberty Magazine*, February 21, 1931, 8.

54. Shephard, *A War of Nerves*, 1–2.

55. Ord, in "Letters from Readers."

56. Saunders, Article for Publicity Sheet.

57. Christian Science as a religion had reached an apex in popularity in the 1930s in the US. Nikki's reference to it seems to be an illustration of her mother's neglect and hints at a traumatic childhood.

58. Saunders, *Single Lady*, 10–11.

59. John V. Wilson, letter to Hal Wallis. Wilson wrote three pages of notes on areas of concern in the script for *Spent Bullets*, which was the working title for *The Last Flight*. He noted that the lines such as "He went off to shave a horse" "contain a vulgar inference in that they convey the idea that the person in question has gone, or is going, to the toilet. We believe that this inference is likely to cause offense to many people."

60. Saunders, *Single Lady*, p. 85.

61. D.H. Lawrence, "Pansies," in *Complete Poems*, 535.

62. Anonymous, "Review: The Last Flight," *Variety*, August 25, 1931, 14.

63. "The Last Flight," *Film Daily*, August 23, 1931, 18.

64. Mordaunt Hall, "After the Armistice," *New York Times*, August 30, 1931.

65. John V. Wilson, 2.

66. Saunders, *Single Lady*, 158.

67. Anonymous, "Review: The Last Flight."

68. In the 1930 novel *Scarface* by Armitage Trail, Tony Guarino is rumored to have been killed in the war. At the beginning of chapter 6 is an account of Guarino's natural leadership abilities learned during his wartime service in France. However, he is also predisposed to being a killer, which sits in line with prevailing medical discourse. See Trail, *Scarface*, 38.

69. Bordwell, *Poetics of Cinema*, 189–252.

70. *Grand Hotel*, Play Script.

71. Vieira, *Irving Thalberg*, 176.

72. *Grand Hotel*, Script Conference Notes.

73. Ibid.

74. Ibid.

75. Peeler, play review for MGM of *Grand Hotel*.

76. *Grand Hotel*, Serial Story on Publicity, 1.

77. Baum, *Grand Hotel*, 251.

78. Jacobs, *The Decline of Sentiment*, 273.

Chapter 6

1. The term "b'gosh," shortened from "by gosh," was a name given to dramas set in rural New England that "featured the lives of village and country folk linked to farmland and/or seacoast and far removed from the sophistications and perceived moral evasions and relativisms of city life." Mayer, *Stagestruck Filmmaker*, 193.

2. Faust, *This Republic of Suffering*, 263; Keene, *Doughboys*, 163.

3. Gregory, *The Silence of Memory*, 8–41.
4. Schatz, *The Genius of the System*.
5. Balio, *Grand Design*, 281.
6. Schatz, *The Genius of the System*, 139.
7. Lord, Letter to Warner Brothers.
8. Anonymous, "The Girl Who Stayed at Home," *Film Daily*, March 30, 1919, 9.
9. Anonymous, "The Shadow Stage," *Photoplay*, February 1922, 65.
10. I am indebted to Helen Day Mayer and David Mayer for drawing my attention to the importance of the integration and movement of gestures in acting style of the late nineteenth and early twentieth centuries and their impact on film acting and film style of the silent period. I am especially grateful to Helen for her thoughts on Barthelmess's performance style.
11. Alison Smith, "The Screen in Review," *Picture Play*, April 1923, 52–53.
12. Mordaunt Hall, "The Screen: Enchantment of Love," *New York Times*, April 14, 1924.
13. Wilson, "Sixty-five Years of Realism."
14. John Corbin, "Barrieized Pinero," *New York Times*, April 8, 1923.
15. Keene, *Doughboys*, 162.
16. Hale, *The Rise and Crisis of Psychoanalysis in the United States*, 20–21.
17. Anonymous, "Pinero's War Fantasy: Love in an Enchanted Cottage," *Daily Express*, March 9, 1922; Anonymous, "Duke of York's Theatre: The Enchanted Cottage," *Daily Telegraph*, March 2, 1922; Anonymous, "A New Pinero Play," *The Times*, March 2, 1922; from *The Enchanted Cottage* Folder in The Billy Rose Collection at the New York Public Library.
18. Arthur Roland, "Seeing Sights on First Nights," *The Official Metropolitan Guide*, April 1, 1923, 29.
19. Corbin, "Barrieized Pinero."
20. Anonymous, "The Enchanted Cottage," *Film Daily*, April 20, 1924, 13.
21. Anonymous, "The Enchanted Cottage," *Film Daily*.
22. Maurice Henle, "'Another Miracle Man' Says Syndicate Writer." Chaney had by this time had become the standard in the performance of disability on screen, particularly as Quasimodo in *The Hunchback of Notre Dame* a year earlier and the legless gangster Blizzard in *The Penalty* in 1920. Chaney's star persona, as it circulated in the fan and trade press, centered on the virtuosity of his performance as a means of justifying the grotesque and gruesome nature of his characters.
23. Louella Parsons, "Louella Parson Recommends It To All Lovers of Good Pictures," *New York American*, April 12, 1924.
24. Lawrence Langdon, "Barthelmess is Enthusiastic," *Cinema Art*, July, 1924.
25. Josephine Lovett, "The Enchanted Cottage," 1–6.
26. The same scene appears in a *Motion Picture Magazine* short story of the film that appeared in April 1924. See Peter Andrews, "'The Enchanted Cottage' A Short Story," *Motion Picture Magazine*, April 1924, 60–61.
27. Lisa Budreau, *Bodies of War*, 142–144.

28. Stallings, *Plumes*, 347.

29. Don Ryan, "The Wherefore of Great Lovers: A Psychoanalyst Compares The Divergent Attractions of Menjou, Meighan, Barthelmess and Valentino," *Picture Play*, August 1924, 112.

30. Ibid.

31. Hansen, *Babel and Babylon*, 253.

32. Barthelmess played non-white roles throughout the 1920s and early '30s. His role as "The Yellow Man" in *Broken Blossoms* (1919) was central in establishing him as a "versatile" actor. While I have not dealt with this aspect of his persona it is important to note the centrality of his whiteness in the emphasis on his performance in these ethnic masquerades.

33. The name "doughboy" held the connotations of the transformative force of battle and whiteness that were enshrined in Ernest Moore Visqueney's statue *Spirit of the American Doughboy*. At the time Moore's sculpture had been a popular choice for memorials and monuments that were being built throughout cities and towns in the United States, and it was mass produced in miniature throughout the 1920s. Budreau, *Bodies of War*, 139.

34. Anonymous, "Brief Reviews of Current Pictures," *Photoplay*, February, 1926, 16.

35. Landy, Pressbook notes for *The Patent Leather Kid*.

36. Jacobs, *The Decline of Sentiment*, 178.

37. Ibid., 178–179.

38. Mordaunt Hall, "Mr. Barthelmess at his Best," *New York Times*, August 16, 1927.

39. Zanuck, Inter-Office Memo to William Wellman.

Chapter 7

1. Rhodes, *The Birth of the American Horror Film*, 10.
2. Balio, *Grand Illusions*, 298.
3. Thomson, *Extraordinary Bodies*, 6.
4. Stallings, *Plumes*, 277.
5. Norden, *The Cinema of Isolation*, 56–57.
6. Ibid., 57.
7. Thomson, *Extraordinary Bodies*, 57.
8. Ibid., 58.
9. Ibid., 78.
10. Ibid.
11. Gunning, "The Horror of Opacity." See also Gordon, *The Grand Guignol*.
12. See Kevin Brownlow, *Universal Horror*, documentary film (Universal Television and Photoplay Productions, 1998); Skal, *The Monster Show*, 67–71; Skal, *Dark Carnival*; Studlar, *This Mad Masquerade*.

13. Skal, *The Monster Show*, 67–71.
14. Skal, *The Monster Show*.
15. Kaes, *Shell Shock Cinema*, 4.
16. Ibid.
17. Skal, *The Monster Show*, 65.
18. Ibid., 66.
19. Skal, *Dark Carnival*.
20. Bogdan, *Freak Show*, 11.
21. Adams, *Sideshow U.S.A.*, 4–5.
22. Allen, *Only Yesterday*, 94.
23. Clodfelter, *Warfare and Armed Conflicts*, 51.
24. Grey, "Introduction," in Priestley, *Benighted*, vii.
25. Deborah Cohen, *The War Come Home*, 16, 62.
26. Keene, *Doughboys*, 162.
27. Budreau, *Bodies of War*, 168.
28. Morris, *The Penalty*, 47.
29. Witt, "The Accidental Republic," 2, 6.
30. Morris, *The Penalty*, 58–59.
31. Ibid., 59.
32. Norman Cohen, *The Long Steel Rail*, 197–223.
33. Aldrich, *Death Rode the Rails*, 3.
34. Crosby, *America's Forgotten Epidemic*, 206.
35. Doležal, "'Waste in a Great Enterprise,'" 95.
36. Anonymous, "Influenza Epidemic Working West: Boston Theatres Opening, While Chicago and Mid-West Close—Houses in San Francisco Capitulate, Making the Coast Practically Restricted in Amusements," *Moving Picture World*, November 2, 1918, quoted in Koszarski, "Flu season," 470.
37. Longmore and Goldberger, "The League of the Physically Handicapped," 891.
38. Ibid., 893–894.
39. Linker, *War's Waste*, 62.
40. Ibid.
41. Ibid., 60
42. Longmore and Goldberger, "The League of the Physically Handicapped," 921.
43. Keene, *Doughboys*, 209.
44. Kaes, *Shell Shock Cinema*, 3.
45. Ibid., 98. The quote is from Sigmund Freud, "Thoughts for the Times on War and Death," 289.
46. Ibid., 6.
47. Curtis, *James Whale*, 149.
48. Ibid., 3.

49. Richard Watts Jr., "Our Ways, Their Ways and a Play: Inevitable Comparisons of What Price Glory to Journey's End," *Herald Tribune*, reprinted in *Boston Transcript*, November 9, 1929.
50. Rhodes, *The Birth of the American Horror Film*, 169.
51. Priestley, *Margin Released*, 181, quoted in Curtis, *James Whale*, 173.
52. Priestley, *Benighted*, 7.
53. Priestley, "Five Persons," quoted in Curtis, *James Whale*, 173.
54. Priestley, *Margin Released*, 111.
55. Ibid., 89–90.
56. Priestley, *Benighted*, 134.
57. Ibid., 136–137.
58. Curtis, *James Whale*, 182. Curtis surmises that R.C. Sherriff wrote the new ending, as Benn Levy had left Hollywood for England by the time it was rewritten.
59. Mordaunt Hall, "Reflections and News of the Screen: Success of a Young Studio Head," *New York Times*, November 6, 1932.
60. Abel Green, "Old Dark House," *Variety*, November 1, 1932, 12.
61. Anonymous, "The Old Dark House," *Harrison's Reports*, November 5, 1932, 179.
62. Anonymous, "Armistice Day Suggestions," *Universal Weekly*, November 5, 1932, 6–7.
63. Gemünden, *Continental Strangers*, 25.
64. Elsaesser, "Ethnicity, Authenticity and Exile," 114.
65. Gemünden, *Continental Strangers*, 15.
66. Land, "Film Reviews: The Black Cat," *Variety*, May 22, 1934, 15, 29.
67. Anonymous, "Reviews of the New Features: The Black Cat," *Film Daily*, May 19, 1934, 3.
68. Gemünden, *Continental Strangers*, 26–27. He cites the Nouvelle Vague critic/directors François Truffaut and Bertrand Tavernier along with American auteur critics Andrew Sarris and John Belton and Ulmer's interview with Peter Bogdonovich as central to raising Ulmer to the status of "auteur."
69. Anonymous, "Film Reviews: They Gave Him A Gun", *Variety*, May 19, 1937, 22.
70. Anonymous, "Reviews of New Films: They Gave Him A Gun," *Film Daily*, May 17, 1937, 21.
71. Keene, *Doughboys*, 204.
72. Allen, *Since Yesterday*, 270.
73. Anonymous, "Showmen's Reviews: They Gave Him a Gun," *Motion Picture Herald*, May 15, 1937, 50.
74. See Hammond, "'Good Fellowship.'"
75. Frank Nugent, "The Screen: Reviews and News," *New York Times*, November 11, 1939.
76. Trout, *On the Battlefield of Memory*, 252.
77. Jay Winter, *War Beyond Words*, 76–81.

BIBLIOGRAPHY

Adams, Rachel. *Sideshow U.S.A.: Freaks and the American Cultural Imagination*. Chicago: University of Chicago Press, 2001.
Aldrich, Mark. *Death Rode the Rails: American Railroad Accidents and Safety, 1828–1965*. Baltimore: Johns Hopkins University Press, 2006.
Allen, Frederick Lewis. *Only Yesterday: An Informal History of the 1920s*. New York: Harper and Brothers, 1931.
———. *Since Yesterday: The 1930s in America*. London: Hamish Hamilton, 1940.
Alvey, Mark. "The Cinema as Taxidermy: Carl Akeley and the Preservative Obsession." *Framework: The Journal of Cinema and Media* 48, no.1 (Spring 2007): 23–45.
Andrews, Peter. "'The Enchanted Cottage' A Short Story." *Motion Picture Magazine*, April, 1924, 60–61.
Anonymous. "Influenza Epidemic Working West: Boston Theatres Opening, While Chicago and Mid-West Close—Houses in San Francisco Capitulate, Making the Coast Practically Restricted in Amusements." *Moving Picture World*, November 2, 1918.
———. "Sure Fire Timely Fun That Will Delight Any Audience." *Film Daily*, November 17, 1918, 32.
———. "The Screen." *New York Times*, March 24, 1919.
———. "The Girl Who Stayed at Home." *Film Daily*, March 30, 1919, 9.
———. "Announce Names of Notables Selected to Act as Judges of The Lost Battalion." *Moving Picture World*, June 28, 1919, 1961.
———. "Historic War Episode Reenacted by Survivors: The Lost Battalion." *Wid's Daily*, July 6, 1919, 3.
———. Advertisement for *The Lost Battalion*. *Moving Picture World*, August 2, 1919, 641.
———. "A Humdinger of a Comedy: The Virtuous Vamp." *Wid's Daily*, November 30, 1919, 23.
———. "How the Lost Battalion Helped to Make History." *Moving Picture Age*, December 1919, 12.
———. Untitled. *Wid's Daily*, February 24, 1920, 1.
———. "Snug Harbor for the Shell Shocked." *New York Times*, January 2, 1921.
———. "The Shadow Stage." *Photoplay*, February 1922, 65.
———. "Duke of York's Theatre: The Enchanted Cottage." *Daily Telegraph*, March 2, 1922.
———. "A New Pinero Play." *The Times*, March 2, 1922.

———. "The Best Picture Norma Has Had in a Long Time." *Film Daily*, March 5, 1922, 2.

———. "Pinero's War Fantasy: Love in an Enchanted Cottage." *Daily Express*, March 9, 1922.

———. "The Enchanted Cottage." *Film Daily*, April 20, 1924, 13.

———. "Brief Reviews of Current Pictures." *Photoplay*, February, 1926, 16.

———. "The Unknown Soldier at the Rivoli." *Film Daily*, June 16, 1926, 7.

———. "Behind the Front." *Film Daily*, July 16, 1926, 3.

———. "The Unknown Soldier." *Film Daily*, August 6, 1926, 8.

———. "Sunday Shows Up at Wayland." *Film Daily*, December 22, 1926, 2.

———. "Comparison of Estimate with Actual Cost." Production 618, "Wings." *Wings*. Paramount Scripts Collection. Margaret Herrick Library, Academy of Motion Picture Arts and Sciences, Beverly Hills, CA, 1927.

———. "'Wings' A Truly Great Picture." *Film Spectator*, March 3, 1927, 10.

———. "$6000 in San Antonio." *Variety*, June 1, 1927, 13.

———. "The Shadow Stage." *Photoplay*, September 1927, 52.

———. "Personal Glimpses: When War-planes Flame and Audiences Gasp." *Literary Digest*, November 12, 1927, 36–40.

———. "Fonck, World's Greatest War Aviator Has Seen Wings Three Times." *Paramount Around the World*, March 1, 1928, 24.

———. "And Now the Triumph of 'Wings' in Los Angeles, The City Where Motion Pictures Are Made." *Paramount Around the World*, April 2, 1928, 22.

———. "Stars Aid Legion Show." *The Film Daily*, July 27, 1928, 2.

———. Advertisement for *Journey's End*. *Film Daily*, May 16, 1930, 6–7.

———. "The Dawn Patrol." *Variety*, July 16, 1930, 15.

———. "Hell's Angels." *Film Daily*, August 24, 1930, 10.

———. "Becky and Joe Were Told to Write Dialogue, and Certainly Wrote It." *Film Spectator*, November 8, 1930, 8.

———. "Beyond Victory." *Variety*, April 8, 1931, 19.

———. "Beyond Victory." *Film Daily*, April 12, 1931, 32.

———. "The Last Flight." *Film Daily*, August 23, 1931, 18.

———. "Review: The Last Flight." *Variety*, August 25, 1931, 14.

———. "The Mad Parade." *Film Daily*, September 20, 1931, 10.

———. "The Old Dark House." *Harrison's Reports*, November 5, 1932, 179.

———. "Armistice Day Suggestions." *Universal Weekly*, November 5, 1932, 6–7.

———. "Private Jones." *Variety*, March 28, 1933, 15.

———. "The Eagle and the Hawk." *Film Daily*, May 6, 1933, 4.

———. "Pilgrimage." *Film Daily*, July 17, 1933, 7.

———. "Reviews of the New Features: The Black Cat." *Film Daily*, May 19, 1934, 3.

———. "Showmen's Reviews: They Gave Him a Gun." *Motion Picture Herald*, May 15, 1937, 50.

———. "Reviews of New Films: They Gave Him A Gun." *Film Daily*, May 17, 1937, 21.

———. "Film Reviews: They Gave Him A Gun." *Variety*, May 19, 1937, 22.

Baird, Robert. "Hell's Angels Above the Western Front." In *Hollywood's World War I: Motion Picture Images*, edited by Peter C. Rollins and John E. O'Connor, 79–100. Bowling Green, KY: Popular Press of Bowling Green State, 1997.

Balderston, John. "Valedictory Memo." *Smilin' Through* File. Part 1, Folder 2. MGM Script Files, USC Cinematic Arts Library, February 27, 1932.

Balio, Tino. *Grand Design: Hollywood as a Modern Business Enterprise, 1930–1939*. Berkeley: University of California Press, 1995.

Basinger, Jeanine. *The World War II Combat Film: Anatomy of a Genre*. Middletown, CT: Wesleyan University Press, 2003.

Baum, Vicki. *Grand Hotel*. London: Queensway Library, 1929.

Behlmer, Rudy. "World War One Aviation Films." *Films in Review*, August–September 1967, 413–433.

———. *Inside Warner Bros. (1935–1951)*. New York: Viking, 1985.

———. "Deja View: A Fond Look Back at Movie Studios' Use of Recycled Footage." *American Cinematographer*, June 1999, 128–138.

B.F. "Love and Duty Play Is Presented at Cohan Theatre." *New York Tribune*, October 12, 1921.

Black, John. "The German Veteran Speaks." *American Legion Monthly*, September, 1929, 42, 66–67.

Boetticher, Budd. "Entretien Avec Budd Boetticher." *Cahiers du Cinéma*, September 1963, 11.

Bogdan, Robert. *Freak Show: Presenting Human Oddities for Amusement and Profit*. Chicago: University of Chicago Press, 1990.

Borden, Mary. *The Forbidden Zone: A Nurse's Impressions of the First World War*. London: William Heinemann, 1929.

Bordwell, David. *Poetics of Cinema*. London: Routledge, 2008.

Bordwell, David, Kristin Thompson, and Janet Staiger. *The Classical Hollywood Cinema: Film Style and Mode of Production to 1960*. London: Routledge and Kegan Paul, 1985.

Boyd, Thomas. *Through the Wheat*. New York: Charles Scribner's Sons, 1923.

Brand, John P. "How the 'Lost Battalion' Helped to Make History." *Moving Picture Age*, December 1919, 11.

Bruccoli, Matthew J., and Judith S. Baughman, eds. *The Sons of Maxwell Perkins*. Columbia: University of South Carolina Press, 2004.

Budreau, Lisa M. *Bodies of War: World War I and the Politics of Commemoration in America, 1919–1933*. New York: New York University Press, 2010.

The Caddo Company, Inc., a corporation, Plaintiff vs. First National Pictures, Inc., a corporation, et al. Affidavit from Howard Hughes in "Order to Show Cause Why Injunction Pendente Lite Should Not Issue" [1930] (District Court of the United States for the Southern District of California, Central Division). Papers held at Warner Bros. Archive, University of Southern California.

The Caddo Company, Inc., a corporation, Plaintiff vs. First National Pictures, Inc., a corporation, et al. Affidavit from John Monk Saunders in "Order to Show Cause

Why Injunction Pendente Lite Should Not Issue." [1930] (District Court of the United States for the Southern District of California, Central Division). Papers held at Warner Bros. archive, University of Southern California.

The Caddo Company, Inc., a corporation, Plaintiff vs. First National Pictures, Inc., a corporation, et al. Affidavit from Joseph Moncure March in "Order to Show Cause Why Injunction Pendente Lite Should Not Issue." [1930] (District Court of the United States for the Southern District of California, Central Division). Papers held at Warner Bros. archive, University of Southern California.

Cameron, R. S. "Irreconcilable Differences: Divorce and Women's Drama before 1945." *Modern Drama* 44, no. 4 (Winter 2001): 476–490.

Carroll, Noël. *Comedy Incarnate: Buster Keaton, Physical Humor and Bodily Coping.* New York: John Wiley and Sons, 2009.

Chaplin, Charles. *My Autobiography.* London: Penguin, 1966.

Clodfelter, Michael. *Warfare and Armed Conflicts: A Statistical Reference to Casualty and Other Figures, 1500–2000.* Jefferson, NC: McFarland, 2001.

Cohen, Deborah. *The War Come Home: Disabled Veterans and Germany, 1914–1939.* Berkeley: University of California Press, 2001.

Cohen, Jeff. "Of Magnascope and Vitalite." *Vitaphone Varieties: Observations on Film Imagery and Music of the Past.* http://vitaphone.blogspot.com/2026/12of-magnascope-and-voccalite.html. Accessed December 21, 2009.

Cohen, Norman. *The Long Steel Rail: The Railroad in American Folksong.* Urbana: University of Illinois Press, 2000.

Cooper, Willard. "Maybe Your Old Buddy Fights in Films." *American Legion Weekly,* January 1926, 4–5, 11.

Corbin, John. "The Play: A New Hamlet." *New York Times,* November 17, 1922.

———. "Barrieized Pinero." *New York Times,* April 8, 1923.

Cozzolino, Robert, Anne Classen Knutson, and David M. Lubin, eds. *World War I and American Art.* Princeton, NJ: Princeton University Press, 2016.

Cripps, Gladys M. "To C.A.L." In *The Spirit of St. Louis: One Hundred Poems,* edited by Charles Vale, 73. New York: George H. Doran, 1927.

Crosby, Alfred. *America's Forgotten Epidemic: The Influenza of 1918.* Cambridge: Cambridge University Press, 1989.

Curtis, James. *James Whale: A New World of Gods and Monsters.* Minneapolis: University of Minnesota Press, 1998.

Daly, Phil M. "And That's That." *The Film Daily,* November 1, 1926, 1.

Danes, Clemence. *A Bill of Divorcement: A Play in Three Acts.* London: William Heinemann, 1921.

Delluc, Louis. *Charlot.* Paris: Maurice de Brunhoff, 1921.

Doležal, Joshua. "'Waste in a Great Enterprise': Influenza, Modernism, and One of Ours." *Literature and Medicine* 28, no. 1 (Spring 2009): 82–101.

Dumont, Hervé. *Frank Borzage.* Jefferson, NC: McFarland, 2006.

Elsaesser, Thomas. "Ethnicity, Authenticity, and Exile: A Counterfeit Trade? German Filmmakers and Hollywood." In *Home Exile, Homeland: Film, Media, and the Politics of Place*, edited by Hamid Naficy, 97–123. New York: Routledge, 1999.

Emerson, John, and Anita Loos. *How to Write Photoplays*. New York: The James A. McCann Company, 1920.

Emmert, Scott D., and Steven Trout, eds. *World War I in American Fiction: An Anthology of Short Stories*. Kent, OH: Kent State University Press, 2014.

Fagan, John. *Smilin' Through*. Shooting Script, Production no. 625. MGM Script Files, USC Cinematic Arts Library, June 7, 1932.

Faust, Drew Gilpin. *This Republic of Suffering: Death and the American Civil War*. New York: Alfred A Knopf, 2008.

Fiala, Andrew. "General Patton and Private Ryan: The Conflicting Reality of War and Films about War." In *The Philosophy of War Films (The Philosophy of Popular Culture)*, edited by David LaRocca, 355–384. Lexington: University of Kentucky Press, 2014.

Fisher, James. Memorandum re: *Hell's Angels*. Hell's Angels folder, PCA Collection. Margaret Herrick Library, Academy of Motion Picture Arts and Sciences, Beverly Hills, CA, June 27, 1930.

Fitzgerald, F. Scott. "Letter to Maxwell Perkins, dated Jan. 21, 1930." In *The Sons of Maxwell Perkins*, edited by Matthew J. Bruccoli and Judith S. Baughman. Columbia: University of South Carolina Press, 2004.

Freud, Sigmund. "Thoughts for the Times on War and Death." In *The Standard Edition of of the Complete Psychological Works of Sigmund Freud*, vol. 14, 273–300. London: Hogarth Press, 1957.

Funderburk, T.R. *The Early Birds of War: The Daring Pilots and Fighter Airplanes of World War I*. London: Arthur Barker, 1968.

Gallagher, Tag. *John Ford: The Man and his Films*. Berkeley: University of California Press, 1988.

Gardiner, Becky. "Notes on War Nurse to Mr. Thalberg." Folder 29, Box 3607. War Nurse files from Turner/MGM Script Collection, Margaret Herrick Library, Beverly Hills, CA, July 24, 1930.

Gemünden, Gurd. *Continental Strangers: German Exile Cinema 1933–1951*. New York: Columbia University Press, 2014.

Gledhill, Christine. *Reframing British Cinema, 1918–1928: Between Restraint and Passion*. London: British Film Institute, 2003.

Grand Hotel. Play Script. Folder 2 of 5. MGM Script File, USC Cinematic Arts Library, May 8, 1930.

Grand Hotel. Script Conference Notes. USC Cinematic Arts Library, November 17, 1931.

Grand Hotel. Serial Story on Publicity. MGM Script File notes, University of Southern California., 1932.

Gordon, Mel. *The Grand Guignol: Theatre of Fear and Terror*. New York: Da Capo Press, 1997.

Green, Abel. "Old Dark House." *Variety*, November 1, 1932, 12.

Gregory, Adrian. *The Silence of Memory: Armistice Day, 1919–1946.* Oxford: Berg, 1994.
Gunning, Tom. "The Horror of Opacity: The Melodrama of Sensation in the Plays of André de Lord." In *Melodrama in Stage, Picture and Screen*, edited by Jacky Bratton, Jim Cook, and Christine Gledhill, 50–61. London: British Film Institute, 1994.
———. "Landscape and the Fantasy of Moving Pictures: Early Cinema's Phantom Rides." In *Cinema and Landscape, Film, Nation and Cultural Geography*, edited by Graeme Harper and Jonathan Rayner, 31–71. London: Intellect Books, 2010.
Hale, Nathan G., Jr. *The Rise and Crisis of Psychoanalysis in the United States: Freud and the Americans 1917–1985.* New York: Oxford University Press, 1995.
Haley, Mary Anderson. "A Faithless Generation Asked a Sign." In *The Spirit of St. Louis: One Hundred Poems*, edited by Charles Vale, 121. New York: George H. Doran, 1927.
Hall, Mordaunt. "The Screen: Enchantment of Love." *New York Times*, April 14, 1924.
———. "The Screen: A Lost Chance." *New York Times*, May 31, 1926.
———. "Mr. Barthelmess at his Best." *New York Times*, August 16, 1927.
———. "After the Armistice." *New York Times*, August 30, 1931.
———. "The Screen." *New York Times*, September 27, 1931.
———. "The Screen is Indebted to the Stage." *New York Times*, October 9, 1932.
———. "Reflections and News of the Screen: Success of a Young Studio Head." *New York Times*, November 6, 1932.
———. "The Screen: Frederic March, Jack Oakie and Sir Guy Standing in a Drama of World War Air Fighting." *New York Times*, May 13, 1933.
Hammond, Michael. "'Good Fellowship': Carole Lombard and Clark Gable." In *First Comes Love: Power Couples, Celebrity Kinship and Cultural Politics*, edited by S. Cobb and N. Ewen, 53–72. London: Bloomsbury, 2015.
Hansen, Miriam. *Babel and Babylon: Spectatorship in American Silent Cinema.* Cambridge, MA: Harvard University Press, 1994.
———. *Cinema and Experience: Siegfried Kracauer, Walter Benjamin, and Theodor W. Adorno.* Berkeley: University of California Press, 2012.
Harding, Alfred. "What Price Censorship." *American Legion Weekly*, November 28, 1924, 3–5, 14–16.
Henle, Maurice. "'Another Miracle Man' Says Syndicate Writer." *Newspaper Enterprise Association*. In the Richard Barthelmess Collection Scrapbook, No.13, 38. Margaret Herrick Library, Academy of Motion Picture Arts and Sciences, Beverly Hills, CA, 1924.
Hitchcock, Alfred. "Why 'Thrillers' Thrive." *Picturegoer*, January 18, 1936, 15.
Hughes, Howard J. Letter to Col. Jason S. Joy. PCA Collection, The Mad Parade file, Margaret Herrick Library Academy of Motion Picture Arts and Sciences, Beverly Hills, CA, February 5, 1931.
Ibáñez, Vicente Blasco. *The Four Horsemen of the Apocalypse.* Trans. Charlotte Brewster. Boston: E.P. Dutton, 1918.

Isenberg, Michael T. *War on Film: The American Cinema and World War I, 1914–1941.* Madison, WI: Fairley Dickenson University Press, 1981.
Jackson, Robert. "The Secret Life of Oscar Micheaux: Race Films, Contested Histories, and Modern American Culture." In *Beyond Blackface: African Americans and the Creation of American Popular Culture, 1890–1930*, edited by W. Fitzhugh Brundage, 215–238. Chapel Hill: University of North Carolina Press, 2011.
Jacobs, Lea. "Men Without Women: The Avatars of What Price Glory." *Film History* 17 (2005): 307–333.
———. *The Decline of Sentiment: American Film in the 1920s.* Berkeley: University of California Press, 2008.
Jividin, J.M. "Power of Attorney: Business Friendship Between Ernest Hemingway and Maurice J. Speiser." PhD diss., University of South Carolina, 2008.
Johnson, James Weldon. "Saint Peter Relates an Incident of the Resurrection Day." In *James Weldon Johnson: Complete Poems*, edited by Sondra Kathryn Wilson, 49–54. New York: Penguin, 2000.
Joy, Jason. Memo to Heads of Studios, November, 1927. PCA Files for *Wings*, Margaret Herrick Library, Academy of Motion Picture Arts and Sciences, Beverly Hills, CA.
Kaes, Anton. *Shell Shock Cinema: Weimar Culture and the Wounds of War.* Princeton, NJ: Princeton University Press, 2009.
Kardiner, Abram. *The Traumatic Neuroses of War.* New York: Harper and Brothers, 1941; reprint, Mansfield, CT: Martino Publishing, 2012.
Keene, Jennifer. *Doughboys: The Great War and the Remaking of America.* Baltimore: Johns Hopkins University Press, 2001.
Keire, Mara L. "Swearing Allegiance: Street Language, US War Propaganda and the Declining Status of Women in Northeastern Nightlife, 1900–1920." *Journal of the History of Sexuality* 25, no. 2 (May 2016): 246–266.
Knutson, Anne Clusson. "Hidden in Plain Sight: World War I in the Art of John Marin, Georgia O'Keefe, and Charles Burchfield." In *World War I and American Art*, edited by Robert Cozzolino, Anne Classen Knutson, and David M. Lubin, 57–72. Princeton, NJ: Princeton University Press, 2016.
Koszarski, Richard. "Flu season: Moving Picture World reports on pandemic influenza, 1918–19." *Film History: An International Journal* 17, no. 4 (2005): 466–485.
LaMotte, Ellen N. *The Backwash of War: The Human Wreckage of the Battlefield as Witnessed by an American Hospital Nurse.* New York: Knickerbocker Press, 1916.
Land. "Film Reviews: The Black Cat." *Variety*, May 22, 1934, 15, 29.
Landy, G. Press book notes for *The Patent Leather Kid*, File 2834A. Warner Bros. Archive, University of Southern California, July 13, 1927.
Langdon, Lawrence. "Barthelmess is Enthusiastic." *Cinema Art*, July 1924. In the Richard Barthelmess Collection Scrapbook, no. 13, 76–77. Margaret Herrick Library, Academy of Motion Picture Arts and Sciences, Beverly Hills, CA.
Lawrence, D.H. *Complete Poems.* London: Penguin, 1994.

Lewis, T.H. "Pollack Returns to Cohan Theatre." *Morning Telegraph*, March 11, 1921. From *Bill of Divorcement* clippings file, Billy Rose Collection, New York Public Library.

Lindbergh, Charles A. "They'll Be Glad To See You." *American Legion Monthly*, September 1937, 6.

Linker, Beth. *War's Waste: Rehabilitation in World War I America*. Chicago: University of Chicago Press, 2011.

Longmore, Paul K., and David Goldberger. "The League of the Physically Handicapped and the Great Depression: A Case Study in the New Disability History." *Journal of American History* 87, no. 3 (2000): 888–922.

Lord, Daniel A. Letter to Arthur H. DeBra, copied to Col. Jason S. Joy of Hayes Office. *Hell's Angels* folder, PCA Collection, Margaret Herrick Library, Academy of Motion Picture Arts and Sciences, Beverly Hills, CA, August 28, 1930.

Lord, Robert. Letter to Warner Brothers. *Heroes For Sale*, File 1740. Warner Bros. Archive, University of Southern California, November 16, 1933.

Lovett, Josephine. "The Enchanted Cottage." = *The Enchanted Cottage*, Draft Script. USC Cinema Arts Library, 1923.

Lubin, David M. *Grand Illusions: American Art and the First World War*. Oxford: Oxford University Press, 2016.

Lusk, Norbert. "Screen in Review." *Photoplay*, November 8, 1930, 64.

Lynd, Robert S., and Helen Merrill Lynd. *Middletown: A Study in American Culture*. New York: Harcourt, Brace and Co., 1929.

———. *Middletown in Transition: A Study in Cultural Conflicts*. New York: Harcourt, 1937.

Lynn, Kenneth Schuyler. *Hemingway*. New York: Simon & Schuster, 1995.

Macgowan, Kenneth. *The Theatre of Tomorrow*. New York: Boni and Liveright, 1921.

Maland, Charles. *Chaplin and American Culture*. Princeton, NJ: Princeton University Press, 1989.

Marinetti, Filippo Tommaso. "The Founding and Manifesto of Futurism." In *The Documents of 20th-Century Art: Futurist Manifestos*, edited by Umbro Apollonio, 19–24. Trans. Robert Brain, R.W. Flint, J.C. Higgitt, and Caroline Tisdall. New York: Viking, 1973.

Marion, Frances. *How to Write and Sell Film Stories*. London: J. Miles, 1938.

Martin, A.L. *Smilin' Through: A Romantic Comedy in Three Acts*. New York: Samuel French, 1924.

Mayer, David. *Stagestruck Filmmaker: D.W. Griffith and the American Theatre*. Iowa City: University of Iowa Press, 2009.

McBride, Joseph. *Searching for John Ford*. London: Faber & Faber, 2003.

McGuire, John Thomas. "Filtering and Interpreting The Great War: *All Quiet on the Western Front, Journey's End, Westfront 1918*, and Their Perspectives on World War I." *Quarterly Review of Film and Video* 33, no. 7 (2016): 667–680.

McLoughlin, Kate. *Veteran Poetics: British Literature in the Age of Mass Warfare*. Cambridge: Cambridge University Press, 2018.

Mencken, H.L. "The Flapper." *The Smart Set*, February 1915, 1–2.

———. *The American Language: A Preliminary Inquiry into the Development of English in the United States*. New York: Alfred A. Knopf, 1919.

Merchant, Carolyn. *Reinventing Eden: The Fate of Nature in Western Culture*. New York: Routledge, 2003.

Miller, Alisa. "'An American Soldier Poet': Alan Seeger and War Culture in the United States, 1914–1918." *First World War Studies* 1, no. 1 (2010): 15–33.

Miller, Angela. "Nature's History: The Changing Cultural Image of Nature, From Romantic Nationalism to Land Art." In *Nature's Nation Revisited: Images of the US American Landscape through Changing Times and Media, Kunsttexte* 1 (April 2015): 1–10.

Miller, Llewellyn. Unspecified article, *Los Angeles Record*, quoted in advertisement for *All Quiet on the Western Front*. *Variety*, April 30, 1930.

Morris, Gouverneur. *The Penalty*. Rockville, MD: Wildside, 1913.

Morrison, Michael. "The Voice Teacher as Shakespearean Collaborator: Margaret Carrington and John Barrymore." *Theatre Survey*, November 1997, 129–158.

Morsberger, Robert E., Stephen O. Lesser, and Randall Clark. "John Balderston." In *American Screenwriters: Dictionary of Literary Biography*, first series, vol. 26, edited by Stephen O. Lesser and Randall Clark, 24–29. Detroit: Bruccoli Clark, 1984.

Mortimer, Maud. *A Green Tent in Flanders*. New York: Doubleday, 1918.

Mosse, George L. *Fallen Soldiers: Reshaping Memory of the World Wars*. Oxford: Oxford University Press, 1991 (Kindle version).

Norden, Martin F. *The Cinema of Isolation: A History of Physical Disability in the Movies*. New Brunswick, NJ: Rutgers University Press, 1994.

Nugent, Frank. "The Screen: Reviews and News." *New York Times*, November 11, 1939.

Ord, George M. In "Letters from Readers." *Liberty Magazine*, February 21, 1931, 8.

Overstreet, Richard. "George Cukor." In *George Cukor: Interviews*, edited by Robert Emmet Long. Oxford, MS: University of Mississippi Press, 2001.

Owen, Wilfred. "Spring Offensive." In *Wilfred Owen: War Poems and Others*, edited by Jon Silkin, 108–9. London: Chatto & Windus, 1978.

Parsons, Louella. "Louella Parson Recommends It To All Lovers of Good Pictures." *New York American*. In the Richard Barthelmess Collection, Scrapbook no. 13, 38. Margaret Herrick Library, Academy of Motion Picture Arts and Sciences, Beverly Hills, CA, April 12, 1924.

———. Unspecified article, *Los Angeles Examiner*, quoted in advertisement for *All Quiet on the Western Front*. *Variety*, April 30, 1930.

Peeler, Clare. Play review for MGM of *Grand Hotel*. In *Grand Hotel* Script File Notes, USC Cinematic Arts Library, September 20, 1929.

Priestley, J.B. *Benighted*. With introduction by Orrin Grey. London: Heinemann, 1927; reprint, Kansas City, MO: Valancourt Books, 2013.
———. *Margin Released: A Writer's Reminiscences and Reflections*. New York: Harper & Row, 1962.
———. "Five Persons." *J.B. Priestley: An Exhibition of Manuscripts and Books*. Austin: University of Texas Press, 1963.
Reed, Langford. *The Chronicles of Charlie Chaplin*. London: Cassell, 1916.
Reilly, William J. "Sell History in Lost Battalion." *Moving Picture World*, September 6, 1919.
Resina, Joan Ramon, and Dieter Ingenschay, eds. "Preface." In *After-Images of the City*. Ithaca, NY: Cornell University Press, 2003.
Rhodes, Gary D. *The Birth of the American Horror Film*. Edinburgh: Edinburgh University Press, 2018.
Robertson, Linda R. *The Dream of Civilized Warfare: World War I Flying Aces and the American Imagination*. Minneapolis: University of Minnesota Press, 2003.
Robinett, Jane. "The Narrative Shape of Traumatic Experience." *Literature and Medicine* 26, no. 2 (Fall 2007): 290–311.
Robinson, David. *Chaplin: The Mirror of Opinion*. London: Secker and Warburg, 1983.
———. *Chaplin: His Life and Art*. London: Penguin, 2001.
Roland, Arthur. "Seeing Sights on First Nights." *The Official Metropolitan Guide*, April 1, 1923, 29.
Rollins, Peter C., and John E. O'Connor, eds. *Hollywood's World War I: Motion Picture Images*. Bowling Green, KY: Popular Press of Bowling Green State, 1997.
Ryan, Don. "The Wherefore of Great Lovers: A Psychoanalyst Compares the Divergent Attractions of Menjou, Meighan, Barthelmess and Valentino." *Picture Play*, August 1924, 47–49, 112.
Sandburg, Carl. "Grass." In *The Complete Poems of Carl Sandburg*, 136. New York: Harcourt, 1970.
Sargent, Epes Winthrop. *The Technique of the Photoplay*. New York: Chalmers, 1913.
———. *Picture Theatre Advertising*. New York: Chalmers, 1915.
——— (aka "Chic"). "Eagle and the Hawk." *Variety*, May 16, 1933, 21.
Sargent, Epes Winthrop, and John F. Barry. *Building Theatre Patronage: Management and Merchandising*. New York: Chalmers, 1927.
Saunders, John Monk. *Wings*. New York: Grossett & Dunlap, 1927.
———. *Single Lady*. New York: Brewer and Warren, 1930.
———. Article for Publicity Sheet. *The Last Flight* Production File, Warner Bros. Collections, University of Southern California, 1930.
———. "Deposition: August 1930." In *Inside Warner Bros. (1935–1951)*, edited by Rudy Behlmer, 338–340. New York: Viking, 1985.
Schallert, E. "Ideal Romance Wins the Tear." *Los Angeles Times*, September 8, 1932. From Norma Shearer Collection, Box 1:8, USC Cinematic Arts Library.
Schatz, Thomas. *The Genius of the System: Hollywood Filmmaking in the Studio Era*. New York: Henry Holt, 1988.

Selznick, David O. *Memo from David O. Selznick*, Modern Library edition, edited by R. Behlmer. New York: Random House, 1977.
Shephard, Ben. *A War of Nerves: Soldiers and Psychiatrists, 1914–1994*. London: Jonathan Cape, 2000.
Sherwood, Robert E. "EXTRA! Hollywood Declares War!" *American Legion Monthly*, September 1926, 36–40.
Silverman, Sidne. "Hell's Angel's." *Variety*, June 4, 1930, 25.
Silverman, Sime. "Chaplin's Shoulder Arms." *Variety*, October 25, 1918, 36.
———. "All Quiet on the Western Front." *Variety*, May 7, 1930, 21.
Skal, David J. *The Monster Show: A Cultural History of Horror*. New York: Faber and Faber, 2001.
———. *Dark Carnival: The Secret World of Tod Browning*. New York: Anchor/Doubleday, 1995.
Slater, Thomas. "June Mathis's Valentino Scripts: Images of Male 'Becoming' After the Great War." *Cinema Journal* 50, no. 1 (Fall 2010): 99–120.
Slotkin, Richard. *Lost Battalions: The Great War and the Crisis of American Nationality*. New York: Henry Holt and Company, 2005.
Smith, Alison. "The Screen in Review." *Picture Play*, April 1923, 52–53.
Smith, Patsy. "Among the Women." *Variety*, March 28, 1919, 90.
Stallings, Laurence. *Plumes*. New York: Grosset and Dunlap, 1924; reprint, University of South Carolina Press, 2006.
———. "The Big Parade." In *World War I in American Fiction: An Anthology of Short Stories*, edited by Scott D. Emmert and Steven Trout, 177–179. Kent, OH: The Kent State University Press, 2014. Originally published in *New Republic*, September 17, 1924, 66–69.
———. Memo to Irving Thalberg, "Original Story." *The Big Parade*. King Vidor Collection. MSS 1372, manuscript 11, box 1, L. Tom Perry Special Collections, Harold B. Lee Library, Brigham Young University, Provo, Utah, n.d.
Stallings, Laurence, and Maxwell Anderson. Promptbook for *What Price Glory*. Billy Rose Theatre Collection, New York Public Library, 1925.
Stenn, David. *Clara Bow: Runnin' Wild*. New York: Cooper Square Press, 2000.
Stewart, John Ogden. *Smilin' Through*. Shooting Script. MGM Script Files, USC Cinematic Arts Library, July 13, 1932.
Stimson, Edna. "Lindberg. May 1927." In *The Spirit of St. Louis: One Hundred Poems*, edited by Charles Vale, 225. New York: George H. Doran, 1927.
Studlar, Gaylyn. *This Mad Masquerade: Stardom and Masculinity in the Jazz Age*. New York: Columbia University Press, 1996.
Thompson, Kristin. *Exporting Entertainment: America in the World Film Market, 1907–1934*. London: British Film Institute, 1985.
Thomson, Rosemarie Garland. *Extraordinary Bodies: Figuring Disability in American Culture and Literature*. New York: Columbia University Press, 1997.
Tinée Mae. "Nikki Charms Her Flock of Warbirds." *Chicago Tribune*, September 19, 1931, 15.

Trail, Armitage. *Scarface*. New York: Edward J. Clode, 1930; reprint, London: Bloomsbury, 1997.

Trout, Steven. *On the Battlefield of Memory: The First World War and American Remembrance 1919–1941*. Tuscaloosa, AL: University of Alabama Press, 2010.

Turner, George. "Wings—Epic of the Air." *American Cinematographer*, April 1985, 34–41.

Vale, Charles, ed. *The Spirit of St. Louis: One Hundred Poems*. New York: George H. Doran, 1927.

Vasey, Ruth. *The World According to Hollywood, 1918–1939*. Exeter, UK: University of Exeter Press, 1997.

Vidor, King. Notes to assistant director David Howard, from *The Big Parade* file. King Vidor Papers, UCLA Film and Television Archive, 1920–1965.

———. Director's personal notes on *The Big Parade*, King Vidor Collection, MSS 1732, box 1, folder 12. L. Tom Perry Special Collections, Harold B. Lee Library, Brigham Young University, Provo, Utah, n.d.

———. *A Tree Is a Tree: An Autobiography*. Hollywood, CA: Samuel French Trade, 1981.

———. *On Film Making*. London: W.H. Allen, 1973.

Vieira, Mark. *Irving Thalberg: Boy Wonder to Producer Prince*. Berkeley: University of California Press, 2009.

Watts, Richard, Jr. "Our Ways, Their Ways and a Play: Inevitable Comparisons of What Price Glory to Journey's End." *Boston Transcript*, November 9, 1929. *Journey's End* clippings file, Billy Rose Theatre Collection, New York Public Library.

Wear. "Film Reviews: Dawn Patrol." *Variety*, December 14, 1938, 14.

Wellman, William, Jr. *The Man and His Wings: William A. Wellman and the Making of the First Best Picture*. Westport, CT: Praeger, 2006.

Whitman, Walt. *Specimen Days, Democratic Vistas and Other Prose*, edited by Louise Pound. New York: Doubleday and Doran, 1935.

Williams, Linda. *Playing the Race Card: Melodramas of Black and White from Uncle Tom to O.J. Simpson*. Princeton: Princeton University Press, 2001.

Williams, Wythe. "Eaglet Grave Lies Out of Legion Path." *New York Times*, September 23, 1927.

Wilson, E. "Sixty-five Years of Realism." *New Republic*, June 1925, 101.

Wilson, John V. Letter to Hal Wallis. First National Studios. Production Code Administration Files, Margaret Herrick Library, Academy of Motion Picture Arts and Sciences, Beverly Hills, CA, April 1, 1931.

Wingate, James. Letter to Harold Hurley of Paramount Studios. Report on *Eagle and the Hawk*. PCA Collection, Margaret Herrick Library, Academy of Motion Picture Arts and Sciences, Beverly Hills, CA, February 6, 1933.

Winter, Jay. *War Beyond Words: Languages of Remembrance from the Great War to the Present*. Cambridge: Cambridge University Press, 2017.

Witt, John Fabian. "The Accidental Republic: Amputee Workingmen, Destitute Widows, and the Remaking of American Law, 1868–1922." PhD diss., Yale University, 2000.

Wohl, Robert. *The Spectacle of Flight: Aviation and the Western Imagination, 1920–1950*. New Haven, CT: Yale University Press, 2005.

Woolcott, Alexander. "Second Thoughts on First Nights." *New York Times*, March 21, 1920.

Zanuck, Daryl. Inter-Office Memo to William Wellman. *Heroes for Sale*. Warner Brother's Archive, File 1740, March 8, 1933.

FILMOGRAPHY

Absent. Dir. Harry A. Gant. Rosebud Film Corporation. USA. 1926.
Ace of Aces. Dir. J. Walter Ruben. RKO Radio Pictures. USA. 1933.
The Air Circus. Dir. Howard Hawks and Lewis Seller. Fox Film Corporation. 1928.
Air Mail. Dir. John Ford. Universal. USA. 1932.
All Quiet on the Western Front. Dir. Lewis Milestone. Universal. USA. 1930.
Angels with Dirty Faces. Dir. Michael Curtiz. Warner Bros. USA. 1938.
The Best Years of Our Lives. Dir. William Wyler. The Samuel Goldwyn Company. USA. 1946.
Beyond Victory. Dir. John S. Robertson. RKO-Pathé Pictures. 1931.
The Big Parade. Dir. King Vidor. MGM. USA. 1925.
The Big Red One. Dir. Sam Fuller. Lorimar Productions. USA. 1980.
A Bill of Divorcement. Dir. George Cukor. RKO Pictures. USA. 1932.
The Birth of a Nation. Dir. D.W. Griffith. David W. Griffith Corporation. USA. 1915.
The Blackbird. Dir. Tod Browning. MGM. USA. 1926.
The Black Cat. Dir. Edgar Ulmer. Universal. USA. 1934.
Born on the Fourth of July. Dir. Oliver Stone. Ixtlan. USA 1989.
The Bride of Frankenstein. Dir. James Whale. Universal. USA. 1935.
Broken Blossoms. Dir. D.W. Griffith. D.W. Griffith Productions. USA. 1919.
The Cabinet of Dr. Caligari. Dir. Robert Weine. Decla-Bioscop AG. Germany. 1920.
The Cabin in the Cotton. Dir. Michael Curtiz. First National Pictures. USA. 1932.
Captain Newman M.D. Dir. David Miller. Universal. USA. 1963.
The Cat and the Canary. Dir. Paul Leni. Universal Pictures. USA. 1927.
Central Airport. Dir. William A. Wellman. First National Pictures. USA. 1933.
Children of Divorce. Dir. Frank Lloyd. Famous Players-Lasky. USA. 1927.
Christopher Strong. Dir. Dorothy Arzner. RKO Radio Pictures. USA. 1933.
Coming Home. Dir. Hal Ashby. Jerome Hellman Productions. USA. 1978.
The Crowd. Dir. King Vidor. MGM. USA. 1928.
The Dark Angel. Dir. Sidney Franklin. The Samuel Goldwyn Company. USA. 1935.
The Dawn Patrol. Dir. Howard Hawks. Warner Bros. USA. 1930.
The Dawn Patrol. Dir. Edmond Goulding. Warner Bros. USA. 1938.
Dead Presidents. Dir. Dir. Allan and Albert Hughes. Caravan Pictures. USA. 1995.
Death in the Air. Dir. Elmer Clifton. Fanchon Royer Features. USA. 1936.
Dinner at Eight. Dir. George Cukor. MGM. USA. 1933.
The Divorcée. Dir. Robert Z. Leonard. MGM. USA. 1930.
Dr. Jekyll and Mr. Hyde. Dir. Rouben Mamoulian. Paramount. USA. 1931.

Dracula. Dir. Tod Browning. Universal. USA. 1931.
The Eagle and the Hawk. Dir. Stuart Walker. Paramount. USA. 1933.
The Enchanted Cottage. Dir. John S. Robertson. Inspiration Pictures. USA. 1924.
The Enchanted Cottage. Dir. John Cromwell. RKO Radio Pictures. USA. 1945.
A Farewell to Arms. Dir. Frank Borzage. Paramount. USA. 1932.
The Fighting 69th. Dir. William Keighley. Warner Bros. USA. 1940.
Flight. Dir. Frank Capra. Columbia. USA. 1929.
The Flying Ace. Dir. Richard E. Norman. Norman Film Manufacturing Company. USA. 1926.
For Valour. Dir. Albert Parker. Triangle Pictures Corporation. USA. 1917.
The Four Horsemen of the Apocalypse. Dir. Rex Ingram. Metro Pictures Corporation. USA. 1921.
Four Sons. Dir. John Ford. Fox Film Corporation. USA. 1928.
Frankenstein. Dir. James Whale. Universal. 1931.
A Free Soul. Dir. Clarence Brown. MGM. USA. 1931.
Full Metal Jacket. Dir. Stanley Kubrick. Stanley Kubrick Productions. UK/USA. 1987.
Gentlemen Prefer Blondes. Dir. Malcolm St. Clair. Paramount. USA. 1928.
The Girl Who Stayed at Home. Dir. D.W. Griffith. D.W. Griffith Productions. USA. 1919.
Gold Diggers of 1933. Mervyn LeRoy. Warner Bros. USA. 1933.
Gone with the Wind. Dir. Victor Fleming. Selznick International Pictures, MGM. USA. 1939.
Grand Hotel. Dir. Edmund Goulding. MGM. USA. 1932.
The Great Gatsby. Dir. Herbert Brenon. Famous Players-Lasky. USA. 1926.
Greed. Dir. Erich von Stroheim. MGM. USA. 1924.
Hearts of the World. Dir. D.W. Griffith. Paramount. USA. 1918.
Helen's Babies. Dir. William A. Seiter. Principal Pictures. USA. 1924.
Hell's Angels. Dir. Howard Hughes. The Caddo Company. USA. 1930.
Heroes for Sale. Dir. William Wellman. Warner Bros. USA. 1933.
His Trust. D.W. Griffith. Biograph. USA. 1910.
His Trust Fulfilled. D.W. Griffith. Biograph. USA. 1910.
Humoresque. Dir. Frank Borzage. Cosmopolitan Productions/Paramount. USA. 1920.
The Hunchback of Notre Dame. Dir. Wallace Worsley. Universal. USA. 1923.
I Am a Fugitive from a Chain Gang. Dir. Mervyn LeRoy. Warner Bros. 1932.
In Search of a Sinner. Dir. David Kirkland. Constance Talmadge Film Company. USA. 1920.
In the Valley of Elah. Dir. Paul Haggis. Warner Independent Productions. USA. 2007.
The Invisible Man. Dir. James Whale. Universal. USA. 1933.
It. Dir. Clarence Badger. Paramount. USA. 1927.
Journey's End. Dir. James Whale. Gainsborough Pictures/Tiffany Productions. UK/USA. 1930.
La Grande Illusion. Dir. Jean Renoir. Réalisations d'Art Cinématographique. France. 1937.

The Last Flight. Dir. William Dieterle. First National Pictures. USA. 1931.
The Legion of the Condemned. Dir. William A. Wellman. Paramount/Famous Players-Lasky. USA. 1929.
Lilac Time. Dir. George Fitzmaurice. First National Pictures. USA. 1928.
Little Caesar. Dir. Mervyn LeRoy. First National Pictures. USA. 1931.
Little Women. Dir. George Cukor. RKO Radio Pictures. USA. 1933.
The Lost Battalion. Dir. Burton King. MacManus Corporation. USA. 1919.
The Love Expert. Dir. David Kirkland. Constance Talmadge Film Company. USA. 1920.
Lucky Star. Dir. Frank Borzage. Fox Film Corporation. USA. 1929.
The Mad Parade. Dir. William Beaudine. Paramount. USA. 1931.
The Man Who Laughs. Dir. Paul Leni. Universal Pictures. USA. 1928.
Manslaughter. Dir. Cecil B. DeMille. Paramount. USA. 1922.
M*A*S*H. Dir. Robert Altman. Aspen Productions. USA. 1970.
The Men. Dir. Fred Zinnemann. Stanley Kramer Productions. USA 1950.
Menschen am Sonntag (People on Sunday). Dir. Robert Siodmak and Edgar G. Ulmer. Filmstudio. Germany. 1930.
Metropolis. Dir. Fritz Lang. UFA. Germany. 1927.
The Miracle Man. Dir. George Loane Tucker. Mayflower Photoplay Company. USA. 1919.
My Four Years in Germany. Dir. William Nigh. Warner Bros. USA. 1918.
My Man Godfrey. Dir. Gregory La Cava. MGM. USA. 1936.
Nosferatu. Dir. F.W. Murnau. Jofa-Atelier Johannisthal. Germany. 1922.
The Old Dark House. Dir. James Whale. Universal. USA. 1932.
One Exciting Night. Dir. D.W. Griffith. D.W. Griffith Productions. USA. 1922.
Only Angels Have Wings. Dir. Howard Hawks. Columbia Pictures. USA. 1939.
Our Daily Bread. Dir. King Vidor. Viking/United Artists. USA. 1934.
The Patent Leather Kid. Dir. Alfred Santell. First National Pictures. USA. 1927.
Paths of Glory. Dir. Stanley Kubrick. Bryna Productions/United Artists. USA. 1957.
The Penalty. Dir. Wallace Worsley. Goldwyn Pictures Corporation. USA. 1920.
The Phantom of the Opera. Dir. Rupert Julian. Universal. USA. 1925.
Pilgrimage. Dir. John Ford. Fox Film Corporation. USA. 1933.
Pioneer Trails. Dir. David Smith. Vitagraph Company of America. USA. 1923.
Platoon. Dir. Oliver Stone. Hemdale, Cinema 86. USA. 1986.
Private Jones. Dir. Russell Mack. Universal Pictures. USA. 1933.
The Public Enemy. Dir. William A. Wellman. Warner Bros. USA. 1931.
Random Harvest. Dir. Mervyn LeRoy. MGM. USA. 1942.
Red Tails. Dir. Anthony Hemingway. 20th Century Fox, Lucasfilm Productions. USA. 2012.
The Road Back. Dir. James Whale. Universal. USA.1937.
The Road to Glory. Dir. Howard Hawks. Twentieth Century Fox. USA. 1936.
The Roaring Twenties. Dir. Raoul Walsh. Warner Bros. USA. 1939.
Saving Private Ryan. Dir. Steven Spielberg. Dreamworks, Paramount. USA. 1998.
Scarface. Dir. Howard Hawks. Caddo Company. USA. 1932.

Sergeant York. Dir. Howard Hawks. Warner Bros. USA. 1941.
The Service Star. Dir. Charles Miller. Goldwyn. USA. 1918.
7th Heaven. Dir. Frank Borzage. Frank Borzage Production. USA. 1927.
The Shock. Dir. Lambert Hillyer. Universal Pictures. USA. 1923.
Shoulder Arms. Dir. Charles Chaplin. Charles Chaplin Productions. USA. 1918.
The Singing Fool. Dir. Lloyd Bacon. Warner Bros. USA. 1928.
Smilin' Through. Dir. Sidney Franklin. Norma Talmadge Film Corporation. USA. 1922.
Smilin' Through. Dir. Sidney Franklin. MGM. USA. 1932.
A Society Scandal. Dir. Alan Dwan. Paramount. USA. 1924.
Source Code. Dir. Duncan Jones. Summit Entertainment. USA. 2001.
Star Wars. Dir. George Lucas. Lucasfilm, Twentieth Century Fox. USA. 1977.
Stella Dallas. Dir. King Vidor. Samuel Goldwyn Company. USA 1937.
Strange Interlude. Dir. Robert Z. Leonard. MGM. USA. 1932.
Sunrise. Dir. F.W. Murnau. Fox. USA. 1927.
Test Pilot. Dir. Victor Fleming. MGM. USA. 1938.
They Gave Him a Gun. Dir. W.S. Van Dyke. MGM. USA. 1937.
The Thin Red Line. Dir. Terrence Malick. Fox 2000 Pictures. USA. 1998.
This Woman. Dir. Phil Rosen. Warner Bros. USA. 1924.
Tol'able David. Dir. Henry King. Inspiration Productions. USA. 1921.
Too Fat to Fight. Dir. Hobart Henley. Goldwyn. USA. 1918.
Underworld. Dir. Josef von Sternberg. Paramount. USA. 1927.
Universal Horror. Dir. Kevin Brownlow. Universal Television and Photoplay Productions. USA/UK. 1998.
The Unknown. Dir. Tod Browning. MGM. USA. 1927.
The Unknown Soldier. Dir. Renaud Hoffman. Charles A. Rogers Productions/Renaud Hoffman Productions. USA. 1926.
The Virtuous Vamp. Dir. David Kirkland. Constance Talmadge Film Company. USA. 1919.
Das Wachsfigurenkabinett (*Waxworks*). Dir. Paul Leni. UFA. Germany. 1924.
War Horse. Dir. Steven Spielberg. Dreamworks, Amblin Entertainment. USA. 2011.
War Nurse. Dir. Edgar Selwyn. MGM. USA. 1930.
Way Down East. Dir. D.W. Griffith. D.W. Griffith Productions. USA. 1920.
West of Zanzibar. Dir. Tod Browning. MGM. USA. 1928.
What Price Glory. Dir. Raoul Walsh. Fox. USA. 1926.
The White Black Sheep. Dir. Sidney Olcott. Inspiration Pictures. USA. 1926.
Wings. Dir. William A. Wellman. Paramount. USA. 1927.
A Woman of Paris. Dir. Charles Chaplin. Charles Chaplin Productions. USA. 1923.
Wooden Crosses (*Les croix de bois*). Dir. Raymond Bernard. Pathé Natan. France. 1932.

INDEX

Absent, xxiv
Ace of Aces, xxix, 82, 86, 87
Adams, Claire, 25
Adams, Edgar, 48
Adams, Rachel, 202–3
Adjusted Compensation Bill, 183
Adorée, Renée, 25, 37
Adrian, xvii
Afghanistan, war in, 237
African Americans: exclusion of, xxiii–xiv, 248–49n1; in D. W. Griffith films, 240n22; soldiers, 21; veterans, 40; segregated graves at Arlington cemetery, 45
Air Circus, The, 85
Air Mail, 94
Aiken, Conrad, 155
Akeley, Carl Ethan, 74; Akeley "pancake camera," 74
All Quiet on the Western Front, xxii, xxvii, xxix, 5, 6, 52, 53, 62, 63, 86, 90, 99, 120, 123, 136, 221, 230, 231, 235; analysis of, 46–51
Allen, Frederick Lewis, 127, 204
Altman, Robert, 237
American Battlefield Monuments Commission, 188
American Cinematographer (journal), 74
American Expeditionary Force (AEF), 21
American Field of Honor Association, 21
American Legion, 21, 71, 183, 205, 211, 229; and Hollywood industry, 40, 242n34; and *What Price Glory?*, 41, 52
American Legion Monthly, The (magazine), 39, 41, 49, 50, 71
American Legion Weekly, The (magazine), 41
American Magazine, 58, 72
The American Museum (New York City), 196
Anderson, Maxwell, 24, 36, 118, 119, 122, 191
Angels with Dirty Faces, 60

Anna Christie (play), 36
Arlen, Richard, 66, 69, 76
Armistice Day, 40, 188
Arthur, Jean, 120
Arzner, Dorothy, 120, 154
Ashby, Hal, xxxi

Baker, Charles Graham, 84–85
Balderston, John, 171, 173; script work on *Smilin' Through* (1932), 136–44
Barnum, P. T., 196
Barratt, Robert, 178
Barrie, J. M., 183
Barrymore, John, xvi, xvii, xviii, 148–49, 155, 167, 173, 176; acting style, 150, in *Bill of Divorcement*, 151–52; in *Dinner at Eight*, 153
Barrymore, Lionel, xvi, xviii, 167, *168*
Barthelmess, Richard, xxiii, xxix–xxx, 14, 82, 94, 102, 156, 157, 176–92; acting in *Patent Leather Kid*, 190
Basinger, Jeanine, 60
Baum, Vicki, xv, xvii, xviii, xxv, 164
Beaudine, William, 100, 120, 122
Beery, Wallace, xvi, xviii, 167
Behlmer, Rudy, 77
Behn, Harry, 32, 77
Benét, Stephen Vincent, 24
Benighted, xxx, xxxi, 205, 215; depiction of veteran 218; comparison with *The Old Dark House*, 220–21
Bergman, Henry, 8
Bern, Paul, 168
Bernard, Raymond, 53
Best Years of Our Lives, The, 144
Beyond Victory, 53–54
Black, John, 49
Big Parade, The, xxiii, xxv, xxviii, 23, 39, 41, 42, 43, 44, 50, 52, 62, 63, 68, 70, 72, 90, 107, 112, 116, 118, 120, 154, 230, 231, 237;

Big Parade, The (continued)
  analysis of, 24–35; adaptation from short story, 36
Big Red One, The, 235–36
Bill of Divorcement, A, play, xxv, 144–49, 152
Bill of Divorcement, A, film, xxiii, xxix, 149–54, 172
Birth of a Nation, The, 10, 12, 16, 39, 240n22; racist sensibilities in, 43
Bitzer, Billy, 15
Blackbird, The, 199–200, 203
Black Cat, The, xxiii, 215, 222–26; reception of, 225–26
Boetticher, Budd, 99
Bogart, Humphrey, 233
Bogdan, Robert, 202
Bond, Lillian, 217
Bonus March, xxvi, xxx, 88, 173, 183, 211, 227
Booth, Maud Ballington, 10
Bordon, Mary, 99
Bordwell, David, 129, 248n5
Born on the Fourth of July, xxxi
Borzage, Frank, xxiii, xxvi; and *Humoresque* (1920), 129, 131, 133, 221
Bosworth, Hobart, 25
Bow, Clara, 66, 68, 69, 96, 101, 105, 111, 116; and flapper persona, 106–9; and vernacular in *Wings*, 108–9
Bowen, R. Sidney, 75
Boyd, Thomas Alexander, 32–35; *Through the Wheat* (novel), 32–35
Breil, Joseph Carl, 12
Brenon, Herbert, 112
Brent, Charles H., 21
Brent, Evelyn, 101, 120
Bride of Frankenstein, 215
Brittain, Vera, 100
Broken Blossoms, 181
Brooke, Rupert
Brown, Clarence, 139
Browning, Todd, xxx, 194, 199, 202–3, 213
Budreau, Lisa, 21, 40, 58
Burchfield, Charles, 23
Burke, Billie, 148
Bryant, William Cullen, 16

Cabin in the Cotton, The, 180
Cabinet of Dr. Caligari, The, xviii, 200, 213
Caddo Company, 83, 85
Cagney, James, 60, 227, 233
Caldara, Orme, 135
Captain Newman M. D., xxxi
Carradine, Robert, 236
Carrington, Margaret, 151
Carrol, Noël, 6
Cat and the Canary, The, 214, 215, 223
Central Airport, 94, 191
Chandler, Helen, 160
Chaney, Lon, xxx, 185, 194, 196–204, 208–9, 212–13, 223
Chaplin, Charles, xviii; and slacker controversy, 6, 239n3; and *Shoulder Arms*, 4–8; and *A Woman of Paris*, 136, 172
Chatterton, Ruth, 120
Cher Ami, 10, 14
Chicago Tribune, 127; "Mae Tinée" in, 127–28
Christopher Strong, 154
Chronicles of Charlie Chaplin, The, 6
Children of Divorce, 106
Cinema Art (magazine), 186–87
Civilian Vocational Rehabilitation Act, 1920, 195
Clary, Charles, 198
classical Hollywood style, 129, 223, 248n5
Clifton, Elmer, 94
Clive, Colin, 215
Clyde, June, 120
Cohan, George M., 229
Cole, Sgt. John Joseph, 41
Cole, Thomas, 16
Colman, Ronald, 236
Coming Home, xxxi
Cook, Donald, 227
Coolidge, Calvin, 10, 233
Cooper, Gary, 85
Corbin, James, 151, 184
Cornell, Katherine, 146, 148, 152
Cosmopolitan (magazine), 72, 100, 190
Costes, Dieudonné, 65
Cowl, Jane, xxiii, 133–34, 135, 212
Crawford, Joan, xvi, 167
Cromwell, John, xxxii

Index

Crosman, Henrietta, 59–60
Crowd, The, 28
Cukor, George, xxiii, *145*, 148, 149, 150–52, 154
Curtis, James, 214, 215, 219
Curtiz, Michael, 60
Custis, Mary Anna Randolph, 45

Daily Telegraph (London newspaper), 184
Dane, Clemence, xxv, 144–46, 149–52
Dane, Karl, 25
Dark Angel, The, 144
Darrow, John, 77
Dawn Patrol, The (1930), xxii, xxv, xxvii, xix, 90, 99, 156, 176, 180, 191; lawsuit with Howard Hughes, 82–86; reception of, 86
Dawn Patrol, The (1938), xix, 95–96
Dead Presidents, xxxi, 237
Dean, Basil, 146
Dean, Faxon, M., 75
Death in the Air, 94
DeBra, Arthur H., 80
Delluc, Louis, 8
De Lord, André, 197
De Mille, Cecil B., 39, 204
Dempster, Carol, 102
Dillingham, Charles, 146
Dieterle, William, xxv, 127, 163–64, 223
Divorcée, 139
Dix, Otto, *Skingraft* (painting), 202
Dix, Richard, 87
Doherty, Ethel, 101
Donovan, Major "Wild Bill," 61–62
Dos Passos, John, 34; *Three Soldiers* (novel), 34
Douglas, Melvyn, 215, 221
Dracula (film, 1931), 136, 194, 200, 213, 223
Dr. Jekyll and Mr. Hyde (film), 143
Dudgeon, Elspeth, 217, 220
Duffy, Father Francis Patrick, 60
Dumont, Hervé, 131
Dunn, Harvey, 38; *The Machine Gunner* (painting) 38, 39; *The Sentry: Front Line in the Morning* (painting), 38
Durand, Asher Brown, 16; *Progress: The Advance of Civilization* (painting), 16; *Kindred Spirits* (painting), 16; 45
Dwan, Allen, 204

Eagle and the Hawk, The, xxii, xxv, xix, 82, 96, 143; production and reception of, 86–94; erotic energies in, 91–92
Eddy, Helen Jerome, 112
Edeson, Arthur, 48
Edward MacManus Productions, 8
Elsaesser, Thomas, 223
Enchanted Cottage, The (play), xxv, xxxi, 181–82, reception of 183–85; 193, 215
Enchanted Cottage, The (film, 1924), xxv, xxix, 44, 156, 175, 176–77, 181–89, 212–13; reception of, 185
Enchanted Cottage, The (film, 1945), xxxii
Englebrecht, H. C., *Merchants of War*, 229
Essanay Studios, 6
Evans, Harry, 51

Fagan James, 142
Fairbanks, Douglas, 6, 197
Fairbanks, Douglas, Jr., 82
Famous Players, Lasky, 72
Farar, John, 24
Farewell to Arms, A (film, 1932), xxvi, 99, 221
Farnham, Dorothy, 42
Farnham, Joe, 112, 118, 122
Fiala, Andrew, and "representational realism" in Hollywood war film, 245–46n33
Fighting 69th, The, xxi, xxiv, xxvii, 60–63, 235; rejuvenation of nature in, 61
Film Daily (journal), 8, 43, 53–54, 58, 79, 89, 122, 136, 162, 184, 226, 230
Film Spectator, The, 106–7
First National Pictures, 84, 133, 179, 182, 189–90, 191
Fisher, James, 80
Fitzgerald, F. Scott, 32–33, 154
Fitzmaurice, George, 85
Fleming, Victor, 94, 132
Flying Ace, The, xxiv
Flynn, Errol, 96
Foncke, René, 65
Forbidden Zone, The, 99
For Valour, 180
Forbes, Charles R., 183
Ford, John, 54–60, 94

Forenger, A. E., *The Greatest Mother in the World* (poster), 221
Fort, Garrett, 214
Four Horsemen of the Apocalypse, The, xxiv, xxviii, 24, 25, 35, 36, 45, 50, 63; analysis, 18–22
Four Sons, 54
Fox Film Corporation, xxv, xxvi; marketing of *Pilgrimage*, 58–60; 68, 72, 222
Frankenstein (film, 1931), cxxxi, 136, 200, 213–214, 215, 223
Frankenstein; or, The Modern Prometheus (novel), 194
Franklin, Sidney, 133, 144
freak show, 196; traditions of, 202, 203
A Free Soul, 112, 139
Freud, Sigmund, 147, 213
Freund, Karl xxx, 200
Full Metal Jacket, 236
Fuller, Sam, 235–36
Futurism, manifesto of, 67

Gable, Clark, 94
Gainsborough Film Studios, 83, 86
Gallagher, Tag, 59–60
Gant, Harry A., xxiv
Garbo, Greta, xvi, xvii, xviii, 167
Gardiner, Becky, xxii, xxvi, xxix, 112, 119, 122, 124; script work on *War Nurse*, 114–18
Gemünden, Gerd, 222, 226
Gentlemen Prefer Blondes, 111, 112
geometry of remembrance, 4, 62–64, 67–69, 71–73, 237; vertical, 82, 236; horizontal, 86, 90, 96; 193, 231
George, Gladys, 233
Gerard, James W., 9
Gibbons, Cedric, xvii, 169, *170*, 171
G. I. Bill, 211
Gilbert, John, 25, 37
Girl Who Stayed at Home, The, xxviii, 14–18, 25, 45, 101–3, 180
Gliese, Rochus, xxvi
Glyn, Elinor, 106
Gold Star mothers, 54, 58, 60, 188; and pilgrimages, 244n70. *See also* Service flag
Gold Diggers of 1933, 157, 177

Goldberger, david, 210
Gone With the Wind, 132
Goulding, Edmund, xvii, 167–68, *168*, 171
Grand Guignol theatre, 197
Grand Hotel (film), xvi–xviii, xxiii, xxix, xxxi, xxxii, 193; analysis of, 164–73
Grant, Cary, 87, 92
Great Gatsby, The (film, 1926), 112
Great Gatsby, The (novel), 154
Green, Abel, 221
Griffith, D. W., xxviii, 3, 10, 12, 13, 21, 39, 43, 176, 180, 215; and *The Girl Who Stayed at Home*, 14–18; vernacular and tradition in, 101–3. *See also* African Americans
Gulf War, 237
Gunning, Tom, 48–49
Gyllenhaal, Jake, 237

Haggis, Paul, xxxi
Hale, Alan, 62
Hall, James, 77
Hall, Mordaunt, 42–43, 46, 88–89, 91, 122, 162, 164, 183, 191, 221
Hamilton, Neil, 82
"Hanging on the Old Barbed Wire" (song), 219–20
Hanko, Arthur, 166
Hansen, Miriam, 189
Harrison's Reports (journal), 58–59, 221
Harron, Robert, 102, 180
Havoc (play), 24
Harding, Alfred, 41
Harlen, Kenneth, 198
Harlow, Jean, 77, 78, 80
Hawks, Howard, xxx, 53, 60, 84, 86, 96, 164, 191, 227
Hays Office, 80, 91, 104, 109, 122, 154, 155, 160, 161, 223, 226
Hearts of the World, 10
Hecht, Ben, 119
Helen's Babies, 105
Hell's Angels, xxii, xxviii–xxix, 51, 75, 77–82, 194, 237; reception of 79–81; Baron von Richthofen's Flying Circus in, 78, 81, 83, 90
Hellinger, Mark, 233
Hemingway, Anthony, 237

Hemingway, Ernest, xxvi, 60, 99, 154, 219; and *The Last Flight*, 250n52
Henle, Maurice, 185
Hepburn, Katherine, 148, 149, 152, 154, 173
Herald Tribune, 52
Heroes for Sale, xxvi, xxix, xxx, 133, 157, 175, 189, 191–92, 211, 227, 230, 237; production of, 177–80
Hilyer, Lambert, 199
Hitchcock, Alfred, 78–79
Hitler, Adolf, 96, 222, 233
Hoffman, Renaud, 42
Homer, Winslow: *The Veteran in a New Field* (painting), 55–56
Hoover, Herbert, 157, 233
hoovervilles, 88, 234
Howard, Sidney, 36
Hubbard, Lucien, 73, 74, 75
Hudson River School, 15, 45, 52
Hughes Brothers, xxxi, 237
Hughes, Howard, xxviii, 51, 75, 194; and *Hell's Angels*, 77–82; lawsuit with First National and Howard Hawks, 83–86
Hughes, Robert, 190, 191
Hugo, Victor, 222
Humoresque (film 1920), xxiii, 140, 143, 155, 172; analysis of, 129–33
Hunchback of Notre Dame (film), 194, 201–2
Hurst, Fannie: and *Humoresque* (novella), 130–31

I Am a Fugitive From a Chain Gang, xxv, xxx, 157, 164, 177–78, 211, 227, 237
Ibáñez, Vicente Blasco, 18, 19–20, 21–22
Iliad, The, xxvii
Illustrated Daily News, 66
In the Valley of Elah, xxxi
influenza epidemic 1918, 203, 209
Ingram, Rex, xxviii
Inspiration Pictures, 182, 190
Iraq, war in, 237
It, 106–107
Invisible Man, The (film), 215

Jacobs, Lea, 36, 37, 54, 70, 109, 118, 136, 172, 190–91
Jagger, C. S., 219

Jennings, Emil, xxx
Jim Crow era, 43
Johnson, Julian, 66
Jolson, Al, 84
Jones, Duncan, 237
Journey's End, xxii, xxvii, xxix, 5, 6, 62, 63, 82, 83, 84, 86, 90, 99, 120, 121, 123, 136, 156, 214, 215, 218, 219, 235; reception of 51–52;
Journey's End (play): comparison with *What Price Glory?*, 52–53
Julian, Rupert, 194
Jung, Carl Gustav, 147

Kaes, Anton, xviii–xix, 47, 200, 202, 213–14, 223
Kardiner, Abram, 148–50
Karloff, Boris, 216, 218, 221, 224
Keene, Jennifer, 205, 211
Keighley, William, xxvii; directing *The Fighting 69th*, 60–63
Keire, Mara, 110, 123
Kellogg-Briand Pact (1928), 52
Kilmer, Joyce, 61–62
King, Burton, xxviii, 9, 10, 12, 15
King, Henry, 176
Knutson, Anne Classen, 241n3
Krotoshinsky, Abraham, 10, 13, 14
Kubrick, Stanley, xxxi, 236

Laemmle, Carl, 50, 99, 218
La Grande Illusion, 235
La Motte, Ellen, 100
Lane, Priscilla, 233
Lang, Fritz, xviii, 223
Lasky, Jesse, 72
Last Flight, The, xxv, xxix, 82, 86, 87, 96, 127–28, 132, 166, 172, 173, 176, 191, 193; analysis of, 155–62; reception of, 162–64
Laughton, Charles, 217, 218
Lawrence, D. H., 161–62
League of Physically Handicapped, 210
Le Brix, Joseph, 65
Lee, Robert E., 45
Legion of the Condemned, xxix, 82
Leni, Paul, xxx, 201, 214, 215, 222
Leonard, Robert Z., 139

LeRoy, Mervyn, xxv, 157, 179, 236
Lestina, Adolphe, 15
Levy, Benn W., 218, 219
Liberty Magazine, xxv, 72, 155, 156, 162
Liberty Pictures, 120, 122
Life Magazine, 51
Lighton, Louis, 66, 96, 105
Lilac Time (film), 85
Lilac Time (play), 134
Lindbergh, Charles A., 66–67, 71–72
Literary Digest (magazine), 75
Little Caesar, 179
Little Women, 154
Logue, Charles A., 9, 10–12
Longmore, Philip K., 210
Loos, Anita, xxvi, 101, 103–4, 124, 151; and *Gentlemen Prefer Blondes* (novel), 111; (play), 112; and *How to Write Photoplays*, 103, 129
Lord, Rev. Daniel A., 80, 90, 193
Lord, Robert, 180
Lombard, Carol, 87–88, 90, 234
Lorentz, Pare, 51
Loring, Hope, xxvi, xxix, 66, 96, 101, 111, 119, 124; script work on *Wings*, 105–9
Los Angeles Evening Herald, 66
Los Angeles Times, 66
The Lost Battalion, 14; popular conception of, 9
Lost Battalion, The (film), xxi, xxiv, xxviii, 16, 17, 24, 25, 50, 63; analysis of, 8–14
Lovett, Josephine, 187
Love Expert, The, 103
Lubin, David, 23, 241n3
Lubitsch, Ernst, 223
Lucas, George, 237
Lucky Star, xxvi
Lugosi, Bela, 223, 225
Lucy, Arnold, 48
Lusk, Norbert, 116
Lynn, Jeffrey, 233
Lyon, Ben, 77

MacArthur, Charles, 119
MacGowan, Kenneth, 26; and *Theatre of Tomorrow*, 147; and realism, 151
McAvoy, May, 182, 184

McClure Newspaper Syndicate, 136
McLagen, Victor, 38, 39
McLoughlin, Kate, xxiii
McManus, Edward, 9, 10–12, 14, 15, 21
Mad Parade, The, xxii, 100, 105, 111, 120–24; reception of 122
Magnascope, 74, 76
Malick, Terence, 236
Malloy, Doris, 120, 122, 124
Man Who Laughs, The, 214, 222
Manners, David, 156, 157, 223
Manslaughter, 204
March, Frederic: in *The Eagle and the Hawk*, 87, 88, 89–90, 92; in *Smilin' Through*, 143–44, 155, 176
March, Joseph Moncure, 51, 77, 84
Marinetti, Fillippo Tommaso, 67
Marion, Frances: and *How to Write and Sell Film Stories*, 131–32; 151
Marvin, Lee, 236
*M*A*S*H*, 237
Massey, Raymond, 215, 218
Mathis, June, 18–22; script notes, The *Four Horsemen of the Apocalypse*, 240n26
Mayer, David, 17, 251n1
Memorial Day, 40
Men, The, xxxi
Mencken, H. L., 111;
Menschen am Sonntag (People on Sunday), 222
Menschen im Hotel, novel, xv; (as *Grand Hotel*), xxv
Merchant, Caroline, 17
Metro-Goldwyn-Mayer (MGM) Studios, 24, 68, 72, 75, 100, 101, 111, 112, 119, 133, 154, 164, 234
Metropolis, xviii, 213, 214
Milestone, Lewis, xxviii, 81, 82, 236; and *All Quiet on the Western Front*, 46–51
Miller, Angela, 16
Miller, David, xxxi
Miller, Llewellyn, 49
Miller, Seton I., 96
Millis, Walter, and *Road to War*, 229
Miracle Man, The, 185
Mizner, Wilson, 180
Montgomery, Robert, 114
Moore, Colleen, 85

Moore, Eva, 216
Morris, Gouverneur, 205–6, 207–8
Morpugo, Michael, 237
Mosse, George L., 45; cult of the fallen, 45, 63
Motion Picture Classics (journal), 105
Motion Picture Herald, 58, 230
Moving Picture World (journal), 10, 185, 209
Moving Picture Age (journal), 9
Muni, Paul, 164
Murfin, Jane xxiii, 133–34, 212
Murnau, F. W. xviii, xxvi, xxx, 200, 222
Murphy, Father Francis D., 61
Mussolini, Benito, 233
mutilés de guerre, 202
My Four Years in Germany, 9
My Man Godfrey, 234

Nares, Owen, 186
Nash, Paul, 23; *We are Making a New World* (painting), 23
Negulesco, Jean, xxvi
Neilan, Marshall, 77, 78, 81
Nerves (play), 24
Neutrality Acts (1935–1939), 230
Nevinson, C. R. W., 23, 31–32, 72; *The Road from Arras to Bapaume* (painting), 23; and *The Big Parade* 28, 241n11
New Republic (magazine), 24, 183
New York Evening Journal, 59, 175
New York Globe, 147
New York Herald Tribune, 155
New York Mirror, 59
New York Morning Telegraph, 75, 147
New York Telegram, 43, 184
New York Times, 42, 71, 88–89, 102, 103, 130, 162, 185, 191, 234
New York Tribune, 146
New York World, 43
New Yorker (magazine), 51
News Weekly (journal), 20
"Nikki and Her Warbirds," 155–56, 157, 163
Niven, David, 96
Norden, Martin F., 195–96
Norman, Richard E., xxiv
North, Robert, 99
Norton, Barry, 38

Nosferatu, xviii, 213
Nugent, Frank, 234

Oakie, Jack, 87, 88, 90
O'Brien, Pat, 60
O'Brien, Tom, 25
Ober, Robert, 25
Odyssey, The, xxvii
Official Metropolitan Guide (New York), 184
O'Keefe, Georgia, 23; *No. 9 Special* (painting), 23
Olcott, Sidney
Old Dark House, The, xxiii, xxxi, 215–22, 223, 224, 226; reception of, 221–22
One Exciting Night, 215
O'Neill, Eugene, 36
Only Angels Have Wings, 191
Ord, George M., 157, 158, 161
Orr, Gertrude, 120, 122, 123, 124
"Over There" (song), 229
Owen, Wilfred, 23

Page, Anita, 112
Paramount Around the World (studio journal), 65
Paramount Studios, xxv, 65, 73, 74, 91, 100, 112; and Artcraft, 131; 143, 154
Parker, Albert, 180
Parker, Dorothy, 119
Parsons, Louella, 49, 185
Patent Leather Kid, The, xiv, 156, 177, 190–91; reception of, 191
Paths of Glory, xxxi, 236
Peeler, Clare, 169
Pelwick, Rose, 59, 175
Penalty, The (film), 203, 205, 212; analysis of, 198–200
Penalty, The (novel), 205–6, 207–8
Perkins, Maxwell, 32
Perry, Harry, 66, 75, 77
Perry, Paul, 75
Phantom of the Opera (film), 194, 201–2
Photoplay (magazine), 136, 181, 189
Pickford, Mary, 6
Picture Play (magazine), 182, 189
Picturegoer (magazine), 78
Pilgrimage, 54–60; reception of, 58–60

Pioneer Trails, 85
Pinero, Arthur Wing, xxv, 181–82, 183–85, 187, 215
Pitts, Zasu, 112, 118
Platoon, 236
Plumes (novel), 24, 188
Poe, Edgar Allan, 197, 226
Pollack, Allan, 146–48
Powell, William, 234
Price, Evadne (aka Helen Zenna Smith), 100; and *Not So Quiet: Stepdaughters of War*, 99–100
Priestly, J. B., xxx, xxxi, 205, 215, and *Benighted*, 218–21
Private Jones, 53–54
Producers Distributing Corporation (PDC), 42, 43, 44
Production Code Administration (PCA), 91, 163
Provost, Marie, 112
Public Enemy, The, xxx, 131, 179, 227

Ralston, Jobyna, 66, 69
Random Harvest, 236
Record, The, Los Angeles (newspaper), 49–50
Red Cross, 121; and *War Nurse*, 248–49n26
Red Tails, 237
Reid, Laurence, 185
Remarque, Erich Maria, 50, 51, 236
Resina, Jaon Ramón, xx–xxi
reunification theme, 17
RKO Pictures, xxxii, 75, 144
Road Back, The, 53
Roaring Twenties, The, 233
Robertson, John S., xxv, *186*
Robertson, Linda R.: "dream of American air power," 68–69
Robinson, Edward G., 179
Rogers, Charles (Buddy), 66, 69, 76
Rogers St. Johns, Adela, 190
Roland, Arthur, 184
Rosher, Karl, xxvi
Roosevelt, Franklin D.: "Forgotten Man" speech, xxvi, 88, 177–78, 192
Roosevelt, Quentin, 71–72

Roosevelt, Theodore, 10, 71
Rosebud Film Corporation, xxiv
Rosen, Phil, 105
Rosher, Charles, 118
Ross, Milton 198
Royal Flying Corps (RFC), xxii, 82, 85, 86, 87
Royer, Fanchon, 94
Ryan, Don, 189

Sandberg, Carl, 23
Santell, Alfred, 190
Sargent, Epes Winthrop, (as 'Chicot'), 89–90, 91, 94; and *The Technique of the Photoplay*, 129
Saturday Evening Post, 181
Saunders, John Monk, xxv, xxvii, xxviii–xxix; and *Wings*, 65–77, 82, 84, 96, 99, 107, 108; and *Last Flight*, 155–68; psychology of characters, 158–59
Saving Private Ryan, 237
Scarface (film), xxx, 164
Scarface (novel), 225–26
Schallert, Edwin, 143
Schenck, Joseph, 134
Schüfftan, Eugen, 222
Schulberg, B. P., 105
Screen in Review, 116
In Search of a Sinner, 103
Seeger, Alan: and "I Have a Rendezvous with Death (poem), 130
Seiter, William, 105
Selwyn, Edgar, 100, 112, *113*, 118
Selznick, David O., 148, 152; and *Bill of Divorcement*, 250n38
Sergeant York, 60, 235
Service flag, 220n19
Service Star, The, 9
7th Heaven, xxvi
77th "New York's Own" Division, 9, 11, 13
Seymour, Clarine, 102–3
Shayer, Richard E., 42
Shearer, Norma, 112, 138–39, 173, 193
Sheen, Charlie, 236
Sheldon, E. Lloyd, 66, 75
shell shock: popular perceptions of, 183–84, 213

shell shock cinema, xvii, 202, 213
Shelley, Mary, 193
Sherriff, R. C., 51, 205, 218
Sherwood, Robert E., 41
Shilling, Marion, 54
Shock, The, 199, 203, 209, 212
Shoulder Arms, xxviii, 4–8
Silverman, Sidne, 80
Silverman, Sime, 8, 50
Signing Fool, The, 84
Single Lady (novel), 159, 162–63
Siodmak, Curt, 222
Siodmak, Robert, 222
Skal, David J., 200–2, 213–14
Smilin' Through (play, 1919), 133, 134–35
Smilin' Through (film, 1922), xxiii, 133, 134–36, 158, 172–73
Smilin' Through (film, 1932), xxiii, xxix, 133, 136–44, 171, 172, 173, 193, 212–13 and script history, 249n18
Smith, Alfred E., 10
Smith, Helen Zenna. See Evadne Price
Smith, Patsy, 102–3
Society Scandal, A, 204
Soldier Rehabilitation Act (1918), 195
Source Code, 237
Spielberg, Steven, 237
Staiger, Janet, 129, 248n5
Stallings, Laurence, xxv, 24, 191 236; work on *The Big Parade*, 26–27, 32–33; and *Plumes* (novel), 188, 195; and *What Price Glory?*, 41, 118, 122
Stanwyck, Barbara, 28
Star Wars, 237
Steene, Burton, 75
Stein, Gertrude, 60
Stella Dallas, 28
Stevenson, Robert Louis, 143, 194
Stimson, Edna, 67
Stone, Lewis, xvi, 167, 176
Stone, Oliver, xxxi, 236
Strange Case of Dr. Jekyll and Mr. Hyde, The (novel), 194
Stuart, Gloria, 215, 221
Sun Also Rises, The (novel), 154–55
Sun Also Rises, The (film), 155

Sunrise, 222
Syria, war in, 237

Talmadge, Constance, 103
Talmadge, Norma, 134–35, 173
Tashman, Lilyan, 121
Taylor, Stanner E. V., 17
Tearle, Noel, 186
Ten Commandments, The (1923), 39
Terry, Ethel Grey, 198
Test Pilot, 94
Testament of Youth, 100
Thalberg, Irving, xvi–xviii, xxv, 24, 32, 112, 115–16, 119, 136, 171–72; in *Grand Hotel* script conferences, 167–69
Thesiger, Ernest, 216, 219
They Gave Him a Gun, 227–33; reception of, 229–30
They Knew What They Wanted (play), 36
Thin Red Line, The, 236
Thompson, Julian F., 148
Thompson, Kristin, 129, 248n5
Thomson, Rosemarie Garland, 195, 196–97, 202
Tiffany-Gainsborough Productions, 214
Tiffany-Stahl Productions, 75
Times, The (London newspaper), 184
Time (magazine), 52
Tol'able David, 176, 181, 183, 191
Too Fat To Fight, 9
Tone, Franchot, 227
Totheroe, Dan, 96
Tracey, Spencer, 228
Trail, Armitage, 226, 251n68
Tranchée des Baïonettes (Trench of bayonets), 39
Trout, Steven, 38, 43, 44, 235
Tucker, George Loane, 185
Turner, Ray, xxiv
Twentieth Century Fox, 155
Tynan, James, 42

Ulmer, Edgar, xxiii, xxvi, 215; and *The Black Cat*, 222–26
Underworld, 191
United States Army Air Corps, 69, 81

Universal Studios, xxxi, 53, 194, 218, 221, 222
Unknown, The, 199–200, 202
The Unknown Soldier: Tomb of, 44; memorials in Arlington Cemetery, 45, 187; in Paris and London, 45, 187–88; in Rome, 188
Unknown Soldier, The (film), xxviii; reception of, 42–44, 243n40

Valentino, Rudolph, 18, 189, 197
Van Dyke, W. S., 227
Variety (journal), 8, 50, 53–54, 80, 86, 95–96, 102, 162, 225–26, 229, 230
Veidt, Conrad, xxx
Veteran's Bureau, 181, 188
Vidor, King, 24, 72, 236; directing *The Big Parade*, 26–35, 241n11
Vietnam War, 235, 237
Viquesney, E. M. 49; *The Spirit of the American Doughboy* (sculpture), 71, 253n33
Virtuous Vamp, The, 103
Von Stroheim, Erich: and *Greed*, 136, 172
Vorkapich, Slavko, 229

Wachsfigurenkabinett, Das (Waxworks), 222
Walker, June, 112, 116
Wall, Harry, 24
Wallis, Hal, 95
Walsh, Raoul, 40, 53, 236; and *What Price Glory*, 36–38; and *The Roaring Twenties*, 233
Walthall, Henry B., 42
War Department: repatriating the dead, 20; and venereal disease propaganda films, 110; and the regulation of leisure spaces, 110
War Horse, 237
War Nurse, xxii, xxix, 100, 105, 111–20, 121, 231
"War Nurse: The True Story of Women who Lived, Loved and Suffered on the Western Front," 100
War Risk Insurance Act, 1917, 195
Warner Brothers: xxiv, xxv, xxx, 95; social problem cycle, xxiv; Warner's/First National, 75; 157, 164; and New Deal, 177; 191, 211

Warner, Jack, 95
Watts, Richard, 52–53, 58, 215
Way Down East (film), 176, 181
Weimar, cinema, xviii,
Weimar culture, xix,
Weine, Robert, xviii
Wellman, William, xxx; and *Wings*, 65–77, 94; and *The Public Enemy*, 133; 157, 175, 179, 192, 227
Wells, Jacqueline (aka Julie Bishop), 223, 225
West, Rebecca, 100
West of Zanzibar, 199–200
Whale, James, xxiii, xxviii, xxxi, 53, 77, 82, 194, 213, 214; and *Journey's End*, 51–52; and *The Old Dark House*, 215–22; 216, 223, 236
What Price Glory (film), xxiv, xxv, xxviii, 43, 44, 50, 52, 53, 61, 63, 68, 70, 72, 85, 90, 107, 116, 118, 120, 122, 136, 154, 191; analysis of, 36–38
What Price Glory? (play), 24, 36–37, 41, 53, 215
White Black Sheep, The, 189
Whitman, Walt, 22
Whittlesey, Charles, 9, 11, 13
Wid's Daily (journal), 11–12, 103–4
Witt, Jason, 207
Wilder, Billy, 222, 223
Wiley, I. A. R., 54–55, 58
Williams, Wythe, 71
Wills, Brember, 220
Wilson, Claggett, 23, 33; *First Attack on the Bois de Beallcau* (painting), 23; 33
Wilson, John V., 163
Wingate, James, 91
Winged Victory of Samothrace, 66–69
Wings, xxii, xxiv, xxv, xxvii, xxix, 81, 85, 90, 96, 105–9, 111, 116, 118, 119, 237; analysis of, 65–77
Winter, Jay, xxviii, 4, 46, 235
Wohl, Robert, 67
Wollheim, Louis, 38
This Woman, 105
Wooden Crosses (Les crois de bois), 53
Woolcott, Alexander, 151
World War II film, 235
Worsley, Wallace, 194; and *The Penalty* (film), 198–200

Wray, Faye, 120
"The Wreck of the Old 97" (song), 208
Wyler, William, 144

YMCA, 122
Young, Loretta, 178

Zanuck, Darryl, xxv, xxx, 175, 176; and *Heroes for Sale*, 177–80
Zinneman, Fred, xxxi, 222
Zukor, Adolph, 131

THE SUNY SERIES

HORIZONS OF CINEMA

MURRAY POMERANCE | EDITOR

Also in the series

William Rothman, editor, *Cavell on Film*

J. David Slocum, editor, *Rebel Without a Cause*

Joe McElhaney, *The Death of Classical Cinema*

Kirsten Moana Thompson, *Apocalyptic Dread*

Frances Gateward, editor, *Seoul Searching*

Michael Atkinson, editor, *Exile Cinema*

Paul S. Moore, *Now Playing*

Robin L. Murray and Joseph K. Heumann, *Ecology and Popular Film*

William Rothman, editor, *Three Documentary Filmmakers*

Sean Griffin, editor, *Hetero*

Jean-Michel Frodon, editor, *Cinema and the Shoah*

Carolyn Jess-Cooke and Constantine Verevis, editors, *Second Takes*

Matthew Solomon, editor, *Fantastic Voyages of the Cinematic Imagination*

R. Barton Palmer and David Boyd, editors, *Hitchcock at the Source*

William Rothman, *Hitchcock: The Murderous Gaze, Second Edition*

Joanna Hearne, *Native Recognition*

Marc Raymond, *Hollywood's New Yorker*

Steven Rybin and Will Scheibel, editors, *Lonely Places, Dangerous Ground*

Claire Perkins and Constantine Verevis, editors, *B Is for Bad Cinema*

Dominic Lennard, *Bad Seeds and Holy Terrors*

Rosie Thomas, *Bombay before Bollywood*

Scott M. MacDonald, *Binghamton Babylon*

Sudhir Mahadevan, *A Very Old Machine*

David Greven, *Ghost Faces*

James S. Williams, *Encounters with Godard*

William H. Epstein and R. Barton Palmer, editors, *Invented Lives, Imagined Communities*

Lee Carruthers, *Doing Time*

Rebecca Meyers, William Rothman, and Charles Warren, editors, *Looking with Robert Gardner*

Belinda Smaill, *Regarding Life*

Douglas McFarland and Wesley King, editors, *John Huston as Adaptor*

R. Barton Palmer, Homer B. Pettey, and Steven M. Sanders, editors, *Hitchcock's Moral Gaze*

Nenad Jovanovic, *Brechtian Cinemas*

Will Scheibel, *American Stranger*

Amy Rust, *Passionate Detachments*

Steven Rybin, *Gestures of Love*

Seth Friedman, *Are You Watching Closely?*

Roger Rawlings, *Ripping England!*

Michael DeAngelis, *Rx Hollywood*

Ricardo E. Zulueta, *Queer Art Camp Superstar*

John Caruana and Mark Cauchi, editors, *Immanent Frames*

Nathan Holmes, *Welcome to Fear City*

Homer B. Pettey and R. Barton Palmer, editors, *Rule, Britannia!*

Milo Sweedler, *Rumble and Crash*

Ken Windrum, *From El Dorado to Lost Horizons*

Matthew Lau, *Sounds Like Helicopters*

William Rothman, *Tuitions and Intuitions*

Dominic Lennard, *Brute Force*

www.ingramcontent.com/pod-product-compliance
Lightning Source LLC
Chambersburg PA
CBHW022041230426
43672CB00008B/1033